# Out Of The Shadow Of The Sun

## A life that exceeded expectations

*Peter J Venison CVO*

London | New York

*Published by Clink Street Publishing 2020*

*Copyright © 2020*

*First edition.*

*The author asserts the moral right under the Copyright, Designs and Patents Act 1988 to be identified as the author of this work.*

*All rights reserved. No part of this publication may be reproduced, stored in a retrieval system or transmitted, in any form or by any means without the prior consent of the author, nor be otherwise circulated in any form of binding or cover other than that with which it is published and without a similar condition being imposed on the subsequent purchaser.*

*ISBN: 978-1-913568-42-9 – paperback
978-1-913568-43-6 – ebook*

*To my very special Pisces, with whom*
*"There's such a lot of world to see,"*
*and to Rogan, Shea, Briggs, Oliver and Sophie*
*– who have yet to see it.*

Also by Peter Venison

*Managing Hotels*
Heinemann Professional Publishing (London), 1983.
Reprinted 1984,1986,1988

*100 Tips for Hoteliers*
iUniverrse, 2005

*In the Shadow of the Sun*
iUniverse, 2005

*100 Ways to Annoy your Guests*
Clink Street Publishing, 2020

# Contents

| | |
|---|---|
| Introduction | 1 |
| One: THE UNIVERSITY OF THE VEG PREP | 5 |
| Two: A TASTE OF AMERICA | 17 |
| Three: AFRICA CALLING | 32 |
| Four: REVOLUTION | 44 |
| Five: NIGHTMARE ISLAND | 57 |
| Six: PARADISE LOST | 73 |
| Seven: FIVE-STAR ISLAND | 83 |
| Eight: THE RISING SUN | 96 |
| Nine: AMERICAN ADVENTURES | 107 |
| Ten: ABORTED DEALS | 137 |
| Eleven: FIGHTING IN THE SUN | 150 |
| Twelve: FREEDOM | 166 |
| Thirteen: THE NOBLE ART | 184 |
| Fourteen: THE END OF A CHAMPION | 205 |
| Fifteen: AMERICAN ROLL-UP | 217 |
| Sixteen: TREASURE ISLAND | 233 |

| | |
|---|---|
| Seventeen: THE LOST CITY | 266 |
| Eighteen: MADIBA | 284 |
| Nineteen: THE FRENCH CONNECTION | 300 |
| Twenty: ATLANTIS | 326 |
| Twenty-One: GREEK TRAGEDY | 341 |
| Twenty-Two: THE ROYAL MIRAGE | 361 |
| Twenty-Three: AFFAIRS OF THE CROWN | 375 |
| Twenty-Four: TORTUOUS INTERFERENCE | 393 |
| Twenty-Five: CONSULTING | 405 |
| Twenty-Six: LOOKING BACK | 421 |
| Twenty-Seven: EPILOGUE | 433 |

# Introduction

Borders are intriguing places. Before the barriers at frontier-control posts in much of Continental Europe were effectively removed, one always felt a slight sense of uneasiness and uncertainty as one approached a border between one country and the next. Even now, as lines form to pass through the simplest of immigration formalities in many countries, one still senses a heightened feeling of anxiety and foreboding. I have crossed many borders in my life, and some of these passages remain firmly imprinted on my mind, even though nothing of any significance actually happened at the time.

I can see, as clearly as if I were watching a film, my crossing into Laos in the mid-nineties. I was on my way from Bangkok to look at a possible resort and casino site at a waterfall in the Mekong River. I had been transported to the border in a Land Cruiser by the reckless driver the Thai promoters of the scheme had provided. He had not stopped at a single red light on the eighty-mile drive. The plan was for me to pick up a prearranged chartered helicopter on the Laos side of the border, because no permission was available to fly private aircraft from Thailand into Laos. I soon discovered that it was also not possible to drive a vehicle across the border, so I was ejected by the chauffeur and told to walk.

It was an interesting walk. Having lined up in a rather scruffy paper-strewn concrete hut to get my passport stamped by the Thai authorities, I now found myself in the company of other travellers, most of whom who had no shoes, walking down a muddy track of no-man's-land. Fortunately, I had no luggage, but those that did were having great difficulty manhandling their boxes and bags along this uneven route. As always happens in situations where someone is experiencing some difficulty, someone else had figured out how to ease their pain—for a small consideration. As a result, the track was dotted with little piccaninnies pushing handmade wooden carts on bicycle wheels in both directions, loaded with every imaginable shape and type of container. I felt as if I were in one of those pitiful refugee lines that you see from time to time on the television news.

Upon arriving at the Laos immigration building, I realised that the Thai concrete building had actually been a palace. This one was little more than a thatched mud hut. Both the thatch and the mud had seen better days. The unshod were waved by with various friendly local greetings; I was ushered into the mud hut by a man in a military uniform with a gun—the sort you don't argue with. There, I had to explain why I was walking to Laos. My explanation—that I was considering building a casino and a resort fifty miles down the river—didn't actually seem to mean much to my interrogators. Nevertheless, they eventually let me go, having forced me to change every cent I had in my wallet into Laotian notes, which were mainly so torn, ancient and dirty that I wondered whether they would stay intact long enough to change back (if allowed) on the return journey (if it ever took place).

I found myself on the other side of a rickety barbed-wire gate, slightly curious as to how you could hide a helicopter.

Just as I was beginning to think the worst about the promoter, who had allegedly arranged the transport, an almost prehistoric Volkswagen Kombi appeared around a bend, in a cloud of black exhaust vapour. Out jumped a young New Zealander in shorts. "I'm Rik," he beamed. "I'm your pilot."

Having once been reprimanded by Sol Kerzner, my boss at the time, for addressing our pilot as 'pilot', I stuck out my hand and said, "Nice to meet you, captain. I was hoping I was going to find you. Where's the chopper?"

"About five miles down the road. They won't let us land here for military reasons. You know what I mean?"

With that, we wobbled off in the VW until we came to a clearing on the side of the road, where sat the oldest, rustiest helicopter I have ever seen. It had no doors and almost all of its paint had long since peeled off. I assumed it was a relic from the Vietnam War, or maybe the Korean one. "It still flies good," the cheery Rik chirped, obviously reading the look on my face; if he ever did any other charter work, this would not have been the first time he had encountered such a look. "Climb in. Sorry about the seatbelts," which I took to mean, "Sorry they don't work." Actually, there weren't any. "If you're worried," continued the upbeat New Zealander, "we can fly low, although we can't fly too low—we don't want to get shot down."

We never built the casino! But I did have a wonderful ride down the Mekong Delta, with its rich brown waters flanked by bright green pastures, interrupted from time to time by clearings of red soil and little primitive dwellings. I was glad I was not responsible for building there. Someone else will, of course.

Other memorable crossings are mentioned elsewhere in this book. They include walking from Israel to Gaza, where people frequently seemed to get shot in no-man's-land; and from Jordan to Israel, in the pitch black of night, across the Allenby Bridge, where once again I had to convince the disbelieving authorities that I was thinking of developing a casino. They also include a walk across the Komatipoort border whilst escaping from the new communist Frelimo government in Mozambique. And, of course, there is the most spectacular border crossing of all: the magnificent walk across the Victoria Falls from Zambia to Zimbabwe. But I have now crossed a different sort of border: the transition between fulltime work and retirement. Like all borders, you are not quite sure what to expect on the other side. In my case, I crossed voluntarily. I wanted to get to the other side, but I have travelled with a certain amount of trepidation.

Writing this book has been positive therapy. It is a way to put the past behind me—to look back on good and interesting times, while at the same time putting them into context: the context of my life. If the experiences recorded herein are of interest to anyone else, it will be a bonus. I am hoping that this book will also be useful for young persons who are about to cross the border into the hospitality industry, or, indeed, to persons who are now in no-man's-land—not sure how to spend their lives. This book is about a working life in that industry and its closely associated neighbours of sport and entertainment. I have been lucky to cross over 120 different country borders in my life, many of them with my amazing wife, Diana. In our first date we went to see a movie, *Breakfast at Tiffany's*. Its haunting musical theme, 'Moon River', talks about their being "Lots of world to see." I promised Diana that I would show her the world. I didn't realise how successful I would be. Now we are preparing for the Moon.

# Chapter One
## THE UNIVERSITY OF THE VEG PREP

I got into the hotel business for none of the right reasons. Before going to hotel school, I had never stepped foot inside a hotel, let alone actually stayed in one. I had absolutely no idea what it could possibly be like to work in a hotel, or what sort of people worked in them. I'd never cooked more than a boiled egg or a piece of toast. The only jobs that I'd had were a newspaper delivery round and two summers of tying up flowers to little wooden sticks in a nursery in Sussex, at which I was so inept that the flowers almost grew faster than I could tie them. I couldn't honestly say that I went into the hotel business because I 'liked people' as so many recruits that I later interviewed claimed. Of course I liked people, but that was certainly not a driving force in setting me off as a hotelier.

No, I went into the hotel business because of a girl. Here's what happened. I attended high school in the days of O and A levels. For those of you that didn't, these were exams. By some quirk of good fortune, as part of an educational experiment, I was allowed to take my exams one year early on the assumption that I would stay on in the sixth form for an extra year to take a new, higher-grade exam: the S (for scholarship) level. At the time, I had a girlfriend, somewhat older than me, who had long since left school. In fact, most of my friends were older than me, and they had all left school. Being the only one in the group who was still at school made life very awkward, particularly in relation to the girlfriend. But, alas, I was too young, at seventeen, to be accepted into university—which would have been socially acceptable. As with all problems, a solution appeared. A classmate of mine, Stephen Partridge, had decided to enrol at hotel school, or to be more precise, at the Battersea College of Advanced Technology. This was a new breed of college that, because of its infancy (according to Stephen), would be happy to consider applications from seventeen-year-olds.

Despite mild opposition from my parents, and much sterner opposition from my headmaster, who thought I should become a civil servant—how much more wrong could he have been?—I applied to and was accepted by Battersea, to which I went with the full intention of leaving after one year to go to 'proper' university. At least by being there for a year, I could avoid the stigma of being at high school. The upshot of all of this, however, was that after one year at Battersea, I had become so interested in the prospect of hotel-keeping that I stayed on for the full four-year course. Stephen Partridge, meanwhile, left after one year to become an actor, and I left my girlfriend for another—or was it she that left me?

Battersea College was going up in the world. It had been upgraded from a polytechnic to a CAT (college of advanced technology) a year before I went there. A year after I left, it became the University of Surrey and relocated to Guildford, to brand-new premises in the shadow of a newly erected modern cathedral. During my sojourn, it was located in Battersea Park Road, South London, wedged between a high-rise council estate (built in a hurry after the Second World War) and Prince of Wales Drive, an elegant street of Victorian mansions overlooking Battersea Park, which borders the south bank of the River Thames between the Albert and Chelsea bridges. The college occupied a ramshackle, noisy, cold, drab Victorian building, which could equally have been a hospital or a prison. Its most memorable aspects were the adjacent Eagle Pub and the Green Café, a 'greasy spoon' establishment down the road. The former served as a lunchtime retreat when any of us had any money, and the latter, likewise, when we didn't.

The actual course content consisted of theoretical studies, from the incredibly mundane (things like how to remove stains from sheets) to the more complicated but mechanical science of bookkeeping and the more subjective art of managing enterprises and people. These studies were interwoven with practical sessions in which we were supposed to learn to cook and serve.

The hotel department of the college operated a restaurant, which lecturers from the rest of the college departments could attend. Once a week, we students had to operate the kitchen at this restaurant, and once a week we were obliged to 'serve'. The restaurant was the dreariest room imaginable; there was not a hint of quality interior design, which in those days was not apparently considered to be a requirement for the hotel business. It was about as appealing as a British Rail waiting room. In the restaurant, under the guidance and watchful eye of Hector, we had to lay up its tables with starched white damask cloths and silver-plated cutlery to serve a table d'hôte menu, which was reminiscent of something that would have been dished up by Cesar Ritz at the turn of the last century. Hector was like a big bird, with eyes on either side of his head, which he could swivel with great speed and effectiveness to catch one out whilst one was attempting little intricacies, such as filleting a sole in front of the guest while it unhelpfully slid around a plate, or dissecting into portions a roasted chicken with a blunt table knife. It seemed that Hector was permanently staring in disbelief at our incompetence—particularly mine.

I could never make up my mind which of these practical sessions I feared most, being taken apart by Hector's eagle eyes in the dining room in front of the academic body, or being the butt of sarcastic remarks from master chefs in the kitchen. To begin with, it was a toss-up as to where I performed worst, in the back or in the front. In retrospect, it was probably the back. We did not have the benefit of Delia Smith or *The Naked Chef* or a myriad of TV cooking shows; no, we were allowed only one cookery book—at that time the chef's Holy Grail—*Escoffier*. This huge volume, compiled by Ritz's chef, should have been subtitled 'How to make cooking difficult'. It was an extremely comprehensive tome of haute cuisine, but its problem lay with the fact that no one recipe was ever completely encapsulated on one page—and there were no illustrations for guidance. Thus, if you didn't happen to know what a turnip looked like, you could finish up cooking a leek, and unless you could cook whilst keeping your fingers in the various pages of the book that described the different processes required for the dish, you would almost certainly go wrong. Furthermore, although it was written in English, all of the culinary terms were in French, so you were continually having to turn to the index to find out what you were supposed to be cooking. The instructor chefs were about as helpful as drill-sergeant majors; to a man, they seemed to take a delight in seeing us flounder until, as service time approached, they calmly and conceitedly stepped in to save the day.

In addition to the practical sessions in the kitchen, we had cookery exams. They were my absolute worst nightmare. The format was simple. At the start of the exam, you entered a classroom where you were handed a menu and told that you must now order your supplies to prepare a meal for (usually) eight persons. Having collected your supplies, you proceeded to the kitchen to prepare the meal, which had to be ready by a set time. On the day of my finals, the menu, which was written in French, included minestrone soup, dressed crab, *vol au vent de volaille,* and some type of cooked pudding. In my panic to get going, I mistranslated crab for lobster, which obviously made it impossible for me to score much for my dressed crab. I recovered some points, however, with the main course, but only, I fear, because my feeble effort at puff pastry for the *vol au vent* cases mysteriously got switched with a rather better sample in a communal fridge. My pièce de résistance, however, was my pudding, which elicited the comment from the chief examiner, as he prodded it with his finger: "Am I supposed to eat it or dance on it?" I now knew that I might be destined to hire cooks, but certainly never would be one.

At the end of the first year at college, we were expected to get summer jobs—not tying up flowers, of course, but in real hotels. I had spent much of my time as a teen in Bognor Regis, which was, at the time, one of the more elegant English seaside resorts. My, how things have changed! This was, of course, before the average Englishman went to Torremolinos, and before Billy Butlin went to Bognor. There, in Bognor, standing resplendent in its own grounds overlooking the grey English Channel, was the Royal Norfolk Hotel—'Royal' because when King George had bestowed the title 'Regis' on Bognor, he had lodged at the Norfolk Hotel. Despite all of my years in the town, I had never actually been in the Royal Norfolk—it was far too posh for the likes of me. Now, at the age of eighteen, I landed my first hotel job: I became an early shift waiter in the Royal Norfolk dining room, serving breakfast, lunch, and afternoon tea.

I soon discovered that as grand as it was from the outside,

decrepit it was on the inside, particularly the real inside—the kitchens, storerooms, changing rooms, etc. They were all absolutely filthy! Nowhere here were to be found the gleaming polished cutlery from Hector's restaurant, or the shining pots and pans from the drill sergeants' kitchens, but instead battered pieces of plate that hadn't seen a burnishing machine since King George's visit, and cooking utensils that you wouldn't have found at a car boot sale. But worst of all, there were no customers. Despite it being peak season, the word must have gone around about the state of the place, so waiting turned out to be exactly that—waiting for someone to arrive.

Back at college, I became increasingly interested in the management subjects. Case histories from other industries, man management, planning, and controlling were cleverly and interestingly presented to me by a certain Professor Philip Nailon, who set us tasks that activated the brain rather than the fingers, as in holding a fork and spoon. It was Philip who got me interested in what motivates people to work.

After the second year at college, we were 'placed' in a hotel for an 'industrial year', which meant that we had to work as trainees in selected hotel establishments for twelve months in order to obtain on-the-job exposure. Luckily, I was seconded to the Grosvenor House Hotel, Park Lane, London, which meant that I could stay at home in Wimbledon and commute, thereby being able, I hoped, to continue my rather active social life. Grosvenor House, or GH as it was known to insiders, was a large, imposing, privately owned hotel that had been built during the Great Depression by the McAlpine family. It occupied one whole block of Park Lane and consisted of a North Wing of 500 hotel rooms, separated by lounges and restaurants from a South Wing, which contained 150 luxury serviced apartments leased by high-powered companies, individuals, and, in some cases, celebrities. GH was one of the prestige assignments, as it was, at the time, the largest quality hotel in London. It still stands as a proud landmark today. Those of you familiar with the English Monopoly board will know the value of a hotel in Park Lane!

The first four months of my year were spent in the control office. My job was to sift through hundreds of waiters' dockets from the previous day, looking for mistakes and, in particular, undercharges. Items of food and beverage were all hand-priced on order slips, which were then posted by bill clerks onto hotel guests' main accounts. All undercharges were to be corrected and posted to the guests' accounts, if they were still in house. All mistakes were to be noted in a book. This seemed to me to be a ridiculous practice, since my weekly 'find' of errors which were recoverable totalled, on average, about eight pounds, and my weekly salary was about ten.

The control office consisted of around ten clerks, who were overseen by a certain Mr Fairfield, known to us as 'Fairy'. Fairy glared at us all day from behind a desk, which dwarfed him, in the corner of the room. Each waiter's docket that had been checked had to be marked with a red felt-tip pen. Offending mispriced checks were like trophies, each to be recorded in our individual analysis books and handed over to Fairy, who could then trot off to reprimand the relevant guilty member of staff.

Not long after I joined the office, my life was changed by a young woman. She worked in the billing office downstairs behind the front desk, where her job was to post the charges on the hotel guests' bills. From time to time she was sent upstairs to sort out some of the docket queries. I decided immediately that I had to ask her out. At the very first opportunity, I manufactured a reason to take some papers to the bill office, where, without trepidation, in front of her colleagues, I asked her for a date. An embarrassed silence followed. After what seemed a much longer time than girls normally took to accept or reject my invitations, she finally ended the silent tension in the room by smiling and saying maybe. I persisted; she evaded; but finally we agreed to meet outside the Leicester Square tube station.

I turned up early. So, apparently, did Diana, but I did not see her at first, so she watched me whilst I waited. Since I apparently spent the whole time looking at the passing girls (I claimed I was on the lookout for her), she later told me she almost walked away—which she would have done if there had not been the need to clear something up. We walked to Bunjies Coffee House, next to the Ivy, and it was here that Diana gave me her stunning news. She was married, though separated; she had two children, aged four and two; and she was "much older" than me. Now I understood the silent tension in the billing office. Everyone else but me seemed to know about Diana. I was completely taken aback; here was this beautiful girl sitting in front of me giving me the facts, but with each new sentence, I found myself being powerfully drawn to her. I was falling in love. I was nineteen.

I decided to brush aside these minor obstacles. Although she was married, her husband had left her over a year ago. The marriage had been effectively finished for two years. She worked full-time to support herself and the children—something that was very rare in 1960. She lived, with the children, in an apartment in her parents' home in Tufnell Park, North London. She had started dating, though nothing serious, and she had never taken a date to meet the children. She couldn't, she claimed, possibly go out with me, because I was too young; and because of her status, it could not be a relationship that could prosper. That was nearly sixty years ago; we are still together!

Back in the control office, my newfound romance with Diana produced immediate dividends. The 'trophy' errors captured in my weekly analysis book rose rapidly to consistent record highs, and Fairy was very pleased. The performance improvement was, of course, a scam. Through my friendship with the girls in the billing office, they would help me out by making the odd deliberate posting error, of which they would tip me off, so that I could easily identify it and have it corrected before the guest checked out—only after, of course, it had been entered in my little book of errors. As a result of this system, I became quite lazy about putting the little red ticks on the dockets before filing them in the appropriate racks.

One Saturday morning, I was undone. Fairy worked one Saturday in four. It was my misfortune to be there on that fateful morning. He was sitting behind his desk, examining some dockets, which, for some reason, caused him to start a search of the previous day's filed work, which, of course, included my un-ticked offerings. As luck would have it, he pulled out one of my piles and, after flicking through the first few dockets, suddenly discovered no more red marks. At first he was calm, but then he climbed up a ladder to get to more stored dockets, and as he soon discovered more and more batches of unticked paper, he became like a man demented, throwing around waiters' checks and elastic bands like an out-of-control windmill, foaming at the mouth with rage as he flapped about. How he didn't fall of the ladder, I'll never know.

It was not long after this incident that I was transferred to the kitchens. To the North Block kitchen, to be precise—a food factory for the main hotel restaurant, the International Sporting Club (now defunct), the Great Room (still London's largest and glitziest ballroom) and room service to five hundred guest rooms. The 'factory' seemed to be run by the Mafia. The don was the *chef de cuisine*, who would now be known as the executive chef. He was the most experienced cook in the whole place, but he did the least cooking—in fact, he did no cooking, except, I noticed, sometimes his own dinner. Under the don were the 'capos', or sous-chefs, each one with a gang (known in the kitchen as a brigade) of cooks and each responsible for the production of one element of a meal, such as sauce, roast, veg, fish, or pastry. In fact, the kitchen was organised almost on the lines of the *Escoffier* cookery book.

I was dispatched to the vegetable section, the least glamorous of all *parties*—and worse, I was allocated a job in the least glamorous corner of the *partie*: the veg prep. Here, one of my daily jobs was to cut the eyes and bad parts from hundreds of potatoes before throwing them into an automatic peeler, which either reduced them to pulp because I left it on too long or spewed out spuds with bits of peelings all over them, which I was supposed to remove by hand. I then spent hours turning the potatoes into nice shapes like rugby balls, which meant wasting roughly a third of each potato. Although this pastime seemed tedious and wasteful, there were always two trainee chefs assigned to the task (the other position rotated), so it did give me the chance to spend many hours with young men who had decided to make their careers in kitchens—something that in later years was of immense help. I spent many unpressured hours discussing every subject under the sun with men and boys who came, in the main, from far less privileged circumstances than myself, but all of whom had something to teach me—and I don't mean about vegetables.

On the odd occasion, I was sprung from the veg prep to the main ranges where I had to serve up the portions of vegetables, as called for by the *aboyeur*—the man who stands at the pass and yells for the food as it is required. The hierarchy of the kitchen amazed me. During the hectic service period, whilst cooks were scrambling all over the place to produce meals on one side of the pass, the most experienced cooks, the head chef, the first sous-chef, and the second sous-chef all stood on the other side keeping cool.

At the time, perhaps the most useful thing I learned from my fellow veg preppers was how to earn a bob or two by illicitly selling meals to the rest of the hotel staff, not, of course, over the counters of the staff canteen, nor over the pass in front of the don. The market for freshly prepared meals to employees through the back door for a shilling a plate was greatly enhanced by the disgraceful standard of the grub that was on offer in the staff canteen.

After several months wasted in the North Block kitchens, I was transferred to the Burghley Room, a restaurant, which, fortunately for me, was serviced by the South Block Kitchen, so my inept reputation had not preceded me. The hierarchy in the restaurant was equally bizarre. There was one restaurant manager, assisted by three headwaiters. None of them actually ever waited on tables. The room was divided into stations, and at each station there was, in descending order of importance, a station headwaiter, a *chef de rang* and a *commis de rang*. The station headwaiter took the customers' orders, the *commis* ran to the kitchen to place and ultimately collect the order, and the *chef de rang* served the food. Wine and beverages were handled by a separate crew of specialists, also with its own hierarchy. As a result of this traditional and quite ridiculously overstaffed structure, the restaurant frequently had more staff than diners. However, the most glaring organisation fault soon became apparent to me. As the lowliest, least experienced person in the restaurant, it was my job to go to the kitchen and place an order with the most experienced, longest serving, senior person there—the head chef. This interrelationship was fraught with danger because, as a young *commis* waiter, I had to be very careful not to tell the head chef what to cook—which is, of course, exactly what I was doing. Ego frequently got in the way, and it often did not seem to matter to the chef when the customer was ready for his soufflé; what was important was when the chef was ready! Fortunately, modern technology, utilising I-pad type equipment has alleviated much of the aggressiveness between restaurant and kitchen, but dangerous interfaces do still exist.

By working in the restaurant, I discovered, just as I had in the kitchen, that the controls were ineffective. For example, every night the *commis* waiters would vie with one another for the job of putting the cheese trolley into the kitchen refrigerator. This afforded a *commis* (though not me, I must say) with the golden opportunity of stealing a chicken or whatever, which was then conveniently 'warehoused' on a pipe that ran along the wall above the cold room door, until it could be retrieved whilst going off duty, after all of the chefs had gone home. How ticking pieces of paper with red felt-tip pens in the control office could be expected to stop this robbery, I never knew.

As a future manager, the time at GH did not teach me much about standards. It did open my eyes to the crazy organisational structure that had evolved in European hotels, which could actually hamper good standards. I also started to see how job titles almost demanded a certain behaviour that was often neither appropriate nor customer friendly. It also taught me that control of assets couldn't be achieved through paperwork alone, because that is like shutting the stable door after the horse has bolted. Good control takes place through prevention. Most other forms of control are often too late.

## Chapter Two
## A TASTE OF AMERICA

Upon leaving college, I needed to get a job. Most of my fellow graduates had been pointed in the direction of graduate training schemes with a few large hotel chains that were beginning to emerge at the time. My romance with Diana had blossomed. Despite having proposed marriage to her, this was not actually possible, because her departed husband had not agreed to allow a divorce, even though he had made no effort to contact his children for the previous two years. Diana and I decided it would be unwise to live together, but because of my frequent visitations, I had become a sort of surrogate father to Sue and Simon, and I had every intention that one day, as soon as possible, I would regularise the situation by marrying their mother and adopting them. Part of this plan would, of course, require me to become the wage earner for my little ready-made family. Becoming a graduate trainee would not be good enough; I needed a real job that paid real money.

At about the time of my graduation, a new hotel was opening in London's Knightsbridge. It was to be called the Carlton Tower and to be operated by Hotel Corporation of America; it was to be the first new hotel built in London after the war and the first belonging to an American operator. Completely against the advice of my college professors, I applied for, and was offered, a position as a front-desk clerk. "How can you throw away four years of college by taking such a lowly job?" they whinged. It was quite simple: the pay was to be ten pounds per week, with the chance of some extra cash from tips, and I had to do my bit to feed and clothe two children. Something else, however, had stirred in me. By taking this job, I was not following the crowd; most of my fellow graduates were routinely taking positions in executive training schemes with British hotel companies. I was doing something different, and even though it was the lowliest of jobs, I felt that it helped me express my individuality. But most of all, I was putting my foot into the door of America!

As it turned out, my instincts were right. The Americans did things differently from the stuffy English hotel chains, which were steeped in the world of station headwaiters, *chefs de rang,* and *commis*. At the Carlton Tower, we had a Rib Room; we served eighteen-ounce portions of prime rib basted in its own succulent juices, not two ounces thinly sliced with warm gravy. In our lobby, we served sandwiches stacked high with turkey, not two slivers of thinly sliced cucumber. We had hotel rooms put together by Henry End, one of the world's leading hotel interior designers, not by the wife of the hotel's managing director. I soaked up this atmosphere. It challenged me; it invigorated me.

Not all was rosy. I was interviewed and hired by an American, Franklin Vick, who had been sent from Boston to oversee the opening. Playing it safe, however, the company had appointed a well-known European hotel general manager, Antoine (Tony to us) Dirsztay. Tony was a tyrant. He loathed his American boss's democratic and open style, and as soon as Franklin had returned to Boston, Tony set about undoing all that Franklin had achieved. We, the staff, hated Tony Dirsztay. He treated his employees as if they were inmates of a concentration camp. His management style was totally demotivating, not just for a lowly desk clerk, but for his entire management and supervisory team. He ruled by fear. I have never disliked anyone as much as I did this man. But I needed the job, and despite Tony, not because of him, the hotel was turning out to be a huge success.

I was determined to put my best foot forward, to get noticed (if possible, by the visiting Americans from the head office), to get promoted, to get on. Not that being a desk clerk was all bad. At least I got to meet the guests. This was always interesting and sometimes quite profitable. To a desk clerk, the opportunity to hand a room key to a visiting sheikh in return for a five-pound tip, when you were only earning ten pounds per week, was really worthwhile. Years later, I joked with the Maktoum family in Dubai that I had been in business with their late father, Sheikh Rashid: I'd had the room keys; he'd had the money.

This was also an exciting time in the world, and the Carlton Tower became a second home to the movers and shakers. It was here that I met the Beatles, Arnold Palmer, Gary Player, Mark McCormack, Robert Altman, Shirley Bassey, David Frost, Otto Preminger, Dudley Moore, Rod Laver, Jackie Stewart, Sharon Tate and many more. They will not remember me, but they were mostly also just starting out, and it was great to be part of it, albeit on the fringe. It was not just the glamour that was fascinating; for a young man from the suburbs of London, the interaction with seemingly successful people from all over the world—the 'jetsetters', even the international businessmen—was an eye-opener. I hadn't entered the hotel business because I 'liked people', but I now realised that by being at the sharp end, you got to meet lots and lots of people, and, like them or not, it was extremely interesting.

Somehow, I came to the attention of a visiting senior vice president, Carl Albers, who suggested to Tony that I be given a chance in the management services department. This was the American version of the control office at Grosvenor House, but this office exercised real and intelligent control. My new boss was Roger Doswell, an Englishman who had been at Battersea a few years before me, but had taken himself off to America, where he had worked for HCA and impressed them. Roger became my mentor and my friend. Roger hated Tony as much as I did, but Roger was protected, because he had been placed at the CT by 'America'. Roger extended that protection to me. Carl Albers was also an important man in the organisation and, as such, Tony gave him respect. It's strange how bullies become yes-men. Somehow I felt that the door to America was beginning to open up just a tiny crack.

After much difficulty, Diana managed to obtain a divorce—something that was so rare in England at the time that her picture appeared on the front page of London's tabloids and I was cited as 'the other man'. This was perhaps the first time that I learned that justice is not always achieved in a court of law. Nevertheless, the way was now clear for us to marry; after all, I had proposed to her four years earlier, and I was still as keen as mustard.

Not long after we were married, the full impact of the weight of responsibility actually dawned on me. Life seems to have its defining moments, and one now came to me. I had taken Diana and the children in our Mini Minor (on which we couldn't afford to keep up the payments) to the beach on a Sunday. Suddenly, as we were playing together as one happy family, I realised that it was the tenth of the month and I had already spent my monthly paycheque. How was I to feed my family for the rest of the month? This thought hit me like a cold shower. We were living a dream;

we were so happy, but it was still a dream. The reality was that, as a management services clerk at the Carlton Tower, I could not expect to look after my family. On that beach, on that day, I resolved to do something about it.

Within days, I had confronted Roger and then, through him, Carl Albers in Boston. I made is clear that I needed a job with more responsibility and, most importantly, more pay. Thankfully, they listened, and within a few weeks I was the new assistant manager at the Carlton Tower. There were two of us: Hans Apel, a very formal Prussian, and me. Although we were like chalk and cheese, we became very good friends, bound together by the common enemy, our boss, Antoine Dirsztay. Luckily, because I had been forced on him by Vice President Albers, Tony treated me with a certain amount of respect, but he treated poor Hans like dirt, often barking at him in German, their common native tongue. During this time, Tony taught me how *not* to manage; Hans taught me everything he knew, including patience and that the only certainty in life is change. Change came suddenly and surprisingly: Tony dropped dead on the tennis court. The entire hotel breathed a sigh of relief.

Tony's replacement was an aristocratic Hungarian American, George DeKornfeld, who was as much a gentleman as Tony had been a bully. George and his elegant wife, Maria, were the ultimate in good manners, class, and style. But this was not a superficial veneer. With George, this went deep into his character and into his management style. George was fantastic to work for. He instructed, he delegated, and, above all, he trusted. He was always willing to listen to any idea from a subordinate that might improve the standards or profitability of the hotel, and if he gave the green light, he would back you through thick and thin. George understood the importance of the guest.

An in-house meeting with George could be an extremely frustrating affair, because he would always interrupt the proceedings to meet or greet a guest. Frustrating, maybe, but correct.

Shortly after George arrived, he reorganised my responsibilities, and in addition to acting as assistant manager, my brief was extended to include the human resources function. This I tackled with relish, and it was not long before I had grown that function into a full-time job, and after that into a pan-European job, when the company concluded deals to open hotels in Italy and Germany, which in turn fell within George's portfolio. George's ultimate boss was Roger Sonnabend, the eldest of the three sons of Abe Sonnabend, the founder of the company. Roger had, at the time, fallen under the spell of an American behavioural scientist from the Sloane School in Boston, Dick Beckhard. Dick was a pioneer of the 'T-group', which was a controversial form of training utilised to assist with executive personal growth as a way to facilitate organisational change. A T-group takes the form of a group of people (often strangers) being thrown together in a meeting room for a period of at least a week with no agenda, no instruction and no formal leadership. Within the group will be a trainer or trainers, but they will exercise no leadership nor instruction, particularly in the early stages of the group's life. The goal of the T-group is to enhance the participants' self-awareness and their understanding of the effect their behaviour has on others. During the week, the group develops its own particular identity, much as a company does, and lessons on how it functions and changes can be learned and, in some cases, taken back for use in the real world.

Roger Sonnabend had attended some of Dick Beckhard's early T-groups, which had affected him profoundly and had influenced his own management style. Roger was completely sold on the idea that he should share the experience with other executives within Hotel Corporation of America, and, in so doing, create a new corporate 'language' of common understanding that would help the company agree and set its standards of operation for dealing with each other, and ultimately, for dealing with our guests. Roger, of course, was egged on by the good Dr Beckhard, and so when Dick was invited to be senior trainer for the first T-group to be held in Europe, he was able to persuade Roger that there should be at least one attendee from Roger's business in Europe. George was the natural choice, but, for whatever reason (possibly George's fear of the unknown), he ducked it and instead rationalised that it was more important for his personnel director to participate, in order to understand the training technique. I didn't realise it when I agreed to go, but this, for me, was one of those life-defining moments.

The T-group was being held in a castle in the middle of a dense forest in southern Sweden. I had no idea, when I set out from London, what I was going to and what I was going for. The only explanations I had received about the method and purpose of a T-group were confused and, frankly, quite frightening. I flew to Copenhagen, where I was picked up in a bus and driven to Elsinore (Hamlet's castle); then I took a ferry to Sweden, where it seemed we were then driven deeper and deeper into a forest. When I eventually arrived, the T-group castle was strangely reminiscent of the one I'd seen in the Dracula movies. I began to think that George had been right.

The group came together for its first meeting later that evening, and I was immediately immensely surprised and then immensely alarmed. I was the youngest participant by what seemed to be at least twenty years. Since neither Dick nor the other trainer said a word when we all first met, we went through the normal, accepted routine of introducing ourselves to each other—or at least, sharing our job titles. The participants were from all over Europe, and they fell neatly into two distinct categories: they were either the chairmen or managing directors of huge companies, or they were professors of psychology. I was overawed.

The first evening's session was very awkward for me. Of course, what I did not realise at the time was that it was at least as awkward for everyone else. Job titles, as it turned out, were not very important or even useful in this environment. That night, when I went to bed, I tried to think the thing through. I came to the conclusion that I had nothing to lose. The others, on the other hand, in theory had plenty to lose, because here, deep in the forests of Sweden, they were on their own, with no personal assistants, secretaries, or advisers to protect them. Their reputations were at stake; I didn't have one.

The week was an amazing experience. As the unstructured days went by, the group took on a life of its own. Its different members were, one by one, initiated into full membership by sharing something of themselves with the others. Alliances were formed, broken, and reformed. Leaders emerged, and were toppled. Hard truths were told. Behaviour was examined and fed back. Managing directors were reduced to just people. Psychologists became participative, not just reflective. As, one by one, these people exposed themselves, showing both strengths and weaknesses, my confidence grew. As the week wore on, I realised that I might be inferior to them all in terms of experience, but not in terms of being a human being or, indeed, a competent manager. By the end of the week, the group had arrived at a state of harmony. It was at peace with itself; everybody had a place, a role, an equal level of importance. I was as important to the group as the most senior managing director. What that did for my confidence as a young manager was invaluable. I left Sweden knowing that I could conquer the world.

Trying to explain to others in the company what I had been doing proved to be extraordinarily difficult, but somehow the fact that, whatever it was, it was endorsed by the president of the company gave it a certain validity. What I had learned about how a group of disconnected people can, within a week, mould together as a fully functioning team continued to fascinate me, particularly when I looked at the way our hotels were structured in terms of jobs. As a personnel manager, I seemed to be forever in the middle of personality clashes between members of staff, or sorting out operational tangles between different functional heads. Sometimes it seemed to me that the needs and rights of each subsection of the organisation were much more important to the various players than the ultimate service received by our guests. Housekeepers would spend time arguing with front-desk clerks whilst the new arrival waited for a room. A diner would be waiting for food because a chef wanted a waiter to experience difficulty. Why, I wondered, couldn't a hotel function with the same degree of unified purpose that my disparate T-group had done at the end of a week, when we knew and used each other's strengths and did not harp on our weaknesses?

I decided to suggest to George that I be allowed to experiment with a T-group format that I hoped would bond our personnel together. My suggestion was bold and, as far as I am aware, had never been tried before in a hotel organisation. The Carlton Tower had about 450 employees, of which roughly seventy were supervisors or managers in one form or another. In other words, on average, one in six people had at least one person working for him.

On paper, I divided the supervisory organisational chart into diagonal slices of ten per slice, thus creating seven groupings of managers and supervisors, but mixed up by department and seniority. I proposed to George that he allow me to arrange for seven back-to-back T-groups, on the basis that this would be a massive team-building exercise, which could only smooth out the functioning of the hotel, and thus benefit our customers. George was interested, but not convinced. He also pointed out the impracticality of paying for seven weeks of professional trainers.

Undeterred, I discussed my plan with the human resources director in Boston, Alan Marsh, and persuaded him to invite me to Boston for training as an in-house trainer with Dr Beckhard. Dick, of course, thought this was a great idea, and put in a word for me where it mattered—with George's boss—and before I knew it, I was in America as a sort of apprentice T-group trainer with an expert, Jan Clee. Within weeks, I was back in the UK, having sold my back-to-back group idea to all of the people who mattered in the company, and George was now happy to have his Carlton Tower as the focus of a major company behavioural-change experiment. Since I was so inexperienced, the Boston office, with Alan's encouragement, lent me the company's senior training manager, Jim Hynes, to guide me through the first few sessions of the weeklong programs, which we structured as T-groups under the guise of 'communications training'.

Since running these back-to-back programs would require almost total immersion, I decided to hold them in a small hotel in the country, near our home in Sussex. This would allow me, I thought, to be able to sneak home each night and to return to the group before breakfast. This, I thought, would be some comfort to Diana, rather than my disappearing for seven weeks. As it turned out it, was also of immense help to me to be able to break away from the intensity of the sessions. In an environment where there was a danger that I would try to make each successive group more meaningful and powerful for its participants than the last, I needed to talk to someone who would make me keep my feet firmly on the ground. Diana became that person.

On the advice of Jim Hynes, we did not actually run successive sessions, but instead ran two, with a break for a week, then two more followed by another break, and then the final three, back to back. Jim's advice was spot-on. I never could have finished seven in a row, and the intensity of the whole thing would have been very difficult for Diana, an outsider to the groups, to take. As it was, it was exceptionally hard work, and I owed a great vote of thanks to two other people I had enlisted for help upon Jim's departure, my own assistant, Geoff Pye, and my old college professor, Philip Nailon.

The whole team-building plan was a triumph. As each successive group returned to the hotel, emanating warmth and kindness toward each other, the people who had yet to attend were intrigued. At first, of course, the attendees were the oddballs, but as the weeks went by, it was the people who had yet to attend that became the odd men out. Eventually, everyone joined the club, and a team spirit had been created across the departmental barriers of the hotel, wiping out the old enmities that had previously been built into the system. The benefits of this work lasted for well over a year, and a side benefit was that nobody wanted to leave this happy family, so staff turnover dropped to almost nil. Gradually, old bad habits crept in, so two years later, we repeated the same process—this time, of course, with different group mixes. I shall be forever grateful that these early experiments were tolerated, even encouraged, by George. What George got in return for his trust was the most efficient and successful hotel in London. He also got to be godfather to our youngest son, Jonathan.

As part of my pan-European personnel responsibilities, I

was required to help set up and open a new HCA hotel in Milan, Italy. The hotel was a modern building in Via Turani, close to the Stazione Centrale and the famous Gallia Excelsior Hotel. Our new hotel shared the ground floor with Alitalia, which used this building as an in-city terminal.

The general manager of the hotel was an incredible man who had, like George DeKornfeld, escaped from the communist regime in Europe and somehow made his way to the USA, where he had started as a dishwasher. Albert Elovic was a complete extrovert. He claimed to speak seventeen different languages, always had a joke on the tip of his tongue, and made a perfect, if somewhat flamboyant host. As a manager, however, Albert had his shortcomings, not the least of which was a lack of attention to detail—not the sort of details that would concern a guest, for in matters regarding service, he was impeccable—but in boring things like accounting, paperwork, reports, payroll and controls. I was, therefore, quite useful to him, since I attempted to bring some order to his chaos without threatening him.

Despite all of his joie de vivre, Albert never touched a drop of alcohol. One day, I asked him why. One evening, he explained, when he had been the manager of a hotel in Quebec, he'd had as hotel guests the president of Somewhere and the president's wife, who had been allocated a suite not dissimilar to the one that Albert and his wife Ada were living in at the time. The hotel was patronised by the military brass, who were frequently to be found in Albert's cocktail bar getting smashed, with Albert the heaviest imbiber. On this particular night, Albert had left the bar quite inebriated and headed for his suite. Unwittingly, using his master key, he had let himself into the visiting president's suite, which was one floor above his own and presumably looked similar from the hallway—especially if you were drunk. Not wishing to wake Ada, he had found his way to the bedroom and undressed in the dark, leaving a pile of clothes on the floor beside the bed. Once in the bed, he'd decided that he felt like a bit of nookie (his words) and snuggled up to 'Ada'. The president's wife had awakened from her sleep and let out a scream. Albert claimed that, not recognising the scream, he had become instantly sober. He'd jumped out of bed, gathered up his clothes, rushed onto the balcony, swung over the railing, and found himself on the balcony of the suite below, whereupon he had jumped into his own bed just in time for the phone to ring to be informed that somebody had tried to rape the president's wife. Albert never touched another drop of alcohol.

Albert was a great supporter of my behavioural-change activities, and sent several members of his opening team to participate in the T-groups in the UK. He also allowed me free run to engage in some really interesting pre-opening team-building exercises in Milan, and then, after the hotel had been open for a year or so, asked me to devise some bonding sessions for his supervisors. Following the pattern we had established in Sussex, England, I rented a wing of the Grand Bretagne Hotel in Bellagio, Lake Como, in order to get the attendees away from their own work environment. I picked Bellagio because that is where I had stayed for a couple of months with Diana and the children whilst we were opening the Milan hotel. They had absolutely loved it. We had stayed at a little *albergo* where the owner kept rabbits in the backyard, which the children had adored. Little had they known that the 'chicken' they had regularly eaten for supper originally had big ears.

The Grand Bretagne was not as great as it sounds, but then neither, I suppose, is Britain. It looked grand from the outside, but it was like sleeping in the Victoria and Albert Museum: you felt surrounded by the past. In many ways, it was not far removed from the castle in Sweden.

Running T-groups in Italy was a completely different experience from doing so in the USA or England. In these countries, the participants, upon finding out that there was no leadership coming from the trainers, quickly turned on them. In Italy, probably due to the very strong influence of the authoritarian Catholic Church at the time, participants were completely flummoxed in a leaderless vacuum. They were used to being told what to do. As a result of this, the life of each group developed very slowly in the early part of the week, but normally finished with fireworks as they eventually became rebellious with zeal. On the final week, I could not get the group to open up, to be themselves, to shake off their 'uniforms'.

On the last night, I decided to throw a party. Everyone got drunk, and although I was trying not to, because I wanted to keep my wits about me, I probably did have one grappa too many, and finished up standing on a chair leading a chorus of 'God Save the Queen'. Suddenly, something happened. One of the members of the group asked if we could go back to the meeting room, because he had something to say. We quickly agreed, even though it was nearly midnight, that we would return to work. The session that followed was gruelling; all through the night, until the middle of the following afternoon, the participants, one by one, shared their feelings with their companions, and eventually a team was built. I left Bellagio exhausted, but content.

I was so encouraged by, enthused by, and interested in this subject of organisational change that I discussed at length with Diana the possibility of taking it up professionally. To do so would require me to receive clinical training, and *the* place to do that would have been in Bethel, USA. Diana did nothing to discourage me, but we just couldn't work out the practicalities of me not being a wage earner, because not only did we now have Sue and Simon, but they had been supplemented by Sarah and Jonathan. Going back to college was not a practical option for me. Besides, just as this idea was passing, another opportunity appeared. George was promoted to vice president for Europe. The Carlton Tower would need a manager, and I was offered the job. At the age of twenty-eight, I could not turn down the offer to be in charge of London's most successful luxury hotel. It was another defining moment and an opportunity, which I accepted gratefully. I would be the youngest manager of a prestige hotel in London; the trainee manager route would have taken much longer.

# Chapter Three
## AFRICA CALLING

Change, as always, was inevitable. Not long after I had taken up my position as manager of the Carlton Tower, Hotel Corporation of America ran into financial difficulties, not because of the Carlton Tower, but because of dollar-based loans in Europe at a time when European currencies were taking a dive. (This would not be the last time that such a scenario affected me. Many years later, I was a director of a cinema company which built about 400 screens across Europe, only to find that the price of admissions, popcorn, and coke was badly eroded by the fall of the new euro against the dollar—so much so that we lost practically all of our investment.) As a result of this, Roger Sonnabend had to sell something, and, unfortunately for me, the jewel in the crown was the Carlton Tower. There was much mysterious coming and going, and many calls for projections and balance sheets, and requests to show 'friends of Roger' around the hotel. The rumour mill was churning, but (as usual) not without reason. Roger was negotiating the sale of the jewel to Trevor Chinn, the founder of Lex Motors, a company whose meteoric rise had been based on the exclusive rights to sell Volvo cars and trucks in the UK. To me, the manager, it was quite a leap from trucks to luxury hotels, so I naturally expressed an interest to stay with HCA, especially if that meant a transfer to the USA. These requests are never easy when a company is downsizing, but if words are anything to go by, serious efforts were being made to accommodate me, when Sol Kerzner arrived on my doorstep.

Kerzner, a South African, had been trained as an accountant in Durban. His father had owned a small kosher hotel near Durban Harbour. Sol, whilst working for Arthur Anderson, had nursed an ambition to get into the hotel business, which he had observed was very immature in South Africa at the time. The three major cities—Johannesburg, Cape Town, and Durban—each had a few elderly and tired hotels, which claimed to be luxurious, but in fact were practically obsolete and had not been refurbished for years. Most of the rest of the hotel rooms in South Africa were above pubs. There were no decent resort hotels at all, and archaic liquor-licensing laws still prevented women from going to hotel bars, except under special circumstances. Despite this, South Africa was emerging into the world as the economic powerhouse for the region, driven by its huge mineral exports and its strategic geographical position between the Atlantic and Indian Oceans—something of interest to both the free West and the communist East.

Sol had spotted the gap. A few years before, whilst still in his late twenties, he had gathered up his life savings of approximately $25,000 and acquired a small plot of sea-facing land in a village about ten miles north of the main beach area in Durban. He had then set about trying to convince the shareholders in the companies he audited to back him in building an eighty-room resort on the land. Most people thought that he was crazy, a bookkeeper with no hotel experience, trying to build a resort hotel so far out of town. But little by little, by dint of his great self-belief and enthusiasm, he gathered in the pledges.

With limited finances, Sol had set off to visit the premier

resort town in the world at the time, Miami Beach, where he'd met Ben Novak. Ben as the owner of the famous Fontainebleau Hotel, although many would say that Ben was fronting for the Mafia, which allegedly considered Ben's hotel to be the perfect spot for a casino, should Miami Beach ever allow one. There is no question that Ben had some connections, because what other seaside hotel would have been able to feature Frank Sinatra, Sammy Davis Junior, and Dean Martin in a little entertainment room— all on the same bill? When Sol visited Ben, he had just completed a new wing of the hotel, which, unlike every other double-banked hotel on Miami Beach, consisted of a gracefully curved building with a corridor at the back and all guest rooms facing the sea. This was considered in America to be a very inefficient way to build, but it certainly did enhance the guest experience, although there were others that say that Ben built it this way so that the plain-looking corridor wall spoiled the views from the neighbouring Eden Roc's guest rooms. It certainly cast a shadow for most of the day over the Eden Roc's swimming pool.

Sol came back from the USA with a design for his little hotel firmly in his head. The result was a gently curving single-banked building with all rooms facing the sea. It was perched on a platform, housing a restaurant that overlooked a massive swimming pool with the sea beyond; at the lowest level was a nightclub. He named the hotel Beverly Hills and the nightclub Cococabana. Sol had never been slow to copy a good idea, but in so doing, his genius had been to improve it. The Beverly Hills became a great success. Sol hired 'characters' to be in guest interaction positions. His front-desk clerks were pretty; his restaurant manager would remember you, but you would also remember him; and his pool superintendent, Harry, was everyone's best friend. Knowing him well naturally guaranteed a chaise longue in the best position. It was the only genuine resort hotel in South Africa. Soon, every visiting celebrity from overseas—whether film star, politician, or sportsman—had to be seen at the Beverly Hills, and Sol was always there to meet them.

With his first profits, Sol managed to acquire another prime seafront site in a strategic position in Durban. He began to draw up plans for a 450-room hotel, to be called Elangeni, a Zulu word meaning 'place in the sun'. In South Africa, a hotel of this size was unheard of. Since Sol did not have the money to build the Elangeni, he approached South African Breweries (SAB), which owned many pubs and sites in South Africa and was the only brewer, importer, and distributor of beer. The result of these discussions was to be a new company called Southern Sun, 10% of which was owned by Sol Kerzner, his family, and backers from the Beverly Hills; and the rest by SAB. Sol contributed the Beverly Hills and the Durban land; SAB were to contribute several existing 'pub' hotels and all the finances needed to build not just the Elangeni, but also a chain of resort hotels, including additions to many of their existing premises, where appropriate.

It was at this point that Sol walked into my life, or, more exactly, I walked into his. The first time I met Sol, he was causing a fuss—something he never stopped doing. I was called to the lobby of the Carlton Tower to assist with a difficult guest. Sol was being unpleasant, but not without cause. I invited him into my office (loud, offensive language in the lobby was not really appropriate), and we quickly sorted out the problem. Two weeks later, he was back, this time with a job offer. He had heard that I had been the European personnel manager for HCA, and he knew that his newly formed Southern Sun was going to need management. The offer was to be his personnel director, based in Johannesburg. I immediately declined and politely explained that I had no intention of living in apartheid South Africa, that my father-in-law was a leading light in the anti-apartheid movement, that Diana would never come, that I had four children, that I wanted to go to America, and so on. None of this deterred Sol. "Why don't you come down for a week's holiday? Then you can see for yourself that it's not like you read in the papers. I can show you our hotels, and explain our plans for the future."

The thought of a free holiday in South Africa sparked my interest, but I couldn't go on my own. "I don't go on holiday without my wife," I replied. Sol stared out of the window of my office, deep in thought.

"I tell you what," he finally said. "I'll pay your fare and half your wife's. If you join me, I'll pick up the other half."

Instantaneously, I stuck out my hand. "Deal. But I want you to know that I am 99.9% sure I will not be joining your company."

This time, the response was immediate: "I'll take my fucking chances!"

The trip to South Africa was exciting. Diana was adamant that she was only going on vacation, and even then, somewhat reluctantly. She was not looking at a possible relocation. I was intrigued by the job opportunity, but also unhappy about the location. It was also the first time Diana had left the children behind, and Jonathan was only a few months old. In 1970, Boeing 707s did not have the range to reach Johannesburg, so we first placed our feet on African soil in Nairobi, Kenya. We were only there for an hour, but somehow I began to sense the magic of Africa. I had never dreamed that I would travel so far from home. Jan Smuts Airport in Johannesburg had a tiny, one-storey white arrivals building with a prefabricated look about it. There were no jetways or computers. A white immigration official was seated at a little wooden desk; he looked at all foreigners suspiciously and spoke with a very heavy Afrikaans accent. The skies into South Africa were very carefully controlled. South African Airways was owned by the government, and other carriers were not exactly welcome.

We were whisked around South Africa on a whirlwind tour. Sol's planning was meticulous; the only hiccup was that he had not bargained on Diana wanting to visit Soweto, the vast African dormitory several miles from Johannesburg and safely out of view. "You can visit slums anywhere in the world," he protested, but she was adamant and, quite rightly, got her way—although we later realised that she had been taken on a rather sanitised tour. At the end of our trip I was scheduled to meet up with Sol on the Saturday morning before we departed, to review the situation. On Friday, without consulting Sol, I broke away from the 'tour' and insisted on meeting with the personnel director of South African Breweries. He was horrified to learn that Sol, the managing director of a small subsidiary, had flown two people from Europe for a recce without his permission, knowledge, or involvement. This was, apparently, against all group personnel policies. Oops!

News of my visit to SAB had obviously reached Sol by the time I met him the next day. He was clearly unconcerned; in fact, if anything, he was impressed that I had forced my way in. The result of our meeting that morning, however, was not to his liking. I thanked him for the wonderful vacation, but declined his job offer. I explained that, in my view, Sol did not need a personnel director; more exactly, he would not know how to use one. He did his best to convince me that I was wrong, but could see it was to no avail. In a way, by turning down the job, I had found a convenient way of not confronting the real issue: would I be prepared to live in South Africa, or, more importantly, would we be prepared to live in South Africa and could we bring up our children there? This was a far more complex issue to deal with than the job, as despite our misgivings about the country before our arrival, we had found it so varied, beautiful, and interesting, and the people we had met so welcoming and pleasant, that it had started to get its hooks into us.

If we thought that we had avoided having to make a decision on this issue, we were wrong, because as soon as I stepped into my office that Monday, I received a call from Sol. He'd been thinking about things, and would I consider being general manager of operations, with direct responsibility for the management of all of the hotels as they came on line—and a salary that was at least twice what I was getting at the CT, and a contract for two years, renewable if we all got on well?

The rationalisation process that Diana and I went through was fairly swift. After all, it was only for two years; we could probably do more against apartheid by being there than in England; we weren't certain that HCA would come up with an alternative in the USA; and twice the money sounded pretty good. What about the children? It would be no trouble for Sarah and Jonathan; she was only five and he was less than a year old. But Sue was twelve, and Simon ten. Not only was that not a great age to move children around, but I had still not been able to get their birth father to allow me to adopt them—even though he had not seen them since he had left and had never sent either of them a birthday or Christmas card or present. I knew, however, that if I were to ask his permission to take them out of the country, he would refuse.

Probably without giving the matter sensible consideration we decided to go. As far as I was concerned, it was more of an intuitive act than a considered one. I just had a feeling that it would turn out all right. Diana was less sure, but she was supportive, as always. Our respective parents were not thrilled, but they put on a brave face. Off we went, without notifying Sue and Simon's father. If he couldn't be bothered to see them in Horsham, I didn't think he'd be bothering us in Johannesburg. I suppose we broke a law or two in this regard, but, as it turned out, I believe that neither of the children regretted it.

Diana decided that she would like to travel with the children by ship. These were still the days when people went on ships to get somewhere rather than to get away from something. Sol wanted me to start yesterday, so I couldn't afford the time for the leisurely trip. I also thought it would give me a couple of weeks ahead of the family to get organised. I took my little family to Southampton and saw them onto the *Orcades*. Even though I was to see them a couple of weeks later, it was still an emotional moment: another defining one. As it turned out, Diana and the children had a great time on the journey, although as they reached the destination, chicken pox had spread through the ship like a dose of corona A.

My first recollection of our offices in Johannesburg is of one of my new Afrikaans colleagues, Mossie Mostert, shouting down the hallway at a black office cleaner—something about him being a "dumb Kaffir." I was not impressed with Mossie, but I soon learned that he actually was a real softy, and we were to become good friends until the day he passed away. My second recollection is of how scared everyone was of Kerzner. I determined that I would not let this man become my second Tony Dirsztay; I would let him see that I was not going to be intimidated.

During my first week on the job, I had the opportunity to draw a line in the sand. I had flown down to Durban to meet the management of the newly opened Elangeni. I decided to have a series of one-on-one interviews, first with the general manager, and then with his top team. The general manager told me about his people, but was particularly cautious about his rooms' division manager, who had been appointed, like me, by Sol on a European trip and who seemed to have a direct line to the boss. As I interviewed the other executives, I learned more and more about how disruptive this man was being for the rest of the team. When it came to my meeting with him, he was so arrogant and dismissive of me that I, there and then, told him that I, too could be dismissive, and that I didn't want him on my team; i.e. that he was fired. Within minutes, there was a phone call from Joburg. Naturally, it was from Sol. Had I gone mad? What was I doing? I told him that he had hired me to make the operational decisions and that I had made one. Sol was quite impressed; the rooms' division manager was not. A few days after that I was equally impressed with Sol. A labour strike had broken out at the Elangeni and I had begun negotiations with the striking members' union, as was my experience in Europe. "What the fuck are you doing?" he bawled down the phone from Joburg. When I explained that I was negotiating he practically imploded. "Negotiate, fuck! I'm coming down," which he did – on the next flight. When he arrived the striking staff we all assembled in the loading bay area of the hotel, happily singing away in Zulu. "Watch this," barked Sol, as he careered off towards the rear of the hotel. There, standing on the loading platform he addressed the mob, who had fallen silent upon his arrival. "If you are not back to work by the time I count to ten, you are fired," he yelled. "One, two, three…" There was an immediate move, no, stampede, for the employee entrance. Nobody was left in the loading bay. Sol turned round and grinned. "Now you can talk to the union," he gloated, and, with that, caught the next plane back.

I collected Diana and the chicken-poxed children from the ship in Durban. They had originally been booked to Cape Town, but hadn't wanted to leave their newfound friends who were en route to Australia, so we had let them all sail on for a few more days. We moved into the Sunnyside Park Hotel in Joburg as a staging post whilst we looked for more permanent lodgings. I remember that afternoon well. It was raining. It was a weekend. The excitement of the cruise had worn off; the nervousness of the new life ahead was now a reality.

For the children, this was a strange place. I decided to cheer them up—at least the older ones—and take them to the movies. They became even more puzzled; the cinemas were called 'bios', and the movies were 'fillums'. What's more, ladies had actually dressed up in long skirts and white gloves to go there—and the gloves were not to protect them from the popcorn, because there was a 'no food in the bio' rule. Sue and Simon thought they were in a time warp.

We quickly found a house to rent in the northern suburb of Craighall, and went through all of the pain of locating schools, doctors, dentists, and so on—or, at least, Diana went through this particular pain. Diana was terrific; coping with a new life with four children was a monumental task, and clearly others thought so, too. One evening, not long after we had moved into the "rental," there was a knock at the front door. Upon opening it, I was confronted with a very pretty young African girl of about eighteen. "I've come to work for the madam," she announced.

Diana joined me at the door. "I don't need anyone to work for me," she quietly explained.

"But you have four children, madam," the girl replied. "You must have help." Diana had quite decided that she did not like the idea of having an African nanny, even though the rental house had staff quarters in the backyard. But it was hard to resist this pretty young thing, especially when she said, "Well, may I stay for one night, madam? I have nowhere to go."

With that, Diana relented. "You can stay for one night, but then you must go. What is your name?"

"Lisa, madam."

Lisa Mojopelo stayed for ten years.

Diana's task of settling in a new country with four young children was not eased by the fact that the extremely dry climate and high altitude, which they were obviously not used to in southern England, caused a plethora of childhood illnesses. For the older children, the strict school regime also took some getting used to. For example, Simon was sent home one day from school with a drawing of a head, in profile, with an arrow at the back showing the permissible length of hair, together with the clear message that he should not return to school until the back of his head coincided with the diagram. For a youngster coming from the home of The Beatles, this was a cruel and unusual punishment.

In addition to this, I was away from home a great deal, either overseas, looking for staff (of which you will hear later), or in other towns in South Africa where we were either opening hotels or making plans to do so. Though normally able to cope, there came a time when even Diana reached her breaking point, and I foolishly was too busy to notice it coming.

I was in Durban, two days after opening the 400-room Malibu Hotel, when I got a call from an Italian friend in Johannesburg. "Peter, I theenk you shoul'a comer 'ome. Diana, she wanna sella me 'er car to buy e air teekets a Inglittera. I theenk Diana, she is seeck." Given this startling news, I rushed back to Joburg. Upon arrival home, I discovered that Diana was in bed with raging scarlet fever. She had been sent there by our doctor. She had a dangerously high temperature, and it had been in this state of misery that she had decided enough is enough and wanted to take the family back home. The pressures of moving away from family and friends, and of coping with four children in a foreign land without much help from an absentee husband had, like her temperature, boiled over. Obviously, the first priority was to get rid of the fever, which luckily subsided within a few days.

This had, however, been a real reality check, and clearly I would have to make some serious adjustments to how I was behaving. This I really tried to do, but with an exceptionally demanding boss in Kerzner, it was far from easy. Diana, bless her, knew that I had enough pressure to cope with without more from her, but now, at least, we were able to come face-to-face with the realities we were having to deal with, and were talking about them as a shared problem. This we needed to do, because new challenges were about to be faced in Mozambique and at the Beacon Isle Hotel.

# Chapter Four
## REVOLUTION

At the age of twenty-nine, when I was still young enough for travel to be exciting, Lourenco Marques (now Maputo), the capital of Mozambique, was a fascinating, although slightly mysterious place. It was still a proud outpost of the Portuguese empire, albeit one of the last remnants, and it had more continental colonial feel about it than its independent neighbour, 'apartheid' South Africa. To go from South Africa to LM, as it was universally and affectionately described by anyone who had been there, you either flew by South African Airways (or TAP) or you drove from South Africa's picturesque Eastern Transvaal, along the southerly end of Kruger Park, through the border post of Komatipoort, and for about two hours across the shrubby African veldt of rural Mozambique. The road was intermittently tar and dirt, and although only a few African huts were visible from time to time, blanket-wrapped Africans would frequently appear from nowhere, walking bolt-upright and purposefully in all directions, balancing pots or fruit or firewood, or even sometimes a single plastic bottle, on their erect heads. One always wondered where they were going and where they had come from! And, why?

The road from the airport to the town was not impressive, although it did leave a lasting impression. It was a fairly broad carriageway, well past its prime, with potholes and dead shrubs and live weeds in the central island; presumably built for a Portuguese state visit in years gone by, it was now flanked with scenes of intense poverty. Hundreds of poor Africans who had migrated to the edge of LM were living (although that is an exaggeration) in shacks made of cardboard boxes, with the occasional luxury of a corrugated tin roof. Water was drawn from a few taps on the side of the road. God knows where the toilets were; I suppose they weren't.

This was all particularly shocking to me, coming from the comfortable white suburbs of Johannesburg, because it was the first time that I'd seen real shantytowns, with the possible exception perhaps, in those days, of the outskirts of Lisbon. In the northern suburbs of Johannesburg, I hadn't, at that time, seen slums, although if I'd looked beyond my nose (which I later did), I could not have missed one of the worst slums in the world. The Alexandra township was situated smack in the middle of some of the most affluent districts to be found anywhere, an area which in those days made Beverly Hills look like a ghetto. Indeed, flying over the northern suburbs of Johannesburg in the early 1970s, you were struck by the huge number of sparkling swimming pools and green tennis courts. Someone once said to me that it was not chic in Joburg to have a tennis court—but it was chic to have four people on one.

So an arrival in LM from Johannesburg was always somewhat shocking. More shocking still was the employee housing at the Polana Hotel. The Polana was a stunning example of the architecture of Sir Herbert Baker, famous for his design of the Union Building in Pretoria, one of the seats of parliament in South Africa. It stood like a white monument to Portuguese colonialism, on a prominent cliff at one end of the bustling city of LM. Its formal gardens, around which the building wrapped, overlooked the warm waters of the Indian Ocean, whence came abundant supplies of the most marvellous prawns, which appeared as an essential part of every menu in Johannesburg as, simply, 'LM Prawns'. Although its interiors were tired and faded, the Polana still had the presence of a great classical hotel and was, unquestionably, the best address in town. Its front-of-house grandeur, however, contrasted dramatically and horribly with the back-of-house. The service corridors were dirty, as were the kitchens, which were full of obsolete and mostly broken equipment. Its eighty-year-old coal-fired boilers, if cleaned, would have fitted well into the London Science Museum, although miraculously, like cars in Cuba, they still worked.

Immediately behind the boiler room was one of the worst scenes I had yet to witness in Africa. About a hundred employees were living in a filthy, crumbling room that would, perhaps, have been large enough for ten of them, not that even ten would have chosen to live there. When I first visited this room on the day that we (Southern Sun) acquired the leasehold on the Polana, I was so shocked and horrified that I felt ashamed to be a white boss in Africa. There was no heating and no ventilation. The room was crammed full of bunkbeds: some wooden, some rusty metal, and mostly broken. Many bunks were covered with disgustingly soiled mattresses on which were lolling listless off-duty workers who peered at me with sad, tired eyes. Many bunks had men on them, but no mattresses—presumably because, in the end, even a hard wooden base had become more desirable than a putrid mattress. There were no lockers, so the few personal belongings they had were either draped over the ends of the bunks or stashed in cardboard boxes. In some places, the room was so overcrowded that more stinking mattresses had been placed on the floor between the rows of bunks, making it impossible to walk around without treading on someone's 'bed'. The smell was unbearable, probably since it was summer, and LM can be a hot and humid place—even more so next to the boiler room. Bad as it was, nothing could have prepared one for the toilet and washing facilities, which were in such a dilapidated and unclean state that the stench was excruciating.

Why on earth, I asked myself, did these people put up with this treatment? What depths of despair had they reached not to do something about it, and to what depths of depravity had the previous owners of this business sunk to have allowed it? What, I soon discovered, made matters even more unbelievable, was that the wages being paid to most of these poor souls were the monthly equivalent of ten dollars per head. No wonder they had so few possessions!

As the newly appointed general manager of operations for Southern Sun Hotels, I was responsible, amongst other things, for making a commercial success of this new trophy hotel, so my natural desire to tear down and rebuild the employee housing and give all workers a 1000% wage increase would have to be tempered by the financial interests of my shareholders and the opinions of my chairman, Sol Kerzner, who was also, after all, a white South African boss. I also quickly discovered that perhaps half of the residents of this black hole didn't even work for us, but found it convenient to patronise our equally squalid staff canteen. My considered decision was to give everybody (at least, those who were actually on our payroll) a 100% wage increase, followed by a further 100% increase a few months later, after we had pruned out some who, although on the payroll, didn't actually do anything. At the same time I arranged for the black hole, as we came to know it, to be shut down, renovated and re-equipped. Additional premises were found for the overflow staff, although numbers, by this time, had been substantially reduced by the pruning.

As a result of these actions, I quickly became something of a hero to the local staff, although their situation would soon become, for me, a perfect example of the theory that increased pay does not create increased satisfaction. Salary increases, I had been told, are like food: you get hungry, you eat. You are not 'satisfied', you are just not hungry anymore—but now you get hungry again, and guess what? You want more food. Well, I was soon to find out at the Polana that after 100% salary increases, the people got 'hungry' again.

However, the immediate effect of goodwill between staff and management was striking. For example, the hotel had one of those beautiful cage-type elevators, encased in decorative wrought iron, with gates that clanged authoritatively. The lift and the gates were operated by a rather rotund African, whose uniform never quite fitted. Either as a result of previous subservience to the Portuguese, or as a result of his salary increase, he would insist on addressing me as "Your Majesty." On several occasions I told him not to call me Your Majesty—Mr Venison would do—but because his response was always "Yes, Your Majesty," I eventually gave up. A few weeks after the revolution, he was calling me a "capitalist pig."

The revolution came quickly. We had been operating the Polana for just under a year and were busy drawing up plans for a complete and dramatic renovation. During that time, I had begun to be aware of the presence of a rebel force, Frelimo, operating in northern Mozambique. Frelimo, led by Samora Machel (whose widow eventually married President Nelson Mandela), was, according to the press reports in LM, being held at bay by the Portuguese army. In South Africa, there were almost no reports of the fighting in the press, and most South Africans, therefore, were oblivious to the problem. Just as I have experienced in many similar situations of imminent danger, life in LM carried on as if this conflict were on the moon.

As a result of this, it never really crossed my mind that our plans for the Polana could be upset by a few rebels. Nothing could have been further from the truth. What, in fact, was happening was that a huge slew of disgruntled Africans had joined forces under Machel's communist banner, and the demotivated and disinterested Portuguese army was no match for them. Despite being given the impression in LM and, indeed, in the press that everything was under control, suddenly, with no prior notice, the Portuguese army just gave up. Portuguese colonial rule was at an end, Frelimo marched triumphantly into LM, and our plans to renovate the Polana marched out.

The next few months were fascinating. After the celebrations had died down and the transfer of power from Portugal to the communist military regime of Samora Machel had been completed, the Polana emptied like water from a bath. The only guests were from the Chinese embassy and a few observers from the Canadian government; 'guest' was the appropriate word, because payment from the Chinese turned out to be an illusion. The employees were quickly organised into a union, better described as a branch of the Communist Party. All employees were issued with a tiny copy of Chairman Mao's red book, which looked like one of those minute bibles with very thin paper and small print, except that it was red and the words were different! These books had been translated into Portuguese, and they were proudly carried by most of the staff at all times. The union formed a committee (which, incidentally, included the previously super-subservient elevator operator), and we were instructed to give them a committee room, which they promptly plastered untidily with anti-Western and specifically anti-South African posters, dominated by portraits of their victorious leader and hero, Samora Machel. (I have often chuckled about the need of African leaders to have their portraits adorning the walls of every public place in their domain, invariably copied by the fawning private sector—in case, presumably, the boss pays a visit. Maybe they have all stayed at a Marriott hotel!

It was to this committee room that my colleague, Colin Walker (the regional manager who was unfortunate enough to have the Polana within his territory) and I were summoned on our monthly visits to LM after the revolution. Upon arrival in this crowded room, we sat at a table surrounded by triumphant workers, with no choice but to listen to about twenty minutes of rousing revolutionary songs, which were bellowed out in Portuguese. All through the singsong, the committee brandished their little red books. After the songs, the list of grievances was aired, none of which could ever be met, because they all involved money, and naturally, we explained that we had none.

I have vivid recollections of Colin standing at the blackboard in front of the committee, where he proceeded to draw a floating ship. In one end of the ship he placed a bundle labelled 'guests', and into the other end he placed another bundle labelled 'staff'. Naturally, the bundles balanced each other, and the ship drawing floated. He then took the chalk duster and painstakingly rubbed out the 'guests' bundle, as if he were telling a story to a kindergarten. He then started to redraw the ship, sinking at the staff-heavy end, only to be rescued from capsizing by a lifeline drawn to a big hypothetical hook, which he laboriously labelled 'bank'. "There," said Colin. "Our ship is top-heavy with staff, and unless Mr Venison can get some more money from the bank, we will sink, and your jobs will sink with the ship."

The committee, to a man, sullenly stared at Colin, until one of them, grabbing his little red book, frantically searched through. With a look of triumph, he found the passage he had been seeking, and announced, "This is a capitalist trick!"

On the occasions when I also went into lengthy explanations as to why there could be no Christmas bonuses, which ranged from "Karl Marx didn't believe in Christmas" to "South African Exchange Control won't let me bring any money here" (which was not only true, but was the one and only time I have been thankful for South African Exchange Control), the responses from the little red book were always similar: "This is an imperialist ploy!"

It was unfortunately true that the advent of communism to Mozambique, amongst other things, brought an immediate halt to the tourist industry. The naïveté of the new administrators was staggering, and their ineptitude at governing was absolute—through no fault of their own, since their training and experience had been in bush fighting. In practical terms, however, it meant that we, the lessees of the Polana Hotel, had no local currency with which to pay the wages or the rent. As a matter of routine for several months, once per month Colin and I would head off, under unwanted armed escort, to the Ministry of Labour to ask permission to lay off workers. Every month we were received courteously and told that "communism means full employment"—or, in other words, no redundancies allowed. Every month we explained that we had no money to pay the staff, and in return we were handed a note by the minister to take to the governor of the Bank of Mozambique (née Portugal). Still accompanied by our armed escort, we would proceed to the marble halls of the bank (now looking distinctly grubby—the halls, and probably us) to await our turn, in the line of other dismayed foreign businessmen, for a meeting with the bank manager. After some interminable waits each month (lines of people waiting outside African government and para-governmental offices was then, and still is, an indelible feature of Africa), we handed our note to the bank manager, who obviously was a new man in the job, because he wasn't Portuguese; he, in turn, gave us another note which allowed us to collect the payroll as we left, just like passing Go in Monopoly.

It was during these monthly visits to LM (shortly later to be renamed Maputo, as is the victor's way) that I witnessed the rapid deterioration of Mozambique, which had never been the most efficient place before the revolution. Workers suddenly became bosses, and soldiers became bureaucrats; the trouble was that nobody wanted to work anymore, and nobody wanted to tell anyone else to work—or perhaps it was because nobody actually knew what to do at work. On some occasions, Colin and I would drive to Maputo from South Africa, and before our own eyes, we saw the farms in the bushveld grind to a halt as the lack of maintenance began to affect the farm machinery. We literally witnessed the wheels falling off the tractors. Food production virtually ceased. At the Polana, since we had plenty of staff being financed by the Bank of Mozambique, we continued to operate the restaurant, but the menu choices slowly diminished as we used up the stores, until we finally had bread and potato soup… period.

When we flew into Maputo, as the months went by, we witnessed the awful scene of lines of descendants of Portuguese settlers, many of whom had been born in Mozambique, clutching bags full of their most treasured possessions as they waited to take that final flight back to an uncertain future in Portugal. These people, who had been the upper class of LM, enjoying a privileged colonial lifestyle (but in the main, not afraid of hard work), were now a sad, bedraggled bunch, leaving behind their land and their lives to those they had previously lorded over. I often thought that these were the same people who had tolerated our black hole and many others, and that they fully deserved this fate; nevertheless, it was a pitiful sight, and one that made me think hard about the future of my white children in Africa. Just as the Portuguese inhabitants of LM had thought the fighting in the north was on the moon, most South Africans next door thought that the downfall of Mozambique was an unrelated event on another planet. I knew that what I was witnessing was the writing on the wall, but, try as I might, I could not convince the wealthy Johannesburg clientele who migrated to our Plettenberg Bay hotel every Christmas, when I joined my family there after a visit to Maputo. The only person I was able to convince was the most important one: Diana.

The end of our adventure in Mozambique came as quickly as the revolution. On one of our now routine visits to the minister of labour, for the first time ever, he engaged us in polite conversation, which included asking us when we were leaving LM, to which we replied, "On the afternoon flight." Then, to our surprise, the bank manager asked the exact same question, having shown no previous interest in our travel plans. Back at the Polana, while enjoying our bread and potato soup, one of the few remaining Portuguese waiters slipped us a note on which was scribbled, "Secret service—next table—watching you."

At the next table were two Africans, who were obviously strangers to a high-class restaurant, even one with such a limited menu, because they were attacking their bread in a particularly mannerless fashion. Colin and I decided to leave, and together with the elderly Portuguese hotel manager, we withdrew to the safety of the manager's office, where we formulated our escape plan. The manager had an old (very old) Mercedes, and we prevailed upon him to drive us to the South African border, whilst making out to all and sundry that we were actually going to the airport. We gathered up our luggage and met in the lobby, making just enough fuss about flight-departure times and the like for anybody who might be paying attention to be fooled. No sooner than we were in the old Mercedes, with the manager pointing it in the direction of the airport, we realised that we were being followed by the bread-eaters. In one of those classic moves that one used to see in American Westerns, where a small group of cowboys would slip into a tiny crack in the rocks whilst the chasing horde of Indians went hurtling by, we drove around a corner and promptly hid in the front drive of a deserted house, from which vantage point we last saw our pursuers rush past in the direction of the airport. We emerged from the driveway and headed off toward the countryside, as fast as the old Merc would go.

The manager was very nervous. He was not a well man. He was also an elderly man who had been working out of his retirement as a replacement manager since the real manager had left for Portugal shortly after the revolution. He was certain that we would be followed and arrested before we reached the border, and his fears were heightened when, about an hour out of LM but still another hour to the border, we got a puncture. I'm not normally very swift with such things, but the speed with which Colin and I changed that wheel would have qualified us for the Ferrari pits team. When we finally reached the border unapprehended, with much relief, we bade farewell to the manager, and proceeded to walk in the direction of South Africa. The guard on the Mozambique side was asleep, but nevertheless, walking through no-man's-land seemed like an eternity. Upon reaching the South African side, the soldier on duty was equally surprised to see two suited travellers, complete with overnight luggage and no vehicle, but our brief explanation was soon accepted, and he kindly allowed us the use of his radio to summon some transport.

The manager was not so lucky. Halfway back to LM he was stopped, arrested, and taken to prison, where he was unceremoniously dumped into an overcrowded cell, apparently reminiscent of our own 'black hole' and accused of assisting 'currency smugglers' (Colin and me). We, of course, did not immediately know of his predicament, because even after we had reached Johannesburg we were not able to contact the Polana, due to a breakdown in telephone service. We learned of his fate initially by courtesy of another businessman who had been visiting LM, who alerted us upon his return to South Africa.

For the next few days, Colin, myself, and even Sol Kerzner did little else but to try to secure his release. We launched into an aggressive campaign to notify everybody and anybody who might be able to help in our quest to secure the man's freedom. We phoned and telegraphed people nonstop, from politicians to pressmen, from presidents to prime ministers. Finally, after the manager had been incarcerated for four days and three nights, the secretary general of the United Nations, Mr U Thant, responded to our pleas, and applied enough pressure on Samora Machel to have the man released. Apparently, the governor of the jail personally visited the cell in the middle of the night, pulled out the manager, and with the simple words "There has been a mistake," released him. The next day, he joined the line at the airport and flew back to Portugal, the recipient of Colin's and my eternal thanks, and, compared to most of the people in the line, a sizeable golden handshake.

We were now operating a hotel from several hundred miles away with no manager on site, no guests, and several hundred staff: not exactly a recipe for success. Needless to say, despite some less-than-hopeful requests from our board, both Colin and I thought it unwise to go back to Mozambique. Indeed, I have not been back since. Salvation was, fortunately, near at hand. Shortly after the jailing incident, the Frelimo government decided to nationalise all property that had been vacated by its owners. We quickly suggested to the lessors of the Polana (a South African family) that they might like to take up residence in order to protect their investment. They declined—and the hotel was duly nationalised, and we promptly stopped paying the rent. That was in 1972. Twenty-five years later, the government of Mozambique asked us if we would like to buy the hotel. We declined.

# Chapter Five
## NIGHTMARE ISLAND

Beacon Island was, for me, a nightmare. Beacon Island was, for most South Africans in the seventies, *the* place to be. Beacon Island is not really an island at all, but presumably it once was, before the shifting sandbanks at the mouth of the Umgeni River joined it to the mainland, forming a rocky mound of no bigger than three acres, approached by a causeway. This 'island' rock sits between two of the most beautiful beaches in the Cape; one stretches miles to a craggy promontory known as the Robberg, and the other nestles beneath the picturesque village of Plettenberg Bay.

Plett, as it is known to all South Africans, is now a bustling small town; back in 1971 it was a one-street village, reminiscent of those false-fronted main streets that you see in old Westerns. It is set within some of the most beautiful scenery in southern Africa. On a sunny day, of which there are many in Plett, the lushness of the forests on the clifftops contrasts vividly with the rugged mountains on the one side and the gleaming Indian Ocean on the other. Even the whales have selected Plett as the place where they want their babies to be born, and on some days you could count dolphins until you no longer cared to count.

Small wonder, therefore, that Sol Kerzner, whilst touring South Africa in 1970, looking for sites on which to construct hotels for Southern Sun, knew instantly that the little rocky mound called Beacon Island could be the cornerstone of his new company. This site he had to have, for it would be on this site that he could build a resort hotel that would be his 'signature' for many years to come. As it happened, the site was already occupied by a small, ramshackle hotel, which was a financial disaster. Despite warnings from everybody that it would be impossible to make a hotel viable in Plett because the season was too short, the Cape 'coloureds' (staff) were too lazy, and the building costs were too high, Sol, with his newfound fund from SAB, swiftly acquired the property and began planning to put a team of talent together to design a hotel, the likes of which had not been seen before in South Africa.

That talent included Andre Hoff (architect), Gordon Hood (development manager) and Barry King (interior designer)—all local practitioners with very little hotel-design experience, except what they had gained at the time during the construction of other Southern Sun hotels, the Elangeni and Malibu in Durban. However, what they produced, with the constant pushing, pulling, criticism, interference and genius of Sol, was a real gem. Two hundred rooms, all with sea views, in a gleaming sand-coloured building perched impressively on the top of the island. One end (the suites) cantilevered over the sea, which constantly crashed into the rocks below, sending spray high into the air; it was balanced by the other end, overhanging a porte cochere, which led to a spectacular atrium lobby. The floor of the lobby was made of blue-glass uneven tiles, which glistened like water, and its centrepiece was an island garden with three huge palm trees rising the full height of the building to the see-through ceiling. This was the first atrium-style resort hotel. It has been copied and improved upon many times since, but in its day, it was a leader in the

Peter J Venison CVO

field of hotel design, and something for South Africans to boast about.

It was the construction of this hotel, named the Beacon Isle, that kick-started the 'people rush' to Plett and turned real estate in Plettenberg Bay into the most sought-after and expensive in the country. It became the place for wealthy Johannesburgers to have a second home, and many bought plots with an eye to retirement. The land on Robberg Beach, adjacent to the hotel, was snapped up and developed. This would not be the last time that we had made other people wealthy whilst being so focused on the job at hand that we missed the chance for personal enrichment.

My role in the development of the Beacon Isle was to supply the planning team with operational inputs and requirements, as well as to get the place up and running. Sol was concentrating on the design, the construction, and the pre-opening marketing. This was a division of labour that played to our respective strengths and which would work well for many years and many projects. I had to think through how the building (still on paper when I joined the company) would work from a practical point of view. This is a job which consists of considering a million details, from such things as which stoves would be needed, where they would sit, and where plugs and gas pipes should be located; to how many lockers there should be in the staff changing room, how big each locker should be, and what system would be needed to control the locker keys. My job also included the planning of all operational procedures for the rooms, food and beverage, and administrative areas; e.g. what linen we would use, what menus we would serve, and which wines we would offer. This, in turn, meant figuring out how many staff members we would need, and finding and training them. It also meant specifying and buying all operational equipment—every single item, from blankets to bottle openers, from fish fryers to filing cabinets.

For those of you who have ever been involved in refurbishing a home, with all of the decisions that have to be made, deliveries that have to be arranged, appointments that have to be kept, and hassles that have to be endured, imagine the enormity of the task when you are planning and equipping a building for 400 guests, not just for your family. It is a *huge* task, and can only be accomplished successfully if a team of experienced, diligent, and committed people are involved. This was South Africa in 1971; there were no people around with this sort of experience. To educated South Africans, working in a hotel was not a career choice; it was something that blacks did. Hotel-keeping was not seen as giving service; it was perceived as being servile, and being servile is one thing South African blacks were trained to be.

Management of a top-quality resort requires experienced professionals, including a general manager, a food and beverage manager, a rooms manager, a housekeeper, an accountant/controller, a chef (with several qualified assistants), restaurant managers and other peripheral executives, such as those handling public relations, sports and entertainment, maintenance and so on. In 1971, I found myself responsible for the opening of two new hotels, the 400-room Malibu in Durban and this 200-room resort in Plett. At only a few short months before the scheduled openings, I did not have even one of these executives in place. Therefore, with the blessing of Sol, with the buildings nearing completion, and with no hope of finding the right people in South Africa, I set off on a series of recruiting trips that literally took me around the world, in one instance, in less than a week.

Utilising employment agencies to pre-screen my candidates, I met people as and when I could, sometimes in the strangest of places and the most difficult conditions. The manager for the Malibu was interviewed and selected on a bench at Kings Cross Station, London (he turned out to be an alcoholic!); a food and beverage manager at San Juan airport; a chef in a taxi in Paris. When you are recruiting for a company that nobody has heard of in a country nobody wants to go to, not only does the interview process become more of a selling than a selecting job, but there is a high probability of getting it wrong. It was very hectic, and my success rate (of executives who eventually stayed and worked out well) was south of 50%, but gradually, as we replaced the errant fifty, the successes started to outweigh the failures. Some of my selected candidates failed because they were not up to the job, some took fright at the difficulty of the job, but for some I had simply oversold South Africa and they decided it was not for them. Sometimes their decision-making was swift. In one case, an executive stayed only long enough to catch the next plane home; he went on to become the most successful hotel executive in the Middle East.

As luck would have it, I did find an excellent candidate for the management of the Beacon Isle: an Austrian, Gerhard Stannick. Unfortunately, the alcoholic from Kings Cross that I had installed at the Malibu had to be 'dispensed with' soon after the place was open, and I had no choice but to move Stannick to Durban, a move which absolutely thrilled him, having realised, after a few weeks at Plettenberg Bay, that running an hotel in the established city of Durban would be a 'doddle' by comparison. This meant, of course, that the embryonic Beacon Island was still managerless, so back on a plane I got, with the mission not to return until I had found a manager. This time I snared an American with impressive credentials and a very nice wife (who could sing a great aria). Unfortunately, Boston to Beacon Island turned out to be too large a culture shock, and the poor man lasted only until the day after we had opened the hotel, and, regrettably, his marriage didn't last much longer.

Just why it was so difficult revolved almost entirely around the staff. Plett is situated in the Eastern Cape, and Plett, being one of the nicest places in the Cape, had been reserved, under the weird rules of apartheid, for whites. Naturally, the whites needed staff, and to satisfy this need, half-castes (Cape 'Coloureds') were also allowed to reside in the region (though not in the village)—but strictly no blacks! Cape 'Coloureds' were the unfortunate 'stepchildren' of apartheid who neither belonged to the ruling white community, nor to the oppressed black majority. They simply did not belong, and this lack of a clear-cut place in society seemed to make them, not surprisingly, a very morose bunch. Their average life expectancy was very low (around thirty-five years), partly because the alcoholic intake of many of them, particularly the men, was phenomenally high. They were constantly fighting and stealing each other's women. They were not, at the time, the stuff that good service staff is made from.

The government, however, had decreed that we could only employ personnel who had the 'right' to live in the region; this meant they had to be white (fat chance!) or 'coloured'. Since we knew we would need about 400 employees and considered the chances of finding sufficient people from this limited local labour pool somewhat low, we petitioned the government to allow us to bend the rules and recruit some blacks. After numerous visits to Pretoria and much pleading, we were finally given permission to hire about a 120, provided that we recruited them from the King Williams Town area, which was inconveniently located about 150 miles from Plett; it was presumably because that region had an unemployment problem, or because a member of parliament wanted to adjust the black/white balance of the local population. The trouble with King Williams Town was that it didn't exactly have a cordon bleu school of cookery—in fact, it barely had a restaurant—so it was not fertile recruiting ground for employees at a five-star hotel.

In realisation of this, before commencing the recruitment, we made arrangements with a newly opened government hotel school in Pretoria to put all of our recruits through a crash course of six months' duration in food and beverage preparation and service. I provided the school with the proposed Beacon Isle menus (a cycle of fourteen days) and the proposed wine and cocktail lists, and begged the school to teach them these things and nothing else.

With these arrangements in place, a couple of my colleagues and I set off for King Williams Town to recruit. The town was hot, dry and dusty, but it did have a few interesting buildings that were rich in the history of the colonisation of South Africa. The blacks lived in 'townships', desolate places out of sight of the real town, which consisted of row upon row of tiny tin shacks, with little infrastructure, no gardens, and no public amenities. This had to be fertile recruiting ground, for why wouldn't anyone want to leave here? We had arranged to use the local magistrate's court as our recruitment centre, not because we thought that our candidates would be used to visiting it, but because it was the only venue capable of holding a crowd. We had 120 trainee positions available at the hotel school, so we decided to select 140 recruits, in case of attrition. About 400 people showed up for the interviews, which consisted of showing each candidate a place setting of a knife, fork, spoon, etc., muddling them all up, and asking the candidate to reset them correctly. Any candidate who could correctly re-lay the table passed the test. About 150 did. Communicating this simple test, as well as our instructions to the 'winners', was not easy. They all, to their credit, spoke two languages: Afrikaans and Xhosa. My colleagues and I, to our shame, only spoke one: English! Fortunately, the local magistrate spoke all three, so the future success of Sol's fabulous Beacon Isle probably had more to do with the apartheid legal system than he ever realised.

The magistrate instructed all of the successful candidates to return to the courthouse exactly one week later with a bag of personal effects for the six-month stay in Pretoria. They were also told that, upon completion of the course, they would be allowed to return home for one week before reporting to the hotel to start the real job. Their pay, whilst at hotel school, apart from some pocket money, was to be held back until they showed up at Beacon Isle—just to make sure we weren't training them for someone else. I left King Williams Town with a heavy heart. The conditions that these poor people had to endure were appalling, and our chances of turning them into high-quality service personnel seemed slim. I rationalised my distaste for the system that had created such an uneven playing field by convincing myself that we would, at least, be doing something to improve the lives of 120 poor souls and many more dependents. This dilemma of whether it was better to be participating in anti-apartheid demonstrations in Trafalgar Square or actually contributing to black employment, training, and enhancement 'on the ground' in South Africa was to trouble me for many years. I was, however, at this time, simply too busy to dwell on it, and was able to quite conveniently rationalise my role as being helpful—rightly or wrongly.

One week after the cutlery-shuffling, we assembled again at the Magistrate's Court in King Williams Town with a fleet of buses to take our new recruits to the railway station, where we had chartered a train to take them to Pretoria, a journey of nearly one thousand miles. I will not bore the reader with the logistics of train chartering (trains belonged to the government!). To my immense relief, 126 recruits showed up, complete with an amazing assortment of bags that would be the envy of any bag lady. Once we were at the railway station, the helpful magistrate insisted that we lock the recruits into the train. I naturally protested, but he eventually prevailed upon me with the notion that if we did not lock the doors and the windows, the passengers would all jump out when the train passed through Johannesburg, where the streets were rumoured to be paved with gold. To the African, Johannesburg was known as 'Goldies'. Even with the doors locked, only 118 arrived in Pretoria.

Realising that it would be hard to achieve the service standards that we desired with the King Williams Town trainees and the local Cape 'Coloureds', we again requested that the central government show some flexibility in the employment rules. The only place in the country where anything approaching international resort standards existed at the time was in Durban, and even then, most of it was at our own hotels, the Beverly Hills, the Elangeni, and the new Malibu. This was primarily because the predominant racial group in Durban was Indian, descendants of sugar plantation workers brought in by the English settlers. The Indian community was held in much higher esteem by the whites than the blacks or the 'coloureds', and subsequently they had been afforded better opportunities of education and advancement. Furthermore, service positions in hotels were not anathema to the Indian community, which was actually not only very service-oriented, but was also very good at it. Add to this that Durban was the only true resort destination in South Africa at the time, and the result was that the Indian labour pool was well worth drawing upon. The problem was that Indians were not allowed to work in the Cape.

After many requests to the relevant minister, we were finally given permission to relocate, for a maximum of one year, fourteen Indians from Durban to Plett. The next task was to persuade fourteen Indians to go, because the permission did not cover wives and children, and most stable and experienced Indians were very family-oriented. It took all of the not-inconsiderable persuasive powers of Sol Kerzner, who had employed and trained many Indians at the Beverly Hills Hotel, to find me my fourteen. Sol knew, only too well, the useful role these chaps could play as on-the-job trainers amongst our four hundred raw recruits.

Even then, the exercise almost came off the rails, as the vehicles in which the Indian 'volunteers' were traveling the fifteen hundred miles from Durban to Plett were stopped and turned back because "the papers were not in order" (the bribe hadn't been paid). Having exercised all of the diplomacy I could muster with the infuriating bureaucrats, I finally got the police and the politicians to agree to let my workers through.

The next conundrum was where to house all of these people. The apartheid government had strict laws about who could live where and who could cohabitate with whom. 'Living where' was entrenched in a law known as the Group Areas Act; 'Living with' was entrenched in the farcically named 'Immorality Act'. Whereas it was sometimes possible to get someone in central government to turn a blind eye to transgressions of these laws, it was well-nigh impossible to get local politicians to bend the rules, since they relied on the votes of the local whites-only community. Simply put, white voters did not want blacks, 'coloureds', or Indians living next door, nor did they want the possibility of creating more 'coloureds' by crossbreeding. In regard to the 'coloureds', this problem had been conveniently solved (at least as far as the whites were concerned) by the establishment of a ring-fenced 'coloured' community about five miles out of Plett, but as far as the Plett establishment was concerned, Blacks were simply non-persons, with no right to live anywhere—at least anywhere within sight. After numerous entreaties to the local town council about the great potential economic advantages of the upcoming Beacon Isle Hotel, which could not be achieved without the help of my black trainees, we were allocated a plot of land, about ten miles from the village, up a steep dirt road, on the top of a bleak and barren mountainside (out of sight of Plett, of course), upon which we were permitted to build a dormitory. There was, of course, no water and no power—a problem we were left to solve. If I had thought that that I was taking these poor folk from King Williams Town to the Promised Land, this was now proving to be a massive misconception.

As far as my fourteen Indians were concerned, there was simply nowhere for them to live, so they finished up on the roof of the hotel in hastily redesigned storerooms, which, once they were installed, reeked perpetually of dagga—for what else was there for them to do in their off-time? According to the local Plett council, once off duty, these people were invisible.

Notwithstanding all of this, it did not take us long to discover a whole village of non-persons living in a squatter camp in a hidden valley quite close to Plett itself. Where else, of course, were the ladies of Plett to draw upon 'non-persons' to do the household chores? Not only did this fortunate (but previously overlooked) discovery ease my recruitment problems, but once the Pretoria trainees had arrived, they pretty soon abandoned our mountaintop hostel and moved in with the wives and daughters of the squatter camp. This, at least, cut down our staff transport costs.

The challenges I was facing in recruiting and training

staff were no less taxing than the challenges Sol and his team were having in building and fitting out the hotel. Thanks to a stupendously successful pre-opening marketing programme the hotel was completely sold out from day one, so there was no choice but to get it finished. With one month to go before the official opening date, however, the hotel was about three months from being ready. It was at this point that we threw all caution to the wind in regard to government regulations and shipped in manpower from anywhere and everywhere we could get it. This included sending for our wives (or partners), who were not on the payroll, but could certainly be persuaded to help. Diana showed up with the children about a week before we opened. They all got jobs, Diana's first being to stop the bleeding of one poor worker who had just been stabbed with a pair of scissors by another. With three days to go, the hotel was substantially finished but was in the sort of filthy mess that builders always leave, and far from habitable for paying guests, unless they were of the sort that didn't object to concrete in the baths, curtains that wouldn't pull, taps marked cold which ran hot, or windows covered with paint specks.

Whilst all the above had been unfolding, we had, a few months earlier, taken over an operating five-star hotel, the Elizabeth, in Port Elizabeth. Port Elizabeth was an industrial city about five hours' drive from Plett along the coast, some of it through winding mountainous roads. In desperation, with three days to go to 'O Day', I called the manager of the Elizabeth and asked him to go into the Port Elizabeth African township (inappropriately named New Brighton) to hire eighty workers, whom he should load onto two large buses with ample stocks of rags, brushes, brooms, buckets, razor blades, etc. and dispatch them to me post-haste. I promised to send them back after two days, and naturally offered to pay them handsomely. This he did, and when the buses eventually arrived, after an eight-hour chug through the mountains, I was ready for them with a team of eight supervisors, including my Diana and Shirley Kerzner, each of whom had explicit instructions as to what to do with her team. Before letting them disperse to their group work, I laid down the rules, which included a demonstration of sounding a big bell, which was to signify food time. That bit they understood.

The new workers all trooped off with their eager supervisors, but about half an hour later, one by one, the supervisors started to report to me that they had lost most of their crews; they had just disappeared. There was only one thing to do: ring the bell. With this, I understood the derivation of the phrase 'out of the woodwork', as the New Brightoners started to appear from everywhere; that is, everywhere except where they were supposed to be. I read them the riot act, but it was hopeless. My supervisors simply could not recognise their men from any others, and chaos continued to reign. Tired and frustrated, I stupidly decided to send them home—unpaid, but fed—with the job still not done. Realising that the shambles had been the fault of my disorganisation, I decided to try again. This time I asked the Port Elizabeth manager to staple different-coloured plastic luggage tags (ten per colour) onto the clothing of each worker. This worked much better, and quite a bit of cleaning got done that night and day.

The postscript to this story is that two nights later—in fact, on the first operational night of the hotel—the night cleaning crew did not show up for work. I was dead on my feet, and I was now in charge of a 'dirty' hotel full of 400 paying guests, and the only member of the night crew that had appeared was a German auditor. Just as this realisation was setting in, I suddenly spotted an African wandering across the lobby with a green luggage tag appended to his shirt. "When does the bus go?" he cheerfully asked me, obviously fresh from a nice long sleep and oblivious of the fact that the bus had left 36 hours before.

"After you've cleaned this hotel," I replied, and quickly found a vacuum cleaner and broom for him, with the promise that if he vacuumed the restaurant, bar and lounge, and swept the glass-tiled floor, I would happily return him next morning to New Brighton, not in a bus, but a shiny, new chauffeur-driven Toyota.

Unfortunately, the night cleaners were not the only employees who decided to stay at home. I was up very early on day two in the life of the Beacon Isle; if the night crew hadn't shown, I had some misgivings about the day to come. The staff were scheduled to start arriving between six and seven o'clock in the morning, in order to prepare and serve the breakfast. By seven-thirty, only one waiter had appeared, and zero cooks. This sole reportee was reeking of brandy and was not quite suitably attired for work, since he was sporting one black shoe and one white; at least he had got half of it right. "Where are the rest of the staff?" I screamed at him.

"Had a party last night—celebrate opening hotel," he drawled. "All 'sleep."

By eight o'clock, every spare bookkeeper, expatriate desk clerk, housekeeper and executive's wife was squeezing oranges, boiling eggs, and so on whilst I stood by the restaurant door and repeatedly explained the situation to our guests and craved their indulgence. My grovelling must have been effective, because even some of the guests, who clearly understood this "South African problem," pitched in to help. Somehow, we got through the day, but it was, without question, the most difficult day of my hotel-keeping life.

Slowly we began to sort the wheat from the chaff. The aforementioned American manager left on day two, to be replaced by an Italian from one of our other hotels. He turned out to be an Italian stallion who couldn't leave the front-desk clerks alone (at least the female ones), so he, in turn, got replaced by an Englishman, who was actually driven to drink by the job.

Most of the trainees from the train turned out to be hopeless, having bonded so well whilst in Pretoria that they had formed a sort of trade union, the purpose of which seemed to be to organise how to avoid work. Within a day or so of the opening, they appeared to have forgotten almost everything they had been taught at the hotel school, probably as a result of the real-time pressure. They were also living in a rather hostile environment far from their homes and loved ones.

Eventually, having found potential replacements from the 'non-person' community near Plett, on a particularly troublesome day, I gathered about forty of the most difficult trainees in the car park. I asked half of them to get into the hotel truck, and I clambered into the driving seat. They were very cheerful; I suppose they thought they were going for an outing. Actually, they were going back to King Williams Town and out of my life forever. I drove to the nearest town that had a railway station: a picturesque spot called Knysna, about twenty miles from Plett. Once at the station, I unloaded my human cargo, bought them all one-way tickets home, and handed each of them one month's pay in cash. I then went back for the other half, who were still happily sitting in the car park, waiting for their ride. When I returned to the station, the first group had gone—not to King Williams Town, it turned out, but directly to the local bottle store to use up the month's pay. I was not a popular person with the residents of Knysna!

Although I soon had to attend to other responsibilities, it was necessary for me to visit the Beacon Isle frequently.

I used to dread the visits, because every time I drove down the hill from the village to the rocky peninsula, I knew that I was driving toward trouble. But despite this, and despite the continuous personnel changes that I needed to institute, I had to admit that it was a very special and beautiful place. Eventually, after several stressful months, the Beacon Isle began to settle down, and it established itself for many years to come as the most desirable resort in South Africa, a recurring Christmas holiday spot for the wealthy from Johannesburg and a must-see stop on the overseas tourist route. For many years, the hotel enjoyed an excellent reputation, but I could never forget the nightmare that it had been. Having left South Africa, I did not return to Plettenberg Bay for a very long time. When I did go back recently, I was shocked at the state of the hotel. New owners had turned it into a timeshare resort. The beautiful blue glass tiles had gone, the lobby with its waving palms now housed a grubby coffee shop, and Barry King's symbolic carved whale had been painted a luminous green. At the time of opening the Beacon Isle it would have been true to say that we were proud of our creation. It was a game changer in our industry and received much praise. Now it seems just ordinary and proof of something which Sol Kerzner used to say: "Never fall in love with your own creation; it is just a building."

# Chapter Six
## PARADISE LOST

As much as Beacon Island was hell, Chobe was heaven. In the early seventies, the concept of a luxury game lodge did not exist, until we built the Chobe Game Lodge. Living in Johannesburg and opening hotels in cities like Durban and white men's playgrounds like Plettenburg Bay was definitely a far cry from working in Knightsbridge, but it was still predominantly urban Africa, not the real Africa of brilliant night skies, flaming sunsets, and vast empty spaces. To be in Africa—real Africa—you had to get away from the cities and villages. Whether it was the dry, open landscapes of the Highveld, the semitropical lushness of Natal, the waves crashing on the rocks of Zululand, or the unsurpassed beauty of the Cape, South Africa was a magnificent country.

And so were its neighbours. The wilderness of Botswana's Okavango Delta, the starkness of the mountains in the Kingdom of Lesotho, the rolling hills of Swaziland, the flowers in the Namibian desert, the countryside dotted with little thatched rondavels, the upside-down moon, the croaking and clicking of the frogs and crickets at night—these were all part of the sights and sounds of Africa that could not be forgotten. And then there were the animals, even then mainly ushered into game parks, but still magnificent.

Once you have seen wild animals, truly wild ones that survive unaided by man, you will never, ever visit a zoo. Once you have drunk the water of Africa, you will return.

Chobe, before we got there, was completely untouched by man; it was unspoiled. The Chobe River flows into the Zambezi, which it joins about fifty miles before the mighty Zambezi tumbles into a great chasm known as the Victoria Falls. The wedge of land between the Chobe River and the Zambezi which was known as the Caprivi Strip. It separates Botswana from Zambia, and where it comes to a point at the convergence of the two rivers, it abuts Zimbabwe, which at this time was still Rhodesia. The Caprivi Strip was part of Namibia and administered by South Africa, having been taken from the Germans shortly after the First World War. None of this, of course, bothered the wild animals that inhabited this magic corner of the world, because there were no fences between the various countries and not enough people to prevent them from wandering freely. The piece of Botswana on the south bank of the Chobe River had been designated a game park, and as such, any human inhabitants had been relocated.

The Botswana government was very keen to obtain some revenue from tourism, and approached us to build a hotel on the edge of the designated park area. We, however, thinking that it would be more interesting for our guests, persuaded the government to let us build on the riverbank several miles inside the park, where no other human settlers would be allowed. We commissioned Bill Birrer as architect, since Bill had demonstrated in other work his sensitivity to rural surroundings. We were determined that we would not spoil what God had given. Bill's design was simple, yet stunning; it was entirely appropriate for its surroundings, consisting of two-storey blocks, gently rounded, with rough, mud-covered walls. Each of the fifty river-facing rooms had generous balconies, on which visitors could sit and watch the glorious sight of hundreds of elephants that had made the daily trek to drink the waters of the Chobe. On one occasion, prior to the opening, our daughter Sarah, who had accompanied me there, counted almost 300 elephants in one day. In the centre, between the room blocks, was a small public building with reception, bar and restaurant. The rough-hewn walls were dotted with little alcoves displaying a treasure trove of antique African carvings, the drapes were rough Kaffir sheeting, and the doors and balconies were fabricated with Masai spears. The place was perfect.

Getting it built was not easy. There were no trained construction workers in the nearest village, Kazungula, so we had to teach them as we went along. As the job was nearing completion, we taught the same people to be cooks, waiters and room attendants. Although they never achieved great competency at either building or hotel-keeping, the result was charming. The buildings looked appropriately unsophisticated, and so was the service. However, the members of the crew, as well as those in the village, were fiercely proud of their achievement; the spirit of cooperation, at which we had worked so hard to achieve at the Carlton Tower, came here through a completely natural and uncontrived fashion.

From this heavenly spot, we operated boat trips down the river and photo safaris on four-wheel-drive vehicles into the park itself. You did not, however, have to go far to see game. Behind the hotel, on the national park side, we had cleared a stretch of the bush about the size of a football field. As this was the only open piece of land for miles, it immediately attracted the smaller animals, such as bucks and warthogs, because the predators could not easily creep up on them. Conversely, the predators soon got to learn that this field was a natural gathering place for their dinner, and so, from time to time, our hotel 'garden' was a fairly active place. Often, when you left the restaurant or bar at night to return to your hotel room, you were followed the whole way by predators' eyes, sparkling in the torchlight beam, from the bush surrounding the lodge.

Word soon spread that Chobe was the ultimate getaway spot, and the business began very well. It quickly became a favourite with visiting celebrities, and we, of course, for the sake of publicity, were happy to cooperate. Rod McKuen, the American poet and songwriter, was particularly fond of the place, and we arranged for him to view game from a balloon, pioneering a practice that is now commonplace. I also spent a hilarious weekend there with Peter Sellers and Professor Chris and Barbara Barnard; it was hilarious because it turned out that Peter was terrified of animals. On the game drives, he hid on the floor of the four-by-four. In the evening, he entertained us in the Barnards' suite with some of the famous voices we had heard on the radio and in films. His pièce de résistance, however, was his refusal to tell a joke in the restaurant; he claimed that it was impossible, since waiters were guaranteed to spoil the punchline by interrupting at the crucial moment. After much persuasion from the rest of us, he finally demonstrated, naturally timing his punchline to the very second that the poor, unsuspecting waiter arrived at the table to take our order.

Peter was not the only one scared of animals; Sol Kerzner was too. On one memorable occasion, Sol, Diana and I, together with an overseas tour operator from Los Angeles (who was looking to add an overnight stay under canvas to his adventure tour) set off in a light aircraft to go to a remote campsite at Savuti to test the experience. The campsite consisted of a few tiny, low, zip-up (to keep out the snakes) bivouac tents dotted around a campfire, on which a young German couple, who ran the place, cooked us a delicious dinner. The camp was surrounded by wildlife, and the fire served a double purpose: kitchen stove and animal deterrent.

The couple had been forewarned by someone that Sol could knock back the whisky. That evening, driven by his fear of the surroundings and with little help from us, he finished a bottle of Johnnie Walker Black. The Germans had not considered that we might need two bottles of whisky for such a small party, and so were only now able to produce a bottle of brandy. Diana and I decided to retire to our tent. From our sleeping bags, we could hear Sol and the American tackling the brandy. Sol then stumbled noisily to his tent. The silence that ensued was punctuated throughout the short night with animal sounds: the quiet crunching of elephant feet, the howling of wild dogs, the distant roar of lions. Magic! Sometimes a small animal would creep right up to the tent and scratch curiously on the canvas. Diana and I didn't get much sleep.

At first light, I stuck my head out of the tent, only to find Sol, with his head also sticking through the canvas. "Thank God someone's awake," he exclaimed. He was dying to go to the 'john', but there was no way he was going to make the thirty-yard dash to the makeshift latrine on his own. Apparently he had sat cross-legged all night, soaking up the sounds of the night in an alcohol-induced terror, waiting for someone to accompany him, or daylight, whichever came first.

Our most famous visitors to Chobe during that period were Elizabeth Taylor and Richard Burton—at the time, the king and queen of Hollywood. It happened like this. We had just opened the Landdrost Hotel in Johannesburg. It was not in the best part of town, but we were eager to promote it as a five-star hotel. Part of our strategy was to ensure that all visiting celebrities to Johannesburg stayed at the Landdrost until it became known as *the* place to be.

Somehow we had been inveigled into supporting a celebrity tennis tournament at the national tennis stadium, Ellis Park. In exchange for free rooms for the celebrities, the organisers had promised us lots of publicity for the Landdrost. The trouble was that two weeks before the event, there weren't any celebrities.

At about this time, a scruffy young man called Bryan Miller walked into my office. I had never met him before, but I did know his elder brother, Selwyn, an entertainment agent who booked many of our bands and cabaret acts. Bryan informed me that he was willing to go to Europe to find some celebrities if I would pay his fare. Bryan looked about as tidy as the average backpacker after a hard day's hiking, so I was as astounded as I was amused by his proposition. However, because he was Selwyn's little brother, I thought I'd let him down lightly. "If you go to Europe and find me some celebrities, I'll pay your fare and a fee—but only after they have arrived."

"Okay," he agreed, "my fare and 5000 rand."

"Depends on who they are," I replied, wondering why I was even having this conversation.

A few days later, I got a call from Bryan. "Is it all right if I bring Elizabeth Taylor and Richard Burton?" he asked. Naturally, I thought he was pulling my leg. But no, Bryan was actually in Gstaad, Switzerland, standing next to Elizabeth Taylor. This I discovered when Bryan passed the phone to Burton. I would have recognised that voice anywhere. How he got through their door, I'll never know. He claims that he rang the doorbell.

The following week, after the travel logistics and, of course, the payments for tickets had been effected, Bryan arrived at the Landdrost, not only with Elizabeth and Richard, but also with Peter Lawford and Ringo Starr—quite a good tennis team! Bryan got his 5000 rand, and we got a huge bill from the insurance company to cover Elizabeth's famous diamond rings.

On the Saturday morning following their arrival, I was sitting in my office trying to catch up with some paperwork, when the phone rang. It was Bryan. Would Diana and I like to join Elizabeth and Richard et al. for lunch at the Post Office Tower? "Of course," I replied. I phoned home to ask Diana if she would like to come out to lunch with me, without mentioning with whom. No, it wasn't convenient; too many things to do, etc. I then informed her who was coming to lunch.

"Couldn't possibly come; hair's a mess; haven't got anything to wear," and so on.

"You'll figure it out," I said. I knew Diana could not pass up the invitation, and I was right. After a quick visit to the girl next door, who conveniently happened to be a hairdresser, she turned up dressed exactly right and looking lovely. Elizabeth, on the other hand, turned up in jeans and a T-shirt, on which was emblazoned across her ample chest 'Coca-Cola', in Arabic. Elizabeth also looked lovely.

At the time, Elizabeth and Richard were not married; in fact, they had just got divorced. But they were back together, in the loosest sense of the word. Their performance at lunch was straight from the movie *Who's Afraid of Virginia Woolf?* They insulted each other from the appetiser to the dessert, and yet there was electricity between them. During the meal, Elizabeth asked if we could recommend somewhere they could get away to see some animals. Before the meal was over, I had mentally chartered a plane for them to Chobe. This, I sensed, could be a huge publicity coup.

As it turned out, 'huge' was an understatement. After one week at Chobe, which they loved, they advised the lodge manager that they wanted to get married right there on the banks of the river. They asked him to find whomever he could (in this case, the district commissioner) to arrange the private affair as soon as possible, with no leaks, no press and no publicity. The manager and another member of staff were to be the witnesses, and the manager would take the photos using Richard's camera.

Up to this point, we had resisted advising the press about our famous visitors. Communication from Chobe to Johannesburg was not easy at the best of times. The phone and fax lines were more often down than up. There were, of course, no cell phones, WhatsApps or any other communication devices available. Somehow, the manager got through to me. He cautioned me about advising the press for fear that the whole thing would abort. I reluctantly agreed, but asked him to take his own photos and get them to me, as though his life depended on it. I had visions of pictures of Liz and Richard, getting married at our lodge, on the front page of every paper in the world. As it happens, I was not far wrong, but I didn't get them there. After the simple ceremony, during which the manager dutifully took photos with Richard's camera (and surreptitiously with his own), Richard put his arm round the manager, gave him a gold watch as a keepsake, and asked him to hand over all the film. Rumour has it that Richard then sold them to the Associated Press for a very large sum. In any event, they still appeared, all over the world, and Chobe Game Lodge was instantly famous.

In the days that followed the wedding, after the news had leaked, our switchboard was jammed. The world's press wanted every detail. What had she been wearing? What had he said? What had she said? The telephone lines were so busy that we simply could not take any reservations. One of the calls was from Elizabeth's lawyer in Switzerland. "Tell me it's not true," he implored. Apparently, he had not yet finished sorting out the financial mess from their last divorce.

Elizabeth and Richard stayed at Chobe for almost a month. Their lawyer needn't have worried. Before the month was up, Richard had resumed drinking like a fish, the shouting was waking up the animals, and plans were being made for a divorce. Notwithstanding this, the Chobe Game Lodge was well and truly on the map.

During all of this time, the war between Robert Mugabe's African "terrorists" and the white ruling government of Rhodesia was hotting up. Kazungula, a border town, was harbouring freedom fighters, and the fifty-mile dirt road from the Chobe Game Lodge to Victoria Falls (the nearest tarred airport) was regularly infested with land mines. For this reason, I was never keen to be the first one to drive down this road in the morning. I, like a coward, would wait until someone else (whose need to travel was more pressing than mine) would lead the way. I often wondered, however, whether it was better to drive very quickly, in the hope that the landmine exploded behind you, or the other way round. This sort of obstacle course did nothing to attract tourists, and although there had been no mishaps with our transfer buses, they began to be emptier and emptier as word of the danger spread. Soon the Chobe Game Lodge was also empty, and we had no option but to close down. This unpleasant task once again fell to me, along with my colleague from the Polana escape, Colin Walker, in whose region Chobe also fell.

We chartered a small plane to Kazungula, where we met with the district commissioner and advised him, with regret, of our intentions. We explained that we had no options but to close down. We knew that we were the only employer in the village and that it would be a hard blow. We were worried that, egged on by the terrorists in their midst, our staff would become hostile when we broke the news. We advised the commissioner that we would expect protection and safe passage back to our plane. As it turned out, we had no trouble. I was desperately sorry for our staff. They had worked with me through the building, opening, and operation of the lodge. They had been loyal, willing and trustworthy. They were as proud of the place as I was. I hated what I had to do, but, as usual, in the pull between the needs of the shareholders and the people, it was my job to see that the shareholders were protected. I was not to blame if Ian Smith (the prime minister) and Robert Mugabe could not peacefully sort out their problems.

We lined up the staff in the clearing behind the hotel and stood on a little mound to address them. I advised them that, due to the war next door, we had no guests, and we would have to close down. I told them that I hoped the war would soon end and that we could reopen. I thanked them for their contribution to the success of the Chobe Game Lodge. I told them that they had made their mark on the world and that we would not forget them. They listened in silence. I advised them that they would all receive three months' money, but they could leave immediately (as indeed, I wanted to, because I was suddenly feeling threatened and vulnerable on my little mound). Still silence. No questions, no protestations… just silence. Finally, Colin announced that they could keep their uniforms. Instantly, there were cheers of jubilation. Their uniforms, the symbol of their involvement, were more important to them than three months' money. With smiles all round, they wandered off to the village. With much relief, Colin and I did what was necessary to brief the few security men we had kept on, and left for the airstrip thinking that we might never see this wonderful place again. Chobe was going to return to Africa and its elephants.

# Chapter Seven
## FIVE-STAR ISLAND

Mauritius, the island republic in the middle of the Indian Ocean, has become one of the most desirable upmarket vacation destinations in the world. Mauritius, at the beginning of the twenty-first century, had surpassed Barbados as the must-see, must-be-seen-at holiday location for the rich and famous from Europe. It was not always like that. When we first went to Mauritius in 1972, there were no five-star hotels, there was almost no infrastructure, and there was no Air Mauritius. Although it had been an independent nation since 1968, the majority of its wealth was still in the hands of the colonialists—not the British colonialists, who had governed since 1810; nor the Dutch, who had ruled it in the seventeenth century; but the French, who ran Mauritius from 1715 to 1810. Wealth and land had been handed down from father to son for many generations. The principal product of the island was sugar, and all but a few of the sugar estates were owned by a handful of powerful Franco-Mauritian families. The political power, however, was firmly in the hands of the descendants of the imported sugar-farm workers, the Indians—mainly Hindu, with a smattering of Muslims. At the lowest end of the pecking order were the Creoles, Afro-Indians at one end of the scale to almost-pure Africans at the other. Everyone had a vote, so all groups were represented in parliament, and they all insisted that the rights of their groups be properly recognised. The country was broadly socialist, with strong rightist tendencies from the white settlers, and even stronger leftist tendencies from the Creole-backed communist party.

The sugar planters were beginning to diversify, as world sugar consumption and the sugar price fell. Textile production was gaining in impetus; cloth imported from India was turned into finished articles for such giants as Marks & Spencer and Gap. Labour was cheap, and supervision by the settler families was efficient. In addition to this, there were two major trading groups, Rogers and IBL, whose shareholders were predominantly the sugar families, but who had carved up all import agencies and services of note in a greedy race between each other. For example, if one represented British Airways, the other would represent Air France; if one had the agency for Coca-Cola, the other would have it for Pepsi. Nobody else could get a look in.

In 1971, a jovial English expatriate, Colin Hare—who had gone to Mauritius years before as a shipping clerk but had risen to be a senior executive of IBL, despite not having been born to an established Franco-Mauritian family—knocked on our office door in Johannesburg and invited us to Mauritius to investigate building a hotel. Rogers, the competitor, had recently formed a fledgling hotel company called Beachcomber, and was moving quickly to acquire the best sites. IBL wanted to make sure that it was not left behind in this new race, but had no knowledge in the field, and was, therefore, looking for an experienced partner. Rogers had decided to go it alone, and IBL thought that it might have a competitive advantage by bringing in a professional partner, hence the visit and invitation from Colin.

Not long after, Sol set off for Mauritius to negotiate a partnership and management agreement, as well as to look for a suitable site. Site selection was a hallmark of Sol's genius, and during a period that was increasingly frustrating for Colin Hare, Sol turned down site after site. Eventually, after over a year of searching and many trips from Johannesburg to Mauritius, Sol settled on a sandy peninsula near Flacq on the north-eastern side of the island, despite having been counselled against this choice by the conventional wisdom of the locals, who had insisted that "The west is best." The reason for this view was that in winter months, the east coast had a reputation for being windy, which, in fact, was accurate. However, the site Sol selected for the Saint Géran Hotel was spectacular (particularly the colour of the seawater) and was naturally shielded from the wind by a promontory of land to the south. History has proved Sol to be right: year after year, the Saint Géran Hotel has won honours as being one of the best resorts in the world, which it could not have achieved if it had been in the wrong place.

Once again, the team of Bill Birrer as architect and Barry King as interior designer was selected, and once again they were bullied and harassed by Sol into coming up with a masterpiece, which was stunning in its simplicity, and heavily reliant on its surroundings and imaginative landscaping. Being simple, it was also cheap to build, which was necessary, because the newly formed partnership of Southern Sun and IBL had limited capital. In 1973, the Saint Géran was built for about $2.5 million (i.e. under $14,000 per room, including a nine-hole golf course). In 2000, it was levelled and rebuilt for over $300,000 per room. In 2018 it was again completely renovated, testimony to Sol's site selection and demonstrating the inherent value of its location.

My job, as usual, was to plan for the operations of the hotel and to oversee its opening. During my early recces to Mauritius, I stayed at the few established hotels on the island, which were mainly owned by Beachcomber. They were quite obsolete in design, and service was generally unsophisticated and poor. The Mauritians, however, seemed to be very charming. Closer examination indicated that the style of management being adopted by Rogers was not in keeping with the socialist ideals of the employees. Rogers had employed French traditional hotel managers, who were used to behaving more like guests than managers in their own hostelry. I observed them sweeping into busy restaurants to be seated at the best tables, expecting to be served by the most waiters, whilst the paying customers, like me, were kept waiting. These imperialistic managerial dinosaurs literally were treating their staff like servants; as a result, the employees were morose and unhappy. The reconciliation of offering service to wealthy capitalist hotel guests by emergent socialist nation workers is never easy at the best of times. It requires a special effort by way of management; clearly Rogers and company were not achieving this, and so I determined that my colleagues and I would manage these people differently.

The first task was to find some people to manage. We placed an advertisement in the local paper. It asked for applications from persons wishing to receive training as room attendants, cooks, waiters, bookkeepers, and desk clerks. The hotel was to have 170 rooms; we were looking for about 250 trainees. To our amazement, from one ad we received nearly 2000 applications, most of which were in the form of rambling, handwritten letters, averaging two pages in length. Despite forming part of a socialist nation, the letters were typically grovelling. "To the esteemed honourable beloved owners of the Saint Géran Hotel, which will be the zenith of all hostelries, a palace to rival the queen of England's, a tribute to your aptitudes," and so on, and so on. "I have the stupendous honour of offering my humble services to use as you will," etc. After having read about 200 of these flowery tributes, a trend was quite apparent. When you finally got to the part (if you ever did) where the applicant was specific about what they wanted to do, nine out of ten wanted to be bookkeepers, and almost none wanted to be cooks or waiters. Had we been Price Waterhouse, this would have been a good sign, but alas, our intention was to run a five-star hotel.

We set about interviewing candidates. These were selected for interview with the careful use of a pin. We decided to interview 400, and arranged to borrow the premises of the Ministry of Labour for this purpose. Assisted by a small team of colleagues, I set about the interview process, with each interview scheduled for fifteen minutes. (Years later, I was to learn from my good friend Olivier Louis in Dubai that the better way to handle this would have been through a group interview, where one talks and obviously listens to a small group of applicants interacting with each other.) Applicants were asked to arrive at a scheduled time (which they mainly ignored), and whilst waiting for their appointment, were given a questionnaire to complete. Apart from the normal personal enquiries, the questionnaire included a list of jobs not connected or relevant to the hotel business. These were manual jobs, such as sugar-cane harvester, textile machinist, road builder, and so on, but there was also a selection of administrative or desk jobs, such as teacher or accounts clerk. There was also a write-in space. The questionnaire asked each applicant to tick off (or fill in) two jobs they would choose to do in an ideal world, if they were not selected for hotel training. The results were illuminating. 'Teacher' and 'policeman' came easily at the top of their lists, followed by a write-in 'male nurse'. The first two selections seemed to be because they were positions of prestige, and you could sit down whilst performing them (either at a desk or on a motorbike), and the third because the British government was offering free rides to England due to a shortage in the National Health Service of hospital orderlies. One by one, we discarded all applications from candidates who did not seem willing to get their hands dirty, and eventually, more through luck than judgment, selected our 250 trainees. Interestingly, at the hotel's twenty-fifth staff birthday party, over one hundred were still on the payroll.

The Saint Géran was to have a small casino, the first to be operated anywhere by Sun. As operational chief, I knew nothing about casinos. We had the option to 'farm out' the casino management, but it was a small operation, and we decided we would learn to manage it ourselves. Considering that we were to become, within a few years, one of the largest casino operators in the world, this decision was also a defining moment in our lives. To prepare ourselves, it was agreed that one of my ablest and brightest assistants, Don Buch (a Canadian who had been salvaged from the management services office at the Carlton Tower), should go to London and apply for a position as a dealer at the Playboy Club. This he achieved, and he was subjected to the intense training program, which was obligatory for all new recruits to the casino-gaming industry. The speed at which a croupier can recognise the value of chips or cards on a table is vital to the productivity of each table, and all croupiers have to be able to recognise 'setups' instantaneously. Whilst being drilled with the physical skills of dealing, it was Don's task to learn as much as he possibly could about the controls, and, of course, how skilled croupiers learned to avoid them. After several months, Don graduated, resigned, and returned to South Africa, where he became, at the time, our only casino expert. Don and I set out to hire our first croupiers. My philosophy was quite simple. We would look for the prettiest or most handsome as well as most personable young Mauritians we could find, and, oh yes, they would have to be able to add. Finding the pretty ones was easy; finding pretty mathematicians was less so, but we persevered.

In preparation for the opening, I made many trips to Mauritius, usually on Qantas, which in those days flew from Perth to Joburg once per week, stopping in Mauritius for fuel. For Qantas crew, a posting to Mauritius was like being sent to heaven. One day a week, the local crew relieved the Perth crew on arrival in Mauritius, flew the plane to Joburg (a four-hour flight), refuelled, and flew it back, handing it over to the now-rested Perth crew, who flew on to Australia. The entire crew was posted to Mauritius for one year and did one day's work per week. They were devastated when Qantas yanked the flight, bowing to anti-apartheid trade-union pressure in Australia.

On one occasion, I was offered a free ride to Mauritius by boat from Durban. Knowing how much the children had enjoyed their passage to South Africa from England, I jumped at the chance to take the family with me. The reason for the freebie was that this particular ship, the *Oceanic Independence*, was en route from a refit in Baltimore to Taiwan, where it would be offering cruises to the Taiwanese. The *Oceanic Independence* was the ship that had carried Princess Grace across the Atlantic to marry Prince Rainier. It had been acquired by a Taiwanese company and completely refitted. An all-Chinese crew had been sent to the USA to sail it to Taiwan. Along the way, someone had decided that it would be good to give the staff some practice at service before it went into operation in Taiwan, so about a hundred or so 'South Africans' were invited to travel from Durban to Mauritius, to serve as guinea pigs.

The whole trip was hilarious. None of the crew—not one—could speak a word of English, and none of the passengers could speak a word of Chinese. The ship was supposed to dock in Reunion and Seychelles en route. It was too big to get into the harbour in Reunion, and there were no tenders to take us ashore, so we soon discovered that all we were going to do was sail right around the island. It was also too big to get into the Seychelles, but then, so is every other ship. Because of this, some rickety tenders were located to take us to Mahé. This was my first experience of the magic of the Seychelles, unquestionably the most beautiful of all tropical archipelagos. In the early seventies, the Seychelles was really very undeveloped. We found ourselves the most perfect deserted beach, and thanked God for delivering us to such beauty.

The ship had been vitaled in the USA, so whenever the 'guinea pigs' asked for a Castle lager, they got a Budweiser. This did not seem to bother the occupant of the cabin next to us, because he seemed to have his own liquor supply and threw parties every night, particularly for young men. Like a good neighbour, he invited us, and I discovered that he was actually a wine manufacturer from Mauritius. This may not sound odd to the reader, but to me it was very strange, because I had yet to see a grape growing there. I was right. His business was importing the seventh or eighth pressing from the vineyards in France in the form of a powder, which he then mixed with 'secret ingredients' (mainly water) and marketed as French wine. Upon arrival in Mauritius, I went to his 'vineyard', which resembled a milk-bottling plant. There was a 140% import duty on wine into the country, which meant that after reasonable profit mark-ups, wine at the Saint Géran was going to be very expensive indeed. I thought the possibility of having some 'homebrew' would be worth investigating.

Together, my fellow cruiser Vivian and I tested his wine, which didn't taste at all bad. We got quite merry, and I finished up ordering multi cases of two different reds, two whites, one rosé and one sparkling. In our tipsy state, we made up fancy French names for them, and I selected labels decorated with pictures of castles, which he plumbed from a dusty little desk drawer in the corner of the plant. We agreed on a price per bottle of about fifty cents, but he insisted that we pay a deposit of roughly a dollar on each bottle. He obviously valued the bottles more than the wine. The cheapest imported wine from South Africa cost around $5 a bottle, so we positioned the 'homebrew' on the wine list at about a dollar less than the cheapest import. All five flavours turned out to be the best-selling items on the wine list.

As the bulk of the new staff reported for duty and training several months before the scheduled opening of the hotel, I insisted that they be treated with dignity and managed 'Sun-style'. This basically meant that if there was something to do, we, the management, did it with them. For example, if a truck full of furniture arrived, we would help unload, not just stand and supervise. If I needed to go somewhere, I would drive myself, not sit in the back of the car directing a driver. The Mauritians, not used to this type of treatment from their colonialist bosses, appreciated the difference immediately, and the moroseness that we had experienced at the other hotels simply disappeared.

The hotel manager we had appointed to oversee the opening was not working out. 'Five-Star Freddie' was a German named Mr Fred Beurkl, a direct descendant, he claimed, of the Red Baron, the Luftwaffe's ace fighter pilot in the First World War. Freddie was as charming as you would expect from a fighter-piloting family, but the pressures of organising a hotel-opening were too much for him. I was beginning to realise that the set of skills required to open a hotel is different from that required to run one. I had, yet again, made the mistake of selecting a 'runner'. Freddie finally went to pieces on the opening day, which he spent personally cleaning the swimming pool.

Unable to take this anymore, I paid him off, and called for reinforcements from South Africa. Fortunately, my selection of Freddie's assistant as food and beverage manager had been much more appropriate, and having tried several other expatriate general managers over the first few difficult months of the hotel operation, I finally agreed to promote the young food and beverage manager, Paul Jones, to the position of general manager. Paul, one of the most accomplished hotel managers I have ever come across, is still in Mauritius, but in charge of a chain of very special hotels across the Indian Ocean and in the Middle East.

The actual hotel-opening was fraught with technical difficulties. Amongst other things, up until a few days before opening, we had not been able to install any baths. The ship carrying the baths some weeks before had docked in Mauritius, but for some unknown reason, they had not stayed long enough to unload them, with the result that they were now on the high seas somewhere in the Far East. Arrangements had to be made to reship replacements, but this shipment had run into paperwork difficulties. Finishing 170 tiled bathrooms without the baths is not easy. Installing 170 baths a few days before they are going to be used is also a challenge, which on this occasion was met by Gordon Hood, my friend and colleague. Not that Gordon need have worried too much, because on 'O Day' we had no water to fill the baths anyway. We were losing water, somewhere in the system, faster than we could pipe it in. The hotel was completely full, but the toilets wouldn't flush. Bit by bit, our engineers, under Gordon's patient direction, tracked down the problem, after digging up the newly tiled lobby and the kitchen floor during the middle of service. Then the electricity failed, just as Her Royal Highness Princess Alexandra from Great Britain was arriving as a special opening guest. We all, including the royal party, watched in horror as the main supply cable, which had been laid between the entry driveway and the golf course, simply blew up in a series of explosions that worked their way down the drive and golf course, sending up plumes of smoke, until thankfully stopping at a transistor box located just before the front door.

One of the first guests was Frank Muir, the famous British broadcaster and writer. I bumped into Frank on day two. "How's it going, Frank? Is everything all right?" I chirped hopefully.

"Yearse," he drawled in his upper-crust style, "evertheeng is perfect—except the beeeed."

"The bed?" I enquired. "What's wrong with the bed?"

"Eeet's the leeegs. They've broken oarff." He was right. One by one, the beds, which had been made locally to avoid hefty import duties, collapsed because unseasoned wood had been used.

To cap it all, on the night of the official opening party, which was a few days after we had received our first paying guests, the *chef de cuisine* went off his head during the dinner service in the presence of the prime minister and other worthies. I was seated at the prime minister's table and was beginning to be embarrassed by the slow service. I excused myself and went into the kitchen to investigate. This was a mistake, because I was immediately subjected to a barrage of flying *vol au vent* cases aimed in my direction by the head chef. "Please," I pleaded with him, "leave enough for the top table."

I left the hotel a week after the opening to attend to other duties in Johannesburg, but because of the shakiness of the new management, I returned a few days later. I took a taxi from the airport (about an hour's trip) and asked the driver to take me to the Saint Géran. He didn't recognise the name, so I had to give him directions. After a while, he said, "Oh, do you mean that new hotel—the one with the sharks?" I hadn't the first idea what he was talking about, but I was soon to find out. I was greeted by the temporary manager, who quickly explained that a barracuda had practically bitten off the arm of one of our first guests whilst he was swimming directly in front of the hotel. As a result, and not surprisingly, nobody was in the water; in fact, there was an unfriendly hush about the place. Several guests had been waiting for my arrival to complain. Why had we built the hotel in such a dangerous place? Why hadn't we warned them? This had ruined their holiday.

Apparently, there had been a cyclone in the area, which had caused bad weather for a couple of days and stirred up the water. As a result, this barracuda had come inside the reef that protected the Saint Géran beaches, and since the water was still a little cloudy, it had not yet returned to deep water. The unlucky guest taking a morning dip had surprised the barracuda, which had taken a bite out of his arm, and severed ligaments. The hotel lifeguard had rescued him, and he had been dispatched immediately to a clinic in Curepipe, about forty-five minutes away, where they had operated on him in an attempt to repair the damage. Having tried to calm down the irate guests and asked our boathouse to resume operations on the water, including a demonstration of water skiing, I set off to Curepipe to visit the poor patient—with thoughts of a lawsuit jangling in my mind. The man was a Belgian who, as it turned out, bore no malice to the hotel and was grateful for his rescue and the prompt action to save his arm. After about a week, he was allowed to return to the Saint Géran, where almost all of his fellow guests had been replaced by the next group of arrivals. He was good enough not to tell them why he was all bandaged up. Thank God Mauritius was not in America!

Despite all of these setbacks, our guests loved the hotel. It represented a new generation of resort: classy, yet relaxed;

elegant, yet delightfully casual; sophisticated, yet simple. But the real difference was the staff. Their sheer charm and natural willingness to please were irresistible. Our guests just fell in love with our Mauritians. The government maintained sensible policies in regard to planning, so the island was not spoiled with high-rise resorts; it vigorously prevented access to air charter companies, thereby encouraging higher-yielding tourism. There was a political wobbly moment after the left-wing party gained control. During their election manifesto, they announced that they would nationalise the Saint Géran and turn it into a hospital. Once in power, however, these ardent socialists quickly veered to the right, as they always seem to, and the Saint Géran continued to provide good tax revenues for the government. The standards we had set at the Saint Géran were soon matched by the local rival company, Beachcomber, and both Beachcomber and Sun Resorts continued to grow until each had several hotels and over 1300 quality rooms.

# Chapter Eight
## THE RISING SUN

Between 1971 and 1977, Southern Sun continued to grow. Initially the pace was frenetic, either through 'new builds', some of which I have described, or through acquisition. Once we had demonstrated the untapped market for hospitality in South Africa, others rushed to join the race, but typically they were not as prepared or dynamic as us, and for various reasons, many competitive new developments were soon under financial pressure. This often created an opportunity for quicker growth for Southern Sun, and in addition to continuing our own development programme, we began to mop up the opposition. In the cases of acquisition, it was normally because the previous owners were losing money, and my job was to turn things around as quickly as possible. This often started by trimming the payroll, or in some cases slashing it.

I remember one such occasion. We had taken over the Edward Hotel in Durban. This was the 'Ritz' of the Indian Ocean: a hotel that had earned a reputation as one of the great hotels of the world. Unfortunately, it was haemorrhaging money when we moved in. On my first morning, in reviewing the operations, I discovered that the hotel was overstaffed, in my view, by about 100 people. I told the manager, an unhappy Scandinavian fellow, that he would have to analyse the payroll and decide which hundred could be laid off—not in a month, not in a week, but now! Either he did not agree with me, or he simply could not bring himself to do it. I explained that it had to be done, or soon all of the staff would lose their jobs, not just the unlucky hundred. I reasoned with him that he knew best whom to let go, since I knew none of them. Having built up the organisation, he (understandably) just could not bring himself to act, and so eventually I took the payroll sheets and a ruler, crossed out 100 names on a "last in, first out" basis, and instructed his payroll clerk to draw up the pink slips. Decisions like these were not easy, but when a ship is sinking, there is no alternative. It was not unreasonable that for some years I was nicknamed 'Hatchet Man'.

One way or another, between Sol, me, and the rest of our executives, we were making headway, and by 1977 we owned and managed twenty-four hotels and resorts in the region, making us, for a time, the largest hotel operator in the southern hemisphere. We also concentrated on innovation and quality, at one point owning five out of the six officially registered five-star hotels in the country. Sol was a hard taskmaster, but without his drive and determination, this rapid expansion would not have occurred. Sol's single-minded approach was awesome, but it also took its toll on those around him.

The abilities required to successfully develop and run a chain of hotels traverse a scale, which at one end demands great administrative ability, and, at the other end, requires great public-relations skills. Most people excel at one place on the scale; they are either good administrators or good hosts, or somewhere in between. Sol excelled everywhere on the scale, and could move up and down it at will. One minute he could be pulling apart the chief accountant's balance sheet, having spotted a minute error; the next minute pointing out to an architect that his drawings wouldn't work; and, immediately after, bawling out a restaurant manager because the food was cold. Sol could enter a room where his executives had been struggling with a problem for hours and immediately spot the solution. His ability to hone in on the crux of the matter was uncanny. In all departments of our business, through accounts, marketing, public relations, government relations, service standards, controls, deal-making, designing, costing and building, Sol was equal to the best consultant or expert in the field. One of his greatest strengths was his vision, not only in the broadest sense of the word, but also his uncanny ability to visualise one-dimensional plans as three-dimensional structures, a gift which often astounded the architects and designers he had employed. He also had 'balls'. His self-assuredness in proceeding with greenfield developments, based not upon feasibility studies, but on his own instincts, was legendary.

His biggest single weakness, however, was man management, although he was certainly a leader and had enough empathy to know when he had pushed someone too far. The problem was that he was selfish—not with his family or friends, but in business. He had to have things his way. Once he had made his mind up about something, he was, in his opinion, never wrong—which of course meant that anyone who disagreed with him was an idiot. Regrettably, as a result of his own lightning-quick mind, he was very tough on mere mortals, which meant that he was tough on everyone. Sol was, in fact, a bully. He could be extremely intimidating, and the more he became so, the more ineffectual people around him were. Talented people gradually lost their self-confidence, and with it, their ability to perform. This became a vicious circle, until eventually most people that had to work with Sol left unhappy and frustrated, or were asked to go.

When I first arrived to work for Sol, I brought with me several young, bright, talented and hardworking executives from Hotel Corporation of America (Sonesta), who initially made up the bulk of our central office. One by one, they fell by the wayside, either because they were never good enough for Sol, or because they just could not stand the man. Furthermore, when you worked for Sol, he owned you morning, noon and night—weekday or weekend. Trying to have any semblance of a reasonable family life was just impossible. Those that stayed had learned how to play the game. Since Sol always had the right answer, why bother to think? Just wait for Sol, and then tell him how smart he is.

This situation was not something that sat easily with me. I was determined not to be intimidated by the man. I wanted to learn from him, which I did, but I could not accept that he was always right (which of course he wasn't), and I could not accept the bullying approach which stifled others' creativity and contributions. I did my best to come between him and employees and consultants, to take his wisdom and translate it into instructions downward, and to take others' really useful opinions and present them to Sol in such a way that they would not be lost. The result was a huge strain on me personally, and despite a great deal of mutual respect, it often led to a state of conflict between Sol and me. On several occasions, I, too, had had enough, and seriously looked for alternatives. This only occurred when his empathetic skills had let him down and he had pushed me one step too far, and I did so with a large degree of reluctance because I was, frankly, proud of what we had achieved. It was not hard for me to find alternatives. The success of Southern Sun had not gone unnoticed in the international hotel community, and I was constantly being approached by head-hunters from overseas. On two such occasions, these approaches came as I was returning to my office after a disagreement with Sol, and on both occasions, I unhesitatingly expressed an interest.

The first was an invitation to interview for the role of chief executive of Canadian Pacific Hotels. At the time, they owned some fine properties in Canada and were the leading chain of luxury hotels in that country. Also, Diana had three sisters living in Canada, so there was some personal appeal to be considered. The call to action came on a Friday; the interviews were to take place the following week in Toronto. This required some quick decision-making. I knew that if I advised Sol that I wanted to go to Toronto to throw my hat in the ring, he would spend the entire weekend trying to talk me out of it until it was too late to travel. I decided to go without that debate. On my way to the airport, I drove by Sol's house, slipped a letter of explanation under his front door, and hastily beat a retreat. "Coward," I thought to myself. "The only way to do it," I rationalised.

After four days in Toronto, I was offered the job. I was proud and excited. But it's a long flight from Canada to South Africa, with plenty of time to think, and it is amazing how, when reviewing the past, the mind plays tricks with you. You think about the good times and minimise the bad. I reflected on our achievements in South Africa. I reflected on our good friends. I reflected on the stability of our children. I reflected on our privileged outdoor lifestyle. I reflected on the sunny, warm weather in South Africa and the cold, grey, snow-laden skies of Toronto. I reflected on how difficult it had been for Diana to settle down initially, but how she now loved Africa and all her friends. I even reflected on how much I had learned from Sol, and how much I would miss his challenges. By the time I reached Joburg, my resolve to leave had not been changed, but it was certainly susceptible to challenge. Diana was her usual stoic self. She was also torn between the lure of living closer to family and the loss of her family of friends in South Africa. She is also a Pisces, so decisions of this nature are not just difficult, they are almost impossible to make.

I went to see Sol in his office. I fully expected to walk into a tirade of abusive language. After all, I had behaved rather badly, pushing off to Canada with only a note shoved under his door. I informed him that I had been offered the job. Instead of abuse, the charm offensive kicked straight in—"Southern Sun needs you"; " job half-done"; "Stick with me, and I'll make you a millionaire." He was determined, as was his way, to keep talking until I had changed my mind. I resisted bravely, but I was not convinced myself that I should leave, and clearly Sol sensed his gap. Finally, and painfully for him, the offer came: substantially more salary and a bundle of stock options. I agreed to reconsider, and went home to talk to Diana. She seized the window. "It's all right with me if we stay." We had, of course, spoken to the children about the possibility of going to Canada. Children, generally speaking, are not big on change. Diana was worried about it, and that decided things. Just for good measure, though, when I returned to Sol to give him the news he wanted to hear, I decided that there was no harm in getting the stock-option bundle increased. He reluctantly agreed.

For a while, I was treated with more respect, but leopards don't change their spots, and it was not long before I was once again the man in the middle, between Sol's driving leadership and the troops. At times, I looked for help from the parent company, South African Breweries, but none ever came. SAB had long since given up on treating Sol's company as a subsidiary; for them, it was an investment, and a bloody good one too.

A few years after the Toronto incident, there was a replay. Once again, having just left Sol's office after a difficult session (in which I had accused him of countermanding some instructions I had given to our advertising agency), I picked up the phone to find a head-hunter on the line. This time it was for Australia: chief operating executive of Southern Pacific Hotels, at the time owned by Adnan Khashoggi and Peter Munk, latterly chairman of the hugely successful Barrick Company in Canada. This time I advised Sol that I was going to take a look, and he almost seemed resigned to it. For Diana, Australia seemed like a long way away. This time, there would be no relatives to welcome us. She agreed to come on the trip, without too much enthusiasm. The trip did not go well.

The first evening we were in Sydney happened to coincide with the annual managers' meeting of Southern Pacific Hotels. A dinner for the hotel managers, the head-office executives, the owners, and their wives had been arranged. We were invited to attend. Ronnie Corbett, the diminutive English comedian and raconteur, was to be the guest speaker, so despite being somewhat jetlagged, it seemed like a good idea for us to attend. Diana, who had not necessarily packed for formal dinners and obviously had no time to shop, asked the chief financial officer's wife what she should wear. "Oh, just put on a pretty party frock," came the reply, in a broad Australian twang. Unfortunately, pretty party frocks had long gone out of fashion in Johannesburg, so Diana could not exactly oblige. The fact that every other lady at the dinner was wearing something that had gone out of fashion years before in South Africa (and the rest of the Western world) was a little alarming.

Back in the seventies, Australia was a cultural backwater. Ten years later, Australia had caught up. Thirty years later, Australia, on the occasion of the Olympic Games, gave a demonstration to the world that cemented that country's position as a world leader and trendsetter. However, our first visit was forty-five years ago, and the thought of going to settle there did seem like a backward step.

Diana's gut feel for the country was further unsettled by an interesting little demonstration of male chauvinism. On the day after the Ronnie Corbett dinner, whilst I was occupied with the interview process, another of the executive's wives kindly took Diana under her wing. During the day, the lady had cause to take her car to the garage to be serviced, only to be told by the mechanic that she should get her husband to bring the car in. Obviously cars were masculine objects!

In any event, despite being offered the job, circumstances suddenly took a turn for the worse when we received a telephone call to return to South Africa urgently because our son Simon had been taken into hospital with a life-threatening condition. Simon had been doing a vacation job at one of our hotels. Unfortunately for him, a disgruntled employee had, unbeknown to anyone at the time, urinated into the milk used in the staff canteen, with disastrous results for all that had drunk it. Simon had been taken to a rather poorly equipped small-town 'cottage hospital'. According to the doctor with whom we spoke from Sydney, he was too sick to be moved, even by helicopter, to Johannesburg. Needless to say, we forgot all about working in Australia and caught the first flight home.

This was also not without its drama; during a refuelling stop in Perth, an engine failed, and we were advised by the SAA representative that they would have to fly a replacement engine from Seattle. During the wait, we noticed that they kept taking the plane up and down a runway. They then announced that they thought they had fixed the problem and were going to take a trial flight, which, if successful, should allow us to continue on our way before the replacement engine arrived. Under these circumstances, you are never quite sure if you are doing the right thing by re-boarding the plane, and some people refused to get back on board. We, however, were desperate to get home. By the time we eventually left Perth, Diana was wishing she had never set foot in Australia. I am pleased to say that she has, subsequently, changed her mind completely. More importantly, after many weeks of incapacitation, Simon fully recovered.

In 1976, I opted to forego some of my annual bonus in exchange for a couple of round the world air tickets. I was quite keen to take a break for a few weeks with Diana and, at the same time, to take a look at what some of the other growing world hotel brands were doing. We set off in an easterly direction, with pit stops in the Indian Ocean, Thailand, Singapore, Hong Kong, Australia, Hawaii, San Francisco, Los Angeles and New York.

Whilst in New York, we started to hear about troubles back in South Africa, which became known as the Soweto Riots. After years and years of frustration about their role in society as second-class citizens, the fury of black Africans had finally erupted. What started as a student protest to being taught in Afrikaans, a language they hated, turned into a riot. Things got out of hand, culminating on the police firing live ammunition into the crowd. There were many dead. South Africa would never be the same. In the New York media, these events were not given enormous coverage, but they were enormous events.

I had long been troubled with the philosophy of apartheid, and both personally and as a company, we had effectively ignored it, or refused to comply with all of its silly regulations. However, there was no getting away from the fact that we lived in an apartheid state, and whatever we did in regard to our personal treatment of black, coloured, or Asian Africans in our homes and hotels was of little importance in the big picture. Whether we liked it or not, we actually were benefiting from the system. I also knew, as did many others, that the system was unsustainable. I had never forgotten the lines of Portuguese in Mozambique, clutching their few remaining possessions after the revolution. I was convinced that a revolution would occur in South Africa, and I could not imagine that it would be peaceful. I was convinced that I could not change the system; in fact, I was horrified that the system was changing me. My instincts very strongly told me that I should now plan to take my family away from South Africa, even if it cost us everything we had. Sitting in New York reading about the Soweto riots was the catalyst I needed.

It was also a wake-up call for the company. All of our eggs were in the Southern African basket, with the exception of the Saint Géran Hotel in Mauritius. As part of our strategic thinking, it was decided that we should make a real effort to spread our risks: to develop the company overseas. The difficulty was exchange control. We were making healthy profits in South Africa, and the rand was worth US$1.3, but we were not allowed to take any money out. After many discussions with the government and commitments to repatriate any profits we made offshore to South Africa, Sol eventually persuaded the reserve bank to let us invest $1 million overseas.

Not wanting to become a minority partner for the second time, Sol set off to the USA to seek a partner to match our million. At least then we would have two million! After doing the rounds of the merchant banks on Wall Street, it did not take him long to latch on to Oppenheimer and Co.—not the South African family, but the bank. Oppenheimer had just launched a property-investment division under a charming and jolly banker, Jim Levi. Jim and his wife, Connie, were duly invited to South Africa to see what we did. We pulled out all of the service stops. They were blown away. Service did not exist like this in the USA. A joint venture was debated and quickly enacted, with a mission to use the $2 million as seed money to start a hotel business in America. Somebody from Southern Sun had to go to New York to run the joint venture. That somebody had to be someone who could recreate the standards we had achieved in South Africa. Needless to say, I volunteered. This time, I had the unqualified support of Diana; she had dreamed of living in America since the days of the Saturday-morning movies.

# Chapter Nine
## AMERICAN ADVENTURES

Once we had made the decision to move to America, the wait seemed interminable. We had little difficulty selling our home in Bryanston, but because the buyers wanted a quick closure, it meant moving the family back into the Sunnyside Park Hotel, where we had started, whilst we waited for the visas to come through and the joint venture to be cast in stone. Diana's enthusiasm for the USA had rubbed off onto the children, who were initially very excited about the prospect of the move. Television broadcasting, which had been banned in South Africa when we first arrived, was now part of family life, and American culture, as displayed in *Dallas*, seemed very attractive to our youngsters, and they were the envy of their chums.

The pitstop at the Sunnyside, however, dragged on and on. Not only was Diana 'Mom's taxi' having to work overtime, fetching and carrying the children from their suburban school to the city hotel, but the room-service menu, which was designed for businessmen on two-night stays, became a nightmare. The children longed for Diana's home cooking, and for all the simple things that don't feature on that sort of menu. They also had to keep quiet. Need I say more? Tempers began to get frayed, and, as usual, Diana had to bear the brunt. I could not give her a definite answer about when we could leave, because it was beyond my control. We had sold our home, did not have one to go to in the UK, and could not venture into the USA until the paperwork was done. How many international corporate executives have had to suffer similar domestic pain?

In the hopes of getting a clearer picture, Diana resorted to visiting a psychic, Mrs. Eva Brown, who had been introduced to her by a good friend. Mrs Brown gave each client an hour of her time, during which she encouraged them to make notes of what she spouted as she consulted first the tarot cards, then regular playing cards, and then the crystal ball.

Her observations were astounding. Diana had been born illegitimately. Her birthmother had placed her in the care of foster parents, whom she (and I) regarded as her real parents. They had also fostered another boy and girl, whom Diana naturally regarded as her true brother and sister. The birthmother had subsequently married and produced three more daughters and twin sons, all of whom were, therefore, Diana's half-siblings. When Diana had been about eleven years old, the birth mother had tried to remove her from her foster parents, who had successfully fought to keep her. Diana had then entered into her disastrous first marriage and produced Sue and Simon. By the time she was sitting in front of Eva Brown, she also had, of course, remarried, and together, we had Sarah and Jonathan. With a few shuffles of the tarot cards, Eva announced that Diana's circle was complicated, and proceeded to describe, in great detail, every single one of the double family, neatly putting the half-brothers and sisters in one pile and the foster family in another.

Diana was immediately convinced that Eva had a special talent, and asked her for information about the future, without tipping her off that we were destined for America.

"You will shortly be crossing the water," announced Mrs. Brown. "In fact, you will be crossing the water twice." She told Diana, "Tell your husband he will be successful," and, most importantly, "You and he are soulmates."

Not long after this piece of useful and welcome advice, our visas came through, and we crossed the water once, to England, where we parked the children for a while with my parents; and then again, to the USA, where we proceeded through the now-familiar routine of finding homes and schools. The news from Mrs. Brown had not been earth-shattering, but it did give Diana, at the time, a certain comfort, and she was to visit Eva on many more occasions, with far more interesting results.

Oppenheimer Properties' office was at One New York Plaza, the last building on Manhattan before the Staten Island Ferry and the rest of the world. This was in 1977, several years before the completion of the ill-fated twin towers of the World Trade Center, but nevertheless, their building was still part of the world's most famous skyline. Jim Levi made a small office available to me, the new chief executive of the joint venture company and its only employee. (All offices seemed small in New York, after South Africa!).

Jim lived in Larchmont, Westchester County, about an hour's commute in a car from the office in lower Manhattan. Jim encouraged us to find a property in Westchester, which was northeast of the city. The choice seemed straightforward, since we could not afford to live in Manhattan, and did not think it would be child-friendly; our choices seemed to be to go east to Long Island, west to New Jersey, or northeast to Westchester. Not knowing any better, we opted for Westchester; we did not regret it. After a brief search, we found a rental house in Harrison, a suburb about five miles from Larchmont.

The house belonged to an American journalist who had

recently separated from his English wife. He worked for *Newsweek*, where his last assignment had been as bureau chief in Moscow, from where he had imported a cat named Trotsky, who went with the house and formed a love-hate relationship with our own much-travelled cat. He (the landlord, not the cat) was completely zany, but when all was said and done, he was a perfect landlord. The house was ramshackle, but, as you might expect from a journalist, full of interesting books, which included all his diaries, in which he had boldly marked with coloured asterisks each night that he had 'done it' with Mary, the long-suffering English wife.

Our daughter Sue had now left school and had opted to undergo beautician's training in England. The other three children joined us in the journalist's house, but Simon, now ready for college, fairly quickly announced that he wanted to go to hotel school in England. What could I say? This temporary breakup of the family was naturally very hard on us, particularly Diana, but she weathered the storm, and set about making a home for the rest of us in a country that she quickly came to love. Moving to America is a bit like moving onto a filmset. Everything seems so familiar: the yellow cabs and the skyscrapers have been part of all our lives for so long, but they have been on the movies. Now, all of a sudden, we found ourselves part of them, but although we were actually amongst them, we still felt strangely detached.

For me, settling in was more difficult. I had been used to directing operations in a fairly large company, with about 8000 workers under my command, in a country with which I was very familiar. Now I didn't even have a secretary, and I had landed in a very strange environment: Wall Street, New York, New York—the home of some of the toughest nuts in the world. Most of the employees at Oppenheimer were traders; i.e. traders in stocks and shares. These people are a breed apart. Their god is money. Their lives, whilst the markets are open, are spent on the tightrope of buy-and-sell. When they are not at work, their lives seem to be spent in pursuit of gaudy expenditure: McMansions, Porsches, etc. Whilst they keep their jobs (which is only while they are successful), they make plenty of money, whichever way the markets are going.

Jim Levi, however, was not like that. A more likeable, hospitable person would be hard to find, and after the strain of working directly for Sol Kerzner, to team up with a chairman like Jim was pure heaven. Jim went out of his way to make me feel at home, with invitations to Larchmont, Saturday mornings in Long Island Sound on his sailboat, and so on. But Jim was a diamond in the rough, and most of his colleagues at Oppenheimer were very rough indeed. During this early period, apart from Jim, I made no friends of my colleagues at work.

The commute was also a culture shock. In the seventies, New York was one of the dirtiest and noisiest cities in the world. It is still noisy, but thanks to a series of very active mayors, culminating in Rudy Giuliani in the late nineties, it is now one of the cleanest; either that, or I just got used to it! Unfortunately for me, when I arrived in Manhattan, Rudy was still a public prosecutor, and after several years of sedate and gentle commuting for all of five minutes in my air-conditioned Mercedes in Johannesburg, the wait for the train on a freezing or boiling platform in Harrison, the overcrowded and filthy Conrail ride to Grand Central Station, and the stuffy, dirty Lexington Avenue Express subway, all of which lasted about three hours a day from home to office and back, were, for me, very depressing. I was finding it difficult to fit in.

At first, the work was also frustrating, and this had a

negative effect at home: first, because I was bringing home my unhappiness; and second, because our initial acquisition target was taking me away from home and threatened, if we were successful, to involve yet another move, this time to Florida. Heavily influenced by Sol, we had set our sights on acquiring the Fontainebleau Hotel on Miami Beach, the same Fontainebleau that had sparked Sol's creative juices in connection with his own Beverly Hills. Ben Novack, the owner, had fallen upon hard times as a result of the collapse of an uninsured tower block, and had filed for Chapter Eleven bankruptcy. This meant that the operation of the hotel was officially in the hands of the receiver, who was supposed to arrange for a sale of the hotel and its assets to the highest bidder in order to partially settle Ben's not inconsiderable debts. Sol had been in contact with his old friend Ben to establish our interest in acquiring the hotel, and had quickly come to an arrangement wherein Ben could be involved going forward.

I was dispatched to Miami for a few weeks to do due diligence; i.e. to find out as much as possible about the operation, in order to arrive at a reasonable bidding price based upon a detailed feasibility study. For obvious reasons, Ben was a model of cooperation, and I quickly learned that all Chapter Eleven bankruptcy meant was that Ben was continuing to run his hotel without the tiresome need of having to pay his debtors. The receiver and Ben, it seemed to me, were the best of friends. Sol and Ben had figured out that they could steal the hotel from the receiver for about $22 million dollars. Even in those days, you would not have been able to rebuild it for forty. As with all bargains, there were other bargain hunters, though none, we comforted ourselves, had such an inside track as us. Our competitors were not, however, little folk. Effectively there were two, the first being none other than New York's pre-eminent real estate owner, Harry Helmsley, who, amongst other things, owned the Empire State Building; the second was Steve Muss, the largest individual owner of real estate on Miami Beach, and therefore the largest payer of real-estate taxes to the city that had hired the bankruptcy judge.

Both Harry and Steve had plenty of money. Our Oppenheimer–Sun joint venture had just $2 million dollars. Our bidding price would therefore depend upon how much more we could borrow, which in turn revolved around my 'numbers' in regard to how much cashflow the hotel would throw off under our management. The thought of managing the Fontainebleau was also daunting. The hotel was huge. It was one of America's first true convention hotels. The ballroom was bigger than two football fields. The hotel was long past its prime. As a result of his financial difficulties, Ben had severely underspent for many years, and the fabric of the building and the equipment were in very poor condition. Part of my job was to assess the future capital expenditure needs and to estimate the potential returns on the assumption that a refurbishment would revitalise the business. At the back of our minds was the possibility that Florida might revoke its casino-gaming ban. The Fontainebleau would make a great casino venue.

Ben took me under his wing, and provided me with all of the assistance and information that I needed to compile the reports required to assess the bidding value and to convince lenders to associate themselves with our bid. Not only would we need to borrow most of the money to buy the hotel, but also sufficient extra to refurbish it. Sol, on his flying visits from Johannesburg, was his usual bullish self when promoting something that he believed in. Sol reasoned that the Fontainebleau could not be rebuilt for less than $40 million, so if we could buy it for around twenty and spend ten to restore it to (almost) new condition, we would have got ourselves a bargain. He also needed to convince Jim Levi and, of course, the banks, because they would be taking an unusually high risk. Fortunately, our track record as managers in South Africa was second to none. As usual, Sol's ability to get investors behind him worked, and in the relatively short time available, before bids had to be with the receiver, we had enough financial commitment in place to be able to prepare a bid for the bankruptcy court of $21 million.

Sealed bids were to be presented to the court before a set date, and each bidder would then be allotted time to promote the merits of their bid. On the advice of Jim, we decided that we should hire a professional to present our bid, and a lawyer called Shepard Broad was recommended. Shep was a remarkable man. Although he was the founding partner of the law firm Broad and Broad, he was also the president and principal owner of Florida's Bank of America. Shep had come to America as a penniless immigrant. Before long, he owned a successful dredging company, and much of the creation of the intracoastal waterway in the Miami area was his work. Broad Causeway, the toll road spanning the water between Bal Harbour and the mainland, had been built by Shep. For many years, Shep had been the mayor of Bal Harbour; the library in the law school at Fort Lauderdale is named after him. His proudest achievements, however, had been in connection with the founding of the State of Israel. Shep had been one of the ten Americans who had been selected by Ben-Gurion to assist with the establishment of Israel in 1947. All ten had had specific roles to play; Shep's was to organise the transportation of Jewish immigrants, and it was Shep who purchased the ship, which was famously renamed *Exodus* and carried so many Jews to the Promised Land. The modern history of Israel was festooned across Shep's office walls, and pictures of Shep alongside Ben-Gurion, Golda Meir, and Abba Eban were prominent.

When we eventually got to the Miami court where the bankruptcy judge was to adjudicate, I was extremely surprised. I had been used to the formality of courts in England and South Africa, where people stood as the judge appeared and the judge himself was traditionally robed and bewigged. The court in Miami was held in a room reminiscent of an untidy schoolroom, and the judge appeared in an unpressed lounge suit, without announcement and with no presence of authority or formality. People were coming and going, passing notes to each other, having little chats in corners, and so on. I found this quite disconcerting, as did I the actual presence of Harry Helmsley and Steve Muss. For some reason—I don't know why—I had thought that they would send their minions to do their bidding. The very presence in court of these two famous men demonstrated the importance of the occasion and heightened my anxiety. Not so with Shep. He was completely at home in these surroundings. He was also a super showman and a narrator of great confidence and style. He completely dominated the room, and as he stood in front of the judge to explain the merits of our bid, he did so with the flamboyance of an accomplished actor. I felt extremely confident that we were on the verge of acquiring the Fontainebleau. My confidence was not only due to Shep's agile and convincing performance; although the three bids were all presented in differing formats, it was hard to get away from the fact that the Oppenheimer bid was $1 million higher than the other two.

I was therefore astounded, as were Sol and Jim, when the judge announced that it was impossible for him to adjudicate that day on the three bids, because he could not compare "apples with apples." In order to do so, he reasoned, it would be necessary for all three bidders, if they continued to be interested, to resubmit sealed bids five days later along a similar format, which he described. And, of course, if bidders wished to change their offering prices, that would be okay with him. Great! Now the other two knew what we had been prepared to bid, and we were all being asked to enter into a new round of bidding. This wasn't a sealed-bid process—this was an auction!

We realised that during the next five days, we would have to increase our bid, but to what—and with what? We had stretched our borrowings to the limit, and we only had available our fixed two million of equity. We dared not dip into our fund for refurbishment, because Shep had already highlighted to the judge and the others how sound our plan was going forward. After much strategising, we decided to increase our bid by just over a million dollars, and Sol and Jim went rushing off to see the banks whilst Shep and I prepared the new paperwork. Miraculously, they found the extra million in time, and so back to court we went.

The three sealed bids were ceremoniously opened by the clerk of the court, in an atmosphere of great tension and expectancy. The interest of the public and the press had been aroused by the previous session in court, which had been widely reported, and so the little room was packed. One by one, the clerk opened the bids, read out loud their contents, and handed them to the judge. We had been convinced that our extra million would not be enough to win this game of poker, but to our delight and amazement, when all of the bids had been read, ours was still the highest by several hundred thousand dollars.

Shep took his turn to extol the merits of our bid, but this time he was strangely muted. I put this down to the fact that since ours was still the highest bid, there was little point in saying anything other than state this fact. How wrong I was. I will always believe that Shep, wise old boy that he was, knew that whatever he said would have been a waste of breath. A decision had been made—not by the judge: he was just the messenger. Steve Muss was to be the successful bidder: the local man, the man with the political clout. The judge went through unconvincing rhetoric that the South African bid, although indisputably the highest, would lead to racial tensions on Miami Beach and difficulties with the union, but it was obvious that we had been stitched up. Four months of hard work and many days away from home had been completely wasted. Life was not fair.

I was bitterly disappointed, and yet I was strangely relieved. I had not fallen in love with the Fontainebleau Hotel; in fact, I did not like it at all, and I was extremely nervous of my ability to be able to successfully manage it with the same impact I had made in South Africa. In addition to this, we would not have to move to Miami. But what would our Oppenheimer–Sun partnership do next? We'd spent some of our capital on lawyers and travel, and we had nothing to show for it. Would the partnership survive, and if not, what would become of me? I definitely did not want to go back to South Africa.

Sol was also disappointed. He flew home to South Africa, asking me to sit tight, to build up a relationship with Jim and to look around for another opportunity. But his focus was not on America. An opportunity was formulating in South Africa for Sol to create his calling card on the world. Despite the apparent harshness and blatant racism of apartheid, the Afrikaans government presented it to their electorate with a certain logic, which in turn was reinforced by their Christian church, the Dutch Reform Church. Their philosophy was not that blacks and whites were unequal; it was that they were different. They had different cultural backgrounds, different lifestyles, and different needs. This half-truth was packaged and presented to both black and white populations in a very persuasive way, and part of the grand plan was to allocate blacks certain exclusive territories where they could develop independently. Blacks were conveniently divided into tribes and allocated 'homelands' to which they were encouraged to migrate. It always struck me as strange that a Xhosa should be encouraged to separate from an Ndebele, but that a white British immigrant was as welcome to South Africa as a white French immigrant, without the pressing need to allocate separate territories to British or French. Nevertheless, the Nationalist government of South Africa had come up with this incredible plan of creating homelands allocated to the various ethnic tribes of black South Africans, notwithstanding the fact that many of them had intermarried and no longer had a strong allegiance to one tribe or another.

Tribal chiefs were also given substantial incentives to form homeland governments, which, after a period of training by white civil servants, could apply for independence from the motherland. Tribal chiefs who opted for independence were given a huge package of assistance by the South African government to help them organise and train their civil services, armies, police forces, schools and universities. Upon taking independence, each homeland inherited the infrastructure that had been developed by South Africa. Once the leader of a tribe had claimed independence, all tribe members automatically lost their limited rights of citizenship in South Africa and became voting citizens of their new homeland, irrespective of whether they lived there or worked there, which was extremely unlikely, since most of the homelands were situated far from the developed urban areas of South Africa.

The exception to this was Bophuthatswana, the new home of the Tswana tribe, or at least the Tswanas who lived in South Africa rather than Botswana or elsewhere. Bophuthatswana was made up of several scattered pieces of land, dotted around the northern provinces of South Africa like pieces of a jigsaw thrown out of a box. One piece of the puzzle nudged precariously close to Pretoria, conveniently providing a dormitory for labour to the white man's factories of Pretoria and the Witwatersrand. Another piece was next to the old town of Mafeking, and it was this area that became the capital and administrative centre of 'Bop', Mmabatho.

The president of Bophuthatswana, upon its independence, was Chief Lucas Mangope. Chief Mangope was stern and authoritative. A visit to his office was like a visit to the headmaster. Sol had been courting Mangope, as had several others. The reason for this flirtation was because, as an 'independent' nation, Bop would have the right to allow casino gaming in its territory to compete with South Africa's other neighbours, Swaziland and Lesotho, both of which housed Holiday Inns containing small casinos and sufficient raunchy entertainment to attract sex-starved South Africans. It had not escaped our notice that these facilities, bad as they were, were doing a roaring trade despite the five-hour drive from Johannesburg and sometimes-lengthy waits at border posts. It was just proof of the old notion that if you attempt to ban something, people will go to great lengths to get some of it. Just as Sol had recognised a few years before that the hotel needs of the South African public and tourists were not being met, he also perceived that the same was true of their entertainment needs, and if we could fill that gap in Bop, eliminating the five-hour drive and cutting out the border formalities to boot, we could be onto a winner.

The Holiday Inn people also saw the potential of Bop, and courted Mangope with stories of their experience and expertise in the entertainment and casino business, as well as, according to Mangope, with a suitcase full of money. The product they paraded as their 'experience' was, however, very poor indeed, and we played this up to the hilt with the new president. Naturally, we took him to Mauritius, not only because that was where we operated our only casino, as described earlier, but because the Saint Géran Hotel was now renowned as a world-class resort. You cannot just describe these things to an African tribal chief; they have no reference points in their lives by which to make judgments. Fortunately, you have to let them experience the product for themselves, which gives you plenty of time to impress them and gain their confidence.

What we proposed to Mangope was not a get-rich-quick scheme, with a suitcase of money on the side. We proposed that if he were to grant us the casino licenses required, we would literally put his new country on the map. We would develop a tourist infrastructure that would make him the envy of every other African president. At the end of a perfect stay in Mauritius, he agreed to allow us to present our plans to his cabinet, and Sol set about putting together the first of many 'blow you away' presentations that would become a hallmark of the company in later years.

Sol explained to Mangope that the cabinet would have to travel to Johannesburg to see the presentation, because the state offices in Mmabatho were not properly equipped. He then rented a full-sized cinema, complete with 'sound surround'. There, with all of the newly formed Bop cabinet of African elders present, he literally blew them away with his vision of how we intended to transform Bophuthatswana into a vacation and convention paradise. To the sound of stirring music and words, the African statesmen sat in wonderment as a movie unfolded in front of them, juxtaposing pictures of the growth of Las Vegas out of the Nevada desert with futuristic images of part of Bop turning into Sun City and more. The presentation was a resounding success, and very soon after that, papers were signed, giving Sun the exclusive casino-gambling rights to Bop for fifteen years, with certain rights of renewal dependent upon our performance—and we intended to perform!

Mangope and his cabinet were getting ready to take their independence from South Africa, and had set up their parliament and administrative offices in Mmabatho, so the first requirement they had was for us to build a small hotel there. Although we did not believe it would be financially viable, it was, of course, politically necessary to build it. We had not anticipated putting a casino into the Mmabatho Sun, but at the last moment we decided to place a few tables and slot machines into what had originally been planned as a meeting room. This turned out to be a very profitable decision. While I languished in America, pursuing lots of blind-alley deals, Sol threw his energy into getting the Mmabatho Sun built in time for the independence celebrations and the planning of the first phase of Sun City.

Not that life was dull in the USA. Diana, the remaining children and I had moved from Jay's rental in Harrison to our own home in Purchase, a small village not far from White Plains, Westchester. The children had settled down well in their new schools, and Diana was really enjoying being in America. I was gaining some useful experience into the ways of American business and Wall Street, and I was beginning to earn a reputation on the Street as one of the few people working in the investment-bank environment who knew anything about the hospitality industry. As a result, my opinion on various deals was frequently sought, not only by Oppenheimer employees, but also by those at other financial institutions.

One day, I received a call from a Mr Alan Stillman, who had been referred to me by Jim Levi. Alan was a restaurateur who had built up a thriving and lively restaurant in Manhattan called TGI Friday's, a concept he had just sold to Carlson's, who ultimately developed it into a worldwide chain. Alan was not interested in TGI Friday's anymore, because he wanted to create the best steakhouse in New York, a city famous for its steaks. Alan had discovered that a landmark restaurant on Third Avenue at 49th Street called Manny Wolf's was about to close down. Manny Wolf's had once been a very famous watering hole, but over the years, it had fallen out of favour; its standards had slipped, and its red plastic banquets were now stained and tattered. But, Alan explained, it occupied a fantastic piece of real estate. According to Alan, the building could be bought for about $700,000. Alan had already negotiated a mortgage of around $400,000, and he was looking for a group of shareholders to put up the balance of $300,000 and sufficient funds for renovating, re-equipping, and relaunching the restaurant. He had spoken to Jim in the hope that Oppenheimer might be prepared to syndicate the raising of the equity.

Alan suggested that I meet him midtown that afternoon to look at the property, and I agreed to do so. I immediately liked what I saw. Manny Wolf's was a two-storey building on the corner of 49th and Third. Going north on Third, between the restaurant and 50th was a row of one-storey, low-quality retail shops. Behind the building, going east on 49th, was a car parking lot. On the opposite side of Third, diagonally across from the building, was another parking lot. Apart from these vacant lots, all around were cranes involved in building huge, skyscraping apartment and office blocks. To me it seemed that Manny Wolf's was sitting on a real-estate goldmine. Even if the restaurant failed, the site wouldn't.

Alan described his new steakhouse concept with great enthusiasm. He would only serve the very best meat and the very freshest fish and shellfish. Portions would be huge. Décor would be spartan, although not quite the rough sawdust-floored look of some of the other great steakhouses in town. The whole place would have a very masculine feel to it. It would be the first restaurant in New York to have a glass wall between the kitchen and the dining tables. Prices would be very high. I liked Alan a lot; he exuded confidence. But most of all, I liked the site.

The next morning, I met with Jim Levi and reported back on my discovery. Diana and I had very little spare cash available, but by the time I reached Jim's office, I had quite decided to use what we had to deal ourselves into a piece of the action, if I could persuade Jim to put together a syndication. Alan actually needed about $450,000. Jim was very impressed with the fact that I was willing to invest, and he rushed around the partners of Oppenheimer, telling them. By lunchtime, Jim had received pledges for the full amount, and he called me to let me know that this had been the quickest (and most informal) equity syndication he had ever conducted. When Alan phoned later that day to ask if I had considered his request, I gave him the good news. He was ecstatic.

I was nominated as spokesperson for the investor group, to liaise with Alan's management. My contribution to the pre-opening planning was negligible, but I had regular meetings with Alan to monitor the investment. In fact, the only useful contribution that I made involved the name of the place. As we were sitting around one evening, brainstorming potential restaurant names, I happened to be glancing through a newspaper from South Africa that I had somehow acquired. I noticed an article about Rhodesia, the headlines of which mentioned Ian Smith, the prime minister, and Sir Roy Wellensky, the governor. "What about Smith and Wellensky?" I proffered.

"Sounds good to me," retorted Alan, and with that brief interchange, one of New York's most famous landmark buildings was renamed—only somehow, between Alan and the signwriter, Wellensky became Wollensky.

Everything went well until the day before the official opening, when, exactly at noon, a gang of thugs armed with crowbars entered the restaurant through a side door on 49th, lined up the staff against a wall, and proceeded to smash every stick of furniture, every bottle, every plate… everything in the establishment. The place was devastated; so was I, because not only could I see my investment going the same way as the furniture and crockery, but I also had to break the news to the partners of Oppenheimer that they would not be attending the opening function as planned, but instead might be called upon (which they were) for some additional funds to get the place sorted out. This was my first brush with the New York Mafia. Alan had been using non-union labour to save money. He had ignored warnings that this was not to the liking of the mob. This was the last time that Alan ignored such warnings, and protection money (booked as PR and insurance) was paid thereafter.

Unfortunately, a restaurant that has been completely annihilated takes a few months to be put back together. Not long enough, however, to lay off all of the staff, so not only are the costs of renovating incurred, but also the payroll costs, with no offsetting income. The investing partners were not pleased. Nor were they pleased when, once we had opened, the restaurant was a complete flop. Week after week, the costs exceeded the revenues, and soon our cash reserves were so depleted that I, once again, had to go back to the Oppenheimer partners (including myself!) and ask for additional contributions. For me, it was a struggle to find the extra cash, but worse was the feeling that my judgment was being questioned. Alan, Jim and I held a crisis meeting. We had about $20,000 left in the kitty, and Jim warned that the partners were about to draw a line in the sand. In other words, once the twenty was gone, there could be no more.

We decided to take a gamble. We gathered together our rather morose and elderly waiting staff, uniformed New-York-style in sombre black with long grey aprons, and photographed them unsmilingly as a group. We then took out a whole-page advertisement in the *New York Times* which simply showed the picture with a caption that said something like "We have 4000 years of experience; we take our job seriously."

The advert cost $10,000. We booked space for two. We were the first restaurant ever to take out a full-page advertisement in the *Times,* and for them it was such a special occasion that they even included a little article recording the fact.

We never ran the second ad! The day after the first advertisement appeared, Smith & Wollensky was 100% full—and miraculously, it stayed that way. The cash came rolling in, and very quickly the partners had all their money back and a very healthy stream of dividends. The restaurant was expanded, and still we were overbooked. Suddenly, Peter Venison was a favoured son at Oppenheimer. Then, just as we thought things could not get better, they did. A real-estate developer, who had acquired the one-storey retail strip adjacent to the restaurant and the parking lot behind, made us a generous offer to buy the restaurant, with a view to demolishing it to make way for a skyscraper. We declined the offer, despite its ever-increasing nature. We were determined to keep our little gem intact. Finally, we made a deal, not to sell the building, but to sell the 'air' above it. That way, everybody was happy. The developer was allowed to add several floors to the height of his proposed building, because by being able to build right up to our walls, he increased the size of the footprint considerably. We, in turn, sacrificed forever the right to build above our restaurant. This was one of New York's first 'air rights' deals, and in one shot we had all doubled our original investments whilst maintaining our cashflow.

Whilst the Smith & Wollensky story was unfolding, I continued to look at other opportunities for the joint venture. I was not troubled much by Sol as he busied himself with the arrangements of Bop's independence, but one day, out of the blue, I received a phone call from him that took me off on yet another adventure, this time an adventure into the murky world of professional boxing. I had always been mildly interested in boxing; that is to say, I would watch the big fights on television, I was a fan of Cassius Clay/Muhammad Ali, I had once met Henry Cooper in an airport line in Milan, and I had even been to a couple of live world-title fights at the Rand Stadium in Johannesburg. At school, I had once entered the school boxing championships, but soon realised that all my opponent had to do was to hit me on the nose and my eyes would water so much that I was practically rendered blind. I never could have dreamed that this mild interest in the sport would lead me to become so deeply involved in this fascinating business, where characters are really characters.

I had just finished watching (on television) Muhammad Ali lose a fifteen-round heavyweight championship fight to rank outsider Leon Spinks, for whom it was only his eighth professional fight, when Sol called from South Africa. It had been an amazing fight. For seven rounds, Ali had hardly thrown a punch. He had merely let Spinks hit him whilst he clowned around and 'rope-a-doped', as he used to call it. This involved covering both sides of his face with his gloves whilst sticking his elbows out in front of his body to guard against blows to the chest and stomach. Needless to say,

Spinks had won the first seven rounds easily. From round eight, Ali had started to dance, jabbing and hitting Spinks almost at will, despite spirited defence from the challenger. It had been clear who was the better boxer: the ever-popular but controversial Ali. By the end of the fourteenth round, the points had seemed evenly poised, and the last round would clearly be the 'decider'. Ali, however, had misjudged things badly, and by the time the fifteenth started, he was exhausted. Spinks seized his chance, fighting just hard enough for the last three minutes to clinch the decision. Immediately after the fight, Ali declared that he was the 'People's Champion' and that he should be given a rematch. The problem was that under the WBA/WBC rules (the two international governing bodies who, at the time, controlled the sport and who had jointly sanctioned the fight) it was mandatory for the winner to fight the number-one contender, Ken Norton, who had been unfairly passed over by Ali in his selection of Spinks as an opponent. The television commentators had quickly exploited the situation, goading the public to phone in support for the popular Ali to be allowed a rematch, notwithstanding the rules.

"Howzit, Pete?" said Sol down the overseas line. "Did you watch the fight?

"Of course," I replied.

"I was thinking," said Sol, with his customary pause, which made one's mind race to consider all the possibilities that he could be thinking about. "Why don't you see if you can't get the rematch for Bophuthatswana?" All the reasons why I thought this would be impossible instantly flooded my mind like a great tidal wave: "I've never met Ali," "I don't know where to start," "There's not going to be a rematch," "No one in America has ever heard of Bophuthatswana."

"Yes, Sol—sounds like a good idea," I blurted out. "I'll see what I can do."

"Maybe you should start by going to see Bob Arum: he's the guy that promoted the fight. I think it would be worth paying a million dollars for it. It would certainly impress the old man if we could do it." The 'old man' was none other than Chief Lucas Mangope, the president of Bop.

"That's not all it would impress," I thought to myself, as I put down the phone.

As a newcomer to New York, the challenge laid before me seemed crazy. I racked my brains for clues as to how to proceed. I could just call Bob Arum. He would be listed for sure; promoters always are. But it would be better to have an introduction. I did have one friend who claimed to know everybody; I'd first met Gregory Brown, a six-foot-six-inch self-proclaimed black television producer, when he had invited himself onto a freebie Air France trip for celebrities from Paris to Mauritius to celebrate and promote the opening of the Saint Géran Hotel. I wondered if Gregory knew Bob Arum. "Of course I know Bob Arum," he lied, when I called him that night. "Leave it to me; I'll get us an appointment with him tomorrow morning, if he's back in town. I'll call you back."

Gregory was so authoritative that I instantly believed him. Several hours later, he did call back to advise me that he had secured an appointment for us at 11 am the next morning at Arum's Park Avenue office. "Meet me at ten-thirty at the Waldorf," instructed Gregory, "and rent a stretch—we'll be needing one." For those of you who are not familiar with the Big Apple, a 'stretch' is a limousine—which, in New York, is a regular luxury car that has been cut in half, had a ten-foot piece of car added to the middle, and re-joined.

"Why do we need a stretch?" I asked Gregory as we met up the next morning.

"Because we need to impress the man," beamed Gregory.

"But he won't see it," I protested. "His office is only two blocks from here, and it's probably on the fiftieth floor."

"Always be prepared to impress," rejoined Gregory, brushing aside my complaint.

Not long after, we were both sitting in Bob Arum's office, with Gregory reminding Bob where they had met, and Bob looking somewhere between annoyed and puzzled. This expression soon changed into one of interest as I made my pitch—particularly the bit about the million dollars. Bob had never heard of Bophuthatswana, which is not surprising because it did not yet feature on any maps, but he seemed to sense that I might be for real. He explained that he was actively trying to get the WBA and the WBC to bend their own rules and let Ali have the rematch, with the promise that the winner would fight Ken Norton. Bob explained that Ali had only lost the fight against Spinks because he had promised the television company, who were disgusted at his selection of the 'no-name' Spinks for an opponent, that the fight would last for at least eight rounds—the minimum they needed to satisfy the sponsor, and the minimum they needed to be able to screen all of the booked commercials. Ali had deliberately not thrown a punch for seven rounds just to keep his promise, but also to mock the television executives. Now the joke had backfired, and he was hustling for his professional life, stirring up public support on radio and television at every opportunity, of which naturally there were many.

"The WBA might bend," said Bob, "but the WBC are standing firm. What about another million for Norton to go away? Nah, never mind; he wouldn't go along."

The more I told Bob about our company and Sol, the more he seemed to be interested, and after about an hour, he invited Gregory and me to lunch. "Let's go to the Friars Club," said Bob. "It's only a few blocks up the road; we can walk." It seemed inappropriate at that moment to mention that we had a driver and limousine wasting dollars parked outside his office building's door, so we both played it cool. As we stepped out of the lobby into Park Avenue, however, our alert driver, seeing us approaching, jumped out of the car and opened the door. I didn't know whether to pretend I did not know who he was or say, "We're walking today, James, thank you," but Gregory came to my rescue with an appropriate instruction, telling him to wait outside the Friars Club. It was some weeks later that Bob Arum told me that he had never met Gregory Brown before, and asked why I had allowed him to waste my money on limos.

The Friars Club is one of New York's more interesting eateries. To be admitted, you must be a member or a member's guest, and to become a member, you must be associated with showbusiness. As Ali's promoter, Bob Arum naturally qualified. But Bob was about as un-showbusiness in character as you could be. A bespectacled, Harvard-trained tax lawyer who had first met Ali, as Cassius Clay, when he was involved in an IRS investigation, Bob had seen an opportunity to make some real money by promoting Ali's fights, and Ali had taken to Bob. Bob had recently remarried, and Sybil, his attractive Hawaiian wife, who was working as his secretary and assistant, had been left in the office. Bob used the lunch to find out more about Southern Sun, Bop, Sol, and the logistics of putting on a fight there, such as details on television links, security and transport. I did my best to answer like a pro. Sitting there, in the hallowed walls of the Friars Club, surrounded by signed portraits of some of the most famous personalities in America as well as a few in the flesh, debating the possibilities of promoting a world heavyweight fight, did not seem real—and I had to keep reminding myself that maybe it wasn't.

We finished lunch and parted, with Bob assuring me that he would telephone later to let me know if he wanted to meet again. He seemed dubious that we would. That night, he rang. He'd spoken to the WBA. In principle, they were interested in letting Ali have an immediate rematch and making Ken wait. The WBC, however, was adamant that Spinks must fight Norton or they would strip him of his title. For the right incentive, Bob informed me, the WBA officials could see their way to allowing the Ali–Spinks rematch in Bop. It immediately became obvious that there would have to be enough 'meat' in the deal for Arum to take care of the incentives. It was also obvious that this one day of effort was, with surprising ease, leading to the distinct possibility that the impossible could be made to happen.

Arrangements were made to meet in Arum's office the next day, together with the representatives of Ali's management, who would be flying in from Chicago. I was not interested in just any Spinks fight—only Ali–Spinks, and only in Bop—so the first task was to convince Ali's people, and ultimately Ali himself, that it would be all right to go there, that he would be safe, that it would be politically acceptable to the black Muslims, and so on. The second phase was to convince Spinks and the WBA, but achieving that was probably going to be more about money than politics.

Bophuthatswana was the product of apartheid. Although the Tswanas had been given the pre-existing infrastructure as part of the process of separate development, the notion of it being a truly separate and independent state was unworkable, firstly because most of South African industry (and therefore jobs) was still located in South Africa proper; and secondly because the outlawed African National Congress (ANC) saw the "homeland" policy as a way to hive off black South Africans to "countries" outside of the RSA, thereby reducing the future potential black vote. The ANC was strongly represented in exile, and, as a result, exerted sufficient pressure on the international community to stop them from recognising the homelands, such as Bop, as independent states. Bop and the other homelands, although operating independently from South Africa, were not recognised by any countries other than South Africa and were, therefore, forced to trade and talk only with South Africa.

Ultimately, with the release of Nelson Mandela from jail, the unbanning of the ANC, and the establishment of a new constitution for South Africa, the homelands were persuaded to give up their independence and were reunited with South Africa under the presidency of Mandela. At the time of the proposed Ali–Spinks fight, however, President Lucas Mangope of Bop regarded himself as very much the leader of an independent country and would have been very happy to host a world-title fight in his Independence Stadium at Mmabatho.

Back in New York, the meeting with Ali's management (consisting of Herbert Muhammad and his black Muslim advisers) went well. They liked the sound of the money, and they had no idea of the political furore they would create by sending Ali to fight in a pro-apartheid state—in fact they had never heard of Bop and did not realise how their presence there could upset the ANC. I, of course, put across all of the plus points about Bop: how it was a black-run country (true), consisting of mainly black citizens (true) that had escaped from the dominance of white-run South Africa (partially true), and deserved to be given assistance by such prominent black men such as Muhammad Ali. Ali did not attend the meetings in Bob's office, and I would not have known that he was even in the city, except for an incredible coincidence.

On the evening of my meeting with his management, I had agreed that Diana and I would take Gregory Brown out to dinner. We had a lady friend from Italy staying with us, and we had booked a table for four at a little restaurant in Greenwich Village. Taking a leaf out of Gregory's book,

I had rented a limo for the evening. When we arrived at the restaurant to meet Gregory, he was not yet there, but the waiter showed us to a table laid up for ten. "This is not my table," I explained to the maitre d'. I quickly found out, of course, that it was; Gregory had just added a few of his friends!

During the course of the evening, Anna Maria announced that she would like to go on to Studio 54, Manhattan's swingiest nightclub, to which it was almost impossible to gain access without a Gregory Brown. Not wishing to disappoint the lady, we all piled into the limo and headed uptown to the nightclub, where, as usual, there was a large crowd milling around at the door, trying to catch the attention of the doorman who held the key to entrance. To our astonishment, just as we pulled up in the limo, none other than Muhammad Ali waltzed out of the club; he made a beeline for our limo, and opened the passenger door. Realising that he had confused our car for his, which had apparently pulled up behind us, he beat a retreat, but not before his presence had illuminated our vehicle and he had cast his magic spell over Diana and our Italian guest. There was not time to explain that we were the people with whom his management had been busy discussing Bophuthatswana that very day, so I just marked down this chance meeting as being a good omen.

The next day, I went to see Bob again, and this time, to my amazement, he informed me that the Ali camp was satisfied with my explanations about Bop and was keen for Bob to get on with the job of convincing Leon Spinks that there was more money to be made in a rematch with the popular Ali than by following the WBC rules. Spinks also 'bought' it, and Arum did not have a hard time selling the idea of a rematch to the television networks, wherever it was going to be fought. All that remained was for Arum to obtain the official sanction of the WBA and the WBC, or at least one of them. The WBA agreed, and history will show that this was the crucial event that split the WBA from the WBC and led to the spawning of many upstart world boxing authorities, which eventually devalued the meaning of the words World Champion.

All of the above was accomplished in a few days by the canny Arum, and in less than one week, I found myself sitting in Bob's office, signing contracts that would commit Southern Sun to staging the WBA Heavyweight Championship of the World, with the participation of the most famous man in the world, in possibly the least famous place in the world. I signed immediately, but Bob, quite wisely, held back. "I'll leave it one day before I commit," said Bob. "I'm going to announce the fight, but I want to see if there is any negative reaction to Bop before I sign." I was somewhat disappointed, but not unduly surprised, so I went home to Purchase that evening with my fingers crossed. As I walked through the front door, the television news was on and I heard the newscaster announce that Ali and Spinks had signed a rematch to be fought in "Boputate… Boffutat… Bop—oh, shucks: you go to Johannesburg and turn right." All of the media carried the news, and amazingly, because it was seen as a major sports story, their entire focus was on the idea of a rematch, the split of the WBA/WBC, the dumping of poor Norton, and so on. Nobody focused negatively on Bop, the product of apartheid. I was therefore very relieved to receive a call from Bob Arum twenty-four hours later, saying that he had placed his final and crucial signature on the contracts and had couriered them to me.

Within half an hour of receiving the contracts, all hell started to break loose on the airwaves. The anti-apartheid protagonists had woken up and were busy reminding

Muhammad Ali and Leon Spinks that they were now the friends and cohorts of the racist South African government. For several days, I was beseeched by the fighters' camps, by the television network—and eventually by Bob Arum—to tear up the contracts. Budweiser, one of the largest advertisers on the network, threatened to cancel all advertising on the channel if the channel fulfilled its contractual obligations in regard to the fight. For a few days I was quite famous, at least within the confines of the US boxing fraternity. Then, a terrible event occurred that changed everything—forever!

At about 3 am, our bedside phone in Purchase rang. These are the calls we always hate. Calls at this time of the morning are either mistakes (usually because someone can't count across time zones) or are bad news. This call was very bad news indeed. Sol's effervescent and lovely young wife, Shirley, had committed suicide, leaving Sol with their one-year old-daughter, Chantal, and three-year-old son, Brandon—in addition, of course, to the three children from his first marriage. Shirley, despite her bubbly personality, had suffered from manic-depression and had, apparently, previously threatened to take her own life, although Sol had never disclosed this (at least, not to me or my colleagues). Now the threats had turned into a terrible reality with the tube from the exhaust into the car, on an open lot of land in suburban Johannesburg. We were all stunned.

I immediately returned to Johannesburg, where I did what I could to comfort a distraught Sol Kerzner. This was certainly the most difficult time in Sol's life, having to cope with the sudden loss of such a loved one, with the feelings of guilt that maybe his lifestyle had contributed in some way to this disaster, and the realisation that his two youngest had lost their mother forever. I stayed in Johannesburg for the next two weeks or so, doing my best, as did many others, to break Sol out of his state of depression. Many friends gathered round and many helpful suggestions were made, including by Diana, as to how best to look after the children. Two of the most helpful people at this time were Colin Hall, ultimately managing director of Woolworths, South Africa, but who at the time was the SAB representative on the Southern Sun board; and Abe Segal, Sol's amiable and loyal tennis-playing buddy. Between us, we tried to get Sol to see that this tragedy was not, in any way, his fault. Slowly, Sol's spark began to return, but for many years later, when I caught him deep in thought, I wondered if he was reliving these awful moments with regret.

During this period of mourning, we discussed the pending fight and the furore we were causing in the USA. We took a view, under the circumstances, to let Arum and the television company off the hook. Sol was in no mood to be organising a world-title fight in Mmabatho; he first had to reorganise his life, and for a time, he was not even sure if he wanted to continue as chairman of the company. I called Bob Arum from Joburg and gave him the news, but in the same breath told him that if I let him rip up the contracts with no compensation, one day I would be calling on him for a favour. I had no idea what the favour would be, but I assured him that one day I would be knocking at his door. "Whatever it will be," Bob acknowledged, "you shall have." This was a promise I never thought would be kept. I could not have been more wrong.

The Ali–Spinks rematch eventually took place in New Orleans, and Ali won rather convincingly, regaining only half of his 'crown', but to the boxing fans and public beyond, he had re-established himself as the true heavyweight champion of the world. I was quite convinced that my little detour into boxing had been TKO'd by Shirley's death; as it turned out, this was only the beginning, and not the end.

# Chapter Ten
## ABORTED DEALS

I left Sol at his house in Homestead Avenue, Bryanston, Johannesburg, and returned to the USA, not knowing quite what the future would hold for me and my family. It seemed obvious to me that Sol was also very undecided about his own future. He had just embarked upon the building of Sun City, had the rest of the South African hotel empire to run, and was party to the embryonic joint venture with Oppenheimer in New York, which had yet to flourish. There was a lot on his plate, and when I left him, his will to tackle it was in doubt. On the surface, however, his bounce-back was quick. Within a few weeks of my return, Sol called to say that he had decided to visit the USA, for discussions with Jim Levi about the future, and to look at a couple of potential acquisition possibilities that I had unearthed.

One of these was in California, and Sol and I stayed at La Costa, a fancy resort between Los Angeles and San Diego. Sol did not take the potential business opportunity very seriously, but I was amazed to see how aggressively he pursued the young ladies in the bar. Then, on our flight back from Los Angeles to New York to meet with Jim, Sol spied a tall, willowy, and very attractive young lady walking down the aisle. Sol, who had an aisle seat, with a deft action and a cheeky grin stuck out his arm as she went past and wrapped it around her leg, thereby completely arresting her progress. Instead of protesting or whacking him with her handbag, she immediately fell into conversation with him and before long was sitting in the vacant seat between Sol and me, with Sol pulling out his brochures and describing to her his hotel passion. It turned out that she was an Eskimo, so Eskimo is what we called her; it just seemed to fit. She was very beautiful, and perfectly charming. She sat with us for a long time, completely enraptured by Sol and more or less ignoring me—but, I have to say, not in an offensive manner. She explained that her boyfriend would be meeting her at Kennedy, but she nevertheless made sure that Sol had her contact numbers.

When I reached Purchase that evening and related the Eskimo incident to Diana, she was furious. "How can Sol behave like that, so soon after Shirley?" she indignantly exclaimed. It was hard to answer. It was not long, however, before it got even harder. Sol was in Manhattan for the weekend, and he used the time, of course, to see Eskimo. Sol was flying to South Africa on Monday, and Diana had previously arranged to accompany me in taking him to the airport in my car. Diana had not seen Sol since Shirley's suicide, and wanted to personally extend her sympathy and to offer her help with Brandon and Chantal. To our horror, as we pulled up at the Pierre Hotel, Sol was arm-in-arm with Eskimo, who apparently also needed to get to Kennedy for a return flight to Los Angeles. Much to Diana's complete disgust, the two of them canoodled in the back of our car all the way to the airport, so any discussion with Sol about his newly deceased wife or the children was clearly inappropriate. To make matters even worse, two days after his return to Johannesburg, Sol called to announce that he would be returning to New York the next weekend. He had decided that Jim, he and I should go to Atlanta to meet the owners of the Omni hotel chain, which Jim and I had been eyeing as a potential acquisition target. "Pick me up at Kennedy from the SAA flight at 8 am—and, by the way, Eskimo will be arriving from LA at 7:30. Will you pick her up first?"

I arrived at Kennedy in time to meet the LA 'red-eye'. Eskimo was there, looking like a million dollars. Everyone else looked as if they had been on a short overnight flight. I had a big car, a Cadillac Fleetwood, but only just big enough, it turned out, for Eskimo's luggage. "I thought we were just going to Atlanta for the night," I ventured. "Oh no," replied Eskimo, her big eyes sparkling with happiness. "Sol has asked me to go back to Johannesburg with him." Words failed me.

Two minutes later, Eskimo and I, in the overladen Cadillac, wound our way through the terminal traffic to meet the SAA flight. There was Sol, with his garment bag slung over his shoulder, standing on the sidewalk. "It's a good job you didn't bring any luggage," I quipped as I relieved him of his one suit. As he looked at the mountain of Louis Vuitton, even Sol's jaw dropped.

The meetings in Atlanta were a disaster. To Jim's amazement and irritation, Sol's concentration on the deal discussions was seriously interfered with by the presence of Eskimo, and furthermore, it turned out that the sellers of Omni were staunch Southern Baptists who could not understand why Sol had showed up in Atlanta with someone they regarded as little better than a prostitute. Sol spent much of the weekend asking me to tell Eskimo that he could not take her back to South Africa, for all of the obvious reasons—not the least of which that his sisters would kill him. "This is one task you will have to do for yourself," I told him, and for once he was not able to persuade me to change my tune. Naturally, it all ended in tears, firstly from Eskimo, who had to cart all her luggage back to Los

Angeles, and secondly from Jim (irritation and frustration rather than tears), who finally decided that this joint venture was going nowhere.

Although Jim did not formally end the Oppenheimer–Southern Sun relationship at this point, he had clearly made up his mind that it was over, because shortly after the Atlanta debacle, when I approached him about the joint venture acquiring a property in Atlantic City for the purposes of establishing a casino hotel, he declined, on the basis that Oppenheimer could not be seen to be part of casino gaming. This was a shame, because the opportunity I had unearthed was, in my view, a sure-fire winner. A few years later, Oppenheimer was at the forefront of syndicating casino deals.

New Jersey had recently decided to become only the second state in the USA to legalise casino gambling, after, of course, Nevada. In doing so, the state had decided to limit casino sites to a small beachfront area in Atlantic City, a decaying seaside town on the southern New Jersey shore. Before the arrival of the jet plane, Atlantic City had been the premier beach vacation spot for New Yorkers. Situated just two hours south of New York by road and one hour east of Philadelphia, Atlantic City had been a thriving town during the early development of the motorcar. Air conditioning in Florida and Eastern Airlines changed all of that, and Atlantic City had been on a downward spiral for several decades. It had been decided that by allowing casino development on the beachfront and at the marina, the city could be revitalised. In order to obtain a casino license, not only would prospective developers have to pass strict probity requirements, but each development would have to include a minimum of 500 hotel rooms. At the time, one casino was due to open shortly: Resorts International. This project consisted of the complete renovation of an obsolete hotel, onto which had been tacked a barn of a building, which housed about a thousand slot machines and several hundred gaming tables. The game plan of the state was to encourage new buildings, but the rules did allow for conversions such as Resorts.

Through my connections with the Fontainebleau in Miami, I had run across a lawyer, Marty Blatt, who owned a flying school in Miami. Marty practiced law in Atlantic City, and, as such, was *the* expert on New Jersey gaming legislation. Marty had identified another building on the Atlantic City beachfront that, in his view, could be renovated to comply with the regulations, and he had asked me for an opinion. The Ritz, which had once been a beachfront hotel, had long ago been converted into small apartments, or 'efficiencies', as one-bedroom studios with cooking facilities were known in America. The building was capable, without too much difficulty, of being reconverted into a 500-room hotel. Adjacent to the Ritz, separated only by a cul-de-sac that stopped at the beach, was a vacant lot of about 80,000 square feet, a big enough footprint on which to build a medium-sized casino. Marty's plan was to acquire the Ritz from its elderly owner, to acquire the vacant lot and the road from the city, and to fast-track the conversion into Atlantic City's second operating casino hotel.

Marty had put together a small group of local investors, one of which was the mayor of Atlantic City's neighbouring town, Ventnor. This group needed a bona fide casino operator (we operated the Mmabatho Sun and the tiny Saint Géran casinos and were building Sun City at the time), as well as the money to acquire the Ritz. I quickly agreed with Marty that, provided we could buy the Ritz on favourable terms, this could represent a fantastic opportunity to get into Atlantic City 'on the cheap', before it was generally appreciated how successful Atlantic City could become. Marty and

I thrashed out a joint venture agreement between his group and Southern Sun, and then together went to Philadelphia to meet the Ritz's owner, A.P. Sloane, who turned out to be one of the most charming old gentlemen I have ever met.

Our timing was perfect. He had had enough of being a landlord; his property needed work; he did not have the cash to fix it up; he did not want to be part of the new casino city; he remembered the city from its earlier, more prestigious days; and so on. For whatever reason, he seemed to trust me. It appeared that he had affection for the English and was very pro-South African, a state of mind that perhaps had been brought on by the fact that his beloved Atlantic City was now very black. Before long, we had settled on a deal; $12 million for the building, two million upon closing, and very favourable terms for the balance. Marty's group was to put in one million, and Southern Sun, the other. With a bit of luck, we could buy the adjacent plot, renovate the building, and be the second casino hotel open in Atlantic City, all for less than $50 million. This could be a license to print money.

We had allowed ourselves about a month to draw up the documentation before having to put down a $1 million deposit, during which time we feverishly worked on the deal to acquire the second lot, and to get the nod on closing the road, and a host of other local permissions. Since our group consisted of one of Atlantic City's leading attorneys and the mayor of the town next door, these things slotted into place with amazing ease. By the time we were ready to sign the deal, much had been accomplished, and to our delight, Resorts had just opened its doors to huge crowds. Such was the pent-up demand on the east coast for casino gaming that people were forming long lines to get to each slot machine, even at three in the morning. The omens were very good indeed.

During this period, I had, of course, kept Sol in South Africa completely informed. I had expected him to fly over to visit the property, but his life, it seemed, was still in some chaos following Shirley's death, and he declined to do so. The signing of the deal was due in Philadelphia on a Monday. I had alerted Sol well in advance that he would need to wire half a million into the Sun account in New York, so that I could pay our share of the deposit. By late in the week prior to the signing, the money had not arrived, despite assurances from Sol that it would. By Friday, I was beginning to panic, and Sol then admitted that he needed a clearance from Dick Goss, the chairman of South African Breweries, before he could release the funds. On Saturday, he called to say that Dick was not prepared to agree to the deal unless Sol had personally visited the site and met the partners. This was an understandable stance from Dick, but one that had been taken, through no fault of his, far too late to be helpful to me. Sol realised that this had put me in an impossible position with our partners, and promised to "Have another go around with Dick." I explained that on Monday morning I was traveling to Atlantic City on a plane chartered by Marty with the intention of signing the deal; we agreed that I should call him before I left, in case anything had changed. On Monday, I eventually got hold of him from a pay phone in Grand Central Station (these were pre-cell phone days!), only to learn that Dick had not changed his mind, and that I was on my way to a signing ceremony with no cash.

I decided to do my best to string out the signing of the deal as long as possible, in the hope that something would come up. Upon meeting Marty and John Best (the mayor) in Atlantic City, I broke the bad news. To say they were livid would be the grossest understatement ever made. They demanded to speak to Sol; there was much screaming and shouting down the phone lines, but the realisation soon set in that nothing could be achieved by yelling at each other. Marty and John, it turned out, could not raise another $500,000 at such short notice. Sol instructed me to do whatever I could do to help them, and promised that if we could keep the deal alive, he would visit Atlantic City within a week. Marty and John knew that I was the one who had developed the relationship with Mr Sloane, and so we decided that I would continue with the scheduled meeting with him, for the assumed purpose of signing off on the deal, but with a hidden agenda to find a way of delaying whilst they did their best to find a new source of equity.

The next few hours with Mr Sloane and his lawyers were tortuous. I set about reading in great detail all of the documentation, looking for anything, however small, that would need amendment. Sloane was extremely patient as I nit-picked my way through the small print, challenging practically every word on the basis that it was my corporate responsibility to be careful. My performance could have won me an Oscar, but after first receiving Sloane's approval for my diligence, he began to be irritated and tired. Finally, he stated that he was leaving for Philly and that he would give me until five o'clock the following evening to sign at his offices there, but after that, the deal would be off. I had won a respite of twenty-four hours.

Meanwhile, John Best had been busy trying to find a partner to replace Sun. He had phoned practically every number in his Filofax, but it was far too short notice for anyone to be able to make any sort of reasonable assessment. Our best hope seemed to be a large recruitment firm with which John had had previous exposure. The president of this company agreed to meet John, Marty and me that evening in Philadelphia, together with his senior management. They had read about the instant success of Resorts and were looking for a diversification in their business. Marty, John and I agreed that since any new investor would want a casino operator on board, and since Mr Sloane thought he was selling the building to a consortium led by Sun, we had better pitch the opportunity as one that still involved Sun as investors and managers. We decided to hide behind South African Exchange Control as the reason we were 'temporarily' short of $500,000. We rented a hotel meeting room, and for several hours I explained the deal, the nature of the gaming business, the history of Southern Sun, the super prospects in Atlantic City, and so on. This was one of the hardest selling jobs I have ever had to pull off, but finally, at about two in the morning, we reached an agreement. The recruitment firm would put up the money in exchange for half of Sun's share in the business. One month later, at the closing, Sun would put up all of the balance of the money due. Sun would remain as managers under the terms of the management agreement, which I had already settled with Marty and John. The situation was saved.

The next morning, I called Sol to let him know what I was doing, and he approved. Effectively, I had given him a breathing space of one month to visit the site, approve, convince Dick Goss, and send me the money. Later that day, I signed the deal with Mr Sloane, like a lamb. Almost immediately, Marty and John started putting pressure on me to get Sol to Atlantic City, but regrettably, Sol kept delaying the trip. Eventually, he did show up, about ten days prior to the closing, and although he approved of the Ritz and all of our planning work, he expressed his complete disagreement with the terms of the management contract. A huge row ensued, and some sort of compromise was agreed. Marty and John, however, were not impressed. First, Sol had made no real effort to apologise for the disaster of three weeks earlier, and second, he appeared to be undermining my authority, and it was me that they had come to know and trust. At the time, I did not realise how badly affected they had been.

Sol flew back to South Africa, and within a few days, having discussed the matter with Dick, wired the necessary money to New York. Since I needed the money on the following Monday for the closing in Philadelphia, I arranged for a correspondent bank in Philly, located in the building next to the closing attorney, to issue a bank draft for my collection in person. John, Marty, our new partners and I met briefly in Philly prior to the closing deadline, and with about an hour to spare, I proceeded to the bank to get the draft.

To my surprise and absolute horror, as I was about to go through the revolving doors of the bank, the screaming of alarms pierced the air and an armed robber rushed out of the doors past me. Mayhem followed. Security men and police dashed about, sirens blared, and—horror of horrors—no one was allowed into the bank. After all I had been through with this deal, why was this now happening to me? This must be a bad dream. "I have to get in," I pleaded with the armed men at the door.

"Can't you see the bank has been burglarised?" one of them growled. I would not—could not—give in. I had to get my bank draft. I persisted and persisted, until even the hardest of policemen realised that my need was desperate, and finally one of them went in search of a bank official with my tale. Balancing my heartfelt commiserations to the bank official with my urgent need for some banking action, I finally managed to extract the draft from a teller, and sped off faster than the bank robber to Mr Sloane's attorney's office, where, with minutes to spare, I produced the bank draft.

The clerk seemed somewhat perplexed. "They've already

been here," she said. "Just a minute." With that, she disappeared into a back office, clutching my draft. Soon, she reappeared. "They'll be out shortly," she said, as the clock ticked onward to the closing deadline.

"I would like you to record that I have deposited that check with you before 4 pm," I authoritatively instructed her. She just looked puzzled. Not long after, Mr Sloane's attorney appeared to explain. Apparently, someone from Marty's firm had already been around that morning, deposited a check for the balance required for the closing, and signed off on the deal on the basis that Sun was no longer coming on board. "They had no right to do that," I explained, but the penny quickly dropped. Marty and John had been so disgusted with Sol, or so nervous that he would not show with the money again, that they had obviously made other arrangements. I had not, however, been party to any changes in the agreements, and I informed Mr Sloane's attorney of such. He understood, but said that it was not his problem. I insisted that he keep my money and record the fact that it had been deposited on time, in accordance with the original documentation. He reluctantly agreed.

Feeling numb after all that had happened to me that day (and before), I retraced my steps to the office where I had earlier met Marty and John. Only John remained, and he confirmed my fears. I reluctantly notified him that I thought he and his partners had acted illegally (although understandably), and he apologised, but explained that Sol's previous behaviour had left them with little choice. We parted rather sadly. After all we had been through together, I knew that I would now be pitted against him.

Not long after the Philadelphia affair, I flew to Johannesburg. I had had enough of this erratic behaviour, and I could not see a future, either for myself with Sol in America or for the joint venture with Oppenheimer. Upon arrival, I realised that Sol, perhaps for the first time in his life, was not coping well with the tasks on hand. The building of Sun City (or at least the first phase) was a full-time job, but the rest of the company needed attention. It did not take me long to see that the right thing to do was to return to South Africa to do what I could to help out in this situation. But the problems with Marty and John had still not been resolved. Although I had retrieved the deposit, we had still run up considerable costs with no result. It had subsequently become evident that Marty and John had replaced Sun with an English gaming company, Corals. In our view, by usurping us in this way, Marty, John, and, indeed, even Corals had acted illegally. I was therefore determined to get some compensation from them, at the very least to cover our expenses.

Upon my return to the USA, I had to break the news to Diana and the children that the company needed me back in South Africa, and I also commenced some negotiations with Marty for damages. This was difficult, because although it seemed cut and dried that they had broken the law, I had every sympathy with their actions, given the way they had been treated by Sol. Nevertheless, my job was to extract the maximum I could from them before returning to South Africa. After protracted negotiations, we finally settled on an immediate payment from them to Sun of $500,000.

The next problem was that their interpretation of the word 'immediate' and mine were different, and during the few weeks that Diana and I were preparing to leave for South Africa, I could not extract the money from them. Sol, of course, doubted that I would ever get the money, branding them as "crooks and cheats." I was determined not to leave America without the cash, and so, with only a few days to go before our departure, I advised them that unless

I had the money in my hands before I got on the plane, I would rip up our agreement and commence a lawsuit for much larger damages.

They played it right down to the wire—so close, in fact, that Diana, the children and I, in the dying moments before we left for South Africa, with our bags already checked in for the flight, finished up waiting with a clutch of lawyers in the general aviation terminal (for private aircraft) at Kennedy Airport, pending the arrival of a light aircraft from Atlantic City carrying John Best and a cheque for half a million dollars. To the amusement of the other occupants of the tiny lounge (including, by some strange coincidence, our local dry cleaner from Purchase), as Best raced from the tarmac, we were all hastily signing off on a pile of documents as high as the Empire State Building. With the cheque safely in the hands of our attorney, and with seconds to spare, we were whisked off in a little van straight across the tarmac to the steps of the plane. As we jetted off to South Africa, I am sure I was grinning from ear to ear.

Although we were now on our way, the news that we were to go had been a shock for Diana and the children. This was, yet again, an enormous domestic upheaval. Diana understood that Sol needed help. She obviously sympathised with his plight after Shirley's tragic death, and was also anxious to be of help; for this reason and this reason alone, she had agreed to go. But she did not regard our journey to South Africa as permanent. We had made a bridgehead into America, both materially and mentally. Sarah and Jonathan had settled down well; it would be a big upheaval for them to go back to South Africa, and so I promised the family that it would be for a maximum of two years, and duly signed a contract with Sol to reflect that. Little did I know that I would not even last two years.

# Chapter Eleven
## FIGHTING IN THE SUN

My new job in South Africa was to run the company whilst Sol concentrated on building the Sun City Hotel. This would mean that Sol's traveling would be limited to the Transvaal; subsequently, he would be able to spend more time with his semi-orphaned children. There was also a plan on the table to take Southern Sun public, and the preparation for this event would be very time-consuming, but could be led by Sol from the home base in Johannesburg. Before taking this job, I was very clear with Sol how I saw the dividing line between my responsibilities and his, because I realised that I could only be successful if I could operate without interference—not that I did not intend to seek his advice, which I thoroughly respected, but I wanted a hands-free role. In particular, I wanted freedom of action with regard to the marketing function. Sol was a brilliant marketer, but this function was so interrelated with operations that if I had allowed Sol to retain responsibility in this area, I could never have been truly in charge. Leaving this alone was particularly difficult for Sol, and it was to be on the subject of marketing that our relationship eventually soured.

Some months after I had been hard at work as the chief operating officer of the company, I got a call at home one evening, right out of the blue, from Bob Arum. "I want to return the favour," he announced—and what followed was a description of a plan as wild as had been my original presentation to him a year earlier. Put simply, we, the sponsor, Southern Sun, would pay Mohammed Ali $250,000 to retire as heavyweight champion of the world. We would then sponsor two fights between the top four ranked boxers (after Ali), with the two winners fighting for the vacant WBA title. All the fights would be in Bophuthatswana, and Ali would have the option of challenging the winner of this mini-tournament to regain his title. Southern Sun would pay site fees for the semi-finals and finals, Bob would ensure worldwide television coverage, and hopefully we would be able to arrange the Ali return bout in Bophuthatswana as well. And just to make it really interesting for the South African fans and to help with the live gate receipts, Bob would ensure that two South African fighters, Gerrie Coetzee and Kallie Knoetze, currently ranked lower in the top ten, would get elevated to within the top four by having a couple of 'easy' preliminary fights. He would also ensure that the WBA officials would like the idea, and therefore cooperate.

This was a lot to take in from one phone call, but I immediately grasped its potential importance in regard to positioning Southern Sun, particularly with the upcoming opening of Sun City, as South Africa's most enterprising promotional company. I also loved the idea that this would be an unfolding series of events, not just a one-off bash. This would enable us to keep the name Southern Sun in headlines on the back pages of the newspapers (and, frequently, because of the 'depth' of South African newspapers, on the front) for many, many months. If this unlikely scenario were to be true, it was a marketing man's dream.

Unlikely and farfetched as it seemed, as Bob spelled it out to me on the phone that night in his calm, cool, understated way, I knew enough about Bob to know that he was capable of creating reality from fantasy. I thanked him for thinking of us (although I, of course, knew he was also actually thinking of himself), tried not to sound too enthusiastic (in case the price went up), and told him that I would get back to him soon. Although this proposed adventure really fell under my marketing function, it was obviously going to be such a major (and expensive) promotion that I wanted a sign off from Sol. When I told him the plan the next morning, he was ecstatic. Not only was Sol a keen boxing fan (he had been a university boxing champion), but he, too, immediately saw the promotional mileage to be gained. For once, Sol and I were completely on the same page.

Within days of the call, I was back in America, this time with Archie Aaron, one of the leading attorneys in Joburg, to draft and sign the agreements with Bob. During our stay in New York, I introduced Archie, who is a very immaculate and precise man, to Gregory Brown, who promptly invited us to dinner—or, more accurately, to a trendy restaurant where we could buy him dinner. Gregory selected Mortimer's on the Upper East Side. As we swept up to Mortimer's in Gregory's (or someone's) limo, there was a line outside. Ignoring this—and the crowd standing at the bar waiting for dining tables—Gregory marched us to the only vacant table, slap bang in the centre of the room. "This is a good table," remarked Archie. "You can see everybody from here."

"No, Archie," fired back Gregory. "Here, everybody can see you!"

The financial arrangements with Bob Arum were quickly sorted out, and he went to work to find some fighters that Gerrie and Kallie could knock out in Southern Sun promotions in Johannesburg. Gerrie and Kallie were never told the entire plan. We wanted them to believe in themselves as they worked their way up the rankings; we wanted them fighting fit; we wanted them to train hard and look good. A fighter, I subsequently learned, who knows that he is going to win, may not bother to train too hard.

Both Gerrie and Kallie were Afrikaners, but that is where their similarity ended. Gerrie was a brooding, introverted, almost shy giant of a man, with a high-pitched girlish voice—a PR man's nightmare. I later learned he was as sly as he was shy. Kallie was a fun-loving, outgoing, lively, charismatic person who also happened to be a policeman who had achieved a certain notoriety for allegedly shooting a young African in the back as he was climbing a wall whilst escaping from the scene of a robbery. Whilst his personality was a PR man's gift, the notoriety held certain dangers, particularly in the US market, if he were to eventually be victorious. Gerrie Coetzee was definitely the better boxer. He had very, very strong legs (an attribute not often recognised as a hallmark of a good fighter), as well as an accurate left jab and a lethal right knock out punch. He was, however, somewhat lazy in training, and his inward-looking personality seemed to hold him back in the ring from finishing off opponents he had wounded. Kallie was a brawler; he would give everything he could muster up in the ring to slaughter his opponents, but he was like a rampaging windmill. If you happened to be unlucky enough to be on the end of one of his flailing fists, you were a goner; but, fortunately, for a skilled fighter, these same fists were fairly easily avoided.

As a result of these preliminary fights and of a visit Bob made to Panama for reasons he does not disclose, the next set of world rankings published by the WBA after Ali's "shock" retirement were:

| | |
|---|---|
| Number One | Leon Spinks (USA) |
| Number Two | Gerrie Coetzee (RSA) |
| Number Three | John Tate (USA) |
| Number Four | Kallie Knoetze (RSA) |

The South African media were overjoyed, and their enthusiasm knew no bounds when Southern Sun announced that it would be promoting the playoffs for the vacant world heavyweight title, with Number Three and Number Four fighting in the Independence Stadium in Mmabatho, Bop, and Number One and Number Two fighting in Monte Carlo (because Spinks refused to come to South Africa) shortly afterward. For the first time in history, South Africa, it seemed, had at least a fifty-fifty chance of getting a world heavyweight champion.

As the operational chief of Southern Sun, I was responsible for the arrangements. The stadium at Mmabatho was an erector-set affair, and it was already in a state of disrepair. It held about 30,000 people, but lacked any semblance of normal facilities, such as toilets or catering. There was no proper airport, only a tiny grass strip, and, naturally, no air-traffic controllers. Our hotel, the Mmabatho Sun, had less than a hundred rooms, and an appropriately sized restaurant, so both catering and transport would present a huge logistical challenge if we were to come close to selling out. Kallie was by now an Afrikaans hero; not only had he shot a black robber, but he was almost a contender for the most important boxing title in the world. At this stage, because of his personality, despite both Gerrie and Kallie being Afrikaners, Kallie was overwhelmingly the favourite son.

His opponent, Tate, was dubbed in America Big John Tate, and not without good cause. John, however, was a gentle giant: a big, well-built black man with a handsome face, kindly eyes, and a generous smile. The black African community warmed to him instantly, and, as a result, this boxing match became more than just an eliminator for the world title; it symbolised the battle that was being waged in the country between the black community and the white government. It represented good versus evil, but even then, to the many white sports fans who opposed apartheid, it would still be impossible to root for the American against the South African. Given these dynamics, and despite the fact that there was almost no public transport available to Mmabatho from the main urban areas of Johannesburg and Pretoria (some three hours' drive away), the fight was an instant sell-out.

On the day of the fight, the traffic jam extended almost from Pretoria to Mmabatho; the grass airstrip overflowed with private light aircraft (you could not land a jet there), which were marshalled by the local boy scouts; and the Mmabatho Sun catering facilities were overwhelmed. I had corralled catering staff from all the other Sun hotels, and under the expert guidance of our brilliant executive chef, John Zimmerman, we set up field catering services whose product fell little short of Claridge's. As a promotion for Southern Sun, the day was an outstanding success, the weather was kind, and the casino winnings at the hotel were unprecedented. Only one thing went wrong—Kallie lost the fight. To the huge disappointment of the predominantly white crowd (the blacks found the ticket prices too high), the boxer beat the slugger, as Big John gave Kallie a boxing lesson.

The next stop was Monte Carlo, for Gerrie Coetzee versus Leon Spinks. For this, we chartered a 707 to take Gerrie's most ardent supporters, plus some of Sun's best customers, to watch the fight ringside. Although the actual fight took place in the car park of Rainier's Palace, the ring was festooned with Southern Sun images, so to the television audience worldwide, there could be no doubt as to whose promotion this was. On the long trip around the horn of Africa to Nice (South African aircraft were forbidden to fly over the mainland of Africa as part of sanctions against apartheid), the fans consumed the entire stock of the overstocked alcohol supply.

I had handed out yellow Southern Sun T-shirts and hats on the flight. On the next day, the beach at Nice and the Promenade des Anglais was speckled with yellow shirts ogling the topless girls—a sight not allowed in puritan South Africa. So much ogling went on, in fact, that most of the South African fans missed the fight that evening, which was not hard to do, since Gerrie knocked out a surprised Leon within two minutes of the first bell. A disgruntled but not disinterested Ken Norton was in the crowd.

Memories of Kallie were quickly forgotten. Gerrie was the new Afrikaans hero, and he was about to fight for the vacant heavyweight title. He returned to South Africa on our chartered 707 (I happily relinquished to him the seats that Diana and I had occupied on the way up) to a tumultuous welcome.

So there we had it. The final for the vacant title was now on, and any doubt that the event could take place in South Africa was now dispelled, because we had two fighters in Gerrie and Big John who were willing to do so. This was not the fight I had originally pursued with Ali and Spinks; this was much better, because one of the fighters was a white South African. It quickly became apparent that the fight was too big to be housed at the new Sun City, which was in the first phase of its development and at this stage did not have an arena, so a deal was struck with the city of Pretoria to use the home of South African rugby, the Loftus Versfeld Stadium, with a capacity of 70,000 seats. Once again I was in charge of the arrangements, and I set about making this not just a fight night, but a carnival of entertainment, to show the world what the Sun City company could do.

The organisation of the event encountered many difficulties, but one of them was not the demand for ticket sales.

We priced them high and sold the lot. In fact, ultimately, because we were able to place extra seats on the turf, we eventually packed in 83,000 spectators, probably a record for a live gate at a boxing match anywhere. Of these, however, 8000 were staff, for security concerns were high.

In a country that was edging closer to a revolution and where a previous prime minister had been assassinated, the Loftus Versfeld Stadium was a risky place. The president and prime minister of apartheid South Africa would be attending, as well as the president of Bophuthatswana, and almost all members of both cabinets. All of them would be seated in the front few rows of a darkened stadium with the bright lights over the boxing ring spilling onto the closest seats, rendering their occupants clear sniper targets. Senior security officers made me go over and over the seating arrangements, so that they could place their men in protective positions.

Even then, I got into hot water, because the only placing I had not identified to the police was Sol's guest, who was to sit between him and the state president. That is because I did not know at the time that he was going to invite his future wife, Anneline Kriel, the reigning Miss World, who, unbeknown to me, was the subject of some rumours involving alleged 'romps' with a South African cabinet minister. Pictures appeared in the paper the next morning, nicely cropped, showing the state president with Anneline, as if they were the best of buddies. The state president was not amused, and the poor security man in charge apparently felt his wrath for not preventing this embarrassing incident. The poor man got no credit for the fact that the president hadn't been shot.

Loftus Versfeld also quickly attracted the attention of the anti-apartheid movement. To my horror, I soon discovered that this stadium was the home of the staunchest right-wingers, who absolutely opposed desegregated seating, desegregated toilets, and desegregated catering. I approached them to explain that this was potentially such a high-profile event that this policy, once discovered, would lead to huge adverse publicity overseas. After several discussions, the powers that were agreed to waive the segregation for the stadium, but only if we refrained from public statements about it. They did not want to be seen by their supporters to be bowing to pressure; rather that they had taken this wise decision themselves and allowed the change to occur quietly.

Unfortunately, this was not to be, because the segregation, as existed, had come to the attention of the Reverend Jesse Jackson in America, who stormed into South Africa on a highly publicised (but redundant) mission to change things—and at the same time, of course, score political points back home. Sol and I met with Jesse Jackson and told him that his task of change had already been accomplished. We warned him that if he were to shout too loud, it would be counterproductive to his anti-apartheid cause. He didn't, it seemed, give a stuff. He agreed to leave without calling a press conference, but immediately after our meeting, did just that—called a press conference and insisted that the owners of the stadium change their policy. This, of course, had the reverse effect, as we had been warned, and we were now back to square one.

Bob Arum, however, held the trump card, and in a series of press conferences and interviews, he promised that unless Loftus was to be desegregated, he would cancel the fight. Of course he realised that the Afrikaans boxing fans could not bear to lose the opportunity of seeing one of theirs fighting for the world title, and that the resultant pressure on the government to make sure that the rules of the stadium were changed would be huge. He also had no choice but to insist, because back home in the USA, he, like Jesse Jackson, had a constituency to look after—black boxers, not black voters! Ultimately, I am pleased to say, with a few days to go before the fight, Loftus Versfeld was desegregated forever, although very few blacks ever wanted to go there to watch rugby, so from a practical point of view, it was much ado about nothing.

So, indeed, was the fight. In twelve rather monotonous rounds, Big John comprehensively out-boxed Gerrie. I was secretly rather pleased. I had grown to like this gentle giant as the weeks before the fight had gone by. We had set up a training camp for him in the white suburb of Bryanston, about half a mile from our home. Our youngest boy, Jonathan, had taken to visiting Big John after school, and they had "trained" together. Big John was quite shy. He was also completely illiterate (but concealed it quite well), which seemed odd at the time—an American who could not read nor write being idolised by millions of oppressed black Africans who could nearly all read, write and speak at least two languages other than their natural tongue. John related to 'Little Jon', who did not threaten him. Big John revealed to Little Jon his reading disability. Little Jon was seven years old, but obviously knew how to read, so Little Jon took Big John to the video shop and helped him rent the tapes in such a manner that the shop assistants had no idea about Big John's problem. When the scoring for the fight was announced, Big John went straight to ringside, and lifting little Jon into the ring, gave him the biggest and warmest bear hug. "We did it," he proudly announced to our youngest son.

From Bob Arum's perspective, the whole series had been a fantastic success, and now Bob had a new American champion, who would be far easier to control than a white Afrikaner 7000 miles away. In addition to this, before Bob left, I handed him a cheque well north of a million dollars for his share of the 'gate'. It had been fun working with Bob, and I had learned a lot. We also had some good times together. One day I needed to go to the rural area of Venda to look at a potential hotel site. To get there and back in a day, I had chartered a King Air, and I invited Bob and Sybil and Diana along, thinking that Bob and Sybil would like to see a piece of the African countryside. To get to the site from the airstrip, we had the normal bumpy ride in a four-by-four to what turned out to be the home of the machichi palms, and also the home of the rain queen. None of this seemed to impress Bob, so I was a bit worried when he accompanied me to meet the local tribal chief, King Hex. I didn't want Bob's lack of enthusiasm for the area to be too apparent. I need not have worried, because the complete lack of enthusiasm from Hex to Bob made Bob's disinterest look like excitement.

"Allow me to introduce Mr Bob Arum," I started with King Hex. "Bob is a very famous man in America, because, among other things, he is the promoter of Muhammad Ali." Since Ali was the most famous man in Africa, I thought this introduction would impress King Hex.

Bob caught my drift. "Yes," said Bob, "maybe you would like me to bring Ali here one day."

After a moment of thought Hex delivered a perfect put-down. "All right, Mr Bob," he replied, "tell him to come on a Tuesday or a Thursday."

From the company's point of view, the result at Loftus Versfeld was a disappointment, because it represented the end of the boxing promotion. Had Gerrie won, there might possibly have been many defences of the title in front of his home crowd, with Southern Sun and Sun City being touted to the world on the ring posts and his gear. Alas, this was not to be, and I had to look for more conventional ways of advertising our wares—not that the company needed any extra promotion, because things had been going very well. Our profits had been growing at over 20% per year, the public offering had been a huge success, and Sol was gradually recovering his own swashbuckling form.

Much of our attention was now directed towards the opening of the Sun City Hotel. Most people in South Africa thought we were mad. To build a 350-room hotel with multiple restaurants, a 500-seat theatre, a golf course and a casino, in a location at least two hours driving time from Johannesburg, with no rail nor air service, was, to say the least, a gutsy decision. As previously mentioned, the homeland of Bophuthatswana was scattered around the countryside between the Witwatersrand and Botswana. Parts of it were located very close to Pretoria, which is only twenty miles from Joburg, the two cities making up almost half of the affluent population of the country. Most people would have opted to build there, with the emphasis on casino, not resort. But Sol had a vision beyond that. In his mind, this was an opportunity to build a world class resort with a casino, not a casino masquerading as a resort. To do this the nature of the site, as it had been with the Saint Géran, would be crucial to success.

If I had a dollar for all of the people who claim that they were on board the helicopter as we scoured Bophuthatswana for a suitable resort site, I would be a very rich man. As it happened there were three of us, Sol, myself and Barry King, the interior designer. The eventual choice was in the hills of the Pilanesberg, an undulating volcanic area between Rustenburg and the border with Botswana. Not only was it a pretty area but the Government was in the process of setting up the Pilanesberg Game Park, a 550 square kilometer area for wildlife. A resort next to this would be of interest, not only to South African residents but also to international tourists. The site also had a small river which could be dammed to create a recreational lake. The hotel itself could be concealed on approach in a valley next to the proposed lake, so that the arrival experience could be one of surprise.

The Sun City Hotel is built as a sprawling three-storey crescent, wrapping around a spectacular pool area. The huge lobby was full of slot machines, Vegas style, with an adjacent table casino with multiple restaurants and a show room. At the time my general manager of operations was Peter Bacon, who had previously worked as an area manager. As chief operating office of the company it was, however, my responsibility to get the hotel open; in other words, the buck stopped with me. Although the hotel only had 350 rooms, which would equate, if fully booked, to around 800 guests, Peter and I were expecting possibly about another thousand or so day-trippers on the first day. As it turned out, 7000 arrived! We were swamped and many services simply could not cope with the volume. There were lines at the toilets, long queues at the restaurants, overflowing trash cans, etc. We did our best to keep the show on the road but, in my view, we failed. Our planning had been just inadequate. After only a couple of hours sleep, at about 7 am, I got a call from Sol, who had obviously been witness to the chaos. "Meet me in the office behind the front desk. As soon as you can," he instructed. I was quite certain he was going to fire me. When I reached the office Sol was grinning from ear to ear. "Get a sheet of paper," he chirped, "we need to build another hotel – and quick!" Undeterred by the chaos of the day before (something he had faith we would sort out over time) Sol had only seen success. I had seen failure; he had seen vindication for his gutsy decision to build. For the next two hours, whilst Peter Bacon got to work on clearing up the mess, Sol and I sat with pencil and paper sketching out the next hotel – something we could build quickly. A few months later we opened the 200 room Cabanas, a budget version of what became known to all as the Main Hotel.

Although Sun City was a resounding success, operating it continued to be a drama. There had been several fatal accidents during construction and this bad luck continued after opening with a chef killed in a road accident and a small plane crash killing another. Peter Wagner, the General Manager of the hotel, advised me to consult with the Chief of the local Tswana tribe, known for his clairvoyance. I asked him why we were having so much trouble and he told me that the ancestors were annoyed because we had built the hotel on an ancient tribal burial ground. "Is there a remedy?" I asked rather hopefully. "Yes" came the reply, "you must ask the elders in the company to drink the blood of an ox in the lobby. This will appease the spirits." I told Sol what he had to do. He declined. Eventually our bad luck stopped and Sun City went from strength to strength.

With Sun City open, Sol began to take greater interest in the rest of the company and it did not take long for him to start tinkering in my territory, I began to notice the odd attempt at interference. To Sol, it was very difficult, it seemed, to respect the company organigram, and gradually both employees and consultants started to find that they had two bosses. I tried to stem this inevitable tide, but it was impossible, and the more Sol dabbled, the more my authority was dented, and the more the staff was confused. Things came to a head whilst I was out of the country.

Diana and I had been invited to Knoxville, USA, by Big John to witness the first defence of the title he had won in Pretoria. Ali had decided, at the time, not to return from retirement, and so Big John had signed to fight Mike

Weaver, another American. It was, however, rumoured that Ali might well be prepared to fight the winner, and this was certainly a match that I had to get to Sun City. It was, therefore, with Sol's approval that I had travelled to Knoxville.

The trip was a disaster. Mike Weaver was probably the best physical specimen of a man that you will ever see. He was not over-muscled like the Mr Universe types; he was just perfectly developed. But he was also an unwilling boxer. A deeply religious man, his greatest pleasure was playing the piano. He fought reluctantly; he fought for the money. It therefore came as no surprise that Big John coasted through the first eleven rounds of the fight with little resistance or interest from Weaver. On my 'card', John had won at least ten of the first eleven rounds. All he had to do in the last round was to walk backwards. Instead, at the urging of his stupid corner men, he walked straight forward into the biggest haymaker I have ever seen. He fell like a log. It was as if he had been sawn off at the ankles. His head hit the canvas with an awful thump. He lost the fight, and he never really recovered. After one more fight, in which it was clear that he had lost his confidence, he was abandoned by his handlers, quickly used up his money (such as they had left him), took to dope, and eventually died tragically in a truck crash.

The trip to Knoxville was also a disaster from another point of view. I received a call from Jeannie Bestbier, my marketing executive back in South Africa, who also happened to be Sol's ex-sister-in-law. "I thought you should know," said Jeannie, "that Sol has met with the advertising agency and completely changed your campaign. I tried to stop him, to get him to wait—and so did the agency, but you know what he is like. Now they don't know what to do."

"Tell them to do as he says," I calmly told Jeannie. "I will take it up with him when I get back." And take it up with him I did. I was furious. So furious that I told him that, two-year contract or no two-year contract, I was going back to America and he could keep his job. We eventually moved back during the following Christmas holidays, and although I continued to work for Sol for a short time once we were back in the States, I had quite decided that I would rather part as a friend than continue as an employee. I was soon to learn that with Sol, this was impossible. Sol was not at all pleased that I was leaving, and in one very ill-tempered meeting on my first return visit to Johannesburg, he completely lost his temper, with the result that I had to resort to lawyers to prevent him from throwing me out of the Landdrost Hotel. I was extremely upset and hurt by his attitude; we did not speak again for two years.

# Chapter Twelve
## FREEDOM

The plan to leave South Africa again was not a popular one with Diana and the children. Whereas two years before, they did not like the thought of leaving the USA, the same was now true of South Africa. Not that they disliked America; they loved it. It was just that on this occasion, the claws of Africa had dug deep. Old friendships had been strengthened, and new ones had been formed. Life had been exciting. I was running a big company; not only was I involved with hotels, but also with sport and entertainment. This rubbed off onto the family; they felt part of the excitement, and more so than I actually realised.

Nevertheless, I did not feel that I could really go on working with Sol, and although, I suppose, I could have considered other options in South Africa, I was still convinced that South Africa's time of peace was rapidly coming to an end. I knew that apartheid was suffering death throes, and rightly so; I just thought that it would end in bloodshed, and I did not want my family involved.

Back in the USA, we decided to return to Westchester. I had no job to go to, but I was full of confidence that I could create something, especially if I were to operate near to the centre of the world, Manhattan. We settled on living in Scarsdale. We had heard that the school system was second to none. It was also the chosen suburb of Jewish and Japanese families; both groups value highly the education of their children. We acquired a nice family home, enrolled Sarah into the high school and Jonathan into the junior school, and Diana picked up with her old friends, many of whom were immigrants from the UK or South Africa. Sarah did not resettle well, although she continued to be a steady performer at school. Rather than come off the rails, she vented her frustrations and anger at her mother. Sarah's counter-dependent stage of life was, for a while, quite a trial for Diana—and I, of course, as usual, was often not around to assist. Sarah once proclaimed, "I'll never marry a man like Dad," meaning, I assumed, a father who is always away. Notwithstanding this, when she did marry, it was to an international marketing executive of Pepsi-Cola, whose job, of course, took him frequently around the world.

I now had to decide how to earn a living. One of the first things I did was, as it happened, for Sol, who had just completed the Super Bowl at Sun City. As an opening act, he had decided to book Frank Sinatra, and I was asked to get involved in the contracting and to make the arrangements for travel, etc. On New Year's Eve, Diana and I were invited to Atlantic City, where Frank was performing. We were given seats at tables in the middle at the front, next to his wife, Barbara. At the end of the concert, Frank was showered with bouquets, and Diana and I were both surprised to see through the crack in the closing curtains how he tossed the flowers to the floor. He was also quite difficult about the air transportation. He wanted a private aircraft; we balked at this, but did second best.

South African Airways agreed not to sell any other first-class seats on their scheduled flight, thereby effectively turning the first-class section into a private cabin for Frank, Barbara, and Frank's lawyer–manager and wife, Mickey and Mary Rudin. They even went as far as to remove some of the seats to create a 'lounge' and to find out from Frank's personal assistant what menu he and Barbara would like. It was disappointing to learn later, therefore, that their special concern and trouble were tossed aside like the flowers. On the way to Kennedy, Frank and party stopped at a favourite Italian deli, bought some takeaways, carried them onto the plane, and ignored the specially prepared menu. Frank's concerts at the new Sun City Superbowl were, however, a resounding success, and paved the way for many more 'sanction-busting' superstars over the next few years, including Queen, Elton John, Shirley Bassey, Rod Stewart and many more.

As a result, people often used to wonder how Sun City was able to attract and pay for such luminaries. The first reason was that, in the early days, the rand was worth more than the dollar, and secondly because of a special taxation arrangement that we had negotiated with the Bop government. Bop, at Sol's instigation, had passed a law to tax foreign entertainers 50%, which we withheld with their prior consent. In exchange for this withholding, the entertainers were given a tax-credit notice, which they duly presented to their own governments (normally the USA). This automatically reduced their tax liabilities in their own countries by the value of the tax credit. The USA did not recognise the existence of Bophuthatswana, and insisted that it was really South Africa, with whom, fortunately, they had a tax treaty that recognised South African tax credits. Through this device, we were able to get a valid South African tax credit issued by another government, i.e. Bop. Then, through a separate agreement with the Bop government, Sun City would routinely invoice them for 'international promotions'. It was not coincidental that these invoices always equalled exactly 90% of the taxes that had been withheld.

The irony of this situation, which Sol had cleverly engineered, was that 'Uncle Sam', who had been leading the world's anti-apartheid charge, was, through these legally iron-clad arrangements, actually subsidising Sun City.

Having dispatched Frank, I then looked for other ventures, and it was not long before I was asked to assist a South African acquaintance, Dion Friedland, with a potential project in the tiny island of Anguilla in the Caribbean. Dion and his vivacious wife, Hilary, had been vacationing at the Byblos Hotel, Saint Tropez, when they found themselves poolside next to a certain Augusto Marini. Augusto and Yolande Marini lived in Saint Maarten, where they operated a very successful upmarket fashion shop, La Romana, which specialised in famous Italian designer-name clothes. Augusto had heard that the owner of La Samanna (one of the Caribbean's most famous resorts), James Frankel, had acquired a beautiful site on the neighbouring island of Anguilla, but that Frankel had fallen out with the Anguillan government and was looking to sell. Augusto and Yolande had raved about Anguilla and the site, which they described as "spectacular." Dion, having heard that I had left Southern Sun, immediately contacted me and asked if I would be prepared to take a look at it.

Within days, I was in a small boat with Augusto, taking the short trip to Anguilla. Augusto had been right. The 180-acre site was indeed spectacular, consisting mainly of a long, curved beach with the most wonderful soft white sand, bounded by incredibly blue water and, in the distance, marvellous views of the rugged mountains of Saint Martin. Anguilla, itself, is a thin, flat island, hence the name, which is a derivative of the French word for 'eel'. But, as I have often noticed, looking at mountains can sometimes be more attractive than being in them, and Anguilla formed a natural platform from which to view its more scenic neighbour.

The other beauty of the place was the fact that it was completely undeveloped; there were no hotels, not even a restaurant. It was, at the time, one of the world's best-kept secrets. Anguilla was perhaps the smallest independent nation in the world, with just 7000 inhabitants and eight members of parliament. It was part of the British Commonwealth, and had had its fifteen minutes of fame when, having seceded from Great Britain, it was 'invaded' by a force of fifty British bobbies. This had been the original 'mouse that roared'.

I reported back to Dion with enthusiasm, and very soon Dion, Augusto and I had entered into a partnership arrangement with a view to acquiring and developing the site. I had not worked with Dion before, and of course had never met Augusto until this trip, but the vibes seemed right. Dion had a proven track record of commercial success. Straight out of the blocks from university, he had started South Africa's first discount whitegoods chain. Although sold long ago, 'Dion's' still exists today in South Africa and is still going strong. Dion is also amazingly hyperactive; the man hardly sleeps. But although, like most businessmen, his pursuit is money and success, it is not necessarily in that order. He is an extremely likeable and fair man, a person willing to share and a person willing to trust. It was quite a pleasant change from Sol.

Augusto was simply charming. An ex-headwaiter with a flair that he had parlayed into probably the most successful retail store in the Caribbean, ably supported by a talented and beautiful wife, Yolande, who was equally charming, but whose charm masked a steely determination and efficiency that ensured the success of their business. In short order, Augusto arranged for me to meet Jimmy Frankel, who it turned out was quite happy to sell us his leasehold in Anguilla, subject to us getting the approval of the assignment from the government. Jimmy was very forthright about his poor relationship with the prime minister of Anguilla, and, whilst happy to sell to us on the one hand, was busy warning us on the other. I had a certain admiration for Jimmy, because in my opinion, he had developed La Samanna into a fine resort, which was always bustling with celebrities. Jimmy's young daughter, Samantha, was dating one of those famous guests, Ivan Lendl, whom she eventually married and with whom she produced a fine family. Jimmy, unfortunately, had recently learned that he had cancer and was keen to do a deal with us, in order to relieve his only daughter of the burden of a new development.

Having agreed the terms with Jimmy, he then arranged for me to meet the Anguillan prime minister, who in turn delegated the negotiating task to a junior minister, Collins, who later also became prime minister. Mr Collins was determined to extract some blood whilst letting Jimmy off the hook, and this came in the way of us making extra promises about what we would build and when; i.e. more and sooner than under Jimmy's lease. After some months and quite a few trips between New York and Anguilla, the deal was finally done. The result of those endeavours is Cap Jaluca, one of the Caribbean's most exclusive resorts. Although Dion bought out Augusto and myself many years later, I still look with pride upon pictures of the place in glossy magazines around the world, and marvel at the fact that Anguilla has established itself as a haven for exclusive beach resorts, rivalling any others.

As well as busying myself with Cap Jaluca and partly as a result of it, I decided to get into the management-training business. On one sunny day, whilst trying to assist with removing a vehicle that had become bogged down in the sand on the building site in Anguilla, I found that I could not stand up. My back had gone into a complete spasm, and my body had gone L-shaped.

In addition to there being no restaurants in Anguilla, there were no hospitals, or at least, no hospitals in which I intended to recuperate. I was therefore manhandled by my colleagues into a wheelchair, then onto a light aircraft (in excruciating pain) to Saint Maarten, and then onto an American Airlines jet to New York, where I was confined to bed for two weeks. During those two weeks, I dictated a little book about the human side of hotel-keeping to my daughter Sue, who after some delays got it published.

Once up and about again, I decided to take some of the messages from the book and convert them into a training programme dedicated to hotel management. The programme drew upon my earlier T-group experiences and the knowledge I had gained from ten years of running Southern Sun. I set about marketing my training product, in some cases with the help of Dion, who owned, amongst other things, an international retail-training company. I quickly found clients in the US, the UK, Australia and New Zealand, but the week-long training programme was completely dependent upon me acting as trainer, which meant that in order to satisfy these clients, I had to travel. (Sarah had been right!)

Although Diana would have been very welcome on all of these trips, and she did come with me from time to time, it was simply not possible, nor indeed sensible, for us to keep leaving Sarah and Jonathan. She did accompany me on one memorable trip to China. The mainland Chinese government was in one of its thawing phases with the USA. President Nixon had just visited China on a goodwill mission, the first US president to go there since the Communist revolution. The Chinese government was reaching out for aid from the USA, and the USA was responding. Tourism to China had been very small, but its potential to produce foreign earnings had not escaped the notice of the government, who previously had not wanted the people to have any exposure to foreigners or foreign ideas. In this regard, the State Department in Washington had received a request for technical assistance in developing tourism from the Chinese government, and this had been passed on to the American Hotel and Motel Association, which had agreed to organise a posse of lecturers and consultants to visit China for about a month.

I was one of a small group who had agreed to go on the trip; I was probably one of a large group who was asked. We were expected to give a series of lectures on our particular subjects in different cities across China. We were not to get paid; this exercise was to be for the good of international relations… but we could take our wives. Apart from overwhelming curiosity about China, which was just emerging from the terrible period in its history of the Gang of Four and the Red Guard, I had discovered that the trip would be taking in the ancient city of Xian, where the famous terracotta warriors had just been unearthed. The temptation for Diana and me was too great. We decided to sign up for the trip, and, indeed, to extend it to Papua New Guinea and Australia, where I could also arrange to run a training session (for fees!). The whole trip was to take at least six weeks—a long time to be leaving the children, and one that (with hindsight) was rather selfish.

Nevertheless, the journey was fascinating. We met up with the rest of our group at Anchorage Airport, Alaska, from which we flew to Hong Kong with onward connection to Beijing. Technically, it was an onward connection. The carrier was China Airlines, and this was to be the first of our many experiences of their complete disregard for the published schedule. We waited eight hours for our connecting flight, which, when we finally boarded, we mostly wished had never arrived. The plane was an elderly 747. All of the internal signage was in Italian, so we assumed that it was an Alitalia cast-off. When the "fasten seatbelt" sign was switched on, I discovered that the buckle on mine was missing. Upon pointing this out to the Chinese air hostess, she calmly instructed me to tie a knot in it.

Whilst in China on this trip, we travelled exclusively on China Airlines; the average delayed departure time was seven hours. Even Pan Am in its decline could never match that. Also, once airborne, the crew, who were mainly Romanian, had a less-than-reassuring habit of rushing up and down the aisle with screwdrivers and other miscellaneous tools. The only saving grace was that the hostesses always gave the passengers a little present, a bit like British Airways did on the Concorde, although instead of leather diaries or gold cufflinks, these presents were normally things like plastic combs or little Chinese flags. The other difficulty was that once in China, the authorities removed our air tickets and passports—all with a smile—and so there was nothing else to be done but go with the flow.

Before leaving the USA, I had prepared my lectures, and in accordance with the instructions from the AHMA, I had made up coloured slides to illustrate my points. This turned out to be a complete waste of time, because none of our hosts had a slide projector (this being well before PowerPoint presentations), and in many cases, the electrical power supply was spasmodic. Not that this mattered, because it quickly became apparent that my prepared lectures were completely inappropriate. Not only did my audience vary from place to place in its level of sophistication (from completely unsophisticated to almost completely unsophisticated), but the hospitality industry per se was so far behind the USA, Europe, and South Africa that my examples bore no relevance to my audiences' needs. I therefore had to gauge what I thought would be interesting for them to hear and make it up as I went along, without the high-tech assistance of a slide projector. This, it turned out, was relatively easy, because every sentence had to be translated, and the translation always seemed to take ten times longer than my actual words.

It was also easy because the Chinese audiences were desperate to learn about the West. Most of them had been starved of information; worse, they were pumped full of misinformation. As a tourist industry, they had no idea about the needs of foreigners, and as a result had made no attempt to adapt their standards or services to suit. The hotels, in the main, were Russian-built monstrosities: grey, dull, and dirty. The dining rooms were always set up with round tables of eight or ten. Very rarely did menus exist; the food just came, and there was no attempt to Westernise it. We soon learned that Chinese food in China was a far cry from the Chinese takeaway in America or even the English high street—and we soon learned one of the reasons why: there were almost no food supplies available, especially in the north. As a result, every last part of every possible animal was utilised, from bears' paws to chickens' intestines. Dogs and cats were strangely missing from the streets. As a result, our own group suffered.

After a few days, we decided to appoint a food taster at each table, a position that would rotate due to its dangerous nature. The designated taster would gingerly lift a portion of this or that with his chopsticks from the bowls, which were unceremoniously plonked in the centre of the table, and pronounce judgment in one of two categories: edible or inedible. On one occasion, whilst performing my role as taster, I gleefully pronounced something not only edible, but actually enjoyable—only to find out minutes later from the server that I had just downed a mouthful of sea slugs. We all would have starved during the first two weeks of our tour of duty had it not been for the fact that some of the group had brought supplies with them. In regard to food, I have discovered, most Americans need to have some handy, so secret rations of candy bars and other delights kept appearing from suitcases. Not that Diana and I were any different, because during the long wait at Hong Kong Airport, we had bought a box of chocolates. These we rationed (one each per day), and used the others to barter with our colleagues from their suitcase supplies: one chocolate for a cup of instant coffee!

China was, however, simply amazing. It was everything that I had imagined. A sea of grey and black Mao suits and bicycles, which, in the cities, overwhelmed one, wave after wave. The costumes were drab, the cities were noisy and dreary, but the welcome smiles of the people were unforgettable. Some of our party (including Diana and me) were blond. Most Chinese had never laid eyes on a blond human being before; the children just stared and stared; some were frightened.

China was at a turning point. We witnessed major roads being built, but on a ninety-mile stretch, we saw only two pieces of mechanical equipment; everything else was being moved or lifted by hand in wicker baskets. We were taken to assess potential tourist sites, only to find that they had been ransacked by the Red Guard or were falling down through lack of maintenance. Hotel management had no concept of profit or loss. All hotels were owned by the state. All revenues were sent to a central bank, so if a hotel manager wanted to spend something on maintenance, he would have to get in the line behind everyone else in every other industry.

The concept of marketing was not known. On one occasion, I attempted to run a day-long seminar on marketing for a bunch of young hoteliers, who seemed very keen to learn. I walked them through all of the basic steps. Together, we divided the year into platinum, gold and silver seasons in regard to their desirability. We then examined the selling prices of their product, season by season, in the American tour-operators' brochures, deducted airfares and commission, and discovered that they were being ripped off by their trade partners. Bit by bit, we gathered data, and by the end of the day, we had completely changed the pricing strategy of their 2000-room hotel. As we went along, we quantified our potential savings and gains on a makeshift flip chart, and by the end of the day, we were theoretically several million dollars 'ahead'. Everyone sat around, very pleased with themselves, until one of the group piped up, "Ah, there is a problem."

"What is that?" I enquired.

"It is not possible."

"What is not possible?" I said.

"We cannot change prices. Only government can change prices."

"Well ask the government. Show them our workings," I suggested.

"Government no listen. Only come to change prices every two years." With that, everyone in the room agreed that there was nothing to be done.

This blind acceptance of the role of central government and authority was quite frightening. It also manifested itself through the in-tourist guide who escorted us throughout our trip. A kinder, more gentle and considerate man you will never meet, but he was, quite naturally, very difficult to draw into conversation on any matters political. On one occasion I was questioning him about the wisdom of the policy of only allowing each married couple one child. "Who will look after all of the old people when there are two oldies for every youngster?" I enquired.

"The state will provide," was his simple and believed, if not believable, answer.

Toward the end of our trip, Diana was intent on buying our guide a present from the group. She tried for several days to coax out of him what he would like as a useful gift. He steadfastly refused to comment, but Diana can be very persistent in her pursuit of gifts for others, and so finally got him to admit that he would treasure a briefcase like mine. This would have been a tall order for most shoppers in China, but somehow Diana managed to find one, which all of the remainder of our group (some had fallen by the wayside) presented to him at a touching little farewell ceremony. He proudly accepted the gift, and then immediately told us that 'the department' would find it very useful. "It's not for the department," we all cried almost uniformly. "It's for you." After much persuasion, he promised that he would not hand it in. Several weeks after our return to America, I received a letter from the Chinese Department of Tourism thanking us for the kind gift, which 'the department' would find very useful.

Toward the end of the scheduled stay in China, I, too, had had enough. We were in Nanjing; Diana and I both had severe colds from sleeping in damp sheets. (I have no idea where Chinese laundries come from!) When China Air called us to announce that our flights to Canton would be delayed by twenty-four hours, I took myself off, unescorted, to what I had perceived to be a government travel agency near the hotel. I was in search of two train tickets to Shanghai, from where I thought it would be entirely possible that we could find a flight to our next destination, Papua New Guinea. At the travel agency, with much sign language between myself and the clerk, I ascertained that there was indeed a train going that day to Shanghai, and after much more sign language, I ascertained that there were still seats available.

"Excellent," I announced. "I buy two."

"You no buy two," was the immediate response.

Puzzled, I re-trod the old ground, and confirmed that there was a train and that there were empty seats. "Why cannot I buy two?" I asked.

"Can only buy seats one week in advance: government rule."

Even a handful of American dollars failed to change his interpretation of the rule. I concluded that the government needed time to vet the passengers. Giving up, I went back to the hotel to impart the bad news to Diana. But, in fact, it was not to be bad news at all, because Guangzhou (Canton) turned out to be almost like Hong Kong, and we were some of the first people to stay in the famous White Swan Hotel, which was possibly the first privately owned hotel in China.

In retrospect, I was pleased that I had completed my full programme of lectures. Most of my colleagues gave up halfway through, and joined their partners, sightseeing. I was able to do my share of museum visits on the odd days between the lectures. The highlight of these, without question, was the visit to the recently discovered site of the terracotta warriors. At the time, about 2000 of these fascinating, individually modelled Chinese warriors had been unearthed and pieced back together. There they were, row upon row, every one different, lined up in a huge building like an aircraft hangar. You entered through a little door and looked down on the site from a wooden deck. It was literally the most awe-inspiring manmade sight I had ever witnessed, and nothing in my life since has surpassed it. Every worker who had been involved in the production of the warriors had been murdered, and their secret had gone to the grave with them for over 2000 years.

Although I enjoyed the sightseeing, I actually found the interaction with my eager audiences at the lecture sessions stimulating, and I like to think that, in some small way, I contributed to their vision. Upon my return to the USA, I was flattered to be offered a position as lecturer in tourism at the University of Beijing, which I obviously could not accept. I was even more flattered when one day, through the mail, came an unfamiliar and unauthorised copy of my book on hotel management—unfamiliar because this version was in Chinese!

I have visited China on several occasions since this trip, with mixed emotions. Gradually, China has joined the rest of the world. The bicycles have been replaced with motorbikes and cars; the Mao suits have been replaced with Giorgio Armani; and the old Russian 'barracks' have been replaced with Sheratons, Meridians, Ritz-Carltons, and the like. Hotel restaurants are no longer banquet halls; supplies and choices are plentiful. The people still have warm and gentle smiles, but I guess now they have more to smile about.

The next port of call was Papua New Guinea. Since this is not supposed to be a travel book, I have not dwelled upon the many, many places that Diana and I have been fortunate enough to visit, but I would be remiss not to single out Papua New Guinea. It may seem more like going to the Channel Islands to Australians, but to a European, Papua New Guinea was like a time warp. Not a politically created time warp like China, but a natural, Darwinesque one. In Papua New Guinea, you could still buy a cookery book with human parts listed as ingredients. In the mountains, there were still tribes who had not seen Europeans, and everywhere we travelled, there were many who wore no clothes save for a loincloth, which was often no more than a banana leaf. There were over 700 dialects, bound together by a common language: pidgin English. More often than not, you could not understand a word they were saying, even though they purported to be speaking English.

It was these jungles that had finally stopped the Japanese advance on Australia in the Second World War, and the reason was not hard to fathom. It was very difficult to drive from the capital, Port Moresby, to any other towns, because the roads all fizzled out about twenty miles into the mountains. Everything, including us, had to be moved by air. We did manage to take a flight to the centre and 'top' of the country, where I managed to rent an old car, which we used along dirt roads and across rivers on a long, three-day downhill ride to the east coast on the other side of the island from Port Moresby. The locals we saw on this route relied heavily on their skills with blowpipes, darts, and bows and arrows to garner their food. They were so accurate that I seriously thought about signing up a team to challenge England's best on a television special. Papua New Guinea was the only place I have stayed where the hotel security guards had bows and arrows. This was also the only place in the world where I have ever heard Diana say that she was frightened.

Not that the natives were prepared to pass up the opportunity of making a buck. One day, as we were cruising along in our battered Toyota through the forests and jungles on the eastern side of the island, our attention was drawn to a makeshift cardboard sign that read 'Birds of Paradise', with a squiggly arrow pointing into the forest. I slammed on what brakes we had, and reversed, to investigate. Diana, who loves her birds, was very excited about the possibility of actually seeing some almost-legendary birds of paradise. The cardboard arrow pointed down a narrow track. Upon examination, it seemed safe to head down it with the Toyota, because there were tire marks in the mud, although the grassy ridge between the tracks indicated that not too much traffic had passed this way recently. Off we set, down the track, which was so narrow and hemmed in by the forest that once we had committed, there could be no turning back, only reversing. On and on we went, and were just about to give up the idea when we emerged from the tunnel of the track into a clearing with a village of huts on stilts, surrounded by coconut palms. The locals, particularly the youngest ones, swarmed around us excitedly, jabbering away in undecipherable pidgin. Then from amongst the crowd emerged a young man with one eye closed. He introduced himself as Kunick. He, apparently, was the guide. He, for a modest sum, would take us to the birds of paradise, but we would have to walk, following him, through the jungle.

We rather nervously locked up the car and started after our guide. On and on we tramped through the hot steamy forest, clambering over fallen tree trunks and leaping little streams, all the time getting bitten to death by hundreds of mosquito-like creatures. As we trudged on, imagining the villagers ransacking our suitcases in the car, Kunick told us why he was left in the village to be the guide, whilst his male neighbours were out doing more manly things. It was because of his eye. He could not see out of one eye, and the other needed aid. This had also apparently prevented him from marrying, because a man is not allowed to have a wife unless he is able to climb a palm tree to get milk for a baby. Kunick's lack of eyesight affected his balance, and he could not climb trees. It also must have affected his ability to find the birds of paradise, for after what seemed to be an interminably long walk, he suddenly thrust out his arm to halt us and said, "Shhh—listen! Listen carefully. We will hear them now."

We stopped and listened with great anticipation. Maybe the sweaty walk was going to be worthwhile after all. The sounds of the jungle were all around us. For several minutes, Diana, Kunick and I were absolutely quiet.

"What are we listening for?" I ventured, after a while.

"It will sound like 'Caw, caw'," said Kunick, with which he started to "Caw, caw" in all directions. Suddenly he stopped, and turning to me, said, "What's the time?" pointing to my watch.

"Ten past two," I replied.

"Oh, pity," said Kunick. "They only come at two."

With that, there was nothing else we could do but battle our way back to the village. The fee for the trip, however, was still required, and at the time, it seemed like insurance, to be able to turn the Toyota around to face the right direction.

Having emerged from the jungle track, we once again headed down the main dirt road, which soon, thankfully, became a tarred road. On and on we went, now traveling through plantations of coconut palms, millions of them, until we finally reached the coast and our hotel for the night. We were hot, tired, dirty, and thirsty. We dumped our bags and headed for the bar.

"What would you like?" I asked Diana.

"I think I'll have a piña colada," she replied.

"Make that two," I instructed the barman.

"Sorry, sir," came the reply, "we don't have any coconuts."

# Chapter Thirteen
## THE NOBLE ART

It was during this time of 'unemployment' that the dubious sport of boxing came back into my life. The shows that we had put on in Pretoria and Bophuthatswana appeared to have impressed the North American boxing community, including the television presenters and, of course, Bob Arum, and I was frequently called and asked if I would consider putting on some promotions in the USA. To me, this would have been like the Brighton bingo hall trying to move into Vegas; I was convinced that it would be a wrong move, and that I would soon get swallowed up. Boxing in the USA was almost completely controlled by Don King and, to a lesser extent, by Bob. Don, being a charismatic black man, had a near-monopoly of promotional agreements with the black fighters, whilst Bob specialised more in Central and South Americans. Once you have the fighters, you can control the sport.

I did, however, have one fighter. To my great surprise, after his loss to John Tate and despite my obvious friendship with Big John, I was approached by Gerrie Coetzee, who asked me to become his manager. Gerrie was convinced that he could and should have beaten John; he had just frozen on the day. Gerrie was still ranked highly by the WBA, because, after all, he had only suffered one loss, and that was in a world-title fight. Gerrie wanted another crack at the title, and, for whatever reason, he thought that I was the person to get it for him. To me, the challenge of creating a world heavyweight champion was very tempting, but I did not want it to become a mainstream activity. Besides, if you are the manager of a fighter, you are not, technically, supposed to be a promoter at the same time. Don King is a promoter; his son Carl is a manager. Okay? After a little consideration, I agreed to take on Gerrie, on the basis that he should donate 10% of all future winnings to the Alexander Township in Johannesburg, where Diana had been, for many years, a volunteer worker.

I then decided that my part-time niche in the boxing world would be to put on fights in exotic places (like Africa) where Don King and Bob Arum would not really want to venture, and to sell them to US and other worldwide television companies. I would not tie up specifically with Don or Bob, but would work with them as co-promoters as was appropriate, i.e. depending on who controlled the opponent. Having concluded that this was the way to go, I set about letting it be known, and I was fairly quickly approached by several other South African boxers. Then I started to put on bouts in South Africa, which I duly sold, with the help of either Bob or Don, to US networks.

On one such occasion, I was promoting a world junior heavyweight (cruiserweight) fight in Johannesburg between Robbie Williams, a white South African, and Ossie Ocasio, a Puerto Rican who had been supplied to me through Bob Arum. Bob had sold the fight to a US television network, and I had sold a sponsorship to the car company, Mazda, for a nice high six-figure sum. Bob and I were splitting the proceeds. At the same time, I had become embroiled in another promotion regarding another sport, cricket, and the problems of being a one-man band were soon to become apparent.

To white South Africans, cricket was their summer religion, as rugby was the winter's. For most people, the British Commonwealth's obsession with cricket is about as puzzling as America's love of baseball from a European viewpoint. South Africans were enthralled with cricket, but as a result of international sanctions against the apartheid government, no foreign cricket teams had been allowed to travel to South Africa or play against a South African team for several years. These sports sanctions hurt South Africans far more than economic ones, and the politicians on both sides knew it. A great fear was beginning to spread amongst South African sports lovers that, after years of isolation, the standard of their international teams might be seriously deteriorating. Anyone who could break these sporting sanctions would be a hero, at least as far as most South Africans were concerned, including, strangely, non-whites, who also loved their sport. From my perspective, I believed firmly that sport bridges understanding between people, whereas sanctions prevent it. When I had been asked, therefore, by South African Breweries if I could assist in a secret mission to beat the cricket sanctions, I instantly and enthusiastically agreed. SAB, it turned out, would be willing to pay me a substantial sum if I could find a way to bring the entire English national cricket team to play a series of matches against South Africa. Absolute secrecy would have to be maintained, because if the British press were to get wind of the mission, it would be over before it had started.

I discovered that the English team was on a long tour of India and Sri Lanka. I also discovered that there was a window of about twenty days, between the end of the tour and the start of the English county cricket championships, during which all of the English cricketers would be theoretically available. The tour of India and Sri Lanka was almost three months long; the cricketers were being paid about

£5000 for the honour of playing for their country in the off season. I secured a budget of £50,000 per player to play thirteen days' cricket in South Africa: two five-day Tests and three One Day matches. Through SAB's contacts with the South African cricket administrators, I managed to book the cricket grounds in the major South African cities on the excuse that I was going to bring in an international junior, albeit sanction-busting team—and that, therefore, secrecy was required. Through a friend, I managed to make contact with one of the senior English players, Geoff Boycott, who was reaching the end of an illustrious career and would probably be more concerned about the cash than the consequences of sanction-breaking. Geoff told me that the most convenient time to talk to the players would be whilst they were playing a Test match in Bombay. For an extra £20,000 pounds, he would be willing to be my man on the inside. So far, so good!

I set off for India with high hopes, and booked myself into the Taj Mahal Hotel in Bombay, where the English team was staying, along with their management and a whole herd of English sportswriters. Fortunately, only Geoff knew who I was, and one by one, he brought the English players (save for the captain) to my hotel room, where I sold them on the concept of coming to South Africa. The selling was not hard. Thirteen days' cricket in South Africa, with wives allowed too (not the case in India), no Indian food, and £50,000 of tax-free money was not the hardest thing I ever had to sell. Within days, I had signed up nine of the first team, which was my target, including the 'stars': Boycott, Botham, Gooch, etc. The contracts were bizarre. First, instead of mentioning the word 'cricket', they referred to 'chess'—just in case a secretary or hotel cleaner happened to get sight of one. Then, because upon arrival in India I had had to make substantial changes to my preconceived contract, I had found it necessary to retype large swaths of it on a typewriter borrowed from the hotel manager's secretary; this machine was missing an *A* and an *O,* which I had filled in with ink. As a result, the contracts all looked as if they had chickenpox.

I obviously could not talk to the cricketers whilst they were playing India, so Geoff kindly gave me a ticket for the VIP enclosure. I am no lover of cricket, but I thought, under the circumstances, that I had better go. Upon arrival at the enclosure, I saw that the seats were, in fact, benches, on which were painted numbers. When I arrived at my bench, incidentally having been ripped off by the taxi driver on the way to the Wankhede Stadium, I discovered that despite there only being ten seat-numbers on the bench, there were already about fifteen people sitting on it.

"Excuse me," I said as politely but authoritatively as I could, "I think someone is sitting in my seat."

"Oh, no problem," several voices exclaimed. "We will all squeeze up a bit."

I did not go to the stadium for the next few days, preferring to stay at the hotel and watch it on the miniscule black-and-white set in my hotel room rather than be squeezed. When Geoff Boycott asked me if I had admired his shot-making (which I actually found to be excruciatingly slow), I pretended I had been at the stadium all of the time.

Although it had been fairly easy to get the players' commitments, Botham did give me some difficulty. Considering himself the star player, he felt that he should have more money. I knew that if I went down this route, my budget would be shot. Botham came to my room several times and threatened to pull out if he didn't get more. Eventually Boycott, who was getting £20,000 more, unbeknown to the rest of the team, settled him down, saying, "Ee, lad, stop grousing; we're all getting same."

The plan we conceived was real cloak-and-dagger stuff. I was to meet the players in Sri Lanka in about a month's time to hand out their air tickets. They would all return to England at the end of the current tour, to be happily reunited with their families. The tickets to South Africa for the players and their partners were all routed to South Africa via different places, so that upon leaving England, any suspicious journalist would conclude that they were all taking their wives to different places for vacation. All of the ongoing tickets had more or less the same arrival date in Johannesburg, and my plan was to smuggle them in, one by one, at the airport and only reveal them from behind a curtain, one by one, at a press conference. To the sporting world, this press conference was to be a coup.

During the intervening weeks between the signing of the chickenpox contracts in Bombay and my scheduled trip to Sri Lanka, some of the natives had started to get restless, and cracks were beginning to appear in my team. For a start, Botham consulted with his lawyer, who advised him not to go, and others were clearly going to need me to stroke them in Sri Lanka, to make sure that they actually showed up. Some started to be concerned about their public image because of the sanction-busting, and some worried about the reaction of the MCC, the ruling cricket body in the UK. The trip to Sri Lanka was therefore taking on great importance. Unfortunately, it was one trip that I never made, which brings me back to Robbie Williams versus Ossie Ocasio, who, as you will recall, were about to fight for the world light heavyweight crown.

The fight was scheduled for 9 pm Joburg time, which was Saturday afternoon on the east coast of the USA. The fight was being held in the open-air Rand Stadium, with a capacity of about 30,000. We had sold about 18,000 seats. At about 5 pm, as is often the case on the Witwatersrand, the heavens opened and a violent thunderstorm swept across the stadium. Richard Loring, the South African impresario and my friend, who was helping me stage the event, became quite distraught, because not only were all of the seats in the stadium now soaking wet, but the actual ring canvas, which was not protected from sideways-driving rain, was soaked through and would certainly never dry in time for the evening fight. "Not to worry," I explained to Richard quite cockily, "I've been through this before. I have a whole spare canvas and under-felt in the truck."

This was not the first time that I had been through this experience in an outdoor venue. As soon as the storm had passed through, my crew got to work fitting the new canvas. The sun had come out again, the crowd was pouring in, and I was already 'spending' the profits. Then disaster struck.

During the second preliminary bout, about an hour before the main event, the storm returned, this time more vicious than before. The wind howled and drove the sheets of rain horizontally across the ring, soaking the new canvas and making it very slippery. Then, suddenly, the little canopy above the ring could not bear the weight of the water anymore and collapsed, spilling its wet contents all over the ringside television equipment, which immediately ceased working, with a series of little flashes. Then, just as we thought nothing else could go wrong, lightning struck the stadium and all the lights in the place went out. The blazered boxing board of control officials, who were all by now sheltering under the ring, instructed me to abandon the fight—as if it were possible for me to carry on!

Somebody produced a loud hailer, and the sodden ringmaster tried to make announcements. It seemed that at least 10,000 Afrikaners were yelling in the dark for their money back, and my sponsor, Mazda, was extremely perturbed, to say the least, since all their VIP guests were now being jostled by a wet mob. Meanwhile, in America, the television networks were screaming at Bob Arum because they were obviously not getting any feed, and he, in turn, was completely frustrated, because (in these pre-cell phone days) he could not reach me for an explanation, since all the phone lines to the stadium were dead. I was also frustrated. My plan had been to tidy up the accounts for the promotion on the Monday following and then head immediately to Sri Lanka. But how could I leave this mess behind?

Late that night, when the storm had passed and the baying crowd had finally gone home, Richard and I cobbled together a plan. Fortunately, all of the tickets for the fight had been sold through Computicket, which, as the name implies, was a computerised ticketing service with several outlets around Johannesburg and other cities in South Africa. Percy Tucker, the Computicket owner, carefully explained to me that from his records, he could establish where each ticket had been bought, and exactly when and how many tickets had been bought with each transaction. In addition to this, he could identify whether it had been purchased using cash, cheque, account or credit card. Enough information, we concluded, to be able to attempt to offer a "Swap your old (wet) ticket for a new one."

Armed with this information, Richard, the impresario, immediately corralled a bevy of his showgirls to be on duty during the next week as 'swap girls'. Now I had to convince the boxing board of control to let me try again with the fight, and they readily agreed that it could be staged on the following Saturday. Fortunately, the stadium was still available. With all of this done, by Sunday afternoon I was able to go onto the television with an announcement that used ticket stubs or other proof of purchase would entitle fans to replacement seats, if they could get to the Rand Stadium to collect them.

That just left Sri Lanka. Somebody had to go to meet the cricketers. South African Breweries, the sponsor, had the biggest interest, so I appealed to them to send an executive to do my work. That was a big mistake. Putting on sporting events, like many other things in life, is all to do with relationships. Some of the cricketers' resolve to take the easy money had been wobbling, but they knew that they had eyeballed me with their commitments. So when somebody else showed up to give them their final instructions, no matter how accomplished he was, he actually had no chance. The promises had been to me; the bonding had been with me; I was letting these people down. All bets were now off. Despite this, the tour did take place, with at least five of the English first team and some reserves. It was a sell-out tour that made big headlines in the UK. All of the English participants were banned from professional cricket by the MCC for two years, and England, with their team decimated, did not win another match against foreign opposition for a long time to come. My English friends (or those that I managed to keep after this) were convinced that I had single-handedly ruined the national summer sport.

The swap sessions at the Rand Stadium turned out to be hilarious. I thanked the Lord for Richard's pretty girls because almost every boxing fan that showed up had a story about how he had lost his front row tickets in the thunderstorm. Until then, I had not realised that it was possible to fit 18,000 seats in the front row around a twenty-by-twenty boxing ring. The girls were just what were needed to diffuse the tension and to unmask the stories. Eventually everyone was reticketed, and as a result of all of the extra publicity, we sold another 7000 seats. Bob and I lost the television money because of scheduling problems on the following Saturday, but the local sponsor was happy with our recovery, and all was well that ended well, except for Robbie Williams, who finished up on the (dry) ring floor.

Meanwhile, I had brought Gerrie Coetzee to the USA for a fight against number-four-ranked Randy Snipes. The fight was held at the Westchester Arena. I did not know it at the time, but this particular arena was rumoured to be owned by the mob. Nor did I realise that Randy Snipes was 'owned' by the president of the Yonkers Garbage Collection Company, another alleged front for the mob. I was soon to find out. The fight was a ten-rounder, and was broadcast nationally on CBS. Gerrie clearly won eight of the ten rounds, and, just for good measure, knocked Randy to the canvas in two of them. I was therefore flabbergasted when two of the judges announced Randy as the winner by five rounds to four, with one even. They had been nobbled, and unfortunately, I said as much in the post-fight interview with the 'fight doctor', Ferdie Pacheco , which was broadcast live to America. In fact, I was quite uncomplimentary about the mob. That night, when we got home to Scarsdale, we found our house had been ransacked.

Notwithstanding this, I persisted with Gerrie, who unfortunately was developing problems with a fractured bone in his right hand. To ease the pain, it was necessary for Gerrie to get a shot of novocaine into the hand before a fight. But this was not an easy thing to achieve, because boxers' hands are wrapped with bandages prior to a fight, in the presence of an opposition corner man, before boxing gloves are donned, to make sure that there are no bricks beneath the wrap. The effect of the novocaine wears off, but if one administers too much, the fighter can't even feel his hand, which is also not good. To get the injection administered at exactly the right time, so that its effects would last for the duration of the fight, we got up to all sorts of mischief. On one famous occasion in Atlantic City, just as his hands were about to be wrapped, Gerrie made a big fuss about going to the toilet. "Use the one here," said the fight supervisor, who happened to be Smoking Joe Frazier.

"Uh, no," whinged Gerrie, with his high-pitched, girlish voice, "I can't go with people around. I want to go up to my hotel room" (which was luckily in the same building). After some negotiation, which included Gerrie's father screaming in Afrikaans and the television producer imploring, "For God's sake, let him go. We've got a show to start on time," Gerrie was finally allowed to go up to his hotel room, provided that an opposing cornerman went with him. This was perfect because hiding in the hotel room bathroom, behind the shower curtain, was our doctor, needle at the ready. After much huffing and puffing and flushing, Gerrie emerged, ready to fight. This fight was against Pinklon Thomas, another top contender. Despite the novocaine in his right hand, Gerrie fought ten rounds using a left jab; he just didn't trust the right. The fight was a draw.

Gerrie was now getting to be quite well-known in America, but with me living in the USA and Gerrie in Brakpan, South Africa, communications between us were often difficult, and I was never really sure that we had properly bonded, as I believe a manager and a sportsman have to do. Gerrie was very Afrikaans, and I, at best, was an English immigrant to South Africa; this was like oil and water. I also was unsure that Gerrie really put his back into pre-fight training. I was sure that he possessed the legs and the fists to win a title; I was not sure that he possessed the mind. Bob Arum suggested to me that the smart thing to do would be to bring Gerrie and his family to the USA and to establish him in a proper training camp, surrounded by the right people. I agreed with this philosophy, but Gerrie did not want to pay for it.

The opportunity to put this plan into action suddenly

presented itself when I received a call from Don King. Don's fighter, Michael Dokes, had just won the heavyweight title from Mike Weaver, and Don was looking for an easy first defence for Michael, who incidentally was managed by Don's son, Carl. As part of the negotiation for the fight, I insisted that I should bring Gerrie to America to set up a training camp, and that this would be good for prefight publicity. I also insisted that Don contribute $50,000 toward the costs, and he agreed. Gerrie decided that he would like to train in California, so he and I looked around for suitable premises, and together hired the training staff. Gerrie also went for treatment on his hand.

Muhammad Ali was now completely out of the picture, as far as fighting was concerned. His last two fights had done untold damage, and he was beginning to suffer badly from Parkinson's disease. As a result of spending time in California with Gerrie, I did get to meet him one more time. Gerrie and I were invited to Vegas to watch a fight being staged by Bob Arum. Whilst we were there, somebody told Ali, who was also in town, that Gerrie was around, and Ali sent a message inviting us to his hotel suite.

When we entered the suite, the room was full of Ali's friends and hangers-on, but there was no sign of the great man. Somebody told us that he was in the adjacent bedroom, expecting us. Before we knew what was happening, we were ushered through a connecting door and found ourselves at Ali's bedside. It was a sad sight. Ali was half-sitting up in bed, his huge frame obviously not in great shape. He greeted us with his wonderful smile, but his words were slow and slurred. He talked to us in his famous rhyming couplets, but you could see that his lips wouldn't do what his brain was instructing them to do. It was really difficult to hold a conversation, and I could see that Gerrie was struggling with his own emotions, so after a few minutes, we left. On the way back to our hotel, Gerrie said, "Whatever happens, Peter, don't ever let me get like that."

It was around this time that another of my activities started to bubble over. KwaNdebele was a "homeland" in South Africa that was preparing to take its independence. KwaNdebele was important because its territory extended close to the eastern edge of Pretoria, and because it was easily reached by motorway from Johannesburg. It had occurred to me that a casino situated on the edge of KwaNdebele would be far closer to the main market than Sol's Sun City, and so for several months I had been shuttling between New York and South Africa, for the purpose of convincing the fledgling KwaNdebele cabinet that they should offer me the casino rights to their new country, once it had achieved independence. For this purpose, I needed to come up with a project that would be completely different from Sun City, and to find a suitable site. Upon review of all of the available land situated near the border, I decided that none of it was attractive enough to create an international resort that could compete with Sun City, but this did not really matter, because the market for KwaNdebele would be substantially people from the Witwatersrand, and not overseas tourists.

With the help of my old friend Barry King, we eventually came up with a concept that 'blew away' the main man, the chief of the Ndebele. We designed two huge A-frame buildings with swivelling stadium seats on all four sides. The buildings were to be placed on each side of a football pitch, which would be surrounded by a dog-racing track. At one end of the stadium, between the two A-frames, was to be a curved seating section, which would also double as an outdoor stage for concerts (hence the swivelling seats). Running around the pitch would be a section of a motor-racing track, which would use the banking of the curve and then wind its way outside of the stadium to other parts of the grounds, where it could be clearly seen from the seats on the outside of the A-frame buildings. The pits for the cars would be lined up opposite the straight, which was to run parallel with the non-stadium side of one of the buildings. Facing the non-stadium side of the other building would be the straight of a horse-racing track. Inside one of the A-frames would be an indoor sports and entertainment arena for concerts, basketball, ice hockey, or exhibitions, and, of course, inside the other building would be a massive casino. In other words, this would be a multipurpose arena at which every conceivable sport on which one could bet would be available, and which could also house major entertainment events.

Chief Skosana fell in love with our design, as did most of his cabinet. However, the strategic importance of KwaNdebele had not escaped the attention of my ex-employer, Sol Kerzner. Sol was determined that he could not allow a development there that would interfere with the success of Sun City, and he had been very active, therefore, in proposing to the Ndebele that he would build them not a casino, but an entertainment centre, second to none. In fact, he was promising to build Africa's Disney World, and with this in mind, jetted key members of the cabinet off to Disney (Japan and America), to show them what he had in mind. It seemed that Sol had certain of the cabinet in his pocket, and that I had the others. As time went by, it became very frustrating for me that they, despite welcoming and applauding my proposals, would not actually sign my documents. The longer this went on, the more it was costing me, and the more Sol seemed to spend on them.

Our approaches, however, were very different. When I went up to KwaNdebele, I visited these local leaders in their own villages; I ate goat chops with them with my fingers; I stayed and jawled with them. Sol wanted them to visit his offices in the city, on his timetable. When he took them to New York, he stayed at the Towers at the Waldorf-Astoria, they stayed at the Hilton, and he sent a driver to fetch and carry them. When they eventually visited me in New York, they came to my house and I drove them in my car. I also knew something that he was not willing to tell them. When he had signed the deal with Lucas Mangope, the president of Bop, he had agreed that in the event Sun was to develop in other homelands, the president had a right to be a partner. I knew that the Ndebele would never accept a Tswana as their partner.

This struggle for the hearts, minds and maybe pockets of the KwaNdebele ministers was just coming to a head as I installed Gerrie at his training camp in California, as, indeed, was a new multi-hotel deal that I had been working on with Jim Levi at Oppenheimer. For an unemployed person, I was being kept pretty busy, and this was not helped by the uninspiring timekeeping of the African politicians. On one occasion, when I was very pressed for time, I was asked by Chief Skosana to attend a meeting at the Bundu Inn in KwaNdebele on a Sunday morning. The only way I could make it was to fly from New York to Johannesburg on a Saturday (a fifteen-hour trip) and rent a helicopter for the day on Sunday to get me up and back from the Bundu Inn in time to catch the Sunday evening flight back to New York.

I arrived with my helicopter at the Bundu Inn on the appointed hour of 10 am. There was no sign of the chief. This was not unduly troubling. In Africa, the whites had a saying: "The white men have the watches; the black men have the time." I was used to (and even admired, to a degree) the concept that time should not rule our lives. However, two hours later, I was beginning to be concerned, but I kept receiving messages on a scratchy telephone line that the old man was on his way. By three o'clock I was quite annoyed, because I knew that we had to leave in the chopper by five o'clock or I would miss my plane. I had also been hanging around all day at the Bundu Inn, whose name aptly described it: there was absolutely nothing there. Finally, at around four o'clock, the phone tinkled again. This time it was the chief himself.

"Terribly sorry. Couldn't meet you today; had to go to a funeral. Can we meet next weekend?"

When you've put a lot of effort into a deal but you haven't yet secured it, it is times like these that you have to exercise enormous self-restraint. You want to tell the man to stuff his meeting, but you know that that would mean the end, and all of your time and costs would have been for naught.

"Of course I can meet next weekend. I'll just fly back from New York," I meekly replied, as if it were akin to taking the Number 19 bus from Battersea Bridge to the King's Road, Chelsea.

The logistics of the next weekend were even more difficult. On Friday, Gerrie was to have a minor operation on his hand in Los Angeles. He was nervous, and wanted me to be there. I told him I could be there on Friday and Monday but that I had a previous arrangement for the weekend. I also had to address a meeting of the town fathers in Akron, Ohio with Jim Levi on Monday evening. From Los Angeles to the Bundu Inn is a long way. This time, the chief and his cabinet did show up. They still didn't sign the deal, so I invited them (or some of them) to America to see Gerrie's upcoming world-title fight, in the hope that I could persuade them to sign the deal on my home ground. With the meeting over, I took the now-familiar helicopter back to Johannesburg, then the plane to New York, with a connection on to Los Angeles, where I held Gerrie's hand for an hour or two before traveling back east to Akron for my

Monday evening meeting; finally I arrived back in New York on Tuesday. It was on this trip that I taught myself how to have a complete body wash and shampoo in the first-class toilet of a jumbo jet. Diana pronounced me to be 'completely mad'.

Ultimately, my persistence in this regard paid off. Three of the Ndebele—Sam Skosana (the son of the chief), Prince Mahlangu, and another cabinet minister—did come to America a few months later. Gerrie's hand had healed, and he was ready to take on Michael Dokes at the Richmond Arena in Akron. Don King, the promoter, was awesome. He enveloped the event with his personality. This huge black man, who had in his youth been to jail for murder, with his famous hair standing upright like a thorn bush, greeted Diana and me as long-lost friends. "Dinah," he boomed as he hugged her, "I just wanna tell you that your husband is Dinah-mite. Yeah!"

"What a friendly man," Diana exclaimed as we walked away.

"Yes," I replied, then added, "You've just shaken hands with a murderer."

I thought I knew why Don thought I was "dynamite." Although he had agreed to pay $50,000 up front for our training expenses, with only days to go before the fight, we still had not received a dime. I was asked to attend a press conference at the Plaza Hotel in New York, which was being held to publicise the fight. As the questions were fired, Don took it upon himself to answer all of them—as is his way. Finally, a question was directed so specifically at me that he could not answer it.

"What's it like working with Don King?'

"Everything's fine," I quickly replied, "except he owes me $50,000." Guffaws of laughter erupted from Don and everyone else.

The next day, back in Scarsdale, I received a phone call from someone at the Yonkers Garbage Company.

"We heard King owes you fifty gees. You'll get yer money."

"Who are you?" I cautiously asked.

"Remember the Snipes fight? We owe you one—and by the way, bet on your boy."

With that, the phone went dead. The next day $50,000 was wired into my account. For some reason, I figured, Don King thought I had friends.

The weigh-in for the fight was hilarious. Weigh-ins are important for all divisions of prize-fighting except heavyweights, because as a heavyweight, there is no upper limit to what a boxer can weigh. For this reason, heavyweight weigh-ins are held on the day before the fight, and are used to generate publicity photos on the eve of the big event. Gerrie did not notice what everyone else in the room observed. Dokes was so out of it that he couldn't even tie his own shoelaces. The poor boy had a cocaine habit, which apparently had been helped along a little bit by some of my 'friends'. Now I knew why 'my boy' was going to win.

The atmosphere in the arena was electric. I had waited a long time for this. Could it be that I was on the verge of achieving the ultimate boxing goal? Could I be about to win the bet I'd taken with myself? This would be the greatest chance that Gerrie would ever have to win the title, and in some ways, I believed that it was through my efforts that it had now been laid on a plate for him. The question was: would he have the appetite for it?

Dokes climbed in the ring looking awful, and as he moved ponderously around the ring, I could see that he was drooling. There was no question that this man was only half-there. My excitement grew. Even so, it took Gerrie eight rounds to stop him. Despite all of the circumstances,

I somehow felt very pleased—indeed, proud—that I had managed to finally produce a world heavyweight champion. My guests from KwaNdebele were also thrilled to be part of the evening, and my Sarah and Jonathan, who had been seated near them, were highly amused to witness them standing on their chairs yelling "Slam die Kaffir!" They must have been the only blacks in the arena that were on the white man's side.

After the celebrations in Akron, we all went back to New York: Diana, the children, Sam Skosana, the prince, the minister, and me. The next day, we had a barbecue at our home in Scarsdale, and we invited some of the neighbours, who were intrigued to meet a real live African chief and prince. I am pleased to say that they were not disappointed.

During the day, unbeknown to me, the Ndebele had a strange request for Diana. They wanted to see our bedroom. "Upstairs; last door on the right," she volunteered, and apparently, off they all trooped, reappearing about a minute later without comment. It was only later that Diana told me about this. As I was driving them back into town late that evening, they suddenly announced that they were ready to sign my deal. Delighted, I asked them, "Why now?"

"Because today," explained Sam Skosana, "we have seen the bed you sleep in." I did not push the matter further, but having later signed up the prospective government of KwaNdebele to my deal, I learned that it is an Ndebele custom that you can only trust a man after you have seen the bed that he sleeps in. Years later, I told Sol that he could have saved his money on trips for them to Japan, Florida, and New York; all he need have done was to have taken them down Homestead Avenue, Johannesburg and let them look at his bedroom. That, I thought, would have been a good test of the KwaNdebele theory.

A few weeks later, I was back in Johannesburg to finalise

the paperwork. As usual with any deal, there was a 'hiccup'. As a deposit on the government land, the chief wanted one million six hundred thousand rand (about $1,600,000). It did strike me as a coincidence that there were sixteen members of his cabinet. Needless to say, not only did I not have a spare million six hundred thousand dollars, but even if I had, I would not have been keen to leave it in the hands of a cabinet who did not yet have a country to govern. To give myself some time to raise the money, I structured the deal on the basis that all parties had signed, giving me (using the good old excuse of exchange controls) one week to deposit the funds; i.e. the deal was binding on all parties if I showed up with the money within a week. Thus, with the ink barely dry on the Bundu Inn agreement, I hotfooted it to Johannesburg, where I explained to the board of Sol's only competitor in regional gaming, Safmarine, that I was willing to give them 49% of my rights in KwaNdebele, provided that they immediately give me a cashier's cheque for one million seven hundred thousand rand and enter into an agreement to provide all of the finance required in due course to develop the casino rights, in accordance with my plan. I also insisted that they should not be able to sell their rights to a third party without my approval, and especially not to Kerzner.

The full board of directors of Safmarine listened intently to my proposal. They argued they should have time for due diligence. I told them that I would wait for one hour. If they had not agreed to produce the money within that time, I would leave their offices to offer the deal to "one of my many friends." After an hour, a secretary appeared to ask if I would mind holding on for another half an hour. I sent back the message that I would wait for another ten minutes and then I would leave. Five minutes later, they called me back into the boardroom, and, with an ashen face, the chairman gravely told me that in all of his years in boardrooms he had never been faced with such a situation, but basically, they were willing to agree to my terms. Bingo! The paperwork was drawn up, the money was transferred to my bank, and sixteen-seventeenths of it was sent duly on to KwaNdebele. The deal was secure. I was now the 51% owner of potentially the richest casino rights in Africa, and all it had cost me was my expenses and time. I felt like flying home on the Concorde.

As it turned out, KwaNdebele never achieved its independence, and so the development I had struggled to sign off on never saw the light of day; but in my life, this was not to be hugely relevant, because by the time their independence was in doubt, I had long since moved on to other things, during which time, as you will see, I offloaded my KwaNdebele interests to none other than Sol Kerzner.

# Chapter Fourteen
## THE END OF A CHAMPION

During the rollout of the boxing and the KwaNdebele affairs, I had been involved in ongoing discussions with Jim Levi about an idea he had to acquire hotels in the USA. Since Jim's flirtation with the hotel industry through the Fontainebleau, it had continued to fascinate him, but Jim was a banker, and to fulfil his ambitions in this area, he needed advice from an operator. Jim and I had stayed in contact, through our mutual interest in Smith & Wollensky, and so from time to time we had met. Jim had seen that the USA was littered with hotels, small and large, that were privately owned and, in many cases, struggling to survive. He rightly observed that in order to tap into marketing and reservation networks, most of these had sought franchises from Holiday Inns, Ramada, Best Western, and the like, who were charging fairly hefty fees and not always delivering good results. Jim reasoned that if enough of these independents could be bought and amalgamated under one management company, the potential synergies and resultant savings would be huge. Jim's plan was to acquire about 100 properties, renovate them as required, and manage them as a group. To achieve this, he would need someone to visit and select the properties, and someone to form and operate a management company. In Jim's view, I was that person.

Jim's proposed method of acquisition for these properties was ingenious. This was to be a 'roll up' with a difference. His plan was to carefully evaluate each property, agree a price with the seller, and then to pay with shares in a new company to be listed on the American Stock Exchange. For example, assuming that ten hotels were for sale and that they were valued at $10 million each, he would form a listed company with a market "cap" of $100 million; at the simultaneous grand closing of the hotel acquisitions, each seller would receive shares in the new company worth $10 million. Nobody would be allowed to sell their shares for two years, and the ten hotels would all have entered into a management contract with the new listed entity. At the end of this theoretical transaction, a seller, instead of owning one hotel in, say, Ridgefield, Connecticut, would now own one-tenth of the shares in a listed company. After two years, the seller would be able to sell some or all of his shares on the market more easily than perhaps he could have sold the hotel on its own; hopefully, because of the synergies involved in operating all of the hotels as a group, the aggregate increased profitability would have improved the share value.

Jim and I discussed and refined this concept over many meetings and several weeks. In order for it to work, we would have to (amongst other things) convince the American Stock Exchange and the Securities and Exchange Commission that we could list a start-up company, find and convince enough sellers of suitable hotel properties that they would be smart to swap their real estate for shares in the new company, convince their respective lenders that they should roll over the loans on each property, convince the sellers that there were synergies to be had and that their new company would be properly managed, convince the sellers that the properties were all being valued equitably, and so on—quite a lot of convincing!

We started with the stock exchange, because, without their approval, there could be no scheme. Never before had anyone approached the stock exchange with such an idea. The rules of the American Stock Exchange were that a company had to have been trading for a minimum of one year before it could be granted membership and a listing. We were now proposing that they confirm the listing of a company that had not been trading for a year and did not yet exist. Jim, however, could be very persuasive, and after many meetings, he finally got an approval, provided that the initial share offering was in excess of $100 million. In other words, we would have to exchange shares in the new company for at least $100 million worth of equity in hotels. This value could not include debt on the hotels; for example, if the ten hotels described above were bought for $10 million each but there was a $9 million-dollar mortgage on each one (which was to stay in place), the amount of shares we would need to issue to acquire the ten hotels would be only valued at $10 million. In this example, therefore, we would need to acquire a hundred hotels to reach the minimum company size to achieve the listing.

Buoyed by his success with the stock exchange, Jim now wanted a commitment from me to work with him. It was obvious that to turn Jim's idea (for which I was rapidly beginning to share joint ownership) into a reality would take a huge amount of work, with great focus and discipline. I knew that if I committed to Jim, I would have to drop the other projects I had been working on. Jim, who was still with Oppenheimer, had figured out that in order for Oppenheimer and management to benefit from the scheme, 20% worth of additional shares would need to be issued at the commencement of the new company. This would naturally have the effect of diluting the sellers' share value by 20% at the outset, but Jim reasoned that the synergies and performance of the new company would quickly redress this dilution. It was yet another thing we needed to convince the sellers of! The challenge of starting up a new business in the USA and utilising my basic skill sets was appealing, as was the potential of making a lot of money. Jim was so boyishly enthusiastic about the plan that I decided to give it a go; but how was I to disentangle myself from Gerrie Coetzee and the Ndebele?

This question was soon answered for me. First I'll relate the Gerrie Coetzee story. Shortly after Gerrie had won the WBA heavyweight title, he began behaving as if the weight of the crown was affecting his brain. The title 'champion' had gone to his head, and he was convinced that he was the best in the world, notwithstanding the fact that the man he had beaten was a gibbering wreck. Needless to say, there were plenty of Gerrie's friends to fawn around him and reinforce his own feelings of greatness. As a result of this, Gerrie and I differed as to how the title should be defended. Gerrie had got it into his head (because, I later found out, a 'friend' of mine had put it there) that he could get $4 million for an immediate fight with Larry Holmes, the reigning WBC titleholder. This fight would, of course, be a reunification of the WBA and WBC titles, and, as such, sounded attractive. I did not think, however, that such a fight was possible at this stage. Gerrie was not a household name in the USA; Larry Holmes was. If Gerrie were to demand $4 million for this fight, I knew that Holmes would ask for at least $8 million, and in these days before the huge bonanza of pay-per-view television, it would simply not be possible to find enough sponsorship and television money to pay for the fight. It was my view that Gerrie should defend his title a couple of times, so as to establish himself as a true champion, whilst we used the time to hype up a fight with Holmes.

In order to test my theory, I invited Don King to lunch at Smith & Wollensky. Don was late, so I had already taken my seat at the back of the restaurant when he arrived. As he swaggered through Smith & Wollensky to meet me, every head in the restaurant turned. This was one famous man. As we sat down for our oversized steaks, it quickly became apparent that Don's plans for Gerrie, for whom he was now entitled to promotional rights, dovetailed very neatly with mine. Don, it seemed, was embarrassed to be holding rights over a white South African; it did not sit well with his other clients.

Within minutes, he had hatched a plan. Don would sell me his promotional rights in Gerrie for two fights, for $1 million per fight. I would put on these two fights in Johannesburg, where we could be sure of a massive crowd. Don would sell the fights to an American television network; most importantly, Don would supply the opponents, who would both have been primed by Don to lose, hopefully in a fairly spectacular fashion, so that Gerrie's ratings in America would be improved. Meanwhile, Don would arrange with Larry to hype up the unification title fight by denouncing Gerrie as white trash or the like. This way, Don predicted, the eventual fight between Gerrie and Larry would be big enough for Gerrie to get his $4 million—and for Don to get his as well, no doubt!

With the plan mapped out, I jetted off to South Africa to clear some details with the tax lawyers so that Gerrie could benefit from all of the proceeds offshore. The way I saw it, even after paying Don $2 million and the other expenses involved, Gerrie would clear at least $2 million profit from the two fights and then, of course, the $4 million from fighting Larry. He would be set for life, and I would have earned $600,000 for the Alexander clinic—a sum they never would have dreamed of. With everything set, I went to explain it all to Gerrie—everything except the bit about the opponents' instructions. But Gerrie stubbornly refused to listen. He was absolutely sure that he could get a fight with Holmes straight away. I could not convince him that he was wrong—and then I discovered why.

It was Gerrie who blurted it all out to me. It seems that he had been approached by another would-be promoter/manager (a so-called friend of mine), who had promised him $4 million to fight Holmes within a few months. All Gerrie had to do was to sign an agreement, which he stupidly had done, despite the fact that he already had valid agreements with Don King and me. I was incensed. After all of the planning and effort I had put into his elevation to the championship and the defence strategy, now all I wanted todo was to wash my hands of him. I knew that the other promoter would never be able to deliver, and I knew that I could, through the courts, prevent him, but I had no desire to even try. I had had my fun; I had created a world heavyweight champion; I had achieved a certain goal. It was time to move on.

I knew I had made the right decision when I discovered, shortly afterward, that Gerrie also had not been fair with me about the clinic. In order to avoid tax exposure for myself, Gerrie was supposed to have paid 10% of his purse from the Dokes fight directly to the clinic, as was his normal practice. On this occasion, I had not received a note of thanks from them, and was therefore suspicious that the money had not been sent, despite assurances to the contrary from Gerrie. Unfortunately, the clinic never received the money. As far as I was concerned, there could be no turning back.

Don King was not amused. "That bastard will never fight again," he declared after I had broken the news to him of my resolve to leave Gerrie to fight his own battles. "You're right. Let him rot," roared Don. As it happened, Holmes, probably encouraged by Don, refused to fight Gerrie, as indeed did everybody else. Gerrie had overlooked, in his deceit and greed, the fact that King controlled all of the other ranked contenders, and none of them, strangely, wanted to fight a white South African. The WBA had a mandatory title defence policy. If a fighter did not defend his title within one year of winning it, he would be stripped of it.

The end of this story was as strange as the beginning. Just as the WBA was about to take action against Gerrie, I received a call from King. "I need to sort out this mess. I need the bastard to fight again—to keep control. Do you understand?" Then, before I could even reply or object, he asked, "Who's he scared of?"

"Greg Page," I retorted immediately, "and I hope he beats the shit out of him."

"It's done. Bye."

The fight did take place, actually at Sun City. Page knocked out Coetzee after three minutes and fifty seconds of the eighth round. Boxing matches only have three-minute rounds. Gerrie, upon review of the tape, lodged an appeal with the WBA. Nobody was in.

This was effectively the end of my flirtation with boxing. It had been fun. It had been interesting. We had had some exciting times. But at the level I had been playing, it was no longer a sport. Through it, I met some lovely people, and I met some rogues. I met greedy men who preyed on the fighters, and I met fighters who double-crossed their backers. I met sensitive fighters, like Mike Weaver, who would rather have been playing the piano. I met loveable fighters, like John Tate, who was just too nice to be a boxer. I met clever men, like Bob Arum; I met famous men, like Muhammad Ali; and I met sharp men, like Don King. My last touch with boxing was in the courts in New York: the IRS versus Don King. Believe it or not, I was subpoenaed to be a witness for Don King.

Here's what happened with the Ndebele. I was sitting in my new office at One New York Plaza, the last building in Manhattan before the Staten Island Ferry Pier, and the home base of Oppenheimer, when the phone rang. It was an old friend from Sun City.

"Are you sitting down?" he started in his distinctive Austro-Canadian drawl. "I thought you would like to know that a deal has been struck here today. Safmarine have sold their hospitality interests to Kerzner. That includes their interest in KwaNdebele. Can't say any more. Thought you should know." I thanked him profusely for the leak, and sat back stunned. It had been perfectly clear, when I sold Safmarine 49% of my KwaNdebele rights, that they could not sell on to anyone without my approval and that they specifically could never sell to Kerzner. I could not have Kerzner as a partner in an enterprise with the Ndebele, after all I had told them about him. But, it seemed, I might already have him as just that.

I did not need a lawyer to tell me that Safmarine had breached our agreement. I didn't even need to get out the files to check. I was positive, because I had written these particular clauses at the time with great care. It was fairly late in the evening in Johannesburg when I started to call the home of my contact director in Safmarine, Nigel Matthews. There was no answer. I tried again every half hour, and finally, at about 11:30 pm (South Africa time), he picked up the phone. It appeared that he had been out celebrating the deal with his colleagues. He was not prepared for my call.

"Nigel, there is a very strange rumour circulating today on Wall Street. It seems that a deal has been struck between Safmarine and Kerzner. The rumour is that Safmarine have sold their hospitality division and KwaNdebele rights to Kerzner. I'm sure that can't be true," I chattered on with mock incredulity. There was stony silence at the other end, the sort of alcohol-induced silence when the brain can't quite work out what it is supposed to say. I carried on: "It's strange that I should be hearing this rumour here. There normally isn't smoke without—"

"How did you know?" Nigel finally interrupted—and with that he had confirmed what I had been told.

"Everybody seems to know," I retorted. "Why didn't you discuss it with me first?

"KwaNdebele was only a tiny part of the deal," he said lamely. "We were going to call you in the morning."

"The morning is too late. In the morning you will be hearing from my attorney."

The next day, Nigel's chairman was on the phone with a thousand excuses and apologies—none of which I could accept. The truth of the matter was that I had a new partner, one I did not want. This was the stuff of punitive damages. About two weeks later, Kerzner telephoned me. He was polite, but curt. "I see that there is a loan on our books to you from Safmarine of one point seven million bucks. When can we expect payment?"

"Did you notice the coupon and the due date of that loan, Sol?" I replied.

"No, what is it?" he drawled.

"Zero and never," I shot back.

"Some fucking loan," he responded, with a chuckle, "I think we'd better talk about it." After a bit of small talk, I agreed to travel to Johannesburg, at his expense, as soon as was practical.

A few weeks later, Diana and I were on our way back to our beloved South Africa, not quite knowing what to expect. For some time now I had been hearing stories from my contacts in KwaNdebele that all was not well with their quest for independence. The leadership was very corrupt, and young Sam, who had visited with us in Scarsdale, had been sent to jail by the South African government, which was desperate to show the world that the independent homelands were properly governed nations. It could not afford to have any more scandals in its newly created independent neighbours, and in the case of KwaNdebele, it was right to be concerned. At this stage of the game, independence for the Ndebele looked to be a long way off. Without independence, the casino rights would be worthless. I knew that Sol would know that, but I figured he could not be sure, and so I decided to try to sell him my 51% before things got any worse. He might not put any value on it other than 'insurance', but I was determined to extract the maximum I could, or I would go forward with a lawsuit against his new 'partner', Safmarine.

We met at Sun Manor, on Homestead Avenue in Bryanston: Sol's house in the northern suburbs of Johannesburg. This was the house that Shirley Kerzner had left to commit suicide; this was the house where I, and others, had worked so hard to console Sol after that tragic event. This was the house where Diana and I were, in the future, destined to live. Actually, we met in the garden—Sol, Nigel Matthews and I. Sol and I quickly came to an agreed figure. Nigel, on behalf of Safmarine, continued to balk. Eventually, Sol started shouting at Nigel, and he finally agreed. Nigel and I then settled down to spell out the terms of the deal, and we arranged to meet again a couple of days later to sign off.

For some reason that I cannot recall, I could not make the arranged meeting, and had to postpone till the next day, a Saturday. This apparently interfered with Nigel's golf, so instead of meeting me as planned, he sent a very junior lady lawyer, who was armed with his power of attorney. I very quickly discovered that Nigel, in his enthusiasm to keep me as far away from South Africa as possible, had written into the agreement all sorts of restraints and conditions which had never been discussed and to which I would never have agreed. Sensing that I could turn this situation to my advantage and perhaps extract more out of Sol through this act of bad faith, I told the young lady that there was no way I was going to sign such a document, and sent her packing. Within hours, as expected, I had Sol on the phone, shouting and screaming and calling me a filthy reneger, whom he would drum out of the country, never to be allowed to return. I was staying at the Holiday Inn in Sandton at the time. Diana could hear every word of Sol's through the plastic of the handset. Sol had just had a heart attack; Diana was convinced that I was about to bring on another, and pleaded with me to agree to meet him again to settle the matter.

A new meeting was arranged for Monday morning at my attorney's office. I played hardball. My attorney announced that, due to the bad-faith attempt to get me to sign something to which I had not agreed and due to the abuse I had taken from Sol on the phone, I would only consider signing for a higher amount. Sol went ballistic, and, as the South Africans say, "threw all of his toys out of the cot." Just at this moment, a secretary called me out of the room to take a phone call. It was Diana. She was with Mrs. Eva Brown, the psychic. Mrs. Brown was "very worried." She "saw" lots of shouting and screaming going on and lots of shuffling of papers.

"Just ask Mrs. Brown this," I said to Diana. "Shall I take the money, or shall I walk?"

"Take the money," came back the clear instruction. "Please do," added Diana. "You don't want to give him another heart attack."

With that I walked back into the room, where Sol was still fuming, now with a glass of whisky in his hand.

"I've decided to sign," I announced calmly.

"Now you're fucking talking," he retorted. "About fucking time."

With that, the formalities were concluded. The offending pieces were removed from the text, the agreements were hastily signed, and I was duly handed a cheque. As it turned out, I was the only person to make any money from the KwaNdebele casino rights, for it never became an independent state. Mrs. Brown had been right.

When all the shouting and signing was over, Sol and I walked together to the elevator. "What made you change your mind and sign?" he quietly asked.

"It was Diana on the phone," I replied. "She didn't want you to have a heart attack."

"Best fucking thing about you is your wife," he said, as he disappeared behind the closing elevator doors.

# Chapter Fifteen
## AMERICAN ROLL-UP

Hotel Properties of America (HPA) was the rather bland but all-encompassing name that Jim and I chose for our 'roll up' hotel company. Having established that the American Stock Exchange was willing to grant us a listing, providing that our new company's market capitalisation exceeded $100 million, we now needed to get to work. I decided to look for a few key executives to assist, initially with the acquisition process of the hotels, and thereafter, with their management. For starters, I would need a chief financial officer, an operations manager and a project development manager. This was not going to be easy, since I would be asking highly qualified executives to join an organisation that could be stillborn. On the other hand, if they could help me to deliver a large and healthy baby, their individual rewards through HPA stock might be substantially more than the salaries they were currently making. We also needed to ascertain whether any existing hotel owners would be willing to 'sell' their properties in exchange for our stock. To do this, we decided to place an advertisement in the *Wall Street Journal* stating that we, HPA, were in the market to buy privately owned hotels.

No sooner had this advertisement appeared than we were inundated with replies from people who wanted to know more about HPA, our plan, our ownership, our net worth, etc. This, of course, meant that the 'selling' to do our 'buying' had begun. Explaining our 'swap your ownership for a joint share of a larger company' plan was not easy. Effectively, we were asking people to give up physical assets under their individual control in exchange for a piece of paper (albeit, eventually, a tradable one) entitling them to a share of a conglomerate of properties about which they knew nothing, managed by others, of whom, at this stage, they also knew nothing.

Although we had prepared reams of paper to explain the details of the scheme, we quickly realised that the best way to explain it was personally, initially by phone. This enabled us to gauge the reactions of the would-be sellers, to anticipate and answer their questions, and to allay their fears. In many cases, this was simply not possible. A substantial number of enquirers, having heard the pitch, just rang off. Others, however, were intrigued, and the more one could explain the logic of the plan, the more they listened and the more they wanted to know. In some cases, our first contact was with advisers of owners, i.e. accountants or lawyers. In some cases, it was directly with sellers. In all cases, it was very, very time-consuming, and between Jim, Don Buch (an ex-Southern Sun and Oppenheimer employee who had decided to join us) and me, we spent many hours on the phone with over two hundred enquirers.

Before long, we had whittled the list down to about 120 potential hotels to be acquired from possibly eighty to ninety owners, since several sellers were multi-unit owners. The next stage was to visit the properties, which were spread across forty of the fifty states in America. This was something that had to be done quickly, whilst the iron was hot. We agreed that before we would actually put in an offer for a hotel, I must personally inspect it, but for the first round of viewings, we divided the task between Frank Hughes (our newly hired CFO), Jim Levi, and me, whilst Don mainly stayed back in the office as a coordinator. Despite this division of labour, I still had over eighty properties on my initial inspection list, with only about thirty days to complete it. I have done more than my share of traveling, but the schedule I now embarked on for the next thirty days or so was the most strenuous of my career. With Don as my travel coordinator, I crisscrossed the USA by air and road in a nonstop whirlwind of inspections, meetings, questions, and explanations. I visited at least two towns per day, and not only did I have to tour each listed property, but I also had to inspect the competitive properties nearby, as well as to spend time with sellers and their attorneys and advisers, not all of whom, of course, were convinced that this madcap plan was the best thing for the health of their clients' net worth.

Many of the properties were 'dogs' on which I wasted as little time as possible. Some were gems and needed more time, particularly with the sellers. But the most difficult ones to assess were the characterless nationally franchised properties, which almost all looked the same, but with different signage. I walked through so many double-banked, two-storey, flat-roofed, metal-frame-windowed, stale-smelling motel buildings that it became very difficult to summon up any enthusiasm for anything in middle America with the name Holiday Inn, Ramada or Best Western. Nevertheless, they were technically for sale, and although potentially obsolete, were, in many cases, still enjoying high occupancies and had to be considered for our purposes. Under these circumstances, visiting so many towns in such a short space of time, one would have thought that everything would become one massive blur, but surprisingly, perhaps because I had to concentrate so hard on the task, these towns that I visited are still refreshingly clear and distinct in my mind. Not that I could answer a quiz on them, but in most cases, something about each town or city stands out in my head when its name is mentioned. Most towns in the USA might look alike in some respects—with Burger Kings, Pizza Huts and KFCs—but actually, they all have their individual histories and marks. I also have an overriding memory of how polite and helpful people generally were. I was struck by how full the church car parks were on Sundays.

With the initial recce completed, we gathered together at One New York Plaza to compare notes with a view to establishing a hit list of desirable properties for the portfolio. This resulted in a shortlist of about sixty-five properties that seemed to fit our initial criteria and whose owners were still interested enough in the plan, without commitment, to want us to proceed to at least establish a value. We now commissioned an engineering company to carry out a detailed inspection of all sixty-five properties, utilising a thorough checklist drawn up by the engineers, Don and me. This was the sort of inspection that you would ask to have done before buying a home, but it extended into assessments for fixing up any problems that were discovered, though not into the subjective realm of how a property might be substantially transformed to capture its potential.

Then came the hard part: how to actually establish a value for each property in an equitable fashion. Each seller would obviously want to know that his property was being evaluated on an identical basis with the others in the proposed portfolio. Actually, each seller was hoping that his property would be evaluated more favourably than any other in the portfolio, but could be quickly persuaded that any irregularities or inequalities might backfire. In the main, therefore, they would be happy if we could convince them that they were being treated fairly. To achieve this, we commissioned the accounting firm of Laventhol & Horwath to come up with a valuation matrix, as well as to actually carry out a financial feasibility study for each property on the list. It was then planned that we would be able to value each property based upon a multiple of its potential future returns; the multiple would be varied according to the value matrix. For example, one of the considerations in the matrix would be age. A new hotel would score maximum points in this category, and points would be reduced for every year the hotel had existed. At a certain stage, age could mean added value, and hotels of historic interest could even expect to be awarded almost the same number of points as new ones. Most of the categories on the value matrix were quite subjective, and eventually I would find myself spending many hours defending our value decisions in the face of uncomfortable sellers. In the end, I realised that I simply had to convince them that even if our value judgments were wrong, as long as the same judgments were applied to all sellers, ultimately nobody would suffer.

The next complication in the process was to deal with the lenders. In most cases, the hotel properties for sale were heavily mortgaged. If a property were to be sold, either the mortgage would have to be paid off or rolled over to the new owner. Obviously, since the seller was not going to get any cash proceeds from the sale, he could not pay off the mortgage, so this meant that not only did we have to convince the sellers of the merits and safety of our plan, but we also had to convince bankers to leave in place mortgages on properties that would now be owned by a conglomerate.

Banking in the USA was somewhat different from Europe and many other countries. Since the Great Depression, banks had not been allowed to trade on a national basis. Banks were, as a result, very regionalised, and, in many cases, traded only in the small towns where they were domiciled. It was not possible, therefore, to sit down and explain our HPA plan to a few high-powered national bankers. No, we had to visit with and explain HPA to literally scores of small-town bankers across the country. Many of these, although extremely well-thought-of in their own communities, were not exactly men of the world, and were naturally quite suspicious of any financial scheme that had been cooked up by some whiz kids in the Big Apple. They were probably right. Nevertheless, we had to set about convincing them, and, visit after visit, we painstakingly trotted out our plan. Many of them never understood it, or, more likely, did not want to let on that they had understood and rejected it. But some bought in; they were generally impressed with the name Oppenheimer, and, in other cases, thought that their chances of getting their loans back from a company listed on the American Stock Exchange were a good deal brighter than from some of the existing owners.

Gradually, after about three months of nonstop travel, and after the completion of over fifty Laventhol & Horwath feasibility studies (probably the largest job of this nature that they had ever been commissioned to perform), we began to arrive at a point where we had established a list of about forty properties on which we thought we would be able to formulate some sort of purchase offer. What began to emerge, however, was the possibility that unless almost all of the sellers of these forty hotels could be persuaded to accept our offer, we would run the risk of falling short of the $100 million market 'cap' required to obtain our listing. This would obviously represent an 'all fall down' scenario, and months of effort and expenditure would have been wasted.

To play safe, the temptation started to creep into our thinking that we should not pitch our offers too low, because by doing so, we could run the risk of rejection but could also finish up short of the magic $100 million. A strange dynamic, therefore, entered our activities. We were about to formally put out offers to the sellers, but found ourselves very tempted to deliberately overpay. Why would it matter, we rationalised, as long as everybody got overpaid pro rata? The real value, we convinced ourselves, would eventually only be evident by the value of the shares in HPA after we had commenced trading. In other words, if we had indeed overpaid for the hotels, this would be recognised eventually by the market, based upon the future performance of the properties, and a seller would, sooner or later, get the right price for his hotel by selling his shares.

Through this somewhat self-serving logic, we soldiered on with a view that if all of our acquisitions were to go through as scheduled, we would just scrape past the $100-million mark and all would be well. But all was not well. What we had failed to recognise was that whilst we were busy scheming how to manipulate our own rules to keep the plan alive, sellers and their hordes of advisers were also busy scheming how to gain special advantage for themselves.

It had become apparent to a couple of the multi-hotel owners that their particular properties were crucial to the success of the enterprise, and this was particularly true of one owner in California, who had submitted seven properties for sale. With only weeks to go to the grand closing, we were hit by his bombshell. Unless we were willing to grant him additional stock, e.g. half of the stock we had reserved for Oppenheimer and management, he would withdraw his hotels. Without his hotels, he had correctly calculated, HPA would not get to the required market 'cap'. Unfortunately, he was right. We tried talking him out of his stance, which was clearly blackmail, but to no avail. We offered him other inducements, such as a share of the management fees, but also to no avail. We could not give him what he was demanding, because there were a few other multi-owning sellers, and this would clearly be the thin end of the wedge. There was nothing else for it but to abort our plan.

After six months of the most strenuous task I had ever undertaken, we were dead in the water. Not only had Oppenheimer spent millions of dollars on salaries, surveys, travel, feasibilities, valuations and the like, but the few hardworking and enthusiastic executives that I had lured away from their steady jobs would now be thrown out of work. The baby had been stillborn. Jim and I were very distressed, but we only had ourselves to blame. Had we have really thought through our plan properly, we perhaps could have avoided the multi-owner pitfall. Or maybe we were just plain unlucky.

It was now time for a council of war. Jim, Don, Frank, our new recruit Heinz Stiehl (who had been hired as our hotel operations executive) and I sat down with some senior Oppenheimer executives to 'talk salvage'. What, if anything, could we rescue from our creation? We still had a list of hotel properties that were for sale and upon which we had agreed a price. What if we were to abandon our stock-swap scheme and offer cash? Surely the sellers would be happy to receive cash instead of paper. After all, these deals were ready to be done, and indeed, we had even convinced the lenders to stay in place. If, therefore, we could find a pot of cash, we ought to be able to proceed, albeit on an entirely different basis. But now came the $64,000 dollar question: since I had to admit that there had been a tendency for upward drift in the purchase prices whilst I was offering stock, was it feasible to offer the same price for cash? On the other hand, what could the rationale be for offering less? By so doing, one would be admitting that the original prices offered had been improperly inflated.

It was now that the Oppenheimer bankers' mentality

came to the fore. Apparently, there was a flourishing market in creating investment opportunities in companies that would for a few years produce substantial paper losses, through advanced depreciation and capital expenditure, whilst building up substantial asset value in the future. Investors were looking for paper losses, to offset their tax liabilities in other, successful ventures. Hotels for which one was possibly overpaying and which needed immediate renovation seemed to fit neatly into this category, and it was not long before the Oppenheimer accountants were selecting, from the hotels available for sale, those that, if amalgamated into a new company, could provide an interesting tax-shelter investment vehicle for Oppenheimer customers. Through this device, Oppenheimer could recoup in commissions and fees some or all of the expenses incurred during the aborted roll-up.

After much tweaking of financial projections in the computer, sixteen of the hotels from the list were selected as candidates for the new company: those being the ones with the highest debt and the lowest cash required. Even then, the numbers still did not work too well, as it seemed more debt was required. The solution was to offer the sellers some cash, but to ask them to take back some paper (debt) on their properties, which would be subordinate to the existing debt, and therefore at high risk. The other solution was to apply high inflation rates to the financial projections. This had the effect, on paper, of increasing revenues going forward faster than expenses, since interest expense on the debt would be a high fixed proportion of these expenses. It is wonderful what one can do with profits in paper projections!

Finally we got the numbers to look attractive, to both potential investors and the sellers. It was then left to Jim and me—but principally me, because I had the closest personal relationships with the sellers—to advise them that Plan A was dead, but Plan B was better. We succeeded with the owners of fourteen properties; very quickly, Oppenheimer's sales force, armed with an investment memorandum strewn with warnings that this was a high-risk investment, went to the market, and, with a good deal of help on road shows from Jim and me, raised the required money. So we eventually had our 'grand closing', but this time with fourteen properties, four of which were owned by one owner and three by another. Not quite the grand closing we had originally envisaged, but nevertheless, something of a miracle and a tribute to the determination of Jim Levi, who just would not give up.

One of the hotels in the pack was from the Californian owner who had successfully spiked the roll-up. Even after the closing, this seller had a sting in his tail. The San Franciscan was a large property near the Civic Center in San Francisco. As in almost all hotel acquisitions, the seller had provided paperwork that included the number of rooms, and their historic occupancy and average rate. As part of our 'due diligence', we had visited all of the different room-types at random. We had not, however, actually counted them. This, it turned out, was a huge mistake, because it soon became apparent, upon the commencement of business, that our current operational numbers did not relate to the history. There was a good reason. The hotel had 100 rooms less than the seller had purported, and he had fraudulently adjusted the statistics. We were furious, and Jim in particular was apoplectic. Naturally, we sued on behalf of our investors, and eventually damages were agreed, but this was just an example of one of several nasty surprises that we received. I was soon to find out the real meaning of caveat emptor—let the buyer beware!

I now found myself as the president and part-owner of a new hotel-management company with fourteen hotels in nine different states, but mostly in the same state of disrepair. In raising the purchase money from the investors, we had also raised sufficient funds for the renovations, and it was this work that we now attacked vigorously. The results were generally very pleasing, and in some cases, we won some awards, but the operating results fairly quickly started to fall behind the projections, and so, as always, cash (or lack of it) became an issue. Not that we weren't inventive, and we certainly tried as hard as we possibly could to turn the properties around, but in some cases, it was difficult to be original. After all, how much different can you make one Holiday Inn from another? And the synergies regarding costs that we had expected from the original roll-up were not exactly easy to achieve with only fourteen hotels spread across nine states. In each individual case, we came up with a plan, both for refurbishment and ongoing marketing, and there was no doubt that we managed to impress the sellers, who were now still extremely interested because of their retained seller debt.

One of my favourite plans involved the renovation of the old Warwick Hotel in New Orleans. The plant was tired and obsolete, and it had been overtaken by a bevy of shiny new hotels in better locations. The Warwick was, however, situated next door to New Orleans' famous Super Bowl, and any renovation or repositioning cried out to have a sporting theme. With this in mind, I hit upon the idea of the Players Hotel. We decided that each room should not be numbered, but should be named after celebrity athletes and decorated with a few of their personal possessions. The hotel had 180 rooms, and we planned to name at least 100 of them, leaving others for future opportunities. For example, I managed to strike a deal with *Sports Illustrated*, America's leading sports magazine, that each new year we would publish the Players Hotel New Year's Honours List, wherein we would honour five new players per year by naming five additional rooms.

To get the personal possessions from the sports personalities, I decided that they needed to be approached direct. Since the only thing we could offer in exchange for their possessions would be the honour of having rooms named after them as well as free accommodation if they were ever in New Orleans (which we gambled would not be often), I knew that to approach them through their agents or management would be a waste of time, because there could be nothing in it for the middlemen.

It was summertime, and our daughter Sarah was looking for a summer job between university semesters, so here was a perfect assignment. The guys in the office soon came up with a long list of famous sportsmen and women, covering all known sports, with a truly international flavour, but an obvious bias toward the USA. Sarah's job was to find them. I gave her free rein. If she had to talk her way into the locker room at the US Open, that would be okay by me. In some cases, it was easy. Some personalities actually seem to want to be found. In others, it was more difficult, and she had to call in favours from friends and ex-colleagues to get to people, but she was amazingly inventive, and it was not long before we started to fill up a spare office with the craziest collection of sporting memorabilia. In her pitch, she specifically asked that they did not send items of value. What we were looking for were things like photos of the personalities as babies, their first school reports, letters from friends, etc.—things that we could frame and hang on the wall.

What we got was incredible. Racing drivers sent us helmets and whole suits that they had been wearing at Indianapolis, footballers sent us their complete kit, many sent us cups and trophies and medals, and some sent us so much that we could not possibly have used it all. We practically needed a whole room for the English cricketer Geoff Boycott's contribution; he must have been moving home.

Finding enough material to decorate a hundred rooms was proving to be easier than I had envisaged.

For the restaurant and lobby, we had another idea. The most famous sports painter in America was, unquestionably, LeRoy Neiman. Neiman's paintings of landmark sporting events were legendary. We decided, therefore, to decorate the public areas with his work. They would have to be prints, because the originals sold for tens of thousands of dollars, but what, I thought, if I could interest LeRoy in backing a restaurant called Neiman's? With this thought in mind, I tracked him down to his studio on Manhattan's West Side and paid him a visit. My proposition was that in exchange for allowing us to use his name, and for him lending us artwork, we would give him 1% of the restaurant revenue. LeRoy loved the idea, and like all good deals, it was done in a flash, on a handshake.

In the corner of his studio was a painter's filing cabinet, to which he enthusiastically took me. "Choose your paintings," he commanded as he pulled open drawer after drawer in which were stored fine-quality prints of his most famous work. As I sifted through, making my selection, Leroy grasped them one by one, took some coloured cokie pens, and instantly individualised and flamboyantly signed each print. "There," he beamed, when he had finished, "there won't be another restaurant in America like Neiman's." The prints were fantastic. Every one was of a sportsman in action, except one, to which my attention was instantly attracted. This painting was not of a sportsman but a dancer, Mikhail Baryshnikov.

"What is he doing here?" I asked. "He's not a sportsman."

"Sportsman he may not be," came back the reply, "but in my opinion, Baryshnikov is the most gifted athlete in the world. That's why he's there."

This was my lucky day. Our eldest daughter, Sue, had on

many occasions during Mikhail's career stood outside stage doors, hoping for a glimpse of her hero. I explained this to LeRoy.

"Give her this from me," he boomed, and taking out his cokie pen, scrawled all across the picture of the leaping dancer: "To Sue, with best wishes, LeRoy Neiman."

Alas, Neiman's was not to be, nor was the Players Hotel. Cashflows from the unrenovated Warwick were not up to forecast, and before we could proceed, the lenders had moved in, insisting that we sell the place. We pleaded with them to let us continue with the renovations, but to no avail. Eventually, they pulled the plug, and I reluctantly sent back all the helmets, bats, balls, suits, and so on to their owners, with a letter of deep regret—a letter which came straight from the heart.

Most of the other hotels fared better, but, having completed the renovations, and set up the management and reporting systems, the operations became quite boring. It was therefore with some relief that I managed to persuade the partners at Oppenheimer, who had no stomach for expansion, that they should buy me out of the management company and let me go onto other things. I had not actually decided on what the "other things" would be, but I had no appetite for the mundane.

Several years later, I learned that the Oppenheimer partnership that owned HPA had run into financial difficulties. Inflation, which had been running at over 8% during the time of the formation of HPA, had fallen to below 3%. The projected inflation in room rates had, therefore, not materialised, and revenues were falling far short of those described in the offering memorandum. Many investors were challenging the accuracy of the feasibility studies in the memorandum, as well as the purchase prices paid for the properties.

Eventually, a group of investors from Texas initiated a class-action lawsuit against Oppenheimer and Laventhol & Horwath, claiming misrepresentation in the offering memorandum. To prove their point, it seemed, they would be very interested in having me as their witness. To disprove their point, it appeared that both Oppenheimer and Laventhol would be pleased to offer me a consultancy contract to work on their defence. Offers, it seemed, were coming at me from all sides. The investor group was claiming over $50 million in damages, and all parties needed my testimony—as long, it seemed, that my memory would conveniently serve them. When the stakes are high, I get cautious. I decided to reject all offers and to appoint my own legal counsel—but whom to get? It was then that I remembered Shep Broad, the talented attorney in the Fontainebleau case. I tracked him down to his home in Fort Lauderdale, to which he had happily retired, now an old man.

"Of course I remember you. The Fontainebleau!" he bellowed down the phone. "How can I help?"

I briefly explained.

"I'm sorry, my boy, but I'm retired. I don't take on cases now. But this does sound interesting. Big players. Wall Street. Maybe I could help. But I don't travel. If they all want to talk to you, they'll have to come to Fort Lauderdale."

The thought of the top litigators from New York and Texas being forced to come en masse to Fort Lauderdale for discussions with me and my attorney, Shep Broad, obviously appealed to this retiree, whose ego was still intact. After only a short period of consideration—about ten seconds—he suddenly said, "All right, young man. I'll take the case. Come to see me."

Within a few days, I found myself in a dining room at Shepard's house, describing the Oppenheimer HPA syndication. Having heard me out, the old man suddenly said,

"I'm going to give you two pieces of advice. The first is: 'Beware of Greeks bearing gifts.' Has anyone offered you anything?"

"Yes," I replied, and described a proposal I had received from Texas.

"Did you take anything?" he asked.

"No," I said, although I must admit I had been tempted.

"Good. Remember, no matter how careful you are, it always comes out in the end."

For the second piece of advice, he asked me to follow him into his study (or 'den', as it is known in America). There on the wall, behind a desk, was a huge blue marlin trophy with a plaque beneath, on which was inscribed: "I'm here because I opened my mouth!"

"That," said old Shep, "is the best piece of advice I can give you."

The case never reached the courts, but for many months, Shep had real fun, insisting that every lawyer involved from New York (representing Oppenheimer), Washington (representing Laventhol), and Houston (representing the plaintiffs) visit him in Florida. For a few months, Shep was again on centre stage. He loved the attention he was getting, and since he was a legend in his field, the lawyers equally enjoyed their visitations, despite Shep frequently nodding off during the consultations. Not long after the settlements were reached, the famous firm of Laventhol & Horwath went out of business.

# Chapter Sixteen
## TREASURE ISLAND

I had not been sorry to part company with Oppenheimer. I had enjoyed working with Jim Levi very much, and was proud of what we had achieved with our little hotel company. It had been a privilege to work with a team of enthusiastic professionals like Heinz, Frank and Don. Although, shortly after HPA became operational, we had moved out of high-rent Manhattan to our own leased offices at the back of a warehouse in Stamford, Connecticut, we were still very much connected with Oppenheimer, and I was soon to learn that these were investment bankers, not operators of businesses. Their goals were all short-term. They were buyers and sellers of properties. I wanted to be in the hotel business with a longer horizon. I had not been used to buying with a view to selling; I had been used to buying with a view to owning and enhancing value over the long term. In short, Oppenheimer and Venison were not a perfect match. To make HPA work, and to create the synergies that we had been looking for, it had to grow. Oppenheimer, it seemed (having recouped its costs on the aborted roll-up), had lost interest in the hotel-operating business, and was not willing, for the moment, to acquire new properties. It was not prepared to bend, and therefore, I was not prepared to stay.

I also wanted to find a way of life where I could spend

more time with my family, with less business travel and more quality time at home, particularly with my youngest two children. I had not spent enough time with my eldest, Sue and Simon, and now they were gone—not gone off the planet, but far enough removed to have their own lives. Sue was married in London and had started her own family, and Simon was working his way up in the hotel business on various assignments between London and New York. Sarah was still in high school in Scarsdale, but was getting ready to apply to universities in the USA; and little Jonathan, in middle school, was no longer so little. Jonathan was one of the best sportsmen in his class, particularly at soccer, and, like all proud parents, I thoroughly enjoyed watching him score plenty of goals for his team, and was irritable if business kept me away from the matches.

In our school district, the children were given very long summer holidays, and it had become the norm for many parents to send them away to summer camps for anything from one to eight weeks. Jonathan went to various camps each year, although never longer than four weeks per summer. It was on one such camp that he had been spotted by a representative of the Nick Bollettieri Tennis Academy, who wanted him to go to Bradenton, Florida for a trial. Bollettieri was an ex-Marine who had somehow or other become the tennis pro at a resort hotel on Longboat Key, Sarasota. It was here that he had started his first academy, having gathered together a handful of kids with potential, housed them in mobile homes, and drilled them for hour upon hour on a tennis court at the club, until they could return balls almost by remote control. One of his first pupils was a young man called Jimmy Arias, who had gone on to be a top-ten professional and brought Nick a certain amount of credibility in the tennis world.

Nick had subsequently acquired land, with the help of

some backers, in nearby Bradenton, where he had developed a substantial tennis centre with fifty courts and enough quasi-dormitory accommodation for 150 youngsters from eleven to seventeen years of age. He had surrounded himself with a few excellent tennis coaches and a large group of (mainly South American) has-been or would-be players, who were able to 'feed' balls to the students all day, like human ball machines.

During term time, the inmates at Bollettieri's attended one of two local schools for academic training every weekday morning from eight o'clock to twelve noon. They were then bused back to the academy for lunch, and by one o'clock, they were all on the tennis courts being drilled into tennis robots. The academy took in both boys and girls, who were mainly separated on the courts (I say 'mainly' because Monica Seles, who was at the school with Jonathan, almost exclusively hit with the boys). They were both divided into eight talent groups, irrespective of age. Matches were played on a regular basis, and the results were recorded in a ladder for each group. Once per week, players from lower groups could challenge players from the lower echelons of the group above. Two consecutive wins over players from a higher group were required for upward movement from group to group. Nick's academy was highly disciplined. Youngsters spent hour upon hour hitting the same shot until Nick's instructors were happy that they could do it in their sleep. His methods were being rewarded with success, and gradually quite a few of the top hundred players in the world rankings appeared to have spent time at Bollettieri's. Professional players also went there for 'tune-ups' or to iron out difficulties with their game, and when the young inmates were on vacation, the academy was opened up to adults, who paid hefty fees for weeklong tennis instruction, whilst sleeping in the students' fairly basic accommodation.

To keep the flow of potential students from drying up, Nick used to send his spotters to summer camps, looking for youngsters who had some potential and had parents with enough money to pay the fees at the academy. It was one of these scouts that had found Jonathan. The sales pitch was clever. Potential students were told that it was very difficult to get into the academy (and therefore an honour), but that once in, the possibilities of achieving fame and fortune as a professional player were not out of reach of anyone who was prepared to work hard. Parents were told that, at the very least, the students could expect to win lucrative tennis scholarships to universities, thereby holding out the probability that most of the money paid to Nick could be recovered at a later stage. Although this was not entirely unjustified, needless to say, there were variations on the downside, as we were to find out.

Our Jonathan was thrilled with the idea of going to Nick's, and so we somewhat reluctantly consented for him to undergo the trial. By coincidence, my sister and her family had recently relocated from France to Sarasota (near Bradenton) because her husband's company had a factory there, so we justified the trip with a dual purpose. Jonathan had been accepted—the honour!—so we were faced with a decision: not only a financial one, but also because the thought of our last child moving away from home was very tough to take. Diana had, for certain periods in her childhood, been sent away to boarding school, and remembered it as a very happy time, notwithstanding that she had a very loving relationship with her foster parents. She was, therefore, not totally opposed to Jonathan going to Nick's. On the other hand, Jonathan was the last of the brood, and it would be a great sacrifice to let him go. Eventually, his enthusiasm to give it a try won us over, and it was not long before we had tearfully abandoned him in Bradenton.

Now, with the end of my involvement with Oppenheimer, there was no real need for Diana and me to stay in New York. Sarah had started her tour of American universities and was settled into Ithaca College as a boarder, and Jonathan had made good progress at Bollettieri's and wanted to stay there. It was Jonathan who suggested that we move to Florida, and so within weeks, it seemed, we had concluded a deal with Nick to rent a house from him that was superfluous to his requirements. Nick had several houses that were superfluous to his requirements; they had been acquired, it seemed, at about the time of each wife (at the time of writing he is on his ninth – wife, not house!). In this case, he had only ever used the house for one night. He loved it, but not so the wife of the day. It was located right on the most fabulous beach at the north end of Longboat Key, about a fifteen-minute drive from the academy, so Jonathan could now live at home and still attend his beloved tennis school. Longboat Key is a long, thin barrier island stretching from Sarasota in the south to Bradenton in the north. Diana described the north end as "the Harlem of Longboat Key," because it was the poorer end and somewhat unkempt. The south end, by contrast, had been very heavily manicured and was full of high-priced condos, golf courses and private marinas. Diana and I loved this spot. We could walk on a wide, deserted white-sand beach every morning and witness dolphins and pelicans and other seabirds of all sorts. Even turtles cried on our beach as they annually laid their eggs. We loved it so much, in fact, that we soon bought the place from Nick, and I opened a consultancy office a few miles away and acquired a fixed-keel sailboat for when the phones didn't ring.

Our deal with Jonathan was that he could stay at the academy as long as he advanced upwards by at least one talent group every year. This he invariably did by the skin of his teeth—often, it seemed, during the last week of term; but to his credit, for the last two years of his stay, he was good enough to be in the top group with some pretty talented players such as Andre Agassi, Jim Courier, David Wheaton, Mark Knowles and several others who would go on to become successful professional tennis players. In the summers, it was too hot and humid to stay in Florida, and so Diana, with me tagging along when possible, became a tennis parent, carting her offspring to tournaments far and wide, but particularly in Europe and England, for whom Jonathan was allowed to play, having been born in (but never lived) in Surrey.

To be a tennis parent can be a gut-wrenching experience. Tennis is a game with huge swings between sweet success and inexplicable failure—even within the confines of a single match. On the tour, even at junior level, the joy of triumph can be replaced so quickly with the pain of defeat that one's emotions can be in constant turmoil. Your son can be holding aloft the trophy at one tournament on a Sunday afternoon, and be knocked out in the first round of the next tournament by an 'unknown' on Monday morning. Nothing can be taken for granted. Nevertheless, for several years, the tennis circuit became very much part of our lives on a journey that took us (and Jonathan, of course) through US East Coast junior tournaments, to UK junior summer tournaments, to the national championships in both the UK and the USA, to international duty for England, to Ivy League tournaments, and eventually, albeit briefly, to the ATP Pro Tour. On this journey, we met parents who violently chastised their offspring for not winning; players who consistently cheated on line calls; others that tanked matches deliberately; youngsters who could have been the greatest, but did not have the money to stay the course; and petty officials (particularly in England) who were more concerned about the strawberries, cream and blazers than they were about the standard of the tennis.

We also met some charming and often colourful people who enriched our lives. Amongst these was Nick Bollettieri himself. He had never been a great player, but he was someone with an uncanny eye for spotting a flaw in another player's toolkit and suggesting sometimes even the subtlest of change to correct it. Since my office was only a few minutes' drive from the academy, I would sometimes sneak out for half an hour or so and sit unnoticed in the bleachers, watching Nick in a coaching session. He was part bully, part motivator, and the kids either loved him or hated him. Jonathan was an admirer, but unfortunately, Nick was only really interested in the students with the absolute highest levels of talent, and for 'average' students like Jonathan, time on the court with Nick was a rare commodity. Nick would get extremely enthusiastic over a few star pupils and nurture them with a love and dedication far beyond the call of duty. The result of this policy was often disappointing, firstly for Nick, because the star pupils frequently abandoned him as soon as they were famous; and secondly, for all of the other kids at the academy, like Jonathan, who idolised Nick and would have loved to have spent more one-on-one time with him.

Diana and I would sometimes meet Nick on the beach during our early morning walks, and he would tell us how he had high hopes for this player or that player. There was a time when, having been let down by some boys, he told us that he was putting all of his personal efforts behind a young girl he had discovered by the name of Monica Seles. Nick had 'imported' Monica's parents from Eastern Europe, rented them a house next to the academy, and given them both jobs. Monica was to have been Nick's retirement package. Monica's folks, however, had different ideas. In what was almost Monica's first senior tournament, the French Open, she demonstrated everything she had learned from Nick, and, to his utter joy, won it in emphatic style. The joy was short-lived, because at the press conference after the match, Monica's father abruptly told the audience that he, not Nick, would henceforth be Monica's coach. Tough and brusque as he was, after all the devotion to and hopes for Monica that he had expressed, you had to feel sorry for the man. But for Jonathan, the lessons of life were there to be learned: coping with success and with failure; no pain, no gain; you make your own luck. These were not just clichés to our Jonathan; these were real issues to be faced and dealt with time and time again.

In between the tennis matches and the ongoing interaction with the rest of our growing family of in-laws and grandchildren, I had to find time to earn a living. Having a base on the Gulf of Mexico was great for sailing, but not, it turned out, for business. Nobody really needed the services of a hotel consultant in Sarasota. As always, in this business, to be effective you have to 'be there', wherever 'there' is. Various projects came up, mainly in the arena of feasibility studies for banks, loan agencies or emerging nations. One of these jobs was in Liberia, where I was asked to make an assessment, for an American bank, of the tourist prospects for the country, and, in particular, the viability of a hotel in the capital, Monrovia. There had been a lull in the ongoing civil war that had virtually destroyed Liberia. According to reports, things seemed to be peaceful, so I asked Diana if she would care to accompany me. To my delight, she agreed to come; what she found was not what she had expected.

Liberia, to the uninitiated, is the country founded by African Americans who had returned to their roots in Africa to form their own nation in 1847. Though rich in raw materials and despite the early support of the United States of America, Liberia had, of late, not been a success story. Through a series of disastrous governments and a succession of civil wars, the country's economy was in dire straits. The military was now in control; the president was one Sergeant Doe.

Diana and I were billeted just outside of Monrovia in a hotel that had been built for a conference of the Organisation of African Unity (OAU). It is, it seems, de rigueur for all African states, however poor, to spend huge amounts of money on constructing hotels to accommodate other African leaders on a once-only basis for an OAU meeting. This is normally the only time that such hotels are actually full, and the Monrovia Palace (or whatever it is called) was no exception. Ten years old and apparently operated with a no-maintenance policy, it had mainly been converted to apartments for expats who had been unfortunate enough to be seconded for duty in Liberia. We arrived in the dark after a hair-raising trip with a taxi driver who did not recognise red, as in traffic lights—which, mysteriously, were the only things that seemed to work. When we awoke to see our seedy surroundings, we hoped for better things in downtown Monrovia.

I was scheduled for a meeting with a certain Mrs Doe, the minister of tourism (could she be a relative?), at 10 am in the capital. Diana came along as my 'assistant'. Despite having correspondence to confirm our appointment, Mrs. Doe was 'unavailable' and 'not in' when we arrived at a dirty, ramshackle building, which announced itself with a shabby sign as being the Ministry of Tourism. As always, there were lines of citizens hanging around waiting to see Her Excellency, but, alas, she was not there.

"Come back this afternoon," we were encouraged. "The minister will see you then."

With that, we sauntered off to my next appointment,

which was with the minister of finance. He was housed in another old, dusty building, in which one approached his office by going up several flights of creaky wooden stairs. On each landing were antique chairs, so dirty that the patterns on the upholstery were unrecognisable, and the value of the chairs themselves presumably had gone unrecognised by the inmates. It was as hot as hell, but once we were finally ushered into the inner sanctum of the minister's office, the fierce air conditioning was a wonderful relief, like walking into Saks Fifth Avenue on a muggy day. Liberia was a case study in poverty, but here, proudly displayed on the minister's desk, were photographs: the minister skiing with family in Klosters; the minister at the wheel of a super yacht in Cannes; the minister and friends at the United Nations building in New York; the minister with a Rolls Royce outside Claridge's in London. This was the minister who kindly arranged, a few years later, Liberian diplomatic passports for certain associates of mine, for the healthy sum of $17,000 a pop.

The minister was, of course, once he had shown up, perfectly charming, and said all of the things that ministers of finance are supposed to say when encouraging visitors from overseas whose principals might want to invest in his country. When the meeting was over, Diana and I went in search of lunch. We could not find anything close to a restaurant in 'Main Street', but eventually found a place that didn't look too bad in a side street, into which we ventured. After two bowls of vegetable soup and nothing much else, I managed to get the check from our waiter. It came to just over $10, but, regrettably, the smallest note I had was for $100, which I placed with the bill in the normal way. The waiter scooped it up and sidled off through the door in the direction of the kitchen. He must have kept on walking, right through the kitchen and onwards towards Sierra Leone, because he never reappeared with the change. This caused me to have a huge row with the burly restaurant proprietor, who blamed me for offering such a big note and wanted to be paid all over again. Two bowls of soup: $110!

After lunch, we re-presented ourselves at the ministry of tourism. No, Minister Doe was still not available, but she would like us to meet the deputy minister, whose name, for a change, was not Doe. We were duly ushered into a tiny office full of rusty metal furniture, including a desk behind which sat the deputy minister. I explained my mission and told him that I would like to be provided with a few simple tourist statistics, such as annual arrivals of tourists and returning nationals or relatives, average length of stay, etc. "That would be a good idea, if we had that information," announced the deputy minister, "but we do not have it."

I was puzzled, because at the airport the night before, we had been required to fill out a form which was practically as long as my curriculum vitae. "What do you do with the information you collect at the airport?" I asked hopefully.

"It is not available to me," he replied unhelpfully.

"But why?" I persisted.

"I cannot get that information," he answered. "They will not give me the bus fare to the airport."

On hearing these illuminating words, I concluded that Liberia was not yet ready for a tourist invasion.

Upon leaving the ministry, Diana and I took a detour to the beach. Monrovia is situated on the ocean. The beach was theoretically very pleasant, but alas, a shantytown attached to the capital had spread down to and all along it, and the main tourist attraction had become one huge garbage tip. We watched incredulously as a continuous line of locals with an assorted collection of makeshift wheelbarrows arrived at the beach and added to the pile. Many of them used it as a toilet pit-stop. Such a sad sight!

About a year after our visit, Sergeant Doe was captured by rebels, who took great pleasure in filming him as they cut off various pieces of his body and slowly murdered him. A few weeks after this, Mrs. Doe turned up at a mutual friend's house in London to ask his advice on how to manage her Swiss inheritance. "Would you like to see the video?" she gleefully enquired. My friend declined, and, notwithstanding his advice, Harrods very quickly became the main beneficiary of the loot.

In between these consulting adventures, I also had a little dip into property development in London. Fortunately, I hardly got wet. Together with Andrew de Candole, Diana's cousin, who has spent most of his life successfully riding the waves of property speculation in England, we put together a syndication to acquire a block of Edwardian properties in Kensington, with a view to creating a new upmarket boutique hotel, before boutique hotels were the rage. The block was anchored at either end by hostels, one belonging to Imperial College and the other to a central London hospital. One was, it follows, full of students; the other was filled with nurses. The relevance of this was that hostel zoning was a short step removed from hotel zoning. In the centre of the block were two parcels of property. One of these already was zoned for a hotel, but the other was designated 'residential'. It was these two parcels that were originally for sale. Our plan was to buy the centrepieces, obtain options to buy the two end hostels, produce a master plan for the block, and, having obtained planning permission for the whole entity, proceed with the final acquisitions. Having secured the hostel options, we were able to raise enough money for the entire transaction, so we proceeded to go firm on the centre parcels. In order to have some cashflow, whilst we attempted to remove the residents from the occupied building and whilst we worked up the architectural plans, we immediately started to operate the piece with hotel rights as a flophouse hotel, which our son, Simon, bravely ran.

Then our troubles started. They fell into two categories: planning, and sitting tenants. Despite taking enormous care to preserve faithfully the character of the buildings and the street, and, effectively, to build a new structure behind the existing façade, we ran into roadblock after roadblock at the town hall. Having developed quality hotels around the world, I found it exceptionally frustrating to deal with the layers of bureaucracy that confronted me in my own backyard. Here I was met with such stupidity that it soon became apparent to me why London planning had been such a mess since the Second World War. I was convinced that what I wanted to do was to restore the grandeur of the street in a manner that would enhance the area and provide much-needed quality hotel rooms. The existing buildings were in a terrible state of repair, which naturally worsened as the arguments about what we could or could not build dragged on at the town hall. I began to believe that there is a certain type of Englishman who does not actually want anyone else to succeed, and certainly not to make any money. I started to notice how many articles appeared in the press criticising managers for the size of their bonuses; I sensed resentment against people who were lucky enough to have won the lottery, etc. This attitude was quite different from those I had experienced in America and South Africa, but it was an attitude that, without question, prevailed amongst the bureaucrats at the town hall.

Perhaps I could have stomached this aggravation, had it not been for the other stupidity with which we were forced to deal. As the new landlords of the residential building, which consisted of about twenty short-let apartments, we set about notifying the tenants that their leases would not be renewed because the property was to be redeveloped.

In most cases, this presented no problem, but three of the tenants, smelling money, reached for their lawyers, who in turn immediately raced to the courts for protection. The blackmail had begun. Two of the three tenants were not even living in the building. One was a Rhodesian geologist who visited once every other year for a two-week sojourn, and the other was a local Thai restaurateur who lived in the suburbs but who used the place as a convenient bolthole to take the waitress of his choice in the afternoons—his version of split shifts. The third was an Indian who really lived in Ealing but had been holding onto his filthy little apartment just in case a developer, like me, should appear. The demands of the Thai and the Indian were completely outrageous, but ultimately, in the big scheme of things, would have to be met. The Rhodesian did not want money; he just plain refused to move, and somehow secured the protection of the court.

Coupled with this aggravation were the constant visitations we received from the fire department and other government agencies, who kept asking us to spend money on a building we were about to knock down. I had, in fact, just reached the point of total exasperation when I received, quite out of the blue, an offer for our buildings that would return us a healthy capital gain. I did not hesitate. Andrew was not too happy, and Simon would need to look for another venture, but I took the money, distributed it as fairly as I could (including to them), and ran—vowing that I would never be tempted to develop anything in Great Britain again. There were, however, two benefits stemming from the above episode: I got to work with one of my sons and watch the other play tennis during the summer. Both made it worth all of the aggravation.

Consulting work, which I continued during the above tribulations, does have its drawbacks. One of them is trying to set fees for the work. As a consultant, I would often follow the norm and quote fees on a daily or even half-daily basis. The difficulty arises because in order to cover for overheads and preparatory work as well as for pure thinking time (which can often be substantial), it is necessary to charge a fee that, when divided by the hours in a consulting day, on the face of it, always seems to be exorbitant. The other problem for an individual consultant is that you cannot demand a down payment or deposit before you perform any services or part with any ideas. However, once one has performed and the client is the recipient of the services or ideas, it can sometimes be very hard indeed to collect the fees due, and, in such instances, it is impossible to take back the ideas. Making a sensible judgment about just how many ideas to impart to whet the appetite of the client (without giving away the shop) becomes quite an art. For this reason, it is important for an individual consultant to locate clients who have ongoing needs and are, therefore, willing to retain one's services. I was fortunate to have such a client in Alfred Meister, a German tax exile, living in Nassau, Bahamas.

Alfred had a fascinating background. As a very young man, he had somehow 'escaped' post-war Germany and managed to gain entry to the USA (without any of the proper paperwork), where, incredibly, he had joined the army. His lack of proper credentials was only discovered after he had been assigned to guard duties on a highly sensitive military establishment, from which he was summarily ejected and sent back to Germany. His family had owned a small grocery store, which comprised several counters for meats, cheeses, dry goods, etc, from which customers were individually served. Whilst in the USA, Alfred had seen the beginnings of the cash-and-carry warehouse discount stores, which have since proliferated across North America.

With nothing else to do, Alfred had convinced his mother

that he should rearrange their little store by getting rid of all of the display counters, and most of the staff, and turning it into one of the first self-serve 'brown box' shops in Germany, controlled at the exit by a checkout counter and cash register. The family convenience store quickly became a success, and Alfred had soon rented a warehouse, from which he operated the first of many Meister cash-and-carry outlets, which rapidly spread across southern Germany. Alfred sold anything and everything at a discount, including gasoline, and soon Alfred's chain had become a real thorn in the side of the major German retailers. Alfred was a trader. He was not well-educated, he did not express himself well, he was not particularly numerate, was a very poor manager in the organisational sense, and was not competent in matters of accounting. Nevertheless, he was as shrewd a person as I had ever run across. His business instincts were based on the simple things in life. He believed in narrow margins, huge volume, and low, low overheads. He understood the value of location, and he had faith in land.

One day, he had received an offer for the purchase of Meister Stores from the German conglomerate that now owns Metro. It was an offer he could not refuse. It was also an offer whose proceeds he had had no intention of sharing with the German tax collector, and so both he and the proceeds had relocated quite swiftly to the Bahamas. From there, he had started to acquire land, both in Florida and in the Bahamas. This land included Treasure Cay and most of Great Guana Cay in the Abacos, and Salt Cay, the adjacent island to Paradise Island, Nassau. The Treasure Cay land included several hundred acres of developable property, a Trent Jones golf course, a 100-yacht marina, a ramshackle hotel, and the local power and water plant. Its crowning glory was one of the finest sandy beaches in the world; stretched out like a huge crescent, its soft yellow sand

and sparkling azure water was clearly visible from jetliners at 30,000 feet. Treasure Cay's beach was simply spectacular, and many visitors had bought land from Alfred and his predecessor for the purpose of building second homes. Unfortunately, Alfred had been unable or unwilling to control the style of these developments. Architecture was not important to Alfred. He saw beauty in a warehouse, and to Alfred, the cheaper one could build, the more admirable it was. As a result, real-estate sales had been slow, and Alfred had been recommended to talk to me for advice about how to masterplan the remainder of the site, as well the adjacent Great Guana Cay.

Guana Cay was situated about five miles across protected water (the 'hub of the Abacos') from Treasure Cay. It also boasted a fabulous beach, but one more open to the Atlantic Ocean than that at Treasure Cay. Between the Great Guana beach and Europe was nothing but the vast expanse of the Atlantic, yet despite a feeling of being on the edge of the earth as one walked along this beach, it was quite depressing to be frequently brought back to reality by the selection of ordinary domestic trash that washed up with the tide. Here was paradise, with the odd plastic bottle. The real beauty of this island was that, at this stage, it was uninhabited.

The Commonwealth of the Bahamas consists of over seven hundred islands, many of which are not populated and have therefore retained a wild and rugged beauty. It was to this particular part of the northern Bahamas that the European settlers who fought on the side of England during the American War of Independence fled. Dotted around Treasure Cay are picturesque little island villages such as Marsh Harbour, Hopetown and Green Turtle Cay, where the white Bahamian descendants of the American refugees still live, many of them intermarried. Green Turtle Cay has a population of around 500, but hardly more than half a dozen family names. Each island boasts a quaint little harbour, which for generations were hiding places for pirate ships, but now were home to small gaggles of charter pleasure craft. This was a world that few tourists, except the particularly adventurous or the particularly wealthy, had set eyes on. The airports at Treasure Cay and Marsh Harbour were not capable of handling large passenger jets, and the water was far too shallow for cruise ships.

Alfred had, however, pointed out to me, on several fishing expeditions in his yacht, that less than a few hundred yards from the end of Great Guana Cay lay the edge of the continental shelf, where the water depth suddenly and dramatically increased from a few feet to several thousand feet in almost a sheer wall of coral. On one side of this wall, the water was easily deep enough for oceangoing cruise ships, and on the other side, the seabed was shallow enough and soft enough to be dredged. If we could find a gap in the reef large enough for a cruise ship to pass through, maybe we could figure out how to get the cruise ship up close to Great Guana. We studied the ocean maps and explored in Alfred's yacht. One thing we knew: we would never be allowed (nor would we want) to tamper with the live coral. Dynamiting the reef to make an entrance was not a possibility. We were particularly interested in an area where, according to our maps, there was a natural break in the reef, and after careful examination, we began to believe that we had found the required gap, a fact that we soon had verified by closer examination with divers.

Part of my master plan for Treasure Cay and Guana Cay involved the development of a new commercial airport, but this would take a great deal of time and money to realise. The possibility of opening up the hub of Abaco to cruise-ship passengers was potentially much cheaper and faster. The cruise-ship industry from Miami and Fort Lauderdale was exploding. The most popular cruises were 'short breaks': between three and seven days. The cruise ship companies needed destinations to cruise to, and the closer these were to Florida, the cheaper it would be to operate. Also, I observed, the passengers on these ships were being 'sold' destinations on romantic islands, but all they normally saw of tropical beaches were those they could be reasonably bused to from a commercial port. The beach experience for most cruise passengers was simply unacceptable. What I had in mind was the creation of a Robinson Crusoe experience: a private island created just for ships' passengers, where they could buy beers in Alfred's bars and souvenirs in his shop, and swim in his sea with, of course, the snorkelling equipment rented from his boathouse. For the non-beach-lovers I envisaged catamaran trips to the shallow harbours of all the other little neighbouring islands of historic interest. And for those that wanted to stay on for a few days, where could be nicer than Alfred's new hotel on Treasure Cay? This was the dream, and fortunately for me, not only was Alfred a dreamer too, but he also had the money and the guts to pursue his dreams.

I did a little basic research into the cruise ships that operated from Florida—their length, breadth, draft, etc.—and then studied their current routes to ascertain which ones were potential candidates to come to our dream island. Armed with this information, Alfred and I, who knew very little about how cruise ships were operated, drew an imaginary channel on the map that was twice as wide as the largest cruise ship we thought we could handle, and about three miles long from the gap in the reef to calm water in the lee of Great Guana Cay. We then figured that we would need a huge turning circle, because, obviously, the ships could not be expected to back out of our channel to the sea. After some cursory discussions with a firm of engineers, we decided to take some core samples of the seabed under the lines on our map. If what we found was rock, we surmised, the cost of dredging a channel would probably be horrendous; if, on the other hand, it was sand, it might just be an easy job.

One of Alfred's previous crazy ideas had been to grow coconut palms. On a visit to Costa Rica, he had seen how cheap it was to buy foot-high palm trees. On a whim, he had bought 10,000 of them, but in getting them back to the Bahamas, he had balked at the shipping rates. This problem he had solved when he saw an advertisement for an old freighter and barge, which had been rusting away in the Mississippi Delta; he had promptly bought them, together with the ship's captain/engineer. On his first run, most of the coconut trees had died due to exposure to salt water, but on later runs he had been more successful. Alfred's little freighter now became very useful for our new project, and soon it was the home of divers drilling core samples down the length of our projected channel. As luck would have it, the core samples indicated primarily compacted sand, but here and there, rather worryingly, the drill had encountered some fairly solid rock.

The time had come, in my opinion, for some professional advice, and so I began a tour of marine engineers, to obtain quotes for an engineering feasibility study. The cheapest price I could negotiate for this work was $100,000. Alfred balked. "We don't need a fancy feasibility study," he said. "You find me a cruise-ship customer and a dredging company that can do this, and I'll take a chance."

To get things in the right order, I decided to test the market for, in Alfred's words, "A cruise-ship customer." Great Guana Cay was quite a long way north in the Bahamas, and roughly parallel with Cape Canaveral in Florida. Most of the cruise ships that called into Nassau were based in either Miami or Fort Lauderdale, a hundred miles to the south. One major cruise-ship company operated three Big Red Boats from Cape Canaveral. They specialised in three and four-night cruises to the Caribbean and specifically to Nassau in the Bahamas, where they were already indirectly a customer of Alfred's, since they utilised another island, Salt Cay, which he leased out, as their 'beach experience'. A local Nassau pleasure-boat operator ferried the cruise-ship passengers daily to Salt Cay from Nassau Harbour. The cruise ship paid the ferry company directly, but, as part of my consultancy duties for Alfred, I had negotiated a lease of Salt Cay to them for a rent of $1 for every person they landed on the island. Through this arrangement, Alfred only needed one employee, who stood all day, every day, with a clicker, counting the passengers setting foot off the ferries. For the expense of this 'clicker', Alfred was netting $500,000 per year—not bad out of the 2 million cruise-ship visitors per annum to Nassau.

Premier Cruise Lines (the Big Red Boat company) was the 'official cruise-ship company' for Disney, and by far the majority of its business was 'packaged' as four nights in Disney World and three on the ship, or three nights in Disney World and four on board. Armed with this knowledge, I travelled to Cape Canaveral to meet with the co-chairmen of Premier. I proposed to them that they take their smallest ship, a 1200-passenger vessel, and send it back and forth from the Cape to Great Guana Cay. On the three-night cruise, it could leave Florida in the late afternoon, arrive at Great Guana early in the morning, stay overnight, and cruise back on the third night. For the balance of each week, it could do the same, except on this cruise it could stay for two nights at the Cay. I explained that Alfred and I would arrange to dredge a safe entry and anchorage for the ship, and that on land, we would develop a tropical island facility, which we would lease exclusively to them. In addition to this, I promised that we would supply tenders capable of taking up to 100 passengers a time on morning and afternoon excursions to all of the neighbouring little harbours which, up until now, cruise-ship passengers had been unable to experience.

Bruce Neimann, one of the co-chairmen and the marketing man, immediately loved the idea. Bernd Hermondsen, the administrator and organiser, was more sanguine. He had heard of this 'madman' Alfred from the lessees of Salt Cay, and he was far from certain that, if left to Alfred, the plan could work. There was, however, sufficient merit in the idea for them to agree to pay Alfred and me a visit at Treasure Cay to examine the plan in more detail. Disney also loved the idea, because try as they may, they had not yet been able to create a decent beach experience for their customers, and this idea, to them, could be a good experiment.

With the fish on the hook, I now had to find a dredging company in a hurry. As luck would have it, I discovered that one of the world's leading dredging organisations had contracted for a major job with the Argentine and Uruguayan governments to dredge the mouth of the River Plate. At the time of my enquiry, the world's third-largest dredge was about to leave Holland—destination: Montevideo. One of the biggest costs involved in dredging, I quickly sussed out, was mobilisation, i.e. getting the dredge to the site. Since I figured that the two South American governments had already agreed to pay for the costs of getting the dredge from Europe, I immediately saw the possibility of a win–win situation for Alfred and the dredging company, if they could be persuaded to make a very slight detour via the Bahamas and if they could get our little job done without arriving too late down south.

Over a couple of phone calls, I convinced their

representative to fly down to look at the job. Fortunately for me, everything would have to be agreed in a hurry, because the dredge was already on the way. If this had not been the case, I very much doubt that I would have been able to cut the deal that I did. All we had to show the Dutchman was the site and our few core samples. To this day, I don't know how we did it, but in a very short space of time, we managed to get him to agree to a fixed-price contract for the dredging of our channel and turning circle at a total cost of $4 million. There were no penalties if it took longer than planned, because I knew that the dredge had more important and lucrative work to do elsewhere. In exchange for a no-time-penalty deal, I traded off their right to adjust the price if they hit hard rock. In short, they agreed to fit the job in and take a chance. They knew that if they finished it in two months, as planned, they would make money; if they ran over by more than a couple of weeks, they would be in the red and would run the risk of suffering penalties in South America.

Before I could allow Alfred to sign the deal, I had two other hurdles to jump. First we had to secure a firm deal with Bruce and Bernd, and then we had to convince the government of the Bahamas that it was all right to dig up the seabed and dump the fill. The first hurdle was tough, and Bernd successfully wrote in the deal all sorts of conditions that were going to be hard to meet. The second was easy. Jobs were almost non-existent in the north Bahamas, because everybody migrated to Nassau. Here, for the first time, was a real initiative that would create employment in the north. The local member of parliament, Hubert Ingraham (who later became the prime minister), was well-respected in Nassau and quite influential. I enlisted his help, and he went straight to the prime minister. Permissions flowed rapidly, again due to the pressure of the one-off opportunity to make use of the dredge, which was relentlessly ploughing its way south. Somehow or other, everything came together in a hurry. I wrote the agreements, and Alfred signed them and paid the money. As the huge dredge inched its way through the break in the reef to start its task, Alfred whooped for joy. So much had come together in such a short time.

On the face of it, dredging is not an exact science, but it is an art. This dredge had something akin to a massive drill on its dredging arm, which loosened up the material and then, like a giant vacuum cleaner, sucked it off the bottom of the seabed and then shoved it through of tunnel of floating rusty tubes to be deposited on either a chosen site on shore or out of harm's way at sea. The art came in sculpturing the channel in the seabed so that the walls remained firm and would not fall, during any weather conditions, into the channel, thereby reducing its depth. To check the work of the Dutch, Alfred and I employed divers to constantly report on progress and quality. To their credit, the Dutch did a magnificent job. To their misfortune, they quickly found that our core samples were not typical, and drill upon drill was smashed upon encountering rock. What was to be a two-month job eventually took four. They lost a lot of money; they never complained.

On shore, I was building the desert-island village. Again, luck was with me in my selection of architect. Dan Duckham had a small practice in Fort Lauderdale; he specialised in restaurants and bars. He loved the idea of building a Robinson Crusoe experience. What we needed was a dining hall, shops, bars, boathouses, jetties and an open-air theatre. Dan came up with the idea of using log construction. Alfred came up with the idea of buying all of the wooden telegraph poles that were being replaced with concrete in Florida. Alfred did a great deal on 3000 of them, and shipped them on his old freighter to Great Guana Cay, just like his coconut palms. Alfred, who was always scouring newspapers and magazines for second-hand goods, also came up with another idea for the onsite employee housing that we knew we would need. One day he spotted for sale a twenty-five-bedroom prefabricated building that was perched on a rig in the Mississippi Delta, where it had been used for housing oil-drilling workers. Alfred figured out that if he could position a barge under the rig, maybe the entire building could be lowered onto it and then towed behind his freighter to the Bahamas.

"How would we get it off the barge and onto dry land at Great Guana?" I asked, being somewhat sceptical of the whole plan.

"Easy," replied Alfred. "At low tide, we'll use a digger to cut out a channel from the beach into the land behind those trees. When the tide comes in, we'll float the barge down the channel, and then fill in the channel behind it. Easy!"

This was the same Alfred that had described to me how, back in Germany, in the days he was building Meister Stores, he had convinced the fire authorities to allow him to build fire-escape tunnels under a road at only five feet high, in order to save two feet of building costs.

"Have you ever watched people running away from a fire?" he had explained. "They put their heads down and go like hell!"

I was still far from convinced about the staff-housing scheme, so I left it to Alfred whilst I concentrated on building the prettiest village possible with his wooden poles. One day, he called me up and asked me to join him in his little Cessna to "inspect the progress" of his freighter and barge. He picked me up at Sarasota Airport, and we flew on for an hour across the Gulf of Mexico. There, suddenly, way below us in the water, was the strangest sight. Alfred's little freighter was towing this enormous building about three times its size, and proceeding at a snail's pace into heavy seas. It had apparently been on the water already for several days, and it still had to circumnavigate the Florida Keys and then go several hundred miles north to the Abacos. Alfred was very excited about his project; I just hoped it wouldn't sink. But sink it didn't, and a couple of weeks later, it appeared on the horizon at Treasure Cay, whereupon Alfred demonstrated, with much pride, the next part of his plan.

Our final important task was to source the tenders. Bernd had stipulated in his contract that our tenders must hold 100 passengers each and must be capable of reaching their destinations from Treasure Cay in less than one hour. This, he figured, would be enough boating time for his passengers, many of whom were not young—one hour to the destination, two hours there, and one hour back. This way, he could offer 300 people trips in a morning, and 300 in an afternoon. This meant that Alfred would have to provide four tenders capable of doing these trips (one reserve) and another tender large enough to shuttle the remaining passengers to and from our Robinson Crusoe Land on Guana Cay. When I had agreed to the contract, I had not envisaged that this would be a problem. I had been wrong. To find a craft of the size required, that could travel at the speed required and also gain entry to a tiny harbour with a very small draft, was simply not possible, except via the very, very expensive jet boat or hovercraft route, which we could not afford. "Never mind," declared Alfred, who loved messing about in boats. "We'll build them."

Florida was full of small-time boat builders. Because of the shortage of time, we needed three of them, which, after much driving from town to town on the Gulf coast, we finally found. Alfred drew for them, in a rough sketch, what was required: basically, two-storey, flat-bottomed, flat-topped platforms with huge outboard engines that could be tilted upon arrival in the harbour. They didn't have to look sleek; they had to float, and go at over twenty knots when full. Alfred took on the role of chasing the boat builders. I concentrated on building the village, and the staffing and equipping thereof.

Our pièce de résistance was our dolphin experience. We had heard of a 'swim with the dolphins' program that was operating in Florida, and of another in Freeport. We went to visit. The Florida programme was minimal, because of difficult government regulations. The Freeport scheme was more interesting. Dolphins, which were kept overnight in pens, were released daily in the open sea, and tourists, having paid a small fortune for the experience, were allowed to cavort with them in the ocean. We concluded that a properly organised 'swim with the dolphins' programme could be a really nice extra activity for our visiting 'cruisers', if we could manage to organise it in a humane fashion. We visited the dolphinarium in Nassau, where, to our absolute disgust, we witnessed two dolphins that were cooped up in a tiny circular concrete pool, where they had been trained to perform tricks in front of a paying audience. The conditions were horrific, and the pool was just about big enough for a tadpole, not two fully-grown dolphins. We decided to rescue them, and after a bit of bargaining, we agreed to pay the owner $25,000 for the two animals.

Back at Great Guana, we were busy building a jetty to receive all of the cruise passengers, and as luck would have it, the piledriver for the jetty poles was still on site. We quickly made a new plan, and alongside the jetty we drove in enough poles to create a two-acre pen in the open sea with the jetty on one side and the beach on another. As soon as we had finished, we went back to Nassau to collect our purchases. We wrapped them in wet towels and took them in a taxi (much to the consternation of the taxi owner) to Nassau Airport, where we loaded them into the back of Alfred's Cessna, having removed the back seats. After a one-hour flight to Treasure Cay in their wet towels, we put them in the back of Alfred's pickup truck, and then finally on his boat across the water to their new home in Great Guana. They had been out of the water for about two and a half hours and were, fortunately, none the worse for their experience. I will swear to this day that, as they entered their new home, broad smiles broke out across their faces. To them, two acres instead of two square yards must have been paradise.

Everything was coming together for the arrival of the first cruise ship to the Abacos. Hubert Ingraham, the local member of parliament who had helped us with the dredging permissions, was starting to pay a keen interest in our progress. One day, he called to ask me if he could visit the building site on Great Guana with me, to see for himself what we were doing. At that stage, I had about seventy Bahamians on the site, and I knew quite a few of them by their first name. I was shocked and somewhat ashamed, I must admit, when Hubert walked around my site and addressed every single man by name, and in addition to this, made some pertinent enquiry about their mothers or fathers or twin sister and so on. A truly impressive politician, I thought to myself at the time. I was not, therefore, surprised to find, some years later, that Hubert challenged for and won the position of prime minister.

As all good politicians do, Hubert was also there on the great day that the first cruise ship arrived. The contractual arrangement I had worked out with Bernd at Premier meant that the ship had to be able to enter our anchorage 95% of the time. In other words, we had a 5% leeway for bad-weather days. If we fell below the 95% mark, all bets would be off, the agreement would be null and void, and Alfred would have a very expensive hole to pay for in the seabed.

On the first day of the schedule, the weather was perfect. Nevertheless, for Alfred and me, it was quite a tense moment as the huge ship edged its way through the gap in the reef and down our narrow channel. To avoid being pushed into the side of the channel by the wind, the captain had to keep up quite a good pace, and there was always some doubt in our minds as to whether he would be able to stop the ship before it ran out of deep water in our turning circle. It was, therefore, a huge relief to me and all concerned that, with all engines in reverse, the forward momentum of the vessel ceased with a few yards to spare. Part of our agreement was that we were obliged to provide the services of a tug in order to assist with the anchorage and the turning process. Alfred had point-blank refused to do this, insisting that his old jack-of-all-trades freighter could double as a tug. It did not take us long to find out that freighters and tugs are different animals.

As the first passengers piled off our tender onto Great Guana Cay I watched their faces light up as they caught site of my wooden log Robinson Crusoe village. "Ooh," I heard one of the first off exclaim, "what a wonderful thing Disney have built here." I was really quite proud of myself.

For a while, I continued to make fairly frequent visits to Abaco, to make sure that things were running smoothly. I knew that the relationship between Alfred and the Big Red Boat guys would be difficult. The Greek ship's captains hated coming into the anchorage, and I have to admit that it was not easy for them. The passengers, however, loved the experience, and sales were very brisk. Alfred, if left alone, was unfortunately prone to cut corners, and as my visits tailed off due to other commitments, this tendency started to manifest itself through poor maintenance and hygiene. It did not take long, therefore, for rows to break out between

Alfred and Big Red, which ultimately caused a suspension of the contract. It did not take long, either, for all of the other major cruise-ship companies from Miami to realise that they had lost a competitive advantage, and within a couple of years, all of the majors had their own private Robinson Crusoe islands.

My final job for Alfred was a different sort of negotiation. I suggested to him that he might be wise to sell the ramshackle Treasure Cay Hotel to a proper hotel operator, and offered to find him a buyer. With his blessing, I began to make some approaches to possible candidates, one of whom was Butch Stewart, the legendary owner of Sandals, the chain of 'couples only' resorts with a very strong base in Jamaica. Butch had not trained as a hotelier. In Jamaica, he ran a successful import agency business, but he had seen an opportunity to acquire a group of rundown hotels from the government for a very low price. After giving each one a lick and a polish, he had started to market his all-inclusive products very aggressively. Butch was not hidebound by the accepted norms of the hotel business. He knew nothing of the 'uniform system of hotel accounts'. He just knew that if you took all the costs away from all the revenues and there was anything left, that would be the profit. He didn't worry that his marketing costs were three times higher than his competitors, or that his food and beverage departments did not make the right departmental profits. He just cared about having full hotels and happy customers. He was expanding rapidly, and had been eyeing sites in the Bahamas. I called him to talk about Treasure Cay. He was very approachable, and invited me to come to Jamaica to visit with him at his home.

He lived in Kingston, but out of town a little and a bit up into the hills. Not exactly Beverly Hills, I thought to myself as I pushed open the gate to a distinctly unmanicured garden. I was greeted at the door by his wife, who told me that he was expecting me and that he was 'through there', pointing to a door off the lounge. On going 'through there', I discovered to my surprise that I was in a bedroom where, propped up in bed, naked (at least, at the top), was Butch.

"Excuse me," I stuttered, "I didn't realise that this was your bedroom. I'll wait outside."

"Nonsense," came back the reply. "Nothing wrong with meeting here."

I had done some selling jobs in my time, but this was the first with a naked man in his bed. In any event, we got on quite well, and he agreed to visit the site.

"Where are you going from here?" he enquired, as I was about to leave.

"Back to Miami," I replied.

Without hesitation, he said, "Take my plane. I'll call up the pilots. You'll have to route round Cuba, though, or they'll shoot you down."

Several weeks later, I had cut a deal with Butch. He put a million dollars down, and had one year to commence rebuilding the hotel, or forfeit the money. He never did build. I never knew why, but I do know that Alfred kept the million.

By now, I had begun to tire of consulting work. It had afforded me the opportunity of spending more time with the family, which had been super. It had also allowed me time to enjoy my boat. There was, however, something about it that was unfulfilling. There was never any closure. Good ideas were, it seemed, either ignored or wasted. I just did not feel that I was creating anything that would last, and, quite importantly, I was not doing anything to improve our net worth. It was lovely living in the sunshine, but Florida is the retirement state of the USA, and I certainly was not ready, nor could I afford, to retire. I started thrashing around for new ideas, and before long, I was focusing on one in particular.

A few years earlier, I had done a consultancy job for a motel owner in New England, who operated a small regional chain known as Suisse Inns. They were simple motels, designed with a slight (very slight) flavour of a chalet. They were clean, bright, attractive, cheap and profitable. I had also witnessed the beginnings of the growth of the Hampton Inn chain and its copycats in the USA. I had, at the time, thought that the UK was ripe for the development of a budget chain, and realising that high land costs were the stumbling block, I had hit upon the idea of utilising railway-station shunting yards and car parks for land on which to build. I had approached British Rail with the concept of a chain of British Rail Motels, all built on land that they already owned, slap bang in the centre of most of the major cities in the UK. I had convinced myself that hotel reservations could be handled through the railway ticketing offices, and that combined rail and room tickets could be sold very easily. I should not have been surprised, after my experiences at the Kensington town hall, that my enthusiasm for a new profit centre at British Rail would not be reciprocated by the lazy, disinterested, unimaginative persons who claimed to run it. I quickly renewed my vow to never try to develop anything in the UK.

It was, however, this research into the world of budget inns that took me back to South Africa, for there, at the tip of the world, a Swiss friend of many years standing, Hans Enderle, had developed a chain of the most outstanding budget hotels in the world, City Lodge. I had a very close look at what Hans had achieved, and for a brief period entered into a negotiation with him to take the concept worldwide. Hans was the first to admit that he liked playing golf too much to be bothered to travel far and wide expanding his chain, and he seemed pleased that I might take on this mantle for him. After considerable thought, I decided that rather than work with Hans, I should go it alone, and commissioned my own architects to come up with something completely different, which would incorporate the best of all of the budget product I had looked at. What emerged was a product I called Green Roof Inns, a colonial version of America's Red Roof Inns, but one I thought would fit well on sites in most African and Australian towns. I then set about putting together the finance, which I ultimately found in Johannesburg, and was on the verge of signing the necessary documents to get going when a secretary interrupted me to advise me that there was a certain Sol Kerzner on the phone from England. I put down the pen and took the call. No Green Roof Inns were ever built.

# Chapter Seventeen
## THE LOST CITY

Sol came straight to the point. He wanted to know if I would work for him again, because he had an interesting project on which he needed help. I told him that I was about to start up my own Green Roof Inn chain: the designs were done and the finance was in place.

"Why do you want to mess around with that boring stuff?" he immediately asked. "Anyway, the rates you'd get for it are so low that you'll never make any real money."

I told him that I'd done a lot of work on Green Roof and that for me to give it up, as well as my independence, would be very hard. I reminded him that after we'd 'made up' following the row on my departure, we had agreed that it would be best if I never worked for him again.

"I'll tell you what," persisted Sol, in a manner reminiscent of when I had first met him all those years ago at the Carlton Tower. "Why don't you come to see me in London before you sign your papers? At least give me the chance to explain what I have in mind."

My plan had been to sign the documents and then leave South Africa for Florida and Diana.

"Well," I wavered, "I could fly back to the States via London. But I'd want to go straight on. I've been away from home for a while."

"That's great. Why don't you come out to Ibstone (Sol's house in the Chiltern Hills that once was the home of Rebecca West) tomorrow for lunch? I can have Manuel pick you up and take you back to the airport."

I called Diana and told her that I was routing home via London; that way I could see Sue and Simon. For some reason, I didn't mention the call from Sol.

Lunch was interesting. Sol was at his most charming. There were four normal possible venues for lunch at Ibstone. One was the large formal dining room, which recently had been completely redecorated at huge expense by Trisha Wilson, but was almost never used (and, in any event, would have been far too big for our tête-à-tête). The next was the small formal dining room near the kitchen on the ground floor. Then there was the little breakfast room, and finally, at the top of some stairs, above the garages, the TV room or den, which housed a shiny rectangular farmhouse table used by Sol as a desk and for meetings. On this occasion, lunch was being served on the "desk."

Manuel did the serving; he doubled as the chauffeur. Manuel was Portuguese. He wore a toupee, which often slipped a bit. He was a lovely man, but he could get flummoxed sometimes by his employer, as, indeed, could almost all of Sol's employees. The unfortunate linkage of Manuel's name to the poor, downtrodden soul in *Fawlty Towers* was inevitable, but any resemblance stopped after the broken English and the job itself. It struck me as odd that we should be eating in the TV room, because this meant that poor Manuel had to make repeated trips up and down the stairs to the kitchen. I can hear him to this day, huffing and puffing as he fetched and carried.

Sol, having been asked to resign some years earlier from Kersaf (as a result of allegations that he had paid a bribe to President Matanzima in the Transkei), had moved to

England. This had always surprised me, because many years before, Sol had emphatically pronounced that there was no way he could ever live in such a dreary place. Not that he was exactly slumming it. Ibstone House was a beautiful home with well over 200 acres of the Chiltern Hills attached.

Sol had acquired a third share of the only casino in Nice and a management contract thereon, as well as a management contract on the casino at the famous La Mamounia Hotel in Marrakech, Morocco, and had plans afoot to add three more casino licenses in France. In addition to this, Sol had acquired ownership of a hotel in the Comores, Le Galawa Beach. Le Galawa, about which I shall explain more later, had been operated unsuccessfully by Sun International after Sol's unexpected departure from South Africa—so unsuccessfully that they had closed it down. In Sol's words, "They fucked it up." Since the South African Development Bank had loaned the government of the Comores the money to build the hotel in the first place, the bank had been looking for ways to get their money back when they approached Sol. He had agreed to take on the hotel, reducing in the process their loans to virtually worthless documents, on which they would only get interest after the hotel had passed certain yardsticks of profitability. At the same time, he had persuaded them to lend him an additional five million dollars at an incredibly low rate, in order to 'fix up the place'. In short, Sol had acquired a ninety-nine-year lease on the hotel, as well as a fantastic adjacent beach site—with everybody else's money.

President Lucas Mangope of Bophuthatswana had been extremely unhappy with Kersaf for forcing Sol to resign and had threatened to cancel the management contract between the Bop government and Sun International for Sun City. This crisis had only been averted by Mangope insisting that

Sol remain as chairman of SunBop, the listed company that owned Sun City and the other resorts and casinos in Bop, and which were managed by Sun International, which in turn was owned by Kersaf. The effect of all this was that Sol had moved from being the chairman of the management company to being the chairman of the owning company in regard to Bophuthatswana, a state of affairs that did not rest easy with the remaining board of directors of Kersaf and Sun International.

For some time, Sun International had been promoting the idea that SunBop should commission a fourth hotel at Sun City, and various architectural plans and renderings had been submitted to the board. Without the flair of Kerzner behind them, Sun International's proposals for the new hotel were distinctly mundane, and Sol, in his owner's capacity, was not shy at pointing this out to President Mangope. Sol had been proud of the innovative nature of Sun City, which had always been a trailblazer in the international hotel world, and he was determined not to have its reputation diminished by the incompetence of his previous colleagues. As a result of this lobbying, Mangope had insisted that Sun International hire Kerzner as a consultant to supervise the design and development of the new hotel. This Kerzner had agreed to do, provided that he was given unfettered authority, a very healthy budget, and a $10 million consulting fee.

It was these things that Sol explained to me over lunch. He had apparently bundled the French and Moroccan casinos, Le Galawa Beach, and the consulting contract into a Kerzner family-owned enterprise called World Leisure. Peter Bacon, my ex-regional manager from the Southern Sun days, was already working for him, but since, as he explained, he now intended to use this platform to grow World Leisure into a force that reflected its rather grandiose name, he needed more executive firepower. His proposal was that I join him, firstly to source new deals and management opportunities, and second, to work closely with him on the design, development, operational planning, and opening of what was to be the Palace of the Lost City at Sun City. Although somewhat tempted by the potential glamour of this opportunity and, to some extent, charmed by the man himself, I did not hesitate in turning him down. I had been through too much pain and trauma with him before. I knew that if you worked for Sol, he owned you morning, noon, and night. It would not be fair on Diana. This I told him.

"Why don't you ask Diana what she thinks?" was Sol's immediate response to my rebuttal, and he then went on to spell out the alluring financial advantages that could accrue to Diana and me, if we were successful. Once again I was reminded of his very first sales pitch to me years ago. "Stick with me," he had said, "and I'll make you a millionaire." Rather than remind him of all the reasons why it would not be a good idea to work for him again, I rather lamely agreed that I would, at the first opportunity, speak to Diana to get her reaction to the proposal. I was 100% convinced that Diana would be opposed, and I saw no reason, therefore, to take the conversation any further over lunch.

That afternoon, I called Diana from our apartment in London.

"Guess who I've had lunch with?" I started.

"Sol Kerzner," came back the reply, like a bullet.

"How did you know?" I said, quite surprised.

"I just had a feeling about it. He wants you to work for him, doesn't he?" Why is it that women are so psychic? "What did you tell him?" she carried on.

"That there was no way I could work for him again. It wouldn't be fair on you or the children. You know what it's like working for him. You never get any peace."

"Let me tell you something," said Diana quietly. "I have discussed this possibility often with the children. I knew that one day Sol would ask you to re-join him. After all, he was never so successful as when you were working together, and he knows it. When I asked the children, they all said, 'If it happens, tell Dad to do it.' I know that you have been successful on your own, but we all think that you were never more alive, more vibrant, or more interesting to be with than when you were working for Sol. And some of that, and the excitement and the glamour, rubbed off on our lives. So I'm just going to say this: if you want to do it, we will not stand in your way."

I was completely stunned. I had no idea that they all felt this way. There were times when I must have been impossible to live with when I had been working with Sol. It was hard for me to understand how they felt. I knew that people tend to look back and only remember the good times—the good old days—but Diana seemed to be saying more than that.

"We'll talk about it when I get home," I said. "I'm on the first flight out in the morning."

Indecision is one of the worst conditions known to man, and in any case, I am a very impulsive person, so within a week we had decided. I would accept Sol's offer, we would return to England as a base, and Green Roof would have to wait. Relocating to England would not be a problem, because we already had a home there and did not intend to give up our place in Florida.

The madness started almost immediately. Before joining Sol, I needed to have a hernia operation, so it made sense to do this whilst still in Sarasota. Although it is a minor operation, one does feel a little groggy the day after, and as a result of the anaesthetic and the region of the operation, one's normal body functions don't work too well for a couple of days. On 'groggy day' and before I was even on the payroll, Sol was on the phone, explaining a deal in Panama which required urgent action. Someone had to go to look at the deal immediately, and since I was 'round the corner', perhaps it should be me. The opportunity, which was to take over the ten casinos currently run by the government, was pretty interesting, but, as usual, a middleman would need to be 'accommodated' and a 'contribution' would need to be made to the ruling political party. It is not illegal to hire consultants, nor is it illegal to make contributions to political parties, but the linkage of these to lucrative casino opportunities is not necessarily very smart in the highly regulated casino industry. On top of this, Sol was still battling the allegations regarding his role in the Transkei and would not be easy to convince that a successful business in Panama was worth a jail sentence. When I got back to England from Panama, Sol was already in a bad mood. I wanted to at least examine ways to get the deal done, but after two minutes of explanation, he was completely turned off, and I wondered why I had dragged myself off the recuperation bed in the first place. Still, Panama had been interesting, despite having my briefcase and air tickets stolen at the airport.

The bad mood seemed to be permanent. Peter Bacon was responsible for running Le Galawa Beach in the Comores as well as being responsible for the casinos. Peter was very experienced and very diligent, but nothing he did seemed to please Sol, and at every meeting between Sol and Peter, to which Sol kept inviting me, Sol berated Peter at the top of his voice in the most appalling language. When these meetings took place at our offices in Henley, the shouting was so loud that every secretary in the building heard him. When they took place at Ibstone House, Manuel would run for cover. Sol's behaviour was so disgusting that I immediately regretted my decision to re-join him. To me, however, he was on his best behaviour. I was still on 'honeymoon', albeit a second one. And besides, the project at Sun City started to take up a lot of my time, and when I was working on this with Sol, his attitude and mood were completely different.

The concept Sol had in mind was spectacular. He wanted to build a hotel that would stand out as a very special place. It would be his tribute to Africa. It would be his calling card for the world. It would be something that would forever etch his name in hotel history. Most important, it was part of his grand scheme for the development of World Leisure. Although it would be known as a Sun International hotel, everyone would know that World Leisure was really responsible for it happening, and best of all, someone else was paying for it.

One of World Leisure's assets was quite useful: our own jet, or to put it more realistically, Sol's own jet. This was a Canadair Challenger, one of the nicest long-range executive jets available—nicer, in my view, than the more popular Gulfstream, because the Challenger was a wide-bodied aircraft as opposed to a flying cigar tube. Our Challenger was fitted out with four very large and comfortable 'first class' leather seats (facing each other in pairs), which could be converted into two six-foot-long beds; at the rear were two seven-foot-long couches, which also pulled out into two extremely comfortable beds. In order to keep on top of the planning and building program at Sun City, Sol and I needed to travel to South Africa very frequently, and during the twenty-four-month construction programme, we probably flew from England to South Africa in the Challenger over thirty times.

On the face of it, this was a great way to travel, but the reality was quite different. Sol was not the easiest of traveling companions. His capacity for normal small talk was negligible. His interests were so entirely wrapped up in his work that he was very hard to be with for long stretches of time, since it was difficult to find topics of conversation that interested him. To Sol, the plane was a refuge. As we climbed up the steps of the plane at Lanseria Airport in Johannesburg after a very hectic meeting schedule with architects, designers, kitchen planners, builders, etc., Sol would sink into his usual seat with a great sigh, just as a normal man sinks into his favourite armchair at home. To Sol, the Challenger was home.

Also, by the time we would reach the airport, Sol would already be halfway through a bottle of Johnnie Walker Black Label, and even before we had taken off, would be, in his most hospitable manner, pouring two more, one of them for me. "How do you like yours?" he would ask me for the thousandth time. "Water or soda?" Sol's whiskies were always poured the same way. He would take a large highball glass, scoop up a handful of ice, fill the glass with ice, and then pour whisky over it until the glass was full. By the time we were in the air, Sol's first drink (on the plane) would have been downed, and he would be up again at the bar. "Ready for another?" he would enquire.

"Not yet, Sol. I'm still busy with this one."

Roughly thirty minutes later, Sol's chin would be touching his chest as he slouched in his seat, still clutching the unfinished glass of whisky. "Go to bed, Sol," I would almost shout, at which he would stumble to the back of the plane, disappear into the washroom, and reappear a few minutes later in pyjamas or track suit and fall into bed. At this point, I would gratefully read my book for a while, and then, whilst the going was good, I, too would turn in for the night. Or at least I hoped it would be for the night, because, more often than not, I would get disturbed by Sol, who had the unfortunate habit of shouting obscenities at the top of his voice whilst still asleep. This was the most amazing, and, initially, alarming phenomenon. He seemed to be reliving his time on the building site. He would sit bolt upright in bed and yell things like "I told you fuckers not to fucking build it here," or "Why the fuck don't you fuckers do what I say?" and so on and so forth. The shouted sentences would always be very loud and clear at the beginning but would tail off towards the end, before starting up again after a deep breath. This performance would go on intermittently for up to a quarter of an hour. During this time, he would never wake up, and he would deny any knowledge of the incident in the morning—but, of course, I, and anyone else who happened to be on board, would be wide awake and often too disturbed to easily regain sleep.

On the nights when Sol did not shout, he would often wake up an hour or so after he had fallen asleep as a result of the dehydrating effect of the alcohol. Since Sol never wore a watch, the only way he could tell the time and thereby check on our progress was to consult the screen, which depicted a little plane creeping across the globe. This screen was, unfortunately, placed at the foot of my bed, but was enclosed behind a hinged panel with a seal around it, to prevent the light from the screen illuminating the cabin at night. Sol, anxious to know if we were nearing the end of our flight, without waking me up would fumble his way in the dark to the end of my bed and open the screen door just enough to let him have sight of the map. His disappointment at seeing the little plane still hovering over Botswana would invariably elicit an "Oh, fuck!" loud enough to wake me, if, that is, I hadn't already done so as a result of the sudden flood of light into the cabin from the screen.

Many years later, I had to chuckle to myself when I had arranged for Geri Halliwell, the Spice Girl, to hitch a ride with Sol in the Challenger from Mauritius to Europe. As they were about to leave the hotel for the airport, Geri appeared, clutching a box of Scrabble and some other board games. Seeing my inquisitive look, she cheerfully volunteered, "I thought Sol might like to play something on the way, to while away the time." One look at Sol, who was already in his pyjamas, nursing a glass of Black Label in the lobby of the Saint Géran, should have convinced her that board games were unlikely. I never did ask her afterwards how the Scrabble went.

Despite these petty disadvantages, the work itself was, as Diana had predicted, extremely challenging and interesting. Sol had assembled a team of professionals to design, build, and operate the Palace of the Lost City and the new world-class entertainment centre at Sun City. We had divided the project into two sections, the first composed of the Palace hotel, golf course and club; and the second, the gardens of the Lost City and a huge new casino and entertainment centre. The architecture and interiors for the latter were being handled by Californian architects Henry Conversano and Paul Steelman, whilst the Palace was being designed by Wimberly, Allison, Tong and Goo, also out of California and being led by Gerry Allison, a partner of the firm. The interiors were by Wilson and Associates from Dallas, using principally Trisha Wilson and James Carry.

With the help of Henry and myself, Gerry had written the 'Legend of the Lost City', to give us all a design framework on which to build. In this legend, we dreamed up an imaginary tribe who, years ago, had inhabited this piece of land. They had lived by the water in a village in a valley. Their ruler had lived in a palace on a hill overlooking the valley. One day, some sort of natural disaster had befallen these 'ancients' and wiped them all out. No drawings of the ancients had been ever discovered, but the ruins of their civilisation had been unearthed, and our job, as developers, was to rebuild and refurbish them for present-day tourists.

This basic story was embellished and embellished as we all worked through the project, but every building and every piece of infrastructure was given the 'ancients test' in some way or other: how would the ancients have done this, how would they have done that, what would they have used this for?

Sol led the team from the front. He was determined that the architecture should be original, that it should be something that had not been seen before—something that was unclassifiable. Time and time again, he rejected the efforts of Gerry and Henry with "This looks too African," or "This looks too Moorish," or "This looks too Arabian," and so on. These discussions were not limited to a few of the team. Sol wanted everyone's opinion. It became a real team effort.

Gradually, a distinctive style evolved which excited all of us and from which we drew inspiration for all of the other design work, whether interiors or operating equipment. Finally we settled on a project that included a palace surrounded by spacious gardens that spilled down the hill to the Valley of Waves (an extensive water park with wave pool, lazy river ride, and slide mountain), and on to the Hall of Treasures (the entertainment centre and casino). My job was to feed into the design team all operational requirements, to select and order all operational equipment, and to hire and train all operational personnel. In addition to this, it was my responsibility to organise the opening of the facility, as well as the related marketing.

Everybody involved was fired up for the job. We knew that we were creating something special… something beyond the envelope. We felt privileged that we were involved. We knew that it was an exceptional project. We crossed the barriers between our respective roles frequently. Nobody minded. The talent fed on the talent.

Although Sol was clearly the inspiration for the project,

the glue that held it together was, without question, the project manager, Dene Murphy. Dene was Rhodesian, having moved to South Africa when his homeland became Zimbabwe. Dene had previous experience in handling Sol, having worked for the builder of the Cascades Hotel (the third hotel to be built at Sun City) a few years earlier. Dene was tough but compassionate. Dene had the highest regard for Sol's ability and loved him like a son loves a father. Sol recognised Dene's strengths and used them—some would say abused them, because Dene would frequently have to step into the breach for Sol when Sol had been on a drinking spree and sometimes didn't appear until midday.

Sol was determined that the opening of this project should be without parallel, and he persuaded Sun International to provide a huge pre-opening and opening marketing budget. With the help of Hazel Feldman, Sun's entertainment manager, we put together a spectacular programme. The Palace was immortalised at the opening by a three-day sound and light show produced by Jean-Michel Jarre, the French electronic musical genius; the staging of the Miss World Pageant; and the Million Dollar Golf Tournament—all within the first two weeks. The Jean-Michel Jarre show made such a splash that even the *New York Times,* miles across the ocean, ran a front-page picture showing the Palace in its full glory, with a news story announcing the opening of the world's most special resort.

The place was awash with celebrities, and it was important that we made sure that they had fun. This meant attending party after party, which for me was quite difficult, because no new hotel runs like clockwork in its first few weeks, no matter how meticulous one has been in planning the operations. I gladly would have given the parties a miss, but I recognised the need to schmooze with the celebs; besides, there is no better way to find out how your hotel is performing than by sampling the wares, i.e. by being there.

Here, Diana was a great help, because she was so interested in others, whether unknown or famous, that everybody got on well with her. She had a certain way with famous people that just worked. She was neither too intrusive nor inquisitive. She treated them with respect, not hero worship. She found out what interested them and gave them a chance to express themselves. Somehow they trusted her. She never interfered with the business, but was always there in the background, supporting it. As a result, celebrities didn't see her as an extension of the business; they saw her as just Diana, a nice, empathetic person with whom they could easily relate and on whom they could rely. This had the effect of making our business more human, and after time, celebrities saw themselves as part of our "family," and they did things for us that money couldn't buy.

One celebrity who ganged up on me with Diana at the opening of the Lost City was Bo Derek. Diana had long believed that Bo was my fantasy girl. (It wasn't true, but no amount of protestations could convince Diana otherwise.) On the opening night of the Jean-Michel Jarre show, which was to take place in the Valley of Waves, I had avoided the celebrity cocktail party, in order to supervise the last-minute arrangements, particularly those involving crowd control. We had erected bleachers at various points in the grounds, and I had reserved the front few rows of one of these for our VIP guests. From past experience, I knew that these seats would need to be protected from gate-crashers, and that to rely on African security would be a mistake. I had decided to be there myself to make absolutely sure that nothing went wrong, and as a result, I had asked Diana to attend the cocktail party for the VIPs and celebrities, and to do what she could to entertain them. Diana had already taken Bo Derek and a few others on a hot-air balloon ride across the game park, so I knew that they would be at home with her.

I, at this stage, had not met Bo. The plan was that I would 'protect' the prime seats, and when the crowd had settled down, our public relations people would escort the VIPs through the grounds to my position on the stands. It turned out to have been the right decision for me to be where I was, and I had my work cut out fighting off the gate-crashers, who all had a thousand reasons why they should occupy my empty seats. I was so busy, it turned out, that I did not notice Bo in the dark, with Diana lurking beyond, ascend the steps to my protected zone. Suddenly, I was taken by surprise when Bo appeared immediately in front of me, saying, "Are you Peter Venison?"

"Yes," I responded, a little taken aback.

"Oh, good" she gushed. "I've always wanted to meet you!" Diana swears that she saw me blush in the dark.

The Palace of the Lost City was an instant success. It was just so striking and unusual that it took people by surprise. Even those determined not to like it found themselves grudgingly admiring it. They were normally people who expected it to be kitsch or fake, but it wasn't. It was solid and original. I often watched with amusement as people did things like tapping on the walls to see if they were real. Their expectancy was that they would sound hollow, like a stage set or, as many of them explained, like Disney. It was only when they grazed their knuckles on the rough concrete, stone, or brick that they knew otherwise. It had its operational design flaws (many of them my fault), but its impact on customers was overwhelming. The attention to detail, whether in the furnishings or the architecture, was outstanding. The gardens were (and still are) spectacular, and so they should have been, since we installed over a million trees and plants. In short, Sol, Dene, me, and all of the crew that had worked on it were very proud of what we had achieved, and all of the disturbed nights on the plane were forgiven, if not forgotten.

My role, I am pleased to say, had not gone unnoticed, and no sooner was my consulting assignment over than I was asked if I would relocate (again) to South Africa to take up the position of managing director of Sun International. The incumbent managing director, Ken Rosevear, was leaving to join MGM in Las Vegas, and after all, I had done the job before.

Apart from the family considerations surrounding this offer, which were obviously troubling, the fact that I had done the job before concerned me greatly. I was not being asked to report to Sol this time, but to the chairman of Kersaf who had replaced him, Mr Buddy Hawton. That was a difference, and an advantage. Buddy did not have hotels and casinos in his blood. Buddy was an astute businessman who had let Ken run the business without much interference. That was a plus. However, to go back in life, no matter how different the circumstances, somehow seemed wrong.

Sol, who would be losing me, was also encouraging me to accept. During the frenetic time of building the Palace of the Lost City, we had had little time to develop new business for World Leisure, which still only owned Le Galawa Beach in the Comores and its share of the casino business in France. Sol now saw his opportunity to merge his World Leisure assets with those of Kersaf, by way of forming a new company offshore from Southern Africa, with the purpose of expanding the Sun International brand overseas. Sol would be the chairman of the international arm of Sun International (which became Sun International Hotels Limited), and Kersaf would supply the necessary funding to grow it. At this point in time, however, the merged international company had no projects, and Sol reasoned that it made sense for me to run the Southern African business for Kersaf, whilst he concentrated on growth overseas for the new joint venture. Once he had got going, he argued,

I could re-join him on the international scene. Meanwhile, I could help the company and Buddy by filling the void in Johannesburg.

Much as Diana loved South Africa, she was not overjoyed by the prospect of returning there at this time to live. Sue, our eldest daughter, was in the throes of a messy divorce in England and needed our support. Jonathan was at university in Manhattan. South Africa was too far away. On the other hand, we recognised that South Africa itself needed all hands to the deck. Mandela had just been released from jail. The country had a choice to make between peaceful or violent revolution. It would be exciting to be part of what we hoped would be the most ambitious peaceful revolution yet achieved by man. There was much we felt we could do to assist in the process, and the ability to do so would be greatly enhanced from the seat of managing director of one of the country's most prominent listed companies.

Unlike our previous career decisions, this was not one to be taken quickly or lightly. We debated it back and forth for many days. Eventually, we decided that I should go for it, although Diana's commitment this time was somewhat half-hearted. She insisted, and rightly so, that she should be free to come and go at will, so as to be there when required by the family. Diana could have suggested that I go to do the job whilst she stayed in England, visiting me from time to time. Instead, she opted for the reverse, probably much against her will, but because of her firm belief in how strong marriages work.

Sol was also probably unsure for how long he wanted to lend me to Kersaf and South Africa, and as a result, he suggested that Diana and I could live in his house in Bryanston, Johannesburg. This arrangement, although extremely comfortable, seemed to add to the temporary nature of the affair. Notwithstanding this, I threw myself into the job with great enthusiasm, and was, in the end, extremely pleased and privileged to have been able to participate in this most important period in South Africa's history.

# Chapter Eighteen
## MADIBA

Like most people who have an interest in South Africa, and many who don't, I will not forget the day that Nelson Mandela was released from prison. I was on the road in North America at the time. To be precise, I was in a Red Roof Inn in Toledo. I was glued to the television. The release time had been announced, but there was a delay. The delay, for any other event, would have been irritating. This one only seemed to heighten the sense of occasion. Finally, there he was, flanked by Winnie, walking proudly but a trifle stiffly through the gates of Pollsmoor Prison to a tumultuous welcome and the world's press. I shed a few silent tears in my motel room. Thinking of that day still brings tears to my eyes. This was one of those defining moments in twentieth-century history. I was, of course, watching it before I had agreed to re-join Sol Kerzner; little did I know at the time that I would one day have the privilege of meeting the great man himself, Madiba, President Mandela.

During the period immediately after Mandela's release, it was far from clear what role he would play in the future of South Africa. The Nationalist Party was still in power. Blacks did not have the vote, but there had been a growing recognition amongst the leadership of the Nats that this would have to change. The question was: how? And when? By one of the greatest strokes of good fortune, the Nationalist Party had voted into its leadership F.W. de Klerk. Previously a staunch supporter of the policy of apartheid, de Klerk had come to realise that it was a flawed policy. De Klerk was also a pragmatist. The world was shunning his country. How long could South Africa survive without trading partners? De Klerk had clearly seen the writing on the wall. But instead of retreating into a Boer lager, as his predecessors would have done, de Klerk determined that radical change was required if South Africa was ever to re-join the family of nations. The alternative would be international isolation and increasing internal terrorism. De Klerk decided, bravely, to opt for major change. What de Klerk proposed to his party was shocking: one man, one vote. Or, more dramatically, roughly 30 million black votes against less than 3 million white ones.

To achieve this de Klerk needed an ally. To the black South Africans, Madiba was a God. If Mandela had ordered civil unrest or an armed uprising it would have followed. But de Klerk knew, before Mandela had been released from jail, that he was a man of peace—a man who bore no resentment or bitterness toward his captors, a remarkable human being who, despite years of deprivation, still believed that talking was better than fighting. Mandela fought with his voice, not with his fists. In Mandela, de Klerk had the ally he needed. By promising to deliver to Mandela's people what they so desperately wanted—their civil rights—de Klerk believed that he could work with Mandela to orchestrate a peaceful transfer of political power. Mandela concurred. This coming together of two such bold, brave, and eminently sensible people, one white, one black, at such a crucial time in South Africa, was the most fortuitous occurrence of the last century. Both men had huge obstacles to overcome, mainly from within their own ranks—indeed, even from within their own families. Both men's marriages did not survive the process.

Some of Mandela's problems came from the 'homeland' leaders. As talks progressed in regard to constitutional change, the 'independent' homelands became an issue. As previously described, the apartheid regime had attempted to spin off certain territories and huge numbers of potential black voters into 'homelands'. This policy had never been supported by Mandela's banned political party, the African National Congress. Now that the ANC had been unbanned by de Klerk (a condition of Mandela's cooperation), the ANC and Mandela pressed forward with their demand to reintegrate the homelands into South Africa proper. In principle, this appeared to be a straightforward matter, but politicians are politicians, wherever they are, and the potential loss of political power was a huge problem for the homeland leaders, such as President Lucas Mangope of Bophuthatswana. What role would Mangope and Holomisa and all the others play in the new South Africa? What would happen to all of their perks and trappings of power? They were not going to join the de Klerk–Mandela train easily. And then there was Chief Buthelezi, political leader of the Zulus. Buthelezi had refused to accept the 'independence' of Zululand from the Nats, and now, of course, held the high ground. What role could he carve out for himself alongside Nelson Mandela? After all, he was head of the Zulu nation, traditional enemy to the Xhosas of the Transkei, where Nelson Mandela had been born. Bickering between Mandela and Buthelezi would only add fuel to the fire of the Nats, many of whom who were convinced that a black-run South Africa would quickly deteriorate into tribal warfare.

It was in this area that we came in. It was in this area that we had a crucial interest. Over the previous few years, Sun International had spent millions of rand in developing resort infrastructure in the homelands. In all cases, our shareholders included representatives of the local governments, and many of their officials sat on our boards. Several of the companies involved were listed in the Johannesburg Stock Exchange. SunBop, the Bophuthatswana company, for example, was so highly developed that it ranked in the top twenty listed companies. As a result, many of the homeland leaders were far closer to us than to Nelson Mandela, and certainly far, far closer to us than the Nat leader, F.W. de Klerk. It was, therefore, to us, amongst others, that the two peacemakers turned for help in persuading the homeland leaders to take the sensible direction.

Nelson Mandela made it known to us that he wanted to talk—in private. We invited him to dinner at Sol's house in Bryanston. The diners were Sol, Buddy Hawton, Madiba, and me. We awaited his arrival with some trepidation. Mary and Violet, Sol's housekeepers, were shaking with excitement—such an honour, President Mandela coming to 'our' house for dinner. African leaders, in my experience, are almost always late for appointments. We therefore quite expected 'President' Mandela, as we had been advised to address him (president of the ANC, not the country—yet), to be late. President Mandela, however, was not like other African leaders; he arrived almost exactly on schedule. He did not disappoint. A tall, imposing man with a powerful, resonant voice and a broad, broad smile strode into our living room and lit it up with his presence. Only one other man had ever had that effect on me before, and he was also a black man: Muhammad Ali.

"I'm sorry to be a nuisance," he said, almost before we had exchanged greetings, "but will it be possible to feed my driver and security man?"

"Of course," we replied in unison, like a church choir.

"And will they be able to have the same food as me?"

This time only I replied, perhaps because I was the only one familiar with what had gone on in the kitchen.

"Of course, Mr President, nothing less," said I, mentally starting to explain to Mary and Violet how the portion control would have to be carried out that evening.

Mandela was fascinating. One minute, he could be gentle and the next, stern. His twinkling eyes could, within a flash, become very imposing. He would listen intently, but could tell stories at length. He joked a lot, but could suddenly become serious and sad. He was humble, but proud. He was confident, but impressionable. He admitted he had a lot to learn, but came across as eminently wise. He would be up on every step of the conversation, but somehow seemed distant. He clearly had a lot on his mind, but he knew just where he was going. Above all, his complete lack of bitterness about his captors was astounding. Here, sitting at our dinner table, was living proof that it can be better to forgive but not to forget.

It could have been intimidating having probably the most famous man in the world home for dinner, but it wasn't. We tried to make him feel at home, but, in truth, he did a better job with us. I sat next to him at the dinner table. As we sat down, he started to talk to me about boxing. He knew that I had been responsible for the Coetzee world-title fights, and Mandela was a huge boxing fan. Had I seen the tape of Joe Louis against Max Schmeling?

"No, Mr President, that was before my time."

"Pity," he continued. "It was a great fight. Louis came out with a right and Schmeling countered with a left," he started, and for the next few minutes, he gave me a blow-by-blow account of the fight, as if he had it indelibly painted in his mind.

"I suppose you watched it over and over in prison, sir?" I suggested.

"Oh no," he replied, somewhat startled. "I didn't have a television in prison. They offered me one, but I refused, on the basis that the other prisoners didn't have televisions. No, no. I never saw the fight on television in jail. I saw it on the television at home two nights ago."

Not long after this first dinner, Diana and I were invited to the opening of a luxury-goods store in the Sandton Shopping Mall in Johannesburg. The proprietor of this Dunhill shop was an Indian friend and a leading ANC member, who had, amongst other things, supplied Nelson Mandela with the suit he had worn to walk out of jail. "This I've got to see," I said to Diana. "The president of the quasi-communist but certainly socialist ANC, opening a luxury-goods store. And besides, hopefully I will get the chance to introduce you to Madiba." (Diana had graciously made herself scarce on the night he had been to dinner.)

The opening was scheduled to take place in the evening, after the rest of the shops in the mall had closed. A section in front of the shop had been cordoned off with those red ropes that you find in cinema lobbies. Within this enclosure were scores of white faces busy scoffing canapes and downing Krug. As we arrived, I scanned the scene for President Mandela, who would obviously not be tough to find in this crowd. He was nowhere to be seen! "He's chickened out," I thought to myself. But not a bit of it: there he was, lurking right at the back of the shop behind a rack of logo-emblazoned sweaters.

"Come on," I said to Diana, "let's go and meet the great man." With that, we threaded our way through the crowd until we reached the back of the shop, where Mandela was standing alone. He recognised me immediately, and I introduced him to Diana.

"What do you feel, Mr President, about opening this shop?" asked Diana.

"Upgraded," came back the reply in a flash, accompanied with a broad smile and a twinkle in the eye. Just then, the owner of the shop, Yuseff, came scurrying back to advise Madiba that the time had come for him to take the microphone on the forecourt in Champagneland.

"Ladies and gentlemen," he began, "as you know, I am looking for a job." A slight titter went around the audience. He was, after all, trying to become the president of the country. "And I think I've found the place I want to work," he continued. "I can assure Yuseff, the owner and my good friend, that he would be very happy to have me work here. He could absolutely trust me with the keys to his shop…" There followed a long pause, and then he went on: "…because there's nothing here that I *need*."

Masterful, I thought to myself, as the audience broke into spontaneous laughter.

I didn't see Madiba for a few months. We, particularly Sol and Buddy Hawton, did what we could to interface with the homeland leaders, to convince them to give up their fiefdoms and join the 'union' for the sake of peace, but it was a long, tedious process. And although we didn't meet during this period, I have no doubt that Madiba knew that we were beavering away on his and de Klerk's behalf. The next time we did meet was on an airplane.

Diana and I were flying to London from Johannesburg on British Airways. We were sitting in row one on BA's 747. Row one consists of four seats, two and two, separated by an aisle. I had had great difficulty getting tickets for this flight, which had been overbooked. I therefore considered us lucky to be sitting in the first row, because I knew that BA's policy was to hold it back for politicians and VIPs. The doors were about to be closed on the plane, but seat 1A and 1B were still unoccupied. I sensed then that we were about to be joined by a politician or celebrity, who would be wheeled in from a special lounge at the last moment. I didn't think it could be a white South African politician, because he would be on SAA. I had a hunch it was Mandela, which I shared with Diana. I was right. At the very last moment, when everybody else was seated, in came Madiba, escorted by a British Airways official. I got up to greet him. Again he recognised me, and his face lit up with that familiar broad smile. "And how are you, Diana?" he enquired as he shook her hand warmly. Diana was almost too flabbergasted to reply. After all these months and such a short previous meeting, he had actually remembered her name.

Our journey was interesting. He talked at length about his time in captivity: his friendship with the prison keepers, his despair at not seeing his children and grandchildren grow up, and his efforts to keep his brain active. Diana had lots of questions, and he had lots of answers, but through it all, there was not a hint of bitterness. This was his crowning feat. This role model had cast a glow over the whole of the leadership of the ANC. No matter where one went, in those early days before the constitutional change and the first multiracial elections, the ANC leadership sang from the same hymnbook: a hymnbook that looked forward, not backwards. This astounding fact was absolutely due to the inspired leadership of the man sitting next to us in the plane. This amazing role model ultimately saved millions of lives.

But his charm is also that he can never be serious for long. Diana told him that she had recently seen him in a shopping mall with one of his grandchildren, buying a little bicycle.

"Why didn't you greet me?" asked Madiba.

"I didn't want to intrude on your personal time," explained Diana. "You have missed out on too much of your grandchildren's lives. You don't want people like me getting in the way."

"The next time I see you at the shops, Diana Venison," he retorted, "I shall also not say hello to you!" The twinkle in the eye belied the message.

I was always intrigued by Madiba's ability to memorise things. After all, he was not a young man when we first met, and as we all experience, it seems to get harder, not easier, to remember things as we get older. I had some years ago read a book by a European lady who had been jailed for several years by the Gang of Four in China. Her blow-by-blow account of what had befallen her in jail was startlingly detailed, and she put it down to having forced herself in prison to focus on tiny details, to keep her mind alert. This had involved inventing mind games, such as counting the number of tiles on the wall or noting the speed at which an ant would cross the cell, perfecting her math tables, etc. I assumed that Madiba had done the same. After all, it was he who had studied for a master's degree whilst in jail, and he who had encouraged many of the other prisoners to do the same.

An outstanding example of this attribute was demonstrated to us some years later. During the first year of his presidency, we once again hosted the Miss World pageant at Sun City. As usual, we asked the contestants if there was anything special they would like to do for recreation during the period they were rehearsing the show. They were unanimous: they wanted to meet Nelson Mandela. We called the president's aides to ask if he would be kind enough to come to Sun City to meet the young ladies. After all, this would make for a great photo opportunity. Madiba had never been to Sun City, which, as far as he was concerned, was a product of apartheid and a gambling den. The answer was negative, but instead he told us that he would be willing to have a photo taken with the contestants on the steps of the parliament buildings the next day in Pretoria, if we would take the girls to him. I quickly arranged some buses and asked Julia Morley (co-owner of the Miss World pageant) and Diana to be tour leaders. Madiba had made it clear that he would not have time to meet all eighty-six of the contestants, but would be happy to have the group photograph.

As the girls were exiting the buses, one of them slipped and twisted her ankle. A wheelchair was called for and quickly arranged. The girls were then duly lined up by our photographer to await the arrival of their hero. As soon as he arrived, Madiba spotted the young lady in the wheelchair at the bottom of the steps, enquired of Julia as to her fate, and then immediately proceeded down the steps to offer his commiseration for her misfortune. As he bent down to greet her, she impudently reached up and planted a kiss on his cheek. "Now I've met you," he quipped, "I shall have to meet all of your friends," and with that, he arranged to shake hands with all eighty-six young ladies. To the absolute astonishment of Julia and Diana, as he did so, he asked that his greetings be passed on to every single head of state that they represented. "Send my regards to Prime Minister X," or "Say hello to General Y," or "Please give my best respects to President Z," and so on. In each case, from somewhere in the depths of his mind, he fathomed up a name. The invitation for the girls to come to Pretoria had only been offered one day prior. Either he had stayed up all night memorising eighty-six presidential names, or he already knew them by heart. Diana and Julia opted for the second explanation.

As the peace process, as it became known, progressed, I continued to manage the company. These were exciting but challenging times. I had inherited a company that, in my opinion, was severely overstaffed by as many as 4000 employees. As the hopes of the people of South Africa for the establishment of equal civil rights for all races, colours and creeds were raised, so were the ambitions of the trade unions. Under the apartheid regime, trade unions had been banned. As part of the pre-negotiation conciliatory phase, not only had the African National Congress political party been unbanned, but so had the trade unions. Initially, they were feeling their way, but I knew that with each success, they would grow stronger and stronger. If I was to be able to right-size the company's payroll, I knew that I would have to act quickly, before the influence of the trade unions made action impossible or, at the very least, difficult. I therefore set about the task of staff reduction on a large scale.

As a manager, laying people off is always a difficult and unpleasant job. Laying off poor and rather low-paid Africans, on whom normally at least seven other people are dependent, is harrowing. Naturally, the further one is away from the actual personnel involved, in a sense, the easier it is. Putting a line through someone's name on a payroll list in the head office is far easier than actually having to confront the individual personally, and as a result, there tends to be much ducking and diving amongst lower management ranks, in an attempt to put off the inevitable. I had to be very firm. I knew that the long-term survival of the company and thus the long-term survival of the majority of the jobs would be subject to us achieving staffing efficiency before it was too late.

As a result of this action, we were confronted with a series of strikes, which became increasingly violent. I have always marvelled at how the peaceful, almost laid-back nature of most Africans can so quickly turn to unreasonable violence, particularly if stirred up by a political or ideological agenda. More and more, I was receiving calls of help from besieged managers. When possible, I went myself to the front line. I remembered my earlier experiences in Durban and Mozambique. I reckoned that, despite the influence of the union leaders, most workers would respect authority, and I, as the managing director, represented just that. It was not, therefore, an uncommon experience in these days to find myself facing an angry crowd, armed to the hilt with AK-47s and other handguns, demanding their rights and often a 30% salary increase to boot. As Jerry Inzerillo, the incumbent general manager of Sun City, used to say, "We were either brave or spectacularly stupid." Nevertheless, we persevered, and over the course of about a year, we achieved our redundancy targets. Two years later, it would have been impossible.

Laying off large numbers of personnel and coping with frequent labour strikes is obviously not a normal recipe for the provision of first-class hotel service. I was determined that, as far as possible, this labour unrest would not affect our standards of operation. Reaching into my training background, I decided on a battle plan. This drew heavily on the experiences of British Airways, whose management had recently also been involved in a large redundancy program, but at the same time had dramatically improved their standards of service. British Airways, I discovered, had utilised a training programme called 'Putting People First', with the help of TWI, an Oxford-based training firm. Over a period of several months, British Airways had ensured that every single member of their worldwide staff had attended the three-day training program, wherever they lived or worked, and, more impressively, the managing director, Sir Colin Marshall, had personally either opened or closed each training session, irrespective of where it was being held. In total, this had meant attending over 100 training meetings across the globe.

With the help of TWI's Sue Moore and my human resources director, Rob Rimmer, we drew up our own training campaign, which we entitled World-Class Winners. This entailed the participation of all of our remaining

10,000 employees. We proposed to run 100 three-day training sessions, for 100 people per session. The logistics of this exercise were quite daunting, and, needless to say, were bound to cause considerable inconvenience to line managers, particularly those who could not be initially convinced about the merits of this exercise. Many of my managers were very sceptical about the benefit of such a programme, as indeed were many of my top executives, but I went about it with such a passion that they (either enthusiastically or reluctantly) went along. I actually gave them no choice, in the hope that the results would soon convince the doubters that they were wrong. I really tried to emulate Sir Colin and attend at least the opening or the closing of each session, but in case I could not achieve this, I drew up a roster of my top executive team, so that there was always one of us present to wave the flag and demonstrate to the troops that 'we' at the top of the company thought that this was important.

In the terminology of World-Class Winners, we were trying to build a company manned by 'Double-Baggers'. A Double-Bagger, we decided, was the equivalent of a supermarket checkout employee who, rather than enjoying the sight of your overloaded single bag splitting apart in the car park and spewing your groceries around, would make sure that this did not happen by 'double-bagging'. A Double-Bagger was, therefore, a person who would go the extra mile for the customer: a person who cared! Judging by the number of employees I saw around after these training sessions wearing 'I am a Double-Bagger' T-shirts, I would have to say that World-Class Winners was successful. At the very least, it gave everyone in the organisation something positive to think about during and after the uncertain period of labour unrest and the clouded future of the political peace process.

In that regard, the process ground forward fitfully and

painfully, but inevitably. De Klerk had huge resistance in convincing first his political party and then the voters that a universal franchise was the right way to go for South Africa. Mandela, on the other hand, needed to keep in check the hotheads in his party, including his wife Winnie. Unreasonable demands about the future from Mandela could have derailed the whole peace process, with the danger, then, of armed conflict. Winnie was becoming an embarrassment, and ultimately her outrageous behaviour led to a divorce. Winnie was, however, something of a demigod amongst young blacks herself; as such, she wielded considerable political clout. Unfortunately, Winnie wanted too much from the process. She was bitter about her years in the wilderness during apartheid, and not without reason. The way she had been treated for the twenty-seven long years of her husband's imprisonment was disgraceful. Her life had been one continuous period of harassment by government officials and police. She had been forced to live under the most appalling conditions, had been allowed very little contact with her imprisoned husband, had been required to raise their children alone, and had had no real way to earn a living. The bad times were now over for Winnie, and she was determined to enjoy the good ones. Who could blame her? But many did.

This was a strange time in many ways. As the negotiations between Mandela and de Klerk lurched forward, the future for whites in South Africa was not clear. What was clear was that there could be no turning back. If equal political rights were not to be granted to all citizens, South Africa would become isolated from the rest of the world and probably beset with internal terrorism of the worst kind. But what form would the new constitution take? Would businesses be nationalised? What protection would whites have from the black majority? All in all, de Klerk and Mandela did a magnificent job of steering the nation through this traumatic period.

Whilst the leaders were doggedly sticking to their agenda, there was a lot of jockeying for positions in the side-lines. We were forever being asked to do favours for ANC members, all of whom assured us, of course, that they were going to be important players in the future government and that our kindness would be remembered. We absolutely refused to give handouts, but contributions to political organisations were legal, as, of course, were charitable donations. It was not only money for which we were asked. Certain of the political hopefuls quickly got used to the fast life, and where better to enjoy themselves than at our hotels and casinos? Sun City became a focal point, and its general manager, Jerry Inzerillo, practically became an honorary public relations manager for the ANC! The requests for other services came flying in. Could Winnie borrow my Mercedes, because her car had broken down? I lent her a Toyota; I am not sure if we got it back. Could Peter Mokaba, leader of the ANC Youth Movement, borrow our company jet for a short trip? As it happens, our jet was used to help further the peace process, since on several occasions it was necessary for Mandela to get to Zululand or Bophuthatswana or some other distant point in a hurry at critical moments of the negotiations. This, of course, we did not mind at all.

Finally, all parties agreed on a new constitution, which would allow all citizens of South Africa and the homelands to vote for their representatives in the South African Parliament. The final step was for de Klerk to hold a referendum to get the approval of the existing white voters. They were simply asked to vote yes or no. Despite huge misgivings about their future, the white voters of South Africa voted yes by an overwhelming majority. The revolution was over. President Mandela of the ANC was to become

President Mandela of South Africa. This had been the most peaceful revolution ever. Who could have predicted such a thing a few years before? Certainly not me!

For a few years, during his short presidency, things seemed to go well for Madiba and the country. Commerce prospered and there seemed to be a common goal of black and white citizens to make the rainbow nation work. Madiba, recognising that he was a leader and not a manager, decided to step down and the ANC chose Thabo Mbeki as president, followed eight years later by Jacob Zuma. Corruption became endemic and, as we all know, corruption is the biggest enemy of efficiency. The hope for South Africa now rests with the burgeoning black middle class; they know how much they have to lose if the tide is not turned.

# Chapter Nineteen
## THE FRENCH CONNECTION

Diana and I continued to live in Sol Kerzner's house in Homestead Avenue in Bryanston. This was the first house he had bought in Johannesburg, many years earlier. This had been his home with Shirley. It was from here that she had driven out to commit suicide. This had been, and still was, 'home' to Sol and Shirley's children, Chantal and Brandon, although both of them were now living overseas. This was also the house in which Sol had lived with his third wife, Anneline Kreil, a former "Miss World," together with Shirley's children. So Sun Manor, as it was unashamedly called, was steeped in Kerzner history, much of which both Diana and I had been very close to. Sol, however, did not, to use his words, "fall in love with buildings," and so it did not seem to bother him at all that Diana and I were living in his home. We were made to feel very comfortable. We were allotted the guest suite, but had the full use of the house, the garden, and the staff. Nevertheless, because the temporary situation of my role as managing director of Sun International seemed to be becoming more permanent, we decided that it was time to get another place of our own, a place where we could have our things around us.

We also wanted some privacy, and felt that although Sol only visited occasionally, he was entitled to his as well.

Not that he ever tried to hide anything from us, because when Sol had had a skinful of Black Label, his amorous adventures and overtures could be heard all over the house. We therefore set about looking for and found a new home for ourselves, and Diana started to organise furniture and decorations.

At about this time, Peter Bacon, who was still working for Sol in the UK, had reached the point where he could take no more of Sol's systematic abuse, and asked me if I would consider taking him on in South Africa as deputy managing director—either that, or he would leave the company altogether. This I was happy to do, since it seemed a real shame to lose Peter's depth of experience from the company, and Sol did not appear to care. It was not long before I discovered why Sol didn't care, for no sooner had Peter bedded down in South Africa than Sol was campaigning amongst the board of Sun International to release me from Johannesburg, to help him with his somewhat stalled efforts to expand the offshore company elsewhere. Within months of Peter arriving as my deputy, I was being persuaded that my contribution to the company would now be greater in the international, non-South African arena. This persuasion coincided with the day that Diana advised me she had completed the decoration of our new home. Notwithstanding this, Diana, great trooper that she is, once again accepted the move back to the UK with calm. Peter Bacon was also happy; having escaped the direct clutches of Sol, he now found himself elevated to take charge of the business in South Africa. He was in the process of getting divorced; within a year, having first played the field, he was remarried to none other than the former Miss World, Anneline Kriel, an event amazingly predicted by Diana's dear clairvoyant, Mrs. Brown, some years before.

My new role was to take charge of all of the bits and

pieces of the business that Sol had acquired, but also, more importantly, to help grow the company. Unfortunately, the 'bits and pieces' were to take a lot of my time. The chief culprit, initially, was the Galawa Beach Resort in the Comores. A galawa is a wooden dug-out fishing boat, a sort of crude dhow. The beach was the only really decent beach on Grand Comores, the largest island of the Comores (or Comoros, as they are also called), which are situated north of Madagascar in the Indian Ocean. Like Zanzibar, the Comores is part African, part Arab, and, in this case, part colonial French. The people of these islands are very poor; there is no industrial base, and the only meaningful exports are vanilla and terrorism. (It was from here that the bombing of the American embassy in Nairobi was allegedly planned.) Grand Comores is volcanic (still active) and is also famous for being the last home of the coelacanth, a prehistoric fish. Its recent political history had been tumultuous. In 1980, following the example established some years before in Madagascar, the Comores underwent a classic struggle of independence from its French masters. Not all of the population was in favour of independence, and the smaller islands, realising which side their bread was buttered on, split from their compatriots when independence was granted, and opted to stay as a French département. Grand Comores struck out alone, with no real means of self-sufficiency and no organised leadership. A series of coups d'état took place, and a never-ending power struggle ensued.

The South African government, at this time, was looking for allies in the region, particularly allies offshore from Africa who could offer landing rights for SAA's commercial jets, which were not allowed to refuel anywhere in mainland Africa, as a result of the apartheid boycott. Grand Comores boasted a runway, built by the French, which could handle a 747, and as a quid pro quo for the landing rights, the South African government agreed to lend the newly independent Comorian government enough money to build a beach hotel, the Galawa Beach. This was originally developed by an independent operator, who quickly became overwhelmed by the complexity of the project and was then rescued, at the request of the South African government, by Sun International.

Getting this hotel built had been a masterpiece of ingenuity by Sun International. For a start, the only harbour in the Comores did not have a crane large or strong enough to lift off containers, so all goods, building materials, and supplies had to be off-loaded piecemeal from cargo ships onto *galawas* and transported onto the beach. When the hotel was finally completed, after considerable trauma, the carnival did not stop, for the country was then invaded by French mercenaries under the leadership of the infamous Bob Denard, who proceeded to run it as a private fiefdom. Needless to say, despite the natural beauty of the place, this was not a recipe for successful tourism, and so, after a while, Sun International decided to close the place down and write off its investment. This action was not popular with the South African government, who had, through their African Development Corporation, funded the entire enterprise, and could now see no way to get their money back. All of this had transpired whilst Sol Kerzner was in Europe and in the wilderness as far as Sun International was concerned, having been forced to leave as a result of the alleged Transkei bribery affair. This, however, did not stop a particularly resourceful member of the South African foreign affairs department, Rusty Evans, from approaching Sol to see if he could not come up with of a way to salvage the South African government's investment in Comores tourism. Happily, all of this coincided with the French government's resolve to get rid of the mercenary regime and install a new democratic leader, which they accomplished through the intervention of the French army.

It did not take Sol more than a few minutes on the site of the Galawa to recognise that it had fantastic potential as a resort. In three-sided negotiations between the lenders' in South Africa, represented by Rusty, and the new 'democratic' president of the Comores, Sol managed to extend the land to include an adjacent site with a picture-perfect beach and enough extra to accommodate a golf course; arrange a ninety-nine-year lease on the land and buildings, with payments that only kicked in after substantial profits had been accrued by Sol; and get the South African government to lend him a further $5 million (at a 2% interest rate) to fix the place up, since it had suffered some deterioration during its brief closure.

Since then, Sol had been welcomed back to the Sun International fold and had rolled in his interest in the Galawa Beach as part of his equity in the international subsidiary, which I was now employed to expand. Peter Bacon had been responsible for managing the Comorian investment and it was this unwelcome task that I now inherited.

Airlift was the first problem. The only carrier to the Comores was Air France, which reluctantly flew there from Paris twice per week, via about five other African countries, with what appeared to be its oldest cattle truck of a 747 (into which it had crammed over 500 economy seats). I was sure that this was at the insistence of the French government, which was desperate to see the new democracy work, so that it did not have to take the place back as a dependency of La France. Given the publicity of coups d'état, revolutions, and mercenary takeovers, French tourists were not exactly lining up to visit the place. Its natural local market was South Africa, where it could feasibly be developed as a 'poor man's Mauritius', but there was no airlift from there available, notwithstanding the government's pressure on the management of SAA to fly there, in order to protect their investment in the hotel. Eventually, with the combined pressure of the government and the inventiveness of Bruce Hutchisson (the marketing executive we hired to solve the problem), we managed to persuade SAA to let us charter a 737 once per week from Joburg. On the back of this arrangement we formed a wholesale travel company in South Africa, World Leisure Holidays, which Bruce ran with a passion, under my direction, eventually growing it into one of South Africa's leading travel companies. For a while, the arrangements with SAA worked well, and the Galawa Beach Resort became a favourite destination for South African tourists, and a financial success.

Operating it, however, was a nightmare. Cholera was endemic on the island, as was malaria. This did not help the marketing of the place, nor did it encourage management at all levels to stay there. Luckily, we had found a Frenchman who was willing to do so, but for a number of years, Christian Antoine had a life full of colourful experiences, which included a volcanic eruption, two coups d'état, the return of mercenary rule, a pitched battle between the mercenaries and the French armed forces, and a hijacked Ethiopian airliner crashing onto the hotel's beach. It also included dealing with successive governments whose ministers were, by and large, completely corrupt and only saw their roles in government as a means to self-enrichment. When it came time to pay various taxes, such as casino and tourist taxes, the ministers would come around personally each month for collection—and sometimes even a month ahead of time. Christian soon discovered that this money never went near the national exchequer, but he also discovered that, since governments and ministers changed so frequently, he could get away with telling each successive minister that he had paid the last one, and by this method, cut down on the actual payments made.

Nor was it only the ministers who stole; by the time we had re-equipped the hotel with operating supplies for about the fifth time in our first year of ownership, we reckoned that every Grand Comorian must have a complete set of Galawa Beach linen and cutlery. On one occasion, Christian was invited to a *grand mariage* by one of the employees, who was marrying off his daughter. As its name implied, it turned out to be a rather grand affair to which the whole village was invited. To Christian's surprise, every single piece of equipment used at the wedding had been stolen from the hotel and was being put to use by the host quite unashamedly in the presence of the hotel's general manager, the host's boss. When challenged by Christian on the subject, the host merely responded that he had bought it all in the local market, and that he saw it as his right to use it, since he had (supposedly) paid for it.

The airlift to and from South Africa in the chartered aircraft worked well, but unfortunately, not long after this had been arranged, Air France decided to completely drop the route from Europe. With no possibility of getting any guests from Europe, the business would rely solely on the low-yielding South African market, which was not entirely satisfactory. Our response was to do a deal with a major German tour operator, involving a charter flight from Frankfurt. This worked well for the first year, but once the operators realised that they were the only game in town, on the anniversary of our deal, they took out their pencil sharpeners and offered us the most ridiculously low room rates. I told them what they could do with their business. Once again we were without a carrier from Europe, and as a result, the tour operators in France, Germany, and the UK all removed the Galawa Beach Hotel from their brochures. Try as we may, we could not convince anyone to fly to the place, until a good friend of mine suggested an approach to Emirates, the Dubai-based airline.

Emirates flew from all of the major gateways in Europe to Dubai. They did not, at the time, fly to Johannesburg. If I could convince them to fly to Johannesburg from Dubai via the Comores, they could, I envisaged, funnel all the Comores tourist business from Europe via Dubai, and from the south, could replace our weekly charter from Johannesburg. After several visits to Dubai, I finally managed to convince Sheikh Ahmed Maktoum, the chairman, and Tim Clark, the general manager of the airline, to put on the new service, which they agreed to do on a twice-weekly basis. I then had to convince the South African government to give Emirates the 'fifth freedom' and allow them to pick up passengers in South Africa bound for the Comores, a right that would normally only have been granted to the national airline of the Comores, Air Comores, which at the time only had one propeller aircraft, which was permanently parked at the airport, awaiting spare parts. When all of this convincing was done, Emirates started to fly, and so did the business to the hotel. Unfortunately, within weeks of these arrangements having been put in place, Bob Denard and his mercenaries once again appeared on the scene to rock the boat.

A group of seemingly harmless tourists had checked into the hotel. They appeared to be particularly interested in painting. They carried their easels and sketchbooks with them for several days, visiting various landmarks along the coast. Unbeknown to Christian Antoine, they were the advance party of a mercenary invasion force, who were busy plotting the landing sites. One night, a small merchant vessel anchored off the hotel, and a group of about twenty heavily armed mercenaries made landfall on our beach, where they teamed up with the 'artists'. They then hijacked the van that made early-morning bread deliveries to the president's residence, and were freely allowed to pass through the president's security in a van full of armed mercenaries instead of bread. Once inside the residence, it was only a matter of minutes before the mercenaries were holding the president hostage. Whilst this action was taking place, another group of mercenaries was capturing the radio station. Here, however, they met with some armed resistance, and a few casualties ensued, but it was not long before they were in control and broadcasting to the nation that the government had been overthrown and that Colonel Denard was in charge again. Most nations would have been aghast at being taken over by a small coterie of mercenaries, but such was the distrust and dislike of the existing government that large sections of the population were completely at ease with the notion of being governed again by a benevolent white mercenary. Some troops were, however, loyal to the president, and, having reformed, made several attempts to dislodge the mercenaries from the radio station; for some time, they successfully held onto the airport.

News of the coup reached me in Paris, where I was at the time attempting to organise a sales effort, aimed at the French market, to promote tourism to the Comores. Christian excitedly relayed the recent course of events from his mobile phone. His only casualty, it seemed, had been a member of staff, who had been paid by a freelance journalist (who happened to be staying in the hotel) to take him on his motorbike to the scene of the battle at the radio station. Regrettably, the biker had been hit in the crossfire and had died. The journalist had survived, with only damage incurred from falling off the bike. Christian's hotel, at the time, had about 180 South African tourists as guests.

Making arrangements to evacuate the present hotel guests seemed a more appropriate use of my time at that moment than orchestrating ways to send more, so I cancelled the marketing meeting and set to work on the rescue plan.

No sooner had I put the phone down than the general manager of Emirates, Tim Clark, was on the line, also with the news of the coup, which had been relayed to him by his station manager on the island. According to Tim, there was still fighting taking place at the airport, and the runway had been littered with objects, making it unsafe to land. I was extremely nervous that this skirmish in the Comores would put Tim off from continuing with the route, but as luck would have it, the plane bookings going forward were very strong indeed, and the route, if it could be salvaged, looked as if it could become very profitable for Emirates. Tim's motivation, therefore, was to try to find a way to keep flying, provided, of course, that it would be safe to do so in the future. Tim agreed to keep in constant touch; reassuringly, he offered me the use of his planes to repatriate our guests as soon as practicable. The news of the coup had now reached the world's media, and the French, of course, were particularly interested to learn of the latest exploits of their favourite mercenary. There was considerable conjecture on the television that Bob Denard was, in fact, acting for the French government, as a means of overthrowing their corrupt stepchild in the Comores. The government was, of course, quick to deny this.

Various action groups started to press the United Nations to do something about the coup. After all, what would happen to international law and order if mercenary bands were just allowed, willy-nilly, to overthrow legitimately elected governments? The United Nations, in turn, started to press the French government for action, but the French, at least publicly, seemed strangely unconcerned about the matter, leading to further speculation that they had organised the whole thing.

Meanwhile, Bob Denard started making announcements. He would stay in charge of Grand Comores until either the incumbent president resigned and new elections were held, or the French agreed to recolonise the place. Pressure grew on the French government to rid the island of Denard, but they were saying nothing. Pressure was also growing on me to do something about our stranded guests, and so, in the absence of any tangible actions by the French authorities, Tim Clark and I decided to visit the island ourselves to negotiate directly with Denard, who was now in control of the airport, to allow us to land a wide-bodied Emirates plane in order to remove our customers. With Christian's help, I managed to speak with Denard on the phone, and he told me that he would allow Tim and me to land in a small jet for discussions. We duly made arrangements to charter a Lear in Johannesburg, and having asked the French foreign office, through a friendly insider, if there was any impending military action that might make our trip difficult (to which the answer was negative), we set off to Johannesburg from Europe to pick up our rented plane.

As we were about to board the Lear, I received another excited phone call from Christian. In the background I could hear a great din. "I'm being invaded!" he exclaimed, and went on to describe how over a thousand French troops were swarming across the resort's beach, presumably on their way to rescue the president and arrest the mercenaries. The background noise was, apparently, the support helicopters, which were buzzing over the hotel. Christian followed the progress of this new invasion like a war correspondent, with frequent telephonic dispatches to Tim and myself, as we waited to know whether to take off or not. In the space of a morning the coup was reversed, the mercenaries were captured, and the airport, now with some considerable damage from gunfire and grenades, was retaken.

Tim was now particularly worried about the state of the runway and the arrival and departure buildings, even though Christian was reporting that the French were firmly in control. He felt it was his duty to inspect the condition of the place before putting his big jet and its crew at risk. So it was that a few hours after the French invasion had been completed, and after a rather difficult telephone conversation with the French general in charge, we eventually took off in our Lear, and four hours later were the first aircraft to land after the turmoil, with our pilots skilfully avoiding the odd hole or two on the tarmac. Two days later, with runway repairs completed by French troops, the first Emirates jet arrived to take away our hotel guests, who had, in the main, thoroughly enjoyed their extended holidays laced with excitement.

Things returned to normal for a while in the Comores, and the Emirates route became very successful, with its frequency between Dubai and Johannesburg eventually reaching seven per week, although only two continued to call in at Grand Comores. Then came the next fright.

One morning, I was awakened early in my hotel room in Connecticut, where I was visiting our newly created Mohegan Sun casino, by a phone call from Diana in London. She, it appeared, had just been phoned at our home by someone from the boathouse at the Galawa Beach, who was looking for me to tell me about a plane crash. That's all Diana had heard before the line got cut, so whilst trying to locate me in Connecticut, she had turned on CNN, only to see 'late-breaking' but unconfirmed reports of a plane crash in the Comores. I leaped out of bed and switched on the box. Sure enough, my CNN said exactly the same thing, although just why I thought it would say anything different,

I have no idea. No details were available. A plane crash in the Comores could only mean one thing: one of Tim's planes had come down. What a tragedy! I tried phoning the Galawa Beach—no answer. Next, I tried calling Tim in Dubai. No, Tim had not heard of the crash yet, but he assured me it was not one of his planes. That, at least, was a relief. The news reports on CNN must be wrong.

I tried calling the Galawa again. After what seemed an age, I got through, and eventually found myself talking to Christian. What I heard was astounding. An Ethiopian Airlines 737 had narrowly missed the roof of the hotel and had crashed in the shallow water between the beach and the reef. The plane had broken into two. Part of the wreckage was now within the reef, and the rest had cartwheeled over it and was now in the deep water on the seaward side. All of our staff at the boathouse were busy rescuing passengers in our small boats, which consisted of a fleet of dive boats, lasers, and Hobie Cats. There were many dead. Christian had too much on hand to stay on the line with me. I let him go, asking him to phone back when he had time. By now, CNN was beginning to get other eyewitness stories.

Little by little, the truth came out. The plane was a Boeing 737 from the small Ethiopian Airlines fleet. One of the pilots had survived the crash, and was eventually able to relate the full story. The plane had been hijacked by some extremists, who had demanded, initially, that the pilots fly them to Australia. The hijackers were, of course, armed, and two of them had taken up position in the cockpit, where they had stayed with their nervous fingers on the pins of hand grenades. The pilots had explained that they did not have enough fuel to reach Australia, and had pointed the plane in the direction of the Comores. When the Grand Comores runway had come in sight, the hijackers were apparently incensed and had instructed the pilots to fly the plane directly at the nearest large building, which happened to be the Galawa Beach Hotel. Presumably, they had wanted to die for their cause, in the biggest crash possible. What could be better than a resort full of Western tourists? According to the pilot, as he had approached the hotel at a very low height, the hijackers had realised that he was going to overfly and attempt to land on the water. A scuffle had broken out, with the result that the plane had tipped and veered, causing one wing to hit the beach under the shallow water. As the plane cartwheeled over the reef, it had broken in two, spewing plane parts and passengers all over the place. The hand grenades had not exploded.

What happened on the ground was pandemonium. As the plane had approached most of the hotel guests had been sunning themselves on the beach or messing about in small boats. One alert hotel guest had been quick enough to reach for her video camera and film the whole episode. Within two days, this dramatic piece of film had found its way onto the news networks of the world, and the amazing pictures of the plane breaking up as it crashed were, within a few more days, in picture magazines everywhere. Almost all of the Galawa staff had rushed to the rescue, manning the small boats in a desperate search for survivors. Over 100 passengers were dead, but, to the credit of Christian's staff, many had been saved. As luck would have it, the hotel had been housing a conference of thirty French doctors at the time. They had set up an emergency station right on the beach. Without their help, many more would have perished.

Several days after the incident, I watched the video in full. It was ghastly. Body after body was dragged from the sea. The video had recorded sound as well as pictures, and I was astounded to listen to the calm, matter-of-fact narration and light-hearted comments that had been captured. It was equally astounding to view many of the hotel guests continuing to sit on the beach with their gin-and-tonics, witnessing the whole event as if it were part of the hotel's cabaret. In many ways, they got their just desserts; whilst the hotel staff, including the security department, were busy attempting to save lives, some thieving local Comorians had raided the unguarded hotel rooms and made off with many of the voyeurs' personal possessions—just one more thing for poor Christian to deal with!

The aftermath, of course, made it difficult to keep the hotel in operation. Swimming in bloody water and sunbathing on bloodstained beaches that are littered with airplane parts and the occasional body part is not most people's idea of a perfect holiday. Incredibly, within a day or two, hotel guests were starting to complain to Christian and his staff about the condition of the beach, as if Sun International had been neglectful with its beach-cleaning operation. The truth of the matter was that even if we had been able to move half a commercial jet from the shallow waters of our beach (which, of course, we did not have the equipment to do), the government of the Comores, the government of Ethiopia, Lloyd's of London, the CIA, and countless other agencies forbade us from so doing. Eventually, several weeks later, the half of the plane in the shallow water was dismantled and taken away, piece by piece. The other half is still there and is now the home of countless tropical fish.

After the hijacking incident, things settled down to normal fairly quickly—at least 'normal' by Comorian standards. We were asked to remove the chief accountant, a very reliable fellow, because he was gay, and this apparently offended the Muslim community; the volcano did erupt, but luckily the lava flow just missed the hotel; and so on and so forth. The president, who had been reinstated by the French forces (for the second time), was duly overthrown in another coup, and his replacement, in turn, met a similar fate. These events became so normal that I asked Christian to wait until after breakfast to advise me of any new startling occurrences. Eventually I found myself reading about them in the *International Herald Tribune* before I got Christian's call.

The actual end of our involvement came a little while later. Through all of the above adventures, my trusty ally Tim Clark had kept the planes flying. Firstly, he loved the Comores; like most people living in the desert, the greenery of the Comores was bliss to him. But it was more than that: visiting the Comores was like stepping back in history to a long-lost world. The mixing of Arabs and Africans had produced some very beautiful people, and the mixing of their cultures had produced an interesting blend. It was easy to fall in love with the laid-back life of the Grand Comores. Secondly, the route to Johannesburg from Dubai turned out to be extremely profitable, even the flights that stopped off in the Comores. Our Bruce Hutchisson did a first-class job of filling the planes from Johannesburg, and likewise, Roger Wharton, our European marketing director; Tim's marketing department did so in Europe and Dubai.

Notwithstanding this, Tim did not enjoy the support of his colleagues. To them, stopping off in Grand Comores was an unnecessary chore—indeed, perhaps, even a risk. The pilots were forever complaining that the runway lights were not working and that the navigation beacons were often vandalised. Also, jet fuel was a constant problem; it was either not available or contaminated. And, to make matters worse, the CIA had circulated a report to international airlines advising them that the Comores was a hotspot for terrorist activity and that the bomb that had wiped out the American embassy in Nairobi had been constructed there. This is a little hard to believe, because we had some difficulty getting Comorians to learn how to mix a cocktail, but nevertheless, the airlines could not afford to ignore the warning.

One day I was summoned to the office of Sheikh Ahmed Maktoum in Dubai, who very reluctantly advised me that he could no longer ignore the warnings and that he would have to instruct Tim to discontinue the flights. I offered to build a security fence around the airport, but it was to no avail. Nobody in Emirates wanted to risk having blood on their hands, and who could blame them? So the flights stopped, and so, effectively, did the hotel. I was weary of the whole affair, but Bruce made valiant efforts to replace Emirates with chartered aircraft. Shortly thereafter, when an offer came from some mysterious investors to buy the hotel for cash (not much of it, but nevertheless, cash), we gleefully accepted.

During this whole period, France and the French figured large on my agenda, not only because of the Comores, but also because Sol and Peter had acquired a share of a business in France, and another in French-speaking Morocco. Both of these fell to me to manage. In France, we were in a three-way partnership in a casino business with Accor, the French hotel conglomerate, and the Barrière Group, a small French leisure chain that also owned resorts and casinos there. This had come about through Sol's friendship with the founder of the Barrière Group, Monsieur Lucien Barrière, who owned the famous casinos at Deauville, on the English Channel, and Enghien-les-Bains, in the northern suburbs of Paris. Sol had helped Lucien revamp the Deauville casino, and recognising Sol's genius in these matters, Barrière had proposed a joint venture, together with Accor, to develop new casinos in France, just at the time that the government had agreed to legalise the use of slot machines. The French government's attitude to slot machines had been very dismissive. They did not think that Frenchmen would lower themselves to play on these 'kids' entertainment machines, and as a result, did not initially have any idea how successful they would be, and how much taxation could be raised through them. After all, it was argued, modern casinos were born in France. The games were French: roulette, chemin de fer, baccarat, etc. Gambling was a serious adult business. Slot machines were for infantile Americans.

French casinos were heavily regulated, and licenses were very difficult to come by; they could not be obtained by foreigners, unless they were part of a French-owned company, hence the need for us to team up with Accor and Barrière. Playing in a French casino was not very user-friendly. Gamblers were treated with suspicion. Passports were to be handed in at the door, and all French casinos had a specially seconded police force 'in-house'. If you were lucky enough to win anything, the French Inland Revenue knew about it before your family did.

Luckily, because of the government's dismissive attitude toward and lack of understanding of slot machines, the same restrictions were not placed upon their operation. They could be sited outside of the main gaming room, and there were no controls to enter the slots area. Sol had convinced Accor and Lucien Barrière that slots would be as successful in France as they had been in South Africa, and it was agreed that Sun International would be the managers of the new French enterprise, since neither Accor not Barrière had any slot-machine experience. The new company was called SPIC. Not long after the company had been formed, Lucien Barrière unfortunately died, and he was replaced on the board of the company by his attractive daughter, Diane. Diane was a beautiful young lady who featured regularly in the society pages of the Parisian press. She was married to Dominique Desseigne, and the two made a truly handsome couple. Neither, unfortunately, knew a great deal about the business, but this they would not admit to either themselves or, naturally, to us.

I assumed the responsibility for managing the business shortly after the first casino had been acquired; it was the Casino Ruhl, on the Promenade des Anglais in Nice. This casino had been infamous as a front for the Mafia, which was forced to sell under pressure from the French government. The casino was extremely well-sited, right in the heart of Nice. It was rather run-down (which we quickly addressed), and had space enough in its basement areas for over 300 slot machines. Peter Bacon had appointed Bill Timmins, an Englishman, as general manager, and Bill reported to me. A more knowledgeable, professional, decent man would be hard to find. It was not long before the French discovered our slot machines; as Sol had predicted, far from being reluctant to use them, they flocked through the doors. In fact, by the time we eventually sold this business some years later, the slots at the Ruhl were producing a 'win' per day per machine of the equivalent of over US$500 US, which compared with an average in Vegas at the time of about $120 per day per machine.

We soon acquired three more casinos, two near Marseilles and one in the Alps at Chamonix, and Bill set about renovating them and installing new slot rooms. The renovations were done well, and the business prospered, but the problems of operating were, to say the least, frustrating. The government soon realised that slot machines were cash cows and started aggressively hiking the casino-win taxes, and the unions realised that their members' jobs as croupiers and inspectors were in danger as the action at the traditional table games diminished and the action on the labour-light slots soared. Not only did the government want to get their hands on our slot revenues, but so did the union bosses, and they started to turn Bill's job and my job into nightmares.

Strike upon strike over the most meaningless and trivial matters ensued, and Bill, as the official representative of the company in France, was constantly being harassed by lawsuits involving industrial relations. Unfortunately for Bill, who would not be bullied by anyone, the unions also resorted to intimidation of the worst sort, including placing a bomb through the letterbox of his home. As Bill's manager, I naturally found myself, once again, having to offer continuous support.

As the business prospered and grew, so did the union-engineered lawsuits against the company and against Bill personally. It was as much as I could do to keep him in the job. It was also impossible to win against the unions in the courts, whose judges were undoubtedly in their pay. The lowest court in French employee/employer relationship disputes is the Prudhommes, which supposedly means 'wise men'. The jury in this court consists of two 'independent' appointees from the union and two from the employers' association (not, obviously from the enterprise being sued). If they are in deadlock, the case goes to a judge in the next town. We never won a case, and although we always appealed, the potential fines started to mount up. Amazingly, the union did not believe in waiting for the outcome of an appeal before trying to collect their damages, and on one occasion even hijacked the security van with our Ruhl casino takings on its way to the bank. Nobody was caught!

If the difficulties of running the business were not enough for Bill and me to worry about, our most trying problems, in fact, came from our partners, Accor and Barrière. Diane Desseigne, urged on by her husband and the Machiavellian management of her own casinos, did her best to second-guess Bill, who was constantly on the receiving end of criticism for mismanagement, notwithstanding the fact that our casinos were performing far better than Barrière's. The chairman of SPIC was Sven Boinet, a director of Accor, who gamely tried to keep the peace between the Barrière Group and Sun International, but who was, after all, French, so we felt he could be influenced by the management of Barrière. The attitude of our French partners became increasingly frustrating for Bill, and I found myself furiously defending him at board meetings, which were always held in Paris, and mostly in French. When Sol attended these meetings, which he was obliged to do from time to time, the tension invariably increased, firstly because he had not the patience to listen to the whinging, and secondly because Sven was a notoriously bad timekeeper, and Sol would spend most of the second part of each meeting pointing out that we would miss our "slot" with the Challenger at Le Bourget Airport.

It was against this acrimonious background that tragedy struck, plunging SPIC into a unique crisis. Diane, who it seemed had now separated from Dominique, had accepted a ride in a friend's light aircraft from the south of France to Biarritz. The plane crashed, and Diane was the only survivor. Unfortunately, she was very, very badly burned and disfigured, but was also in a deep coma. Even if she recovered, her life could never be the same. Despite the petty boardroom arguments, we all had a great deal of respect for Diane. She had stepped into a man's world and had learned fast. Now she was a vegetable, no use to her two children and no use to herself. Hard as it was to admit, we hoped she would die. But she didn't. For month upon month, she clung to life, and even came out of the coma from time to time. Months turned into years, and still she held on, but she had no ability to properly read or understand the myriad of papers that an owner and director of a casino business had to deal with. She was neither dead nor alive. She was in limbo, and so, as a result, was our shared business. Under the terms of our partnership agreement, all three parties had to sign off on major decisions, which included the acquisition of new ventures. There was nothing we could do under French law to bypass this. We could not grow the business. We had to wait for Diane to die or recover, and she did neither.

As far as Bill was concerned, sympathy turned to frustration as he saw competitors overtake our business. Eventually, I could keep him no longer, and replaced him with David Marshall, one of our casino execs from the Wild Coast in South Africa, who happened to be fluent in French. The business was going nowhere, and although still profitable (despite the tax-grabbing French government), it still needed to be managed, as did the relationship with Accor. I hated being stuck with this albatross, which was cutting into the time I had to develop other business opportunities. I agreed with Sol that if I could find a buyer for our share of the business at a reasonable price, we should sell. Sol was dismissive of the thought. He rightfully concluded that there could be no buyers for a minority share in a business whose growth was severely restricted. I did, however, have one hope. In the partnership agreement, each party was allowed to sell their piece, but only after the other partners had been given a short period of time to match any bona fide offers received. If I could only interest a rival casino company to offer to buy our share of SPIC, I was fairly confident that Sven Boinet at Accor would not want a rival as a minority (but equal) partner in his business. But why would a rival company want a minority stake, and why would they be interested in putting up a bona fide offer, with the strong possibility that it would be a waste of time when the majority partners exercised their option rights? On the other hand, this was France, the land of subterfuge. Anything was possible.

To help solve the problem, I turned to one of Sun International's old friends, Jean-Yves Olivier. Jean-Yves was our French 'Mr Fixit'. He, it seemed, could fix any problem involving politicians or officials for 5% of the upside, whatever that might be. It was Jean-Yves we turned to if we needed to lobby the government. It was Jean-Yves who had assisted in obtaining our casino licenses. Jean-Yves dealt in the murky world of political favours. His territory included most of the French-speaking world, but he had also been an envoy of France to the emerging Mandela government, and had become quite close to the ANC, and in particular to Winnie Mandela. I wondered if any casino company in France, other than SPIC, owed Jean-Yves a favour. I offered him a commission on the sale of our shares if he could produce a letter of offer sufficiently convincing that Sven Boinet would have to take it seriously. It did not take him long to come up with the goods.

Armed with my letter of offer from a rival French casino company to buy our third of the business for $25 million, I visited Sven at his office in Paris. I told him that we were completely frustrated with the stalemate within SPIC, and asked him if he would be interested in buying us out. He declined. I told him that it was, therefore, my intention to find a buyer. He laughed, and rather smugly informed me that I would never be able to find anyone who could possibly be interested. I produced my letter. If Sven was surprised or shocked, he did not show it, and for a while, I thought that he would call my bluff. I did not believe that my 'buyer' would ever follow through, but I desperately needed Sven to believe it. The clock started ticking. The fuse started to burn. As it turned out, Sven was concerned, and a few days after my visit to Paris, I received formal notification from him that Accor would take up its pre-emptive rights. Within weeks, I was able to hand my company the cheque and I was free, I thought, of French business forever.

Meanwhile, in Morocco, I was also experiencing problems. There we leased and operated the casino at La

Mamounia Hotel in Marrakech. La Mamounia is one of the world's great hotels, and it has a fascinating history. It was here in its quiet-walled gardens that Winston Churchill used to come for relaxation and to paint. The hotel is almost embedded in the ancient city walls of Marrakech. This old city, with its narrow streets and colourful souk, is both charming and interesting. Moroccans are the most artistic clan of all Arabia, and certainly of all Africa. Their natural bent for design has been blended, over the years, with French finesse, and the epicentre of this activity is the old city of Marrakech, which nestles between the desert and the fabulous Atlas Mountains.

In most Muslim countries, casino gambling is off-limits to their citizens. In some, such as Egypt, casinos are legal, but only tourists may enter, including, strangely, Muslim tourists. In Morocco, we were allowed to operate a casino, not through a license, but in the terms of a letter from the king. We were allowed to admit Moroccan citizens, provided that they were not Muslims. This permission was sufficiently vague for us to allow almost anybody through the doors, because the onus was, in effect, on the customers to declare their faith, rather than on us to pick off the Muslims at the entrance. Nevertheless, if any Muslims were caught gambling, not only would the offenders be punished, but so would we. For several years we managed to coexist happily with the authorities by paying the city police 'fees' for vetting our customers at the door and for 'guarding' our premises. The policemen knew that if the casino were to be closed down for any reason, so would the need to guard it.

Notwithstanding all of this, the casino was only marginally profitable. Moroccans in Marrakech had very little spare money with which to gamble. Tourists came to Marrakech for other reasons. The only Moroccan 'high rollers' lived in Casablanca, some three hours' drive away, and to attract them, we had to transport them on weekends at considerable expense. We also tried organising junkets from Paris, but quickly discovered that because there was no legal framework for gambling in Morocco, we were unable to prove in French courts that casino debts were enforceable in law. We therefore found ourselves in the position of having to declare uncollected 'wins' as revenue and pay casino tax on it to the Moroccan authorities. As a result, it was impossible to extend credit to foreign gamblers, and there were not enough local ones to make a real impact. I quickly came to the conclusion that we were also being robbed blind by our employees, but at the rate of potential profitability, it was not worthwhile to spend our executive time trying to control the business on fleeting visits. To do this, one would have to live on the premises, or be lucky enough to have a very sharp local manager who would be willing to live there.

After many frustrating visits to Rabat, the capital, to try to convince the authorities that we should not pay tax on our uncollected 'wins' unless they were willing to properly legalise gaming, we came to the obvious conclusion that someone was waiting to be helped to make a decision. This we were not prepared to do. The casino bumped along, making a small profit of around $1 million a year—not enough to get excited about, but too much to just walk away from. We concluded that an owner/operator who would be willing to live on the premises (or at least visit frequently) would be able to operate it more profitably than us, and would also be able to sort out the government of Morocco without putting other businesses at risk. I set about looking for such an animal, and, as luck would have it, eventually found one in the south of France: the owner of a small hotel near Eze, who was also the European agent for Bally slot machines. After a fairly complicated negotiation, I finally managed to sell him the business. Much to the astonishment of the rest of my board, within the course of one year, I had been able to unload all of our businesses in the French-speaking world, leaving the playing deck free for other things.

# Chapter Twenty
## ATLANTIS

Fortunately, cutting back on 'French affairs' did not mean that there was any serious risk of being idle. I had thought, after my efforts at Treasure Cay and Great Guana Cay for Alfred Meister, that I had done my time in the Bahamas. Not that I hadn't enjoyed it, but I felt the chances of ever being involved there again on a commercial basis were zero. Then one day, whilst Sol and I were together on the Challenger somewhere in the world, he tossed an offering document at me across the aisle, saying "What do you think of this?"

The document was about the Paradise Island resort, on Paradise Island, Nassau. Paradise Island is within sight of Alfred Meister's Salt Cay, the tiny island for which I had assisted him in negotiating a lease for cruise-ship passenger visits, so I knew it well. Paradise Island was also within sight of Alfred's home in Nassau, and we had, on many occasions, wandered over there for an evening's entertainment. The general manager was a well-known Bahamian, George Myers, who had long since stopped worrying too much about his job on Paradise Island, because of ownership changes that never ended and a capital expenditure budget that *had*. Instead, George had become one of Nassau's most successful entrepreneurs, with several small businesses and restaurants in his portfolio—supplied, it was rumoured, with a little 'help' from Paradise Island. At the end of the casino, there was a bar surrounded by a few tables and chairs, perched on a slightly raised platform. It was here, each evening, that George could be found surveying the scene. With his bulky frame falling over the edge of the seat, George had found the perfect spot to greet everyone that entered or left without actually moving. From time to time, Alfred and I would join George for a drink and a chat, and, as a result, I was fairly au fait with the history of the resort being peddled in the brochure.

Over the last few years, prior to this offering document, the resort had had a sad history. It had been bought by Donald Trump, who had seen its potential, but done nothing with it. He, in turn, as part of a more intricate deal, had sold it on to Merv Griffin, the American talk-show host and singer, for a vastly inflated price, which was mainly paid for with high-yielding junk bonds. The high yield, however, was wishful thinking, and it soon became apparent to Merv and his management team that they had overpaid. As a result, not only were they unable to raise the money to refurbish the place, but the cashflows were not equal to the interest on the bonds. As happens in these cases, bondholders take a keen interest in what is going on, and there was immense pressure on Merv to sell the resort and repay the bonds.

Merv's acquisition covered the whole of Paradise Island, all 500-plus acres of it, but many parcels had been sold off for private homes or competing hotels. The Paradise Island Hotel consisted of two main rooms blocks (totalling over 1300 rooms) linked by a shopping arcade and a 30,000 square foot casino. This development spanned a footprint of approximately thirteen acres, much of which was covered with an ugly concrete deck, surrounding an obsolete swimming pool and out-of-condition hard tennis courts, enclosed by unattractive, rusty wire fences. The great feature of the site was a magnificent sandy beach, facing the most brilliant blue sea, but any view of this was completely obscured from the pool deck and the restaurants by a rickety wall consisting of part bricks, part concrete, part wooden fencing, and part various kiosks serving ice cream, hot dogs and so on. Although you could see the ocean from most of the hotel rooms, you had to look at it through an array of tennis-court fences, maintenance huts, delivery bays, etc., and the rooms themselves had not been refurbished for many years. The plumbing was completely shot; the furniture was old, but not, unfortunately, antique; and the softs were faded, dirty, and threadbare. The kitchens looked as if they belonged in a Charles Dickens novel, and the slot machines should have been in a museum. Although Merv was spending close to $10 million per year on maintenance, it was all going on glue and sticky tape; not one cent had been spent on replacing or improving capital assets.

Merv was obviously caught in a classic downward spiral. The resort was not producing enough cash to service its debt, and Merv could not afford to bring it up to an acceptable standard, even if he had known what that standard should be. As the physical condition of the place had deteriorated, so had the morale of the employees, who once had seen themselves as working at the flagship of Bahamian properties, but were now in the fourth division. This combination of poor physical plant and poor morale naturally led to a poor product, which in turn led to a poor reputation, and lowering occupancies and average rates achieved, and, ultimately, less cash with which to pay the bondholders.

On the other hand, Paradise Island had been named as such for a very good reason. Paradise Island, once known as Hog Island, had been aptly renamed. Running the full length of one side of the island is probably one of the finest bathing beaches in the Bahamas, and the Bahamas boasts the best beaches in the world. On the other side of the island lies the city of Nassau, to which Paradise Island was connected by a road bridge (now two bridges), which spanned a wide deep-water channel. Nassau, the capital of the Bahamas, is the international air gateway and is located as close to Boston, New York, Washington, and Philadelphia as is Miami. In other words, the natural market for tourism in the Bahamas is right on its doorstep—the lucrative east coast of the United States of America. Whoever owned Paradise Island, with its perfect beach, its acres of undeveloped real estate, its convenient air access, its deep-water harbour, and its year-round sunny climate, could be sitting on a goldmine—but, just like gold, the cost of digging it out would be high.

"So, what do you think?" Sol repeated.

"It would take big balls," I replied, with a grin. "The place is in terrible condition. It will take huge cash to fix it up, but the site is fantastic," I expanded.

"I worry more about the politics and the people," said Sol.

For the rest of the trip, we debated it back and forth. We had discussed many times before the potential for creating a beach resort on the scale of Sun City for the North American market. We were convinced that a mega beach resort could work in the region. After all, Disney had proved that an inland resort could work, but Disney's biggest weakness was its lack of sea-bathing beaches. They had tried and tried to create beach clubs on the ponds of Orlando, but you just can't replicate an ocean beach. Whilst developing the cruise ship island for Big Red, I had had several discussions with Disney executives, who had all agreed that they lacked a beach resort, but had explained that there was no availability of large tracts of good coastal land in the sunny parts of the USA, and even if there had been, coastal planning restrictions were so difficult that it would be almost impossible to create a resort of sufficient scope to be interesting. Paradise Island could be the solution to this problem. Most Americans thought that the Bahamas were part of America anyway.

We also quickly agreed that if we were to consider developing Paradise Island, we would need to spend a huge amount on capital improvements, not on paying for the property in the first place. The current cashflow before debt service was around $12 million. Merv had paid almost $600 million for the property. We did not think we should pay more than $120 million for the place. Someone would have to take a huge write-off. I was dubious about Sol's ability to pay someone $120 million for something they had paid $600 million for a few years earlier. Sol was bullish; he had already figured that one out.

Sol's concern about the politics of the Bahamas was partially based upon the bad reputation of Premier Pindling, the islands' prime minister for over twenty years. For many of these years, rumours had circulated about Pindling's ties with organised crime, and the drug trade in particular. Pindling had been adamant that drugs were the United States' problem, not his; but there were sufficient gold-bedecked, Armani-dressed young Bahamians driving around in Ferraris for even a casual observer to notice that drug traffic flourished through the Bahamas. Both Sol and I had met Pindling independently, and neither of us had been impressed. Nor had most of the United States' bankers, and if we were going to do anything in the Bahamas, we would need plenty of bank support. As luck would have it, Pindling had recently been defeated in the latest elections, and the new prime minister was the same Hubert Ingraham that had been our local member of parliament at Treasure

Cay: the same Hubert Ingraham that had impressed me so much by remembering the names of all my workers on Guana Cay. I had a very healthy respect for Mr Ingraham; I hoped the feeling would be mutual, because we would, no doubt, need his support, since we were, after all, perceived to be a company with roots firmly based in apartheid South Africa; this would not go down too well with the labour union in a black country. I shared my feelings about Hubert with Sol, and he seemed cautiously encouraged.

I also shared my feelings about the Bahamian workers. Sol had only experienced surly service in the Bahamas, and particularly at Paradise Island, where he had stayed a few years earlier and had his passport stolen. And Sol was not alone. For many years, the Bahamas had been a British colony; i.e. a black country, run by whites from afar. It had also been a playground for wealthy whites from both America and Europe. Not all of the whites had treated the Bahamians with courtesy. After they had gained independence, there had been a certain backlash against foreign visitors, who were mainly from the United States and mainly white. At the same time, the labour unions wielded great political power, and the Pindling government had been unable or unwilling to curtail massive wage hikes, with the result that chambermaids, for example, were earning more than on any other (competitive) Caribbean island and more than they were in Miami. It was not surprising, therefore, that the Bahamas had developed a reputation in America for extremely poor service at a very high price, and, unfortunately, this was true.

On the other hand, it was my view that, properly managed and motivated and given product of which they could be proud, Bahamians, like any other people, could make first-class service personnel. I had proved this point to my own satisfaction at Great Guana Cay. Although we only had a staff of about seventy, their helpfulness and courtesy to our daily army of 1000-plus cruise passengers was outstanding. The visitors were delighted with their time on the Cay, and high amongst their positive comments was always the friendly welcome they had received. Furthermore, once we had set the standard, the island was always absolutely spotless, so much so that Alfred Meister once complained to me that I was keeping his island too clean (which meant spending too much money). This I related to Sol, with a good deal of conviction, and finished by assuring him, "If you can buy the place for a hundred and twenty million, I know we can train those folk to give good service."

We decided to head for the Bahamas to take a closer look. Bad as I thought the place had been during my visits with Alfred, upon closer inspection, I was absolutely shocked. It wasn't in bad condition; it was in appalling condition—so much so that I must admit my confidence was badly shaken. Not so Sol. If anything, having revisited the place, he was keener than ever to pursue the matter. This time, I kept my concerns to myself. I took Sol to meet the prime minister, and the meeting went well. Hubert Ingraham is, on the surface, a man of great warmth and jocularity. Underneath he is astute, tough and determined. Sol and the prime minister hit it off immediately. He was concerned about our South African history, so we suggested he call Nelson Mandela for a reference. That normally gets people's attention.

As it happened, President Mandela was planning to visit the Bahamas shortly as a guest of Tony O'Reilly, who had a home at Lyford Cay, and so it was not long before Mandela and Ingraham had met and struck up a nice friendship.

Sol now met with Merv's advisers and the bondholders to outline his deal. We would value Paradise Island at $120 million. We (Sun International Hotels Limited) would contribute $60 million to this pot. The bondholders, in exchange for writing off their debt entirely, could have $60 million of the equity. Merv would be off the hook. The bondholders could have board representation, and the new company would then borrow a further $120 million to fix the place up. It was now beholden on me to start churning out pro forma financial projections, to demonstrate to the bondholders that, by taking this route, under our management, they would eventually get most of their money back; and to bankers that a newly refurbished Paradise Island would easily be able to meet the debt service on the new loan. Day after day, night after night, we tweaked away at the numbers, until I could first satisfy Sol, and then everyone else. This included, of course, our own board members and investors, who had not, at this point, set eyes on the place.

The Sun International Hotels Limited board that was now formed consisted of Buddy Hawton and Alisdair MacMillan from Kersaf, South Africa; and Peter Buckley and the Honourable Charles Cayzer from Caledonia Investments, London; as well as, of course, Sol Kerzner. Having got the numbers right, Sol and I made presentations to these two groups on their own turf. This got their interest up. Then we invited them on a 'recce' to the Bahamas. We expected them to be shocked at what they saw, and we both realised that the slightest hesitation or doubt on our part would give them the ammunition they needed to run for cover. Sol is a master salesman, and on this occasion, he was at his enthusiastic best, explaining with great gusto to the group how he could turn this 'dog' into America's premier resort. Independently and individually, they all 'collared' me. What did I really think about the place? Did I really think that we could manage it? "Sol tells me that you have previous experience here; tell us what you know." Despite my qualms, I must have answered with complete assurance, because, in the end, everyone signed off on the acquisition. I was full of trepidation.

The deal structure gave us from January to the end of March to finish our 'due diligence' and to put all of the loans together. If we were successful in so doing, the 'closing' was to be on March 31, and all cashflow gained from January 1 to the closing date would be for our account. Since this period was high-season, it was imperative that the cashflows should be maximised during this pre-closing period, but local management, knowing that the place was being sold, would not be too interested in running the business efficiently. It was agreed that I would be allowed to take up residence and oversee management, even though I would have no direct control over them for this interim period. At the same time, we could complete the due diligence process and commence, with Sol, the planning of the massive refurbishment. This also gave me the opportunity to size up the existing management and supervisory staff, as well as to learn some of the many intricacies involved in running a large business—in fact, the largest business—in the Bahamas. This, of course, was not easy, because I needed the cooperation of the management but did not want to hoodwink them into thinking that we automatically intended to keep them on, should we be successful in acquiring the property. The only way I knew how to do this was to be honest with everyone; sure enough, after we had 'closed', there were many casualties, but, I believe, not too many hard feelings.

As we worked up our renovation plans, I could sense that many of the staff were disbelieving. They had seen this all before. Not only had 'The Donald' (Trump) and Merv Griffin trundled out massive refurbishment plans, but so had many others before them. Nevertheless, the place was still falling apart, the kitchens were still infested with cockroaches, and no one had bought them new pots or pans or beds (or anything else) for many years. Why should they believe us? I decided to introduce a little drama into their lives

On the day Sol and our attorneys were up in New York at the closing, I held two huge employee meetings of about 1500 employees per meeting. I gathered them together in the hotel ballroom. I told them what we were planning to do. I told them that whilst we were in our meeting, Sol was in New York with Merv finalising the purchase. I told them of the warnings Sol and I had received from many people, including some of our own investors—warnings that they, the Bahamian people, were lazy, rude, inefficient, slow and expensive; that they were not cut out for the hospitality industry. I also told them that I, personally, did not believe this; that I had first-hand experience of Bahamian courtesy and hard work at Treasure Cay; that I believed in them; and that I had given Sol and the other directors my word that Bahamians knew how to work and how to behave.

The mumblings of discontent during the first part of my speech now turned to murmurings of approval until, as a coup de grâce, I drew back the curtains of the ballroom and showed them bulldozers that we had rented for the occasion, piling into the ugly tennis courts and maintenance huts around the pool deck with almost-exaggerated relish. "We believe in you," I almost shouted. "Now you must believe in us. Together we will get this job done. Can we do it?"

The room, at both meetings, burst into a cacophony of applause and enthusiasm. It was the closest I have ever been to running a Sunday morning revivalist meeting. When the sessions closed, everybody believed that we would get the job done.

It was not easy. We had decided to renovate all 1300

guest rooms, as well as every restaurant, public space and casino. We had also decided to dig up thirteen acres of pool decks and shabby gardens and replace them with a fantasy water-world of aquariums, landscaped into the surroundings with rocky underground and transparent underwater walkways, and thousands upon thousands of tropical fish. We were to totally transform the resort from plain Paradise Island to Atlantis at Paradise Island. We were to do all of this between May and December, and, worst of all, we were to do it without closing down the hotel, because our plan depended on using the summer cashflow, and our promise to Mr Ingraham was that we would not lay his people off.

Once again, Sol and I worked together to pull it off. But it was difficult. Our budget of $120 million was very, very tight. I had to fight for every single cent at the back of the house. I had to fill new positions I knew nothing about (such as aquarium manager). I had to organise the retraining of every existing member of staff. I had to deal with Sol, who, sensing his team was not as strong or talented as the old Lost City team (even though many of them were the same), was quite cranky. I had to deal with the guests, to whom we sold rooms throughout the renovation period, albeit at very low rates. I could not quite put my finger on why the team did not work as well together as before, but I think it was because, when all was said and done, this was a renovation job rather than a new creation, although everyone who saw the finished product commented on just how creative our design team had been.

The Bahamian staff, however, was terrific. They had never seen anything like this before in their lives. Sol was everywhere, night and day. If he wasn't in planning meetings until all hours of the evening, he was stomping around the site with a hard hat, urging, encouraging, showing and shouting. The word went around how hard the boss worked.

The people saw how much money was being spent, and they saw how quickly the place was being transformed, and they, true to their word, entered into the spirit of the task in fabulous fashion. Bahamian taxi drivers were soon heard to be sharing their enthusiasm, telling disbelieving guests that Atlantis would be finished before Christmas. And finished it was—and so were all of us!

Part of my task had been to find a new chief executive for the island. One of my candidates had been a senior member of the Euro Disney opening team. On paper, he looked perfect, and his references were blue-chip. Sol and I interviewed him together in a suite at The St. Regis in New York. I asked the questions. Sol didn't seem to pay much attention to the answers. After the interview, Sol raved about the guy. I had not been impressed. Sol told me I was just plain wrong, and it troubled me that we could have such diametrically opposed opinions based upon the same data. Sol was very influenced by the references, which were from very well-respected sources. I did not feel the man had interviewed well; I thought his management style would be far too abrasive for the Bahamas. We parted that evening in disagreement, but I knew, of course what Sol wanted, although he would far rather have me in agreement. As luck would have it, the candidate was staying over for the night at the St. Regis. I decided to see if I couldn't meet him again on my own. I called his room and invited him to an early breakfast.

Breakfast at The St. Regis is very elaborate and fussy. My approach to the candidate was very direct and straightforward. I told him about my concerns. He told me I was wrong. He convinced me. Later that morning, I called Sol and told him I had had a second meeting with the candidate and that I was now convinced. We hired the chap. I should have followed my instincts. Within three months, with Sol's complete agreement, I was forced to fire him, after he had upset every Bahamian in sight. Once again, I had to step into the breach whilst we sought out a new candidate. This turned out to be an ex-Hyatt man, Pat Cowell. The Bahamians loved Pat, and Pat settled in to do a good job.

The transformation of the old Paradise Island Hotel into "Atlantis" was amazingly successful. The theme, of course, was water—or, more precisely, under water. The old concrete gardens were transformed into a thirteen-acre water park, with much of the rock work, rope bridges, and waterfalls that had featured so heavily in the Lost City at Sun City, but this time with the addition of thousands of gallons of decorative tanks which we filled with 35,000 tropical fish. This was the world's largest aquarium, but it was designed to be part of a natural tropical garden in which the tanks were cleverly melded into the landscape. From the hotel rooms, one could look down into predator pools; but take a stroll in the gardens, and the winding paths would lead you underground into caverns and through glass-tube walkways, where you would be surrounded by a kaleidoscope of coloured fish—including some very large species indeed. But the water park was also action-oriented, with huge swimming pools, lazy river rides, boating lagoons, and children's water playgrounds, all of which abutted the fabulous Paradise Island beach. The North American public loved it, and within a year, the occupancy of the 1300 rooms had risen to over 90%, year round, and the average rate per room achieved had almost trebled.

It did not, therefore, take long for Sol to convince the board that Atlantis should be doubled in size as quickly as possible. The renovations described above had cost about $120 million dollars. The audacious plan that Sol now proposed would cost almost another $600 million. This was to be the Royal Towers at Atlantis, two huge room blocks (totalling 1300 rooms) attached at a high level by a bridge housing the 'Presidential Suite', the whole new edifice rising out of a spectacular pond full of even more spectacular fish. The massive public areas of the Towers would be walled in glass, through which there would be a constant, moving backdrop of tropical fish of all shapes and sizes. Guests would be able to wander through subterranean tunnels flanked by giant saltwater tanks, decorated with the ruins of the Lost City of Atlantis, and through which shoals of colourful tropical fish would be constantly on the move.

At the same time, a state-of-the-art marina was to be built, also abutting the Royal Towers, capable of berthing the largest luxury yachts that existed. To achieve this would be no small task, because a road tunnel would have to be built under the marina for vehicles to reach the new buildings, and a new bridge would need to be built from Paradise Island to Nassau. Sol also proposed a complete rebuild of the luxurious, secluded Ocean Club and a new championship golf course, to be surrounded, of course, by luxury villas.

The opening of the Royal Towers really put Atlantis on the North American map. In the history of hotel openings, there can be nothing to match it before, and there probably never will be anything to match it in the future. You have to hand it to Sol: when he decides to throw a party, he really means it. Jerry Inzerillo, the Brooklyn Italian I had recruited to open the Lost City in South Africa, was in charge of the invitations, and Jerry surpassed himself. This was not your B-list, *Hello* magazine party. This was the A-list! Guests who actually arrived included Michael Jackson, Leonardo DiCaprio, Julia Roberts, Quincy Jones, Stevie Wonder, Oprah Winfrey, Jimmy Buffett, Carmen Electra, Natalie Cole, Denzel Washington, Harry Belafonte, Donald and Ivana Trump (with separate partners, since they were no longer married), Mark McCormack, Monica Seles, Bob Arum, Dr Ruth and Michael Jordan. The cabaret featured Grace Jones, who descended on a high wire from the top of the building to the pool deck in an angel costume; and the singing trio of Michael Jackson, Stevie Wonder and Natalie Cole with the massed church choirs of the Bahamas, all of whom gave their services for the fun of it.

The party was spread over two evenings. The first evening was indoors, in the palatial lobby of the Royal Towers, where a huge champagne fountain served as a backdrop to the Quincy Jones Orchestra and Natalie Cole. The second evening was outside, with lavish buffets surrounding the enormous swimming pools in the gardens. Some of the celebs behaved themselves, and some didn't. The organisation was pretty shambolic, but Sol, who had downed more Black Label than usual, didn't seem to notice. The fireworks display was the best that even this ritzy crowd had ever seen, and everybody seemed to have a great time.

Huge publicity followed the event in the USA, with the result that Atlantis, now with over 2600 rooms, became *the* place to go. For several years following this party and ensuing PR events, Atlantis continued to run a year-round occupancy of over 90%, at an average room rate now four times higher than the original Paradise Island Hotel. Without a doubt, it became the resort success story of the decade—something to rival Disney. Atlantis alone took more food and beverage revenues per day than any other hotel in the world!

# Chapter Twenty-One
## GREEK TRAGEDY

While Sol busied himself with the construction of the Royal Towers of Atlantis (and, at the same time, the Mohegan Sun Casino in Connecticut), I went looking for adventure elsewhere. One of my ports of call was Athens, where the Greek government had announced that it was preparing to make available an exclusive casino license at the site of the old naval academy, at the point where the road out of the city divided, going one way to Piraeus and the other to the airport. This was a perfect location for a casino, and Athens, in my opinion, was the perfect city. Amongst Europeans, it seemed to me, the Greeks were the most sociable, fun-loving, entertainment-oriented people, and an imaginative, modern casino slap-bang in the middle of Greece's biggest city had to be a goldmine for whoever was lucky enough or clever enough to secure the license.

I had dabbled in Greece before. Some years earlier, when I first re-joined Sol in the UK, I had been approached by a young Greek lady, Mrs. L, who was the wife of a leading Greek journalist stationed in London. She had explained to me that the Greek prime minister, to whom she claimed to be 'close', was interested in privatising Greece's only casino, which was situated high on Mont Parnes, the rugged backdrop to Athens. This casino was owned by the government but operated, through management contract, by Casinos of Austria. The government, according to Mrs. L, was not happy with the management and thought that it would be in the national interest to have a change. She assured me that she and her friends were in a position—provided they were rewarded, of course—to steer the casino into the direction of Sun International. Needless to say, I was somewhat dubious about this young lady's ability to deliver what she was promising, because she was just one of a long line of ten-percenters I had encountered in my career.

"How can you prove that you have such influence over the Greek government?" I challenged her. "What can you do to convince me?"

"Tell me what I need to do," she instantly retorted, with the look of supreme confidence that only practiced confidence tricksters can achieve.

After a moment of thought, I said, "I want to meet the prime minister."

"No problem," she beamed. "When would you like to meet him?"

As she left my office, I was rather sure that I would not see her again. I was therefore surprised when, about a week later, she called to say that I was invited to meet Prime Minister Mitsotakis at the official prime minister's residence in Athens the following week. To this point I had not even mentioned Mrs. L to Sol, but since it now seemed that I was about to have an audience with the Greek prime minister, I thought that I should, out of courtesy, let him know. He, naturally, was suspicious of this turn of events, and was deeply cautious about getting involved in Greece. Nevertheless, Sol was never one to pass up the opportunity to rub shoulders with the rich and powerful, so the thought of me representing our company to a European prime minister without him was a little too much to take. I was now told that although he was sure it would be "a fucking waste of time" and was, indeed, a great inconvenience, and "you can never trust a Greek," he would come too.

The following week, we flew to Athens in the Challenger, where we were met on the airside of customs by Mrs. L, all dolled up in a smart red Chanel suit, with plenty of gold bangles. She authoritatively whisked us through immigration formalities and into an old Cadillac stretch limo, instructed the driver to head downtown, and then proceeded to yap nonstop, in such a manner that I could see Sol becoming more and more irritated.

During the yap', she explained that she could not actually be seen with us at the official residence (she was sure we would understand why), and that we were going to drop her off at the home of her 'friend', who was even closer to the prime minister than she was, and that the driver would bring us back there after our meeting with the prime minister to 'talk business'.

Sol clearly did not like all of the inferences, and no sooner had she alighted then he turned to the driver and told him to head straight back to the airport.

"What on earth are you doing?" I exclaimed. "We've got a meeting with the prime minister."

"Fuck that. I don't like the smell of this at all. They're all the same, these fucking Greeks. I told you we were wasting our time." All of this, of course, was at the top of his voice!

However, a few minutes later, having quietly persuaded Sol that we really had nothing to lose by at least attending the meeting, we found ourselves being driven through the decorative iron gates of the official residence and whisked up some steps by Greek guards in skirts and boots. Once inside, we were shown into a large, ornate room, where we were offered coffee, delicately served in demitasse by a footman with white gloves and a gilded uniform. Sol was in a foul mood, and the longer we were kept waiting (which was quite a while), the worse his mood and his language became, although he did at least restrict his swearing to only slightly more than a whisper.

"I don't know what the fuck I'm doing here. I don't know how you persuaded me to come. I shouldn't listen to you," etc. On and on he went, like a morose, mumbling bear; until suddenly, there, standing in front of us, was the enormous frame of the instantly recognisable prime minister, who stuck out his hand with a warm politician's smile and ushered us across the hall into his office—or, at least, into the sumptuously decorated chamber in which he had his desk. Immediately, Sol's mood changed, or at least his outward demeanour did, and he became unrecognisably courteous and charming. Mitsotakis, it turned out, had been extremely well-briefed about Sun International, and he even produced from within his huge antique desk copies of our annual reports, which had miraculously found their way from me to Mrs. L to him. He explained the history of the Mont Parnes Casino, and spoke of his desire to see it better managed. He made it clear that we would have to compete with others for the job but that we were well-placed. The hour that we were with him flew by, and we left, promising to visit the casino, and to later, should we decide to proceed, let him know of our intentions.

As we left the building, Sol was a changed man. "Most impressive," he ventured, as we climbed back into the old limo. His good mood was not to last for long, however, because we were soon being escorted into the rooms of Mrs. L's friend, the 'fixer', who, it appeared, enjoyed a rather special relationship with Mitsotakis. We were then told by the friend how they wished to be remunerated for the 'fixing'. This was just not acceptable, so we swallowed our tea and left rather abruptly, with Sol and I in complete agreement that we could not proceed upon the lines that had been suggested. As we boarded the Challenger, even before Sol had poured the first Black Label, I heard him shout at Martin, our pilot, "If Venison ever gets you to fly me to Greece again, I'll fire you. Understood?"

Despite this incident, I was still convinced that Greece would be a great spot to operate a casino, and so I followed the news from Athens with interest. I even managed to squeeze in a visit to Mont Parnes, which was impressive on two counts: firstly, how badly it was run and what bad condition it was in; and secondly, how many people were gambling there, which in itself was amazing, since the only access to the casino was via a rather rickety cable car holding no more than a dozen people at a time, or up a steep, narrow mountain road, which could be quite treacherous at night, given the combination of darkness and Greek drivers.

Now, a couple of years later, things, it seemed, had moved on in Greece. Mitsotakis had been replaced as prime minister by Georgios Papadopoulos. Nothing had happened in regard to the Mont Parnes Casino, but the new government had decided that a casino more accessible to Athens would be very lucrative. A site had been selected, and official requests for tenders were being prepared. Bidding companies were to have primarily Greek ownership but should involve partners or managers with international casino-operating experience. The successful bidder would also need to ante up $40 million as key money for the license, which would be exclusive, except for the existing and inaccessible Mont Parnes Casino. Despite the heavy upfront payment, the numbers still looked inviting, and I was convinced that if I could find the right local partners, Sun International should be well-placed to win a bid. Sol, however, was less than enthusiastic, but he was so busy in the Bahamas and Connecticut that he did not bother to interfere.

I set about looking for local partners, but soon discovered that because one of the tender conditions was the involvement of an international gaming operator, Greek investors were soon looking for me. When trying to break into a new country or territory, I had long since learned that a great shortcut is to hire the best (or best-known) law firm there, as well as a leading international accounting practice. No sooner are you through the door than they are normally introducing you to their clients, who "might be able to make good use of your specialised services." Such was the case in Athens. Between Mr Lukas Roufos of Vgenopoulos & Partners (the lawyers) and Price Waterhouse (the accountants), I soon found myself being introduced to a consortium of construction companies, who were not only interested in the thought of printing money by owning a casino, but also by making healthy profits through building it. What they were short of was a credible international casino operator, and Sun International obviously fitted the bill. My credibility was also helped by the fact that on the day before I was introduced to this group, we had hosted the Miss World pageant at Sun City, which had been aired on Greek television and seemed to have made a strong impression. I normally would have been hesitant about forming a partnership with a construction company, because of the potential conflict of interest—but four construction companies, and in Greece! However, because it was Greece and you just knew that somewhere along the line you would get fleeced, knowing up front whom the fleecers were going to be was, in a sense, comforting.

What was more important was that the four managing directors of these companies were absolutely certain that they could win the bid, if Sun were to join them. Since it seemed that their need was greater than ours for this partnership, we were able to strike a fairly useful deal for Sun.

Sun would own 10% of the equity in the Greek company, with the balance being shared equally by the four construction companies, but—and this turned out to be the important part—Sun's 10% would be the last cash to go in. Sun would also have a potentially lucrative management contract.

Negotiations between the partners and Sun were noisy and argumentative. On our side of the table were Butch Kerzner (Sol's son, who had recently joined the business), Roufos and me; on the other side, four heavyweight builders and their attorneys. Butch became very frustrated and impatient, and on more than one occasion, I had to dissuade him from walking out. Bit by bit, we hammered out an acceptable agreement, but there still remained a couple of sticking points, and I had reluctantly agreed with Butch that if they were not solved within an hour or so, we would walk away.

Without Butch knowing, I side-lined one of the four, Mr A, who seemed to be exercising the leadership and was definitely the calmest, and warned him that the theatrics had to end. I stressed to him that although I was in charge of our negotiations, the reality was that if Butch walked out, I would not get the sanction of any deal we had done from his father and the board. When we returned to the negotiating table for what was definitely going to be the last time, Mr A produced a couple of bottles of whisky, which he plonked down on the table with a clutch of glasses. "Win or lose," he announced, "let's at least have a drink!" The contents of the two bottles were quickly dispatched, as were the remaining deal points, and, within an hour, we were all shaking hands and toasting the new partnership.

We now set about producing all of the material we needed for the formal tender document, which was detailed and voluminous. Besides preparing all of the necessary paperwork, several of my colleagues and I had to appear before the government commission to explain why we should be the chosen sons. For this purpose, we produced one of Sun's landmark 'blow away the customer' videos, and the resultant 'dog and pony show' that we put on was clearly far more comprehensive than those of our competitors. I was not, therefore, personally surprised when, a few months after the original negotiations, it was formally announced that the Sun consortium was the winner of the coveted license.

That night, Mark Roussos (a Sun executive whom we had put in charge of our project) and I went out for a celebratory dinner. By chance, a Greek friend of Mark's was also in the restaurant, and he came over to congratulate us, word of the tender result having been the object of detailed press coverage. Mark's friend sat down with us for a drink.

"Sixteen million wasn't a bad number," he ventured, after a bit of small talk.

"No," I corrected him, "the down payment for the license was $40 million, not sixteen."

"No, no," he carried on, "I'm not talking about the license fee. I'm talking about the bung. I think you guys did very well to get away with only sixteen. Everybody thought the old man would take more."

"Did they?" I said rather meekly, and changed the subject.

When Mark, at my request, pursued the issue with his friend later, it appeared that every smart businessman with any connection to the government was aware that a massive bribe had been paid by someone in our group to someone in government.

I was not amused. I had naively thought that we had won the bid as a result of my team's super presentations and tender documents. Now I knew why the builders had been so confident. The next day, I tackled Mr A. He confirmed that the number was correct with a shrug and a smile. "This is Greece, Peter," he explained. "This is the way things get done."

I felt annoyed and stupid at the same time. I was also disappointed because I knew that this would be the end of our involvement, one way or another. Thank God, I thought, that we hadn't yet paid over our 10% of the $40 million license fee. The builders, however, had paid, and would shortly be looking for our $4 million.

At this point, I had not shared the bad news with Sol, Butch, or even our attorney.

"Look," I began to say, in the vain hope that I could rescue the situation. "What you guys did before I met you, and before we entered into any agreements, is your affair. Sun will not and cannot be involved. And Sun must not know anything about this. If I ever hear one more word about this matter from you or any of your partners, Sun will withdraw, and maybe we will have to explain publicly why we had to. Is that understood?"

"Okay, okay, Peter," said Mr A. "I hear you. But somehow we will have to account for your share."

"We have no share," I almost shouted. "What you did before I arrived is your affair. There will be no accounting for this amount in our books, or even off them. That is the last I have to say on the matter." And with that, I stomped out.

I went to Roufos, the attorney, whose quiet wisdom I had come to respect. "I think we will have to pull out," I explained, "but we've spent about $400,000 to date on this project, and I want to get our money back. You'll have to threaten to them that if I don't get our money back, I will go to the press."

Roufos was baffled. "But surely you must have known that your partners had to do this to win. This is Greece,

Peter. This is the only way business gets done. This is normal. Nothing will happen. There will be rumours, the opposition will call for an enquiry, there will be an enquiry, maybe even two, nothing will be found, and after a while, everything will be forgotten. This is Greece. You are silly to pull out after you have won."

I explained, for the umpteenth time, that in regard to our casino licenses worldwide, we were subject to very close scrutiny, and that, irrespective of what he had explained, 'mud sticks', and we could not afford to take the chance, no matter how high the stakes were.

Next I called Sol. I need not record what he had to say. I told him that I thought we should pull out, but that I should be a little cautious about how. I told him that I intended to get our costs back. He agreed, but obviously felt that I was wasting my time. He could not, of course, resist from telling me that he had been right about Greece. He had been right!

Shortly after my showdown with Mr A, he called a partners' meeting. The partners, it seemed, wanted to know when Sun would be coughing up our 10%. The question was, it seemed to me, would they be asking for 10% of 40 million or 10% of 56 million? If, as I now hoped, they were to ask me for five point six million, I could legitimately 'blow a fuse' and threaten to walk out of the partnership and to spill the beans about the bribe. I knew that they would not want either to happen. The first might embarrass them, because although they had secured the license by other means, Sun was publicly associated with it, and Sun's disappearance would be difficult to get around. On the other hand, if I went to the press with the full story, I would heap upon them a mountain of trouble.

Mark and I went to the meeting. Capital contributions were indeed the subject, and sure enough, it was not long before one of the group (not Mr A) demanded that Sun participate in its share of all payments. I exploded with feigned surprise and horror. I insisted that I had been deceived, that I could not go along with such behaviour, that all of our work had been for naught, that we could not carry on with the project, and that this had been the result of their wrongdoing. I insisted that we wanted compensation for our expenses and, most of all, for our loss of opportunity. When I claimed that Sun's bid had been the best and that we would have won without their actions, they laughed, and I, of course, knew that they were right. At first they tried to soft-talk me into staying, but only with our 'full contribution'. I flatly refused, and told them that we were out and that the next thing they would hear would be from Roufos. Mr A, as usual, did his best to calm things down; he was the realist in the group. He knew that I could not proceed, and he knew that they had to be pragmatic about it. He asked if Mark and I would excuse ourselves whilst the builders discussed the matter. When we were called back into the meeting, the mood had changed. Aggression had given way to calmness.

How much did I want to leave without fuss was the gist of the question put to me. "Ten million dollars," I calmly replied. The uproar started instantaneously. Nothing else could be achieved, so Mark and I left.

"Fuck!" said Sol down the phone line, when I told him what had happened. "You'd better get your arse out of there before you finish up in the Med with concrete round your feet." This was probably good advice, so Mark and I made our plans to retreat. However, as we were about to check out of the Hilton, the phone rang.

It was Mr A. "We'll give you a million dollars," he stated flatly. "Two hundred thousand now, and the balance in four post-dated cheques over the next four months." I told him that it wasn't acceptable by me, but that I would ask my board. I also told him that the concept of post-dated cheques from Greeks was ridiculous.

"Not so," explained Roufos, the lawyer, when I later described the offer. "In Greece, strangely enough, post-dated cheques are as good as gold. If you bounce a cheque here, you go to jail." This concept did strike me as quite strange. You could get away with a fudged public enquiry if you bribed ministers in the government, but if you bounced a cheque you would go to jail.

"Are you sure?"

"One hundred percent," he said, and the manner in which it was said displayed unusual forcefulness for our gentle attorney.

"Okay," I said, "if you say so. Get in touch with them. Accept the deal, on the basis that I have the first cheque today, before I leave Athens."

And that's what happened. I got the first cheque and Roufos got the four postdated ones. I advised Sol and, in turn, the board. Although the first cheque cleared, to a man, the board and my colleagues did not believe that the post-dated cheques would be honoured. But, to everyone's surprise, every single penny was paid, and although at the time we thought we had lost an opportunity, we did at least turn $400,000 worth of expenses into a return of $1 million.

In truth, however, we were lucky to be out of the deal, because not long after we had split, a group of local residents started a campaign of objection to having a casino on their doorstep. The site was in an upmarket residential area, and they were concerned about the potential for late-night disruption. Remarkably, the government quickly caved in, and announced that it was moving the site of the proposed casino, notwithstanding that it was already holding a $40-million license fee relating to the original site. The problem for the builders was that the new site announced was forty miles away and the government would not refund the $40 million. Mr A and his gang of four were hardly in a position to argue. Ultimately, the whole affair got bogged down, and to this day, no casino has been built in or near Athens. I do not know what happened to the $40 million, but enquiries did take place regarding the sixteen. These, as Roufos predicted, produced no real evidence or result, even though the press printed lots of pictures of a new pink villa that the minister's wife had bought for a price that far exceeded her husband's annual salary.

Many other adventures also came to naught, but they did keep life interesting whilst they lasted. The Middle East figured quite prominently in these, starting with a short brush with Lebanon. The Casino du Liban had originally been something that had stirred our imaginations (as hoteliers and casino operators) back in the heyday of Lebanon, before Beirut was devastated by war. The Casino du Liban, when it was first built, was as sophisticated as Las Vegas (at the time) was brash. The casino was elegant, yet the cabaret was spectacular and rivalled anything that Las Vegas could offer. The clientele was drawn from the top drawer of Europe and Arabia. You did not venture into the casino unless you were properly attired in a tuxedo, be it white or black. This was the real backdrop to a James Bond novel.

I had first experienced it in the days when I was responsible for staffing Le Vendome in the late sixties. Sol had, independently, experienced it whilst he was researching the design for the Beverly Hills Hotel. It had made its impression on both of us. However, it had long since been closed, having suffered severe damage during the Lebanese–Israeli war and having lost its source of business.

In the late nineties, Beirut had settled down; the

attention of Israel had turned to Palestine, and as a result of the Oslo agreement, peace in the region seemed a real possibility. Beirut was being rebuilt in quite a striking manner, and as part of this renovation process, the government had announced that it was looking for international investors and operators to rebuild and reopen the casino. Naturally, I got involved—but not for long.

I met with the minister responsible, and he outlined the general conditions that, he assured me, would shortly be published in a tender document. He wanted to know if Sun International would be interested in bidding, and I assured him that if the conditions were right, we would be doing so. Some time after, he was in England, and at Sol's invitation, I took him to lunch at Ibstone House, where, as usual, Manuel puffed up and down the stairs from the kitchen. We again assured the minister of our interest and he, in turn, advised us that he would expedite a set of the bid papers to us as soon as they were available. This he did, some months later, but to our surprise, they called for bids to be made within a ridiculously short time frame of about three weeks, complete with a bank guarantee of many millions of dollars. There was no time for proper 'due diligence' or any other planning. The conditions were such that they only could have been met by a bidder who had had several months' prior warning in order to 'get his ducks in line'. The whole process was so clearly a setup for an insider that we were neither surprised when the winner was announced, nor surprised that nobody else (including us) had bothered to bid.

In due course, the new casino was opened, but it was not a great success. Times had changed since the original Casino du Liban had enthralled us. In this redesign, huge prominence had been given to the table games in grand, formal, cold spaces, whilst the slots had been squeezed into a cramped corner. As a result, after a couple of years, certain senior Lebanese politicians began to think it was time for a change of management, and once again I was approached, this time via a Lebanese friend in New York. Arrangements were duly made for Butch Kerzner and myself to visit Lebanon, and, just to make sure that we realised that they were serious players, also to meet the president.

Diana had come along for the ride. She had always wanted to see Beirut, having been fascinated with my stories from the Vendome days. By sheer coincidence, our prospective Lebanese partners had booked us into the Vendome, which had recently undergone a refurbishment and was looking good. After a day of meetings with politicians and bankers, whilst Diana looked around, we all visited the casino in the evening.

It was getting late, so Diana and I decided to head back for the hotel, leaving Butch and our colleagues to do whatever they wanted. As we approached the Vendome, all of the lights in the city went out. Undeterred, we went up to our room, retired to bed and soon to sleep. The noise of an Israeli missile zinging passed the Vendome and exploding in a nearby apartment (which allegedly was housing a Hezbollah radio station) woke us up. I switched on CNN only to see the tickertape that shoots across the bottom of the screen with 'breaking news' read: "Beirut under missile attack." We lay in bed, waiting for the next missile to arrive. After a while, when it didn't, I suggested to Diana that we go back to sleep, and amazingly, we did. The next morning I asked Butch if he'd heard the missile. "What missile?" he asked.

Unfortunately, this incident, and of course, many others like it, heralded an escalation of Israeli anti-terrorist activity and a reversal of the momentum that had been building towards peace in the region. Any investment in Beirut was, therefore, put on the backburner—as, indeed, was any ambition that I had been nurturing in Palestine itself. I knew, from previous discussions that Sol and I had had with ministers in Israel, that the chances of a casino license ever being granted there were minimal due to the strong religious lobby. We had at one time been lured into the possibility of developing something in Eilat, in the south, but it had not panned out. We were convinced that any casino catering to Israelis would be a sure-fire success, and had seen how many had managed to cross the border to Taba in Egypt to visit that casino, despite all sorts of border post delays and hassles. So when my friend, Bryan Miller, called me to say that he had just visited a new casino that had recently opened in Hebron (Palestine), just over one hour's drive from Tel Aviv, and that it was 'pumping', I was immediately interested.

At the time, I was pursuing a development project in Amman, so I agreed to go to Hebron to see for myself. I soon discovered that it is not easy to go from Amman to Hebron. I took a taxi to a staging post close to the border at the Allenby Bridge. There, I discovered that the only transport across the border, which was about five miles away, was in a special coach that departed every hour and which, unfortunately, I had just missed. Since I was not thrilled about the idea of waiting at this desolate outpost in Jordan late at night for an hour, I persuaded a taxi driver to take me to the actual bridge, which was the border.

I was, at the time, en route from Johannesburg to London and was carrying an extra empty suitcase, which I had used to take some of my family's discarded clothes to an African family whose need, as they say, was greater than ours. I had put my own over-full suit carrier inside this empty case, which had little wheels on it for easy manoeuvrability. Unfortunately, I now found myself dragging this and my heavy briefcase over the Allenby Bridge in the pitch dark, the taxi driver having turned and left in a great hurry, since he had explained to me that only the bus was actually allowed to go down the road to the bridge. I soon discovered that the Allenby Bridge, which was effectively a no-man's-land between Jordan and Israel, was made up of wooden slats, which now entrapped the wheels of my suitcase and eventually ripped one of them off. (So much for the lifetime guarantee!)

I must have looked a strange sight to the Israeli army as I emerged from the darkness of the bridge, lugging my oversized suitcase in one hand and my overstuffed briefcase in the other. Sure enough, I soon found myself staring down the barrels of some serious-looking guns, brandished by disbelieving Israelis. Any reader who has had the somewhat gruelling experience of checking into or out of Israel will appreciate the interrogation to which I was now subjected. The truth was that I was on my way to visit the newly opened casino in Hebron, Palestine. Unfortunately, this did take some believing, because I only had about $80 in my pocket, hardly enough stake money, they thought, for such a determined gambler. Eventually, the army gave up trying to understand and drove me to the immigration station a few miles up the road. Here the interrogation began all over again, but about an hour later, I was finally released into the night to search for a taxi (and hopefully an ATM) to take me the few miles on to Hebron.

Security at the casino was also extremely tight, and it involved, once again, opening my large suitcase to disclose another suitcase inside. The explanation that one suitcase had been used to carry clothes to Africa did sound a bit farfetched a few miles from the Dead Sea, and the fact that I had no money with which to gamble was even odder. I, of course, had intended to use a credit card, but once inside the casino, I realised that this had seemed even more unusual to these guards, because the clientele in the casino, who were all Israeli, were, to a man, holding huge wads of (untraceable) cash. Although, thank goodness, there was an ATM, it obviously didn't get much use.

The scene in the casino was unbelievable. Hundreds of Israelis were crowded around the gaming tables, almost fighting to put on their bets. The only previous experience I had had of such crowded activity was when Resorts International first opened the only (at the time) casino in Atlantic City, and at Mar del Plata in Argentina. In Mar del Plata, however, there had been roped queue lines leading up to each table, like at an airport check-in; here it looked like a pack of dogs around a food bowl. The din was huge; background music or entertainment would have been a complete waste of time. The casino, which had recently opened, was clearly going to be a great success.

Hebron is situated southeast of Jerusalem, not far from the Dead Sea, but most of the clientele, judging from the plates on the cars in the car park, came from Tel Aviv. Whilst there is a good highway between Tel Aviv and Jerusalem, the road from Jerusalem to Hebron is not so good, particularly at night, when, naturally, the casino was busiest. If, I mused, we could find a way to site a casino in one of the small pieces of land identified to be Palestinian in the Oslo agreement, near Tel Aviv, we could have the most successful casino in the world.

Bryan Miller, who had urged me to visit Hebron, believed he had the answer. Bryan had developed a relationship with several members of Arafat's closest advisory group, who, it turned out, were all investors in the Hebron casino. They, too, were not blind to the fact that their success in Hebron could be multiplied ten times over near Tel Aviv, and had identified a hillside near an Arab settlement that could serve as a perfect site. From this hillside you could actually see Tel Aviv in the distance. The hillside, they explained, was due to be rezoned into Palestine, because all of the important players in the peace talks were on side. Diana, Bryan and I went to check it out. They were right. It consisted of gently sloping olive groves, from which one had a panoramic view of Tel Aviv and the eastern Med beyond. And even better, we saw nearby a double highway in the making, designed to bypass this future piece of Palestine, so that Israeli settlers living to the east could travel safely to and from Tel Aviv.

I met with Arafat's men in Switzerland. They were certain that this venture could be pulled off, provided that the peace process continued. They were very keen to let me know how much carried equity the 'chairman' would require in the deal. They asked me to draw up a plan, and this we did, creating on paper a huge discount-shopping mall, entertainment complex, and, of course, casino. Just to be sure that this project would not get blocked by the Israelis, I managed to secure an appointment with a high-ranking Israeli minister and a leading attorney who was well respected by the government. Yes, there would be support for such a scheme, I was assured, because any investment in Palestine (and subsequent creation of jobs) would be very welcome to the Israelis, and "we could all go shopping there on Saturday."

As a quid pro quo for allowing Sun into this gem of a site, Arafat's men insisted that the 'chairman' needed us to do something to develop tourism in Gaza. After all, they rationalised, Gaza did have a long coastline, and it, too, was close to the major Israeli cities in the west. On the face of it, Gaza and tourism didn't seem to belong in the same sentence. Nevertheless, the prize of the Tel Aviv casino was too tempting, so I could do nothing other than at least examine the sites they had in mind. Diana also came along for the ride—or, as it turned out, the walk, as well.

Driving a taxi or rental car between Israel and Gaza is forbidden. You have to walk across no-man's-land, and although it is only about 100 yards, you really do feel exposed. The welcome we received, however, in Gaza was very special. I suppose not too many potential investors had been there for a while. Unfortunately, the situation in Gaza was so desperate that it would be many years before any sort of tourism prospect would survive, be it international or domestic.

I was, however, spared the difficult task of explaining this to the Palestinians, because events overtook the process. Within weeks of our visit, the peace process began to crumble before our eyes, and a series of suicide bombings in Israel, with subsequent retaliation in Gaza and elsewhere, once again brought chaos to the region. Israelis were stopped traveling to Hebron, and the casino closed. Any hopes of building a new one near Tel Aviv closed with it.

# Chapter Twenty-Two
## THE ROYAL MIRAGE

I was, however, more successful in Dubai, although initially it was an uphill battle, once again through Kerzner's lack of interest and cooperation. Sheikh Mohammed Maktoum, the second son of Sheikh Rashid, whom I had served years ago at the Carlton Tower, was the visionary leader of Dubai, one of seven states which make up the United Arab Emirates. Dubai sits next to Abu Dhabi on the Arabian Gulf. Abu Dhabi had recognised oil reserves for more than ninety years into the future; oil in Dubai was beginning to be exhausted. As a result, the ruling Maktoum family had decided to turn Dubai into the commercial centre of the Middle East, eventually hoping to rival Singapore as the preeminent capital of trade and commerce outside of the West. To do so, the Maktoums realised that Dubai would also need to become the R-and-R capital of the Middle East, and that strict religious codes, as practiced in the rest of the region, would have to be moderated and relaxed for the sake of attracting 'expat' businessmen and their families. The development of a stock of international-quality hotel rooms was to be part of the plan, and Mohammed Maktoum would ensure that funds would be found locally to achieve it. Unusually, foreign investment was not required; foreign knowhow was.

Mohamed's business adviser for many years was the trusted Brigadier Barclay, who had remained in Dubai to help the royal family when the British departed. There was not much that the brigadier did not know about the business and financial affairs of the Maktoum family, and he had obviously earned their respect through his sound advice, care and confidentiality. The brigadier, however, knew little about the hotel business, although at the time of our first meeting, Sheikh Maktoum did own the old but successful Chicago Beach Hotel in Dubai, and the Sheikh's uncle, Sheikh Ahmed Maktoum had just opened the Forte Grand Hotel on the road to Abu Dhabi. Bryan Miller, who lived in Dubai, knew the brigadier, who had helped Bryan locate a rental villa. It was Bryan, therefore, who, having heard of the Maktoums' intention to turn Dubai into the convention and tourist centre of the Middle East, arranged a meeting for me with the brigadier to see if Sun International could feature in the plan in any way.

The brigadier was charming, brusque, and very British. He explained to me that it was Mohamed's intention to knock down the Chicago Beach Hotel and to replace it with two new edifices, one a 600-room hotel on the site of the existing hotel, and the other a massive all-suite tower hotel on a manmade island (yet to be made, of course) in the Gulf, connected by a bridge to the mainland and the other hotel. The architects had already been selected, having been winners of an architectural competition at which they had had to produce models of their proposed designs. The brigadier proudly showed me the two designs of the hotels, which were destined to become the Jumeirah Beach Hotel and the Burj al-Arab, Dubai's 'Eiffel Tower'. The brigadier had been instructed by Sheikh Maktoum to find a management company to assist with the planning of these two projects and to manage them thereafter.

It did not take me long to be useful. It was immediately obvious that despite the architects having won the competition through bold design, which must have looked very attractive to His Royal Highness in model form, they knew zero about practical hotel design. For example, the footprint of the Jumeirah Beach Hotel was almost the same width as the rest of the building, which was a single banked wave of hotel rooms. The result was that the public areas were all long and thin, and the spaces allocated to service them were not adjacent, where they should have been, but were situated under them, with connections via elevators or escalators. Food, it was imagined, would be delivered to the restaurant via an escalator-like conveyer belt from the kitchen, one floor below. Dirty dishes would disappear in the reverse direction. "I hope nobody wants his steak redone," I pointed out to the brigadier, who, having examined the problem, instantly recognised it as one.

After maybe an hour of pointing out similar obvious design faults, such as the pillars in the conference room and the low ceiling heights in the rooftop restaurants, the brigadier seemed very keen to have Sun on board, and he asked me to prepare a one-page description of Sun International for presentation to Maktoum. "I can't describe Sun International on one page," I exclaimed, thinking that I needed to produce a mind-blowing video presentation to properly impress the sheikh.

"One page, and not a sentence more," barked the old man. "None of your ruddy video nonsense. He's not fooled by all that."

Reluctantly, and with some difficulty, I produced the one page, and either Barclay or Sheikh Maktoum was suitably impressed, because I was soon back in the brigadier's office, negotiating terms for the management contract—or, to put it more realistically, being told how much they were willing to pay. Although the terms for management were not too far below our expectations, the brigadier was not prepared to pay anything close to the marketing fees that I requested, because, he pointed out, Sun had no experience of marketing a hotel in the region and all of the business would, in any event, be delivered by their own airline, Emirates, or would come as a result of the huge promotion the government intended to do on behalf of the country. Try as I did to insist that his project should contribute to Sun's international marketing expenses, I could not get through, so we agreed to disagree for a while, whilst we got on with the more urgent job of planning the hotels. I was certain that I would be able to convince him later—and I needed to, because Sol had become adamant that I should not sign the contract unless I got what we wanted.

The architects were under pressure to produce working drawings, but they admitted that this was the first hotel they had ever designed, and they were desperate for input from an operator. Two interior designers, one selected by me and the other by Sheikh Maktoum, had been preparing presentations, and we were all asked to attend a meeting in Newmarket, at the English country home of Sheikh Maktoum, to present our work to date. We all arrived at the gorgeous house, surrounded by little white-fenced paddocks and green, green grass, at eleven in the morning, as requested. Sheikh Maktoum arrived to view the presentation at 10 pm!

Whilst we were waiting, and after the presentation boards had been set up, we asked the butler if we could have a room to work in, and he duly ushered us into a dining room. On the dining-room table were several miscellaneous items, which I requested permission to put on the floor, so that we could have clean space on the table to unfold our plans. As I carefully removed the objects from the table, I could not help but notice that one was the Epsom Derby trophy, another was the Ascot Gold Cup, and so on, all of which I neatly placed on a row on the floor. I never thought I would ever get to see such famous trophies, yet alone be relegating them to the floor.

By the time the sheikh arrived (with many apologies for the delay), we were all quite dishevelled—and hungry. Not thirsty, though, because I had rudely rooted around the pantry to the dining room and found a fridge full of Beck's. With empty stomachs (except for the Beck's), and after a depressingly long wait, Trisha Wilson, James Carry and I were probably not looking our best when the sheikh entered the room from the opposite end to that which we had been advised by the brigadier, who had been hovering around at the other end all day. In fact, Trisha, who is normally never in the slightest way dishevelled, even on a hot or windy construction site, actually greeted His Highness with her shoes off, holding a bottle of beer.

As it happened, Sun International never did the job, much to my embarrassment. Sol was absolutely adamant that I should not sign the management agreement as offered. I argued that whilst we were not getting everything we wanted, these projects could be a calling card for the future in the Middle East and even beyond. I pointed out that Sheikh Maktoum was also the owner of the Carlton Tower in London and that if we were to do the right job for him in Dubai, anything could happen in the future. But it was to no avail. Sol had gone cold on the whole idea of operating in Dubai, and absolutely instructed me—no, forbade me from offering the Sheikh or Brigadier Barclay another ounce of help.

The brigadier was cross when I informed him, but quickly rationalised things by declaring that they didn't really need a management company anyway, with a defiant "We can do it ourselves." When next I heard from the Middle East, the brigadier had hired the man I had earmarked to work for us, Gerald Lawless, and had put him in charge of a newly created management group, owned, of course, by Sheikh Maktoum. It has to be said that in this instance, the brigadier was right; Gerald did a first-class job, although I think he would agree that my free planning advice had been a positive contribution to what could have been an unworkable plant.

Not long after I had been forbidden to talk to the Maktoums, Diana and I received an invitation from Sheikh Maktoum's uncle, Sheikh Ahmed Maktoum, the chairman of Emirates Airlines, to attend the inaugural Dubai Gold Cup, the world's richest thoroughbred horse race. Notwithstanding the wishes of my employer, this was an invitation too good to pass up, and we soon found ourselves staying at Ahmed's hotel on the beach with such racing luminaries as Frankie Dettori, and Burt Bacharach.

This was the year of Cigar. The world's finest horse (sixteen wins from sixteen starts, at this point) would be competing in the world's richest horse race. And Cigar did not disappoint, beating out the rest of the best by a neck, as thousands of dish-dashed Arabs yelled encouragement, whilst concealing their cell phones (for bets to London, since betting in Dubai is illegal) under their flowing robes.

Although we were the guests of Ahmed, the host of the race meeting was Sheikh Mohammed Maktoum himself. As part of the affair, on the night before the race, we (and a few hundred others) were invited to 'dinner with cabaret'. 'Cabaret' turned out to be Simply Red. Most people, I think, would have mentioned that on the invitation! On the night after the race, His Royal Highness hosted a desert party par excellence, to which we were all shuttled in individual Land Cruisers, and at which we sat (somewhat uncomfortably) on our haunches on Arabian carpets under the desert skies and feasted.

During our stay in Dubai, Sheikh Ahmed asked for some advice. The eldest of the ruling Maktoum brothers had a large plot of gulf-side land on which he wanted to build a hotel. He had entrusted Sheikh Ahmed to organise it, and Sheikh Ahmed wanted to do something special for the ruler, even though the site was almost adjacent to his own hotel and would inevitably become competition. I explained that I could not advise him wearing a Sun International hat, but that as plain Peter Venison I would be delighted to help.

"What you should do," I ventured, "is to build something which will mean 'Arabia' to the tourists. With the greatest respect, Your Highness," I continued, "the hotels that you and your family have built until now are architecturally spectacular, but are in the vein of current Western building. They are the type of buildings that Europeans and Americans work in: all steel and glass. They are not, by definition, ones that they want to play in, nor, indeed, that fit their romantic image of Arabia. Arab architecture may remind you of the days when your people were poor, but if it can be recreated in the form of a hotel, it will make the ruler rich." Of this I was convinced, and I really hoped that Ahmed would be able, in turn, to convince his 'employer' likewise. I explained that I could not take part in the development of the site without a conflict with Sun International, but that I would introduce him to a project manager and team of architects that could do the job. The man I had in mind was Dene Murphy, our old friend from the days of the Palace of the Lost City, who responded to the challenge (and the brief) with huge enthusiasm, professionalism, and, ultimately, success.

I followed Dene's progress on the project from a distance, but with great interest. Dene and his team had designed a hotel exactly along the lines that I had in mind, and the building was well out of the ground. Whilst having a conversation with Bryan Miller one day, he told me that he had been asked by Sheikh Ahmed to source a management company to operate the new hotel. When Bryan told me that he had secured a written offer to manage on acceptable terms from Westin Hotels, I was very depressed. "With the greatest respect to Westin," I told Bryan, "it is the wrong company to manage this place. Westin is great at operating city hotels, but not resorts— and, in my opinion, over half of the business on the beach at Dubai will be holiday-makers."

"Well, why doesn't Sun International manage it, then?" Bryan replied. "Sheikh Ahmed would be thrilled if you would, Peter. He is always telling me that."

"Okay, Bryan," I said. "Hold off signing with Westin if you can. It's been almost two years since Sol and I have spoken about Dubai. I'll give him one last chance to change his mind."

After a few moments of picking up from Bryan the relevant details of the Westin management contract, I promised a quick resolution. Not long after, I broached the subject with Sol, who to my surprise was very relaxed, even disinterested about the matter. "If you can get the deal back from Westin, I suppose there's no harm done," he volunteered, with no great enthusiasm. "I'll leave it to you." Which he did.

Sheikh Ahmed seemed very pleased when I told him that we were now willing to manage. He was well aware of Sol's ambivalence on the matter, but that didn't seem to bother him as long as I was involved, which I promised him I would be. The actual negotiation for the contract, which was handled by Ahmed's trusted and experienced financial adviser, was a lengthy and somewhat testy process, but I threw myself into the task of operational planning well before the matters of the small print were finalised, which, eventually they were.

Dene had done a marvellous job of planning and organising, but there were some built-in faults, particularly with the planned food, beverage and entertainment outlets. I was as determined as Dene that this should be the finest hotel in the Middle East. We had some huge differences about how to achieve this, with Dene naturally anxious to preserve his plan (and his budget), and me adamant that my inputs were correct and necessary. The glue that held us together was a mutual desire that this should be 'the best', and so we both understood (and forgave) each other's passion. What we created was the Royal Mirage. Thanks to Dene and his team, and to Olivier Louis, leading my team, and the unfailing support and wisdom of Sheikh Ahmed, it did turn out to be amongst 'the best'.

Sol, meanwhile, left us completely alone, only visiting the Royal Mirage when it was all finished, one week before we opened. Even then, he only went from some sense of duty, and the visit was not a huge success. We had just taken delivery of a new corporate jet, another longer-range Challenger, and Martin and the boys had flown it on an inaugural flight from the USA to South Africa, with Sol on board. There, he picked me up, together with our friend, Abe Segal, the tennis pro at Sun City, who wanted a ride to London (or Wimbledon, to be precise), to which we were headed via Dubai.

Abe was a huge man, both in size and character. As one of the first professional tennis players in the world, Abe had been the funny man of the tour. He had also been a talented player and had earned his place in the Last Eight Club at Grand Slam events. Not one to boast, however, Abe would tell you that his claim to fame was participating in the longest tennis set ever played at a Grand Slam event, actually at Wimbledon, which he lost 34 to 36. In any event, with Abe on board, we knew that we would have a good laugh.

When we arrived at Dubai Airport in mid-morning, it was already very, very hot, and Sol was cursing because he had not brought any shorts. "You can wear some of mine," offered Abe, and promptly rustled around in his bag, from which he pulled out a huge, screwed-up pair of shorts. The fact that Abe is at least one foot taller than Sol did not seem to deter Sol from accepting the offer, and so we set off to the Royal Mirage in the shiny new Mercedes limo, with both Sol and Abe in tennis shorts (Sol's coming almost to his ankles), looking like Laurel and Hardy.

The manager of the Royal Mirage, Olivier Louis, had been nervously awaiting Sol's visit for at least a year and was determined to impress him. For starters, he had organised a tour of the practically finished premises, of which he was also very proud, to be followed by pre-lunch cocktails with all of the department heads and supervisors: a chance for them all to meet the great leader, Kerzner. The tour did not go well. Sol found fault with everything he looked at, Abe cut his arm on the authentic keyhole door to the Moroccan restaurant, and it was hot, hot, hot. Unperturbed, Olivier soldiered on with the tour, talking ten to the dozen, but I could see that all Sol wanted was a cool drink, so eventually I managed to steer the odd inspection group back to the air-conditioned room where we were due to meet the supervisory team. There, assembled, were about thirty people from every corner of the world, who had all put on their best clothes, hair, makeup, etc. for the meeting, which Olivier had billed as being very important. They were therefore somewhat surprised at the sight of Sol, swamped in Abe's creased tennis shorts, and even more surprised when he hardly bothered to talk to them, other than to respond curtly to the warmest of welcoming words from their boss, Olivier.

After about five minutes at the gathering, Sol asked if we could leave to get some lunch at one of the competitors' hotels down the beach. There, from our seats in the restaurant, we could glimpse into the kitchen, where we could just make out staff crowded around what appeared to be a television screen. The manager of the hotel where we were lunching came to sit with us, and quickly spotted that the cricket match on the television seemed to be more important to his staff than the service. It also became more important to Sol than pursuing the purpose of our visit, since South Africa was playing England. So we all soon adjourned, at Sol's insistence, to his suite at the Ritz-Carlton, where Sol, Abe and I watched the television for the rest of the afternoon and Sol knocked back almost a whole bottle of Black Label, kindly provided by the management.

Poor Olivier Louis was somewhat put out. He had, at my request, done quite a lot of preparation for the visit of the chairman of the company, including having prepared detailed budget and marketing presentations. Since he had his top team on standby, on the assumption that Sol would soon be returning to the Royal Mirage, Olivier kept calling me to find out what he should do. After a while, and by the time the Black Label was 'quite low, I told Olivier to take his team off 'alert' and to cancel the dinner arrangements that had been made for later. This turned out to be a wise move, because when the cricket and the scotch were finally finished, Sol asked if there was anywhere casual we could go to dinner, because he did not want to change out of Abe's shorts.

We went to the Hard Rock Café. According to the waitress who served us, Sol was the first person in the history of Hard Rock who had managed to fall asleep with his head on the table between the order and the delivery of a hamburger, notwithstanding the million-decibel music that is the trademark of the place.

We left on the Challenger at the crack of dawn. To round off a thoroughly unpleasant and unsatisfactory trip, no sooner were we airborne than Abe broke the toilet on the new plane, so none of us could use it on the seven-hour flight, and Sol wouldn't talk to him the whole way home. That's what happens when you break a friend's toys!

Although Sol's behaviour in Dubai had been disappointing, to be fair, it was not always like this. I have learned more from Sol Kerzner than from any other manager. I have often not agreed with him, but have always respected his opinion, his knowledge, and his ability. I have also benefited from and appreciated his most generous hospitality. There are many things that Sol can do that I have not mastered, and never will, because, in his way, he is a genius. Firstly, Sol has the ability to move up and down the scale of required management behaviour at will, and in a flash. He can spot a mistake in a balance sheet quicker than Arthur Andersen, or a problem with a building plan before Frank Gehry. He can walk into a room where 'experts' have been puzzling over a problem for hours, and instantly tell them the solution.

He can party all night, but be the first one to work in the morning, with a crystal-clear head. He can push and push, but knows exactly when to stop, or, in realising that he didn't stop in time, can make instant amends. He can be rough and tough, and he can be charming; he can even be charming whilst he is being rough and tough. He is never neutral. He can listen well. He can seek and take advice, but he will always make up his own mind. He is brash and outward-going, but he can keep things very close to his chest. He can be extremely intimidating, and maybe still doesn't realise (or care) how negative this can be. Once he has made up his mind about something, he believes he is right. He is not always right, but mostly he is! He is always strategising.

There is always a plan in his head, sometimes one that goes far beyond the current circumstances.

For someone who can be extremely fiery and short-tempered, his greatest quality is his patience. He is like a predator. He will wait and wait and wait before the kill. You win battles against Sol, but never wars. He leads from the front. He may give his generals a hard time, but his troops love him. He doesn't manage by walking around; he stomps around. Despite all he has achieved, he never seems to be a happy man, and, along the way, he has caused some unhappiness for those around him. If Sol had been born in America and not in the backwater of South Africa, where the politics of the country handcuffed his growth, he could have been the giant of the world's hotel industry. As it is, he is certainly no dwarf.

Sol was also extremely careful in choosing his partners and business colleagues. He had been badly bitten in the Transkei, and had many years of worry whilst the public prosecutor refused to close this case. During this period, I made several sorties into the Far East and India in an attempt to find opportunities for Sun International, particularly in the casino business, but in each case, these had to be stopped abruptly when the request came for the bribe.

At least in India, they were upfront about it. On my first meeting with a famous maharaja, who claimed to be able to 'deliver' a legal casino license, he produced a budget for the project, which actually had the bribes that would be necessary all neatly listed as line items.

In China, no matter how often I explained to potential partners (normally politicians or local officials) that we would not be prepared to offer bribes, and no matter how often they said that they understood, sooner or later the 'request' would come, and I would find myself reluctantly withdrawing. This was not just in mainland China, but in Taiwan as well. The bribe would normally take the form of a contribution to a political party, which I was always assured was perfectly legal. I have no doubt that one day China will be an immensely successful country; the Chinese are extremely clever and likeable, but until they can rid themselves of this cancer of corruption, they will never reach their full potential. If I have learned anything on my travels, it is that corruption is the worst enemy of efficiency. Unfortunately, in many places, it is the lubrication that keeps the wheels turning.

My travels in search of the right opportunity for Sun International took me round the world, but just when it seemed as if a deal was right, for one reason or another, Sol Kerzner didn't want to know. Although he did not control the board, as a large personal shareholder and as chairman of the company, if he did not recommend something, it did not happen. Even in the Indian Ocean islands of Mauritius and Seychelles, it was difficult to drag Sol along with expansion, but at least there he was not the chairman of the local company, and so we were able to grow, and, under my watch (and eventually with Sol's agreement), we built Le Coco Beach and the Sugar Beach, and knocked down and rebuilt the Saint Géran (in an amazing eight months).

As I watched the new Saint Géran rise from the rubble of the old one, I told myself that this would be my last hotel. I was tired, and somewhat frustrated. I felt that my management team had the skills to create the finest resort-hotel chain in the world, but that, for whatever reason, this was not what the Kerzners wanted to do at the time. I knew I had to leave. Two months after I had resigned, and before I had worked out my notice, I found myself under the heart surgeon's knife. It was obviously time for a change.

# Chapter Twenty-Three
## AFFAIRS OF THE CROWN

I did not approach retirement with trepidation; instead I looked forward to it with positive anticipation. It seemed to me that life could be divided into three sections. The first, growing up and education, the second, working to provide for the wellbeing of wife and family, and the third to enjoy the fruit of one's labours with wife and family. In my case I felt that the retirement phase was particularly important because, as a result of the nature of my work, the second phase had been one where I was frequently away from Diana and the family, leaving her with the lion's share of domestic responsibility. It seemed to me that retirement would give us the opportunity to do things together and, particularly, things that Diana would like. My goal had been to retire at age fifty, but I eventually managed it about five years late. That said, although greatly relieved at not having to go to an office or an airport on a daily basis, or incessantly answer the phone or be asked to make decisions, like most retirees, I needed to find something to fill the gap of intellectual stimulation. Shortly before retirement, whilst sitting in a window seat on a plane flying into Heathrow, on an approach from the west, we passed low over Windsor Castle, I happened to notice a golf course tucked into the grounds. I had never seen this before either from the air or the ground, where it is exceptionally well hidden from the road. The thought hit me that if would be rather special to play on this course and that other people might think the same. Gradually I conceived the idea or using the course as a prize to raise money for charity. My plan was to utilise my international contacts in resort hotels around the world to persuade them to organise charity golf tournaments, with the winners being invited to play against each other in an annual tournament (The Duke of Edinburgh Cup) in the grounds of the castle. This would obviously involve flying people to England from far-flung parts and obtaining permission from the Royal Family to use, what is, in effect, a private facility. My goal was to organise up to ten annual national events in different countries. The idea was to raise $75,000 at each event, half of which would be donated to the national branch of the Duke of Edinburgh Award and the balance, with the agreement of the local sponsor, to other charities in each country where the money was raised. The Award is given in the form of gold, silver and bronze medals to young people who have successfully completed a course in life skills and charitable work. Every year around a quarter of a million youngsters are presented with medals on behalf of, and often by, HRH The Duke of Edinburgh.

As luck would have it, I had a friend, Terry Regan, who, in his retirement had been involved in fund raising for the Award. I pitched the idea to Terry, who loved it, and promised to find a way of presenting it to His Royal Highness, Prince Philip. A meeting was duly arranged at which, not only did his Royal Highness approve of the idea, but offered, subject to the Queen's agreement, to allow the visiting golfers to use the state rooms for the prizegiving dinner, which he would personally attend. This was more than I had hoped for, since one is not allowed to dine in the state rooms of Windsor Castle without the presence of a senior member of the royal family. Our prize for the winners of each national tournament was set; one week's holiday (with partner) in the UK, free air travel, three rounds of golf (at two internationally recognised courses in Surrey and Berkshire and the third at Windsor Castle), and a black tie gala prizegiving at the castle with HRH The Duke of Edinburgh as guest of honour.

I set about pitching this idea, with the help of British Airways, who were kindly willing to pony up the air tickets, to various potential sponsors in countries where I had good contacts. Initially this was South Africa, Mauritius, Bahamas, USA and Canada, but over the years the list grew to the UAE, Barbados, Spain, Portugal, Botswana, China, India and several more. Over nearly twenty years, through this simple idea, we have raised and distributed to charities over $10 million, with the lion's share going to the Duke of Edinburgh Award.

Not only did we obtain the blessing of Her Majesty, the Queen, and HRH, The Duke of Edinburgh, but we also were blessed with their enthusiasm for the project, and when the Duke decided to cut back on his extensive workload, his sone, HRH The Earl of Wessex, together with his charming wife Sophie, stepped up to the plate with fantastic and unselfish support, for which I will always be grateful.

My dealings with the Duke were sometimes quite amusing. On one occasion I assisted the Palace by locating and organising an African cabaret to be performed in St. James Palace on the occasion of a 'thankyou' dinner for major donors to the Award, hosted by His Royal Highness. The show, *African Footprint*, was written and produced by my good friend Richard Loring, the well-known impresario in South Africa, and took place in the library at the Palace before the dinner. The show went well and the Duke looked pleased. However, as he left his seat in the library, I ventured to ask him if he had enjoyed it. "A bit loud, wasn't it?" was his brusque reply, although it was delivered with a smile–so I took it to be a bit of a tease. The dinner was a big success and, at the end of the Duke's after dinner speech, he invited all present to follow him down the back stairs to the small garden of St. James, which abuts the Mall. Having lined all of his tuxedoed guests against the wall, with me and Diana standing beside him, he clicked his fingers and, out of the bushes, in the dark, came the Irish Guards, led by their huge regimental dog, complete with kilts and blaring bagpipes. They marched up and down in complete precision in the secondary light of the Palace, and then came to a stop (music too) in front the Duke, with a crisp salute. In the momentary silence that followed His Royal Highness turned to me and said, with considerable pride, "That's what I call 'British Footprint'," whereupon I was able to retort, "It was a bit loud, wasn't it sir?"

I also had the privilege of meeting Her Majesty, the Queen. An invitation arrived one day at home to a cocktail party at Buckingham Palace. It gave no indication as to the reason for the party and it did not seem to include Diana. I called the RSVP number on the card and asked if I could bring my wife. The answer was "No." "In that case, I will not go," I exclaimed to Diana. "Of course you will," she replied. "You cannot turn down an invitation to meet the Queen." I felt very uncomfortable about this but I did, rather reluctantly, agree to go. Upon arrival I was ushered into one of the state rooms, where there were about thirty people sipping champagne and other beverages. I thought I recognised several of them. After a few minutes I was approached by an aide, who ushered myself and four others into an adjacent room. "You will be introduced individually to Her Majesty," he informed us. With that he handed me and the others a little card with my name printed on it.

"When the doors open over there hand the card to the page inside and he will announce you." Seconds later the double doors were flung wide open and there, beyond the uniformed page, was the Queen, much tinier that I had imagined, flanked by HRH Prince Philip. Behind whom stood Sir Miles Hunt-Davis, his private secretary who was one of my Trustees. "Mr Peter Venison" announced the page, giving my name an unusual air of importance, whereupon I found myself stepping forward to shake Her Majesty's outstretched gloved hand. A few polite words later I heard the next name being boomed out, which I took as the clue to move on to the Duke's outstretched hand. "Haven't we met?," enquired the Duke rather quizzically. "This is Peter Venison, sir," whispered Sir Miles, "he helps us raise money for the Award." Then came the next "announcement" from the door, so I moved on again, to be ushered back to the cocktail party, the purpose of which I had still not figured out. When I got home that evening Diana asked me what the Queen had discussed with me during the introduction. I was ashamed to say that, since the whole episode seemed dreamlike, I honestly could not remember.

However, Her Majesty had not done with me for the day. As I stood clutching my champagne flute, I was approached by a young man who appeared to be in charge of the catering. "I expect you won't remember me," he said, as he introduced himself. "I am the assistant catering manager at the Palace. I used to work for you as assistant manager at the Bloemfontein Hotel." Quite a jump upwards, I thought – from me to the Queen and from Bloemfontein to Buckingham Palace. I asked him what the gathering was all about. "You," he stated, "have been selected as a person with current knowledge of South Africa as have all of the other guests. There is a State Visit next week. President Zuma is coming to stay at the Palace. Her Majesty is doing her research so that she is au fait with current affairs in South Africa. The only thing she doesn't know is which of his wives will be staying." Apparently, Heads of State are always invited to stay in the Palace during official State visits, the last from South Africa being Madiba.

Sure enough, at that moment, the diminutive, but immaculate, figure of Her Majesty joined the cocktail party and began to mingle with the guests, making sure that she got to talk to every single guest, including me and the others who had previously been introduced. Her questions about South Africa were piercing. She stayed for at least an hour. I was extremely impressed. She really is a remarkable lady.

When, after many years, I decided to step down as chairman of the golf charity, I was summoned to Buckingham Palace for a meeting with Prince Philip. I was ushered into his private suite and advised by his aide that the meeting would last up to thirty minutes and no more. The room had a strangely old-fashioned appearance, with one much used desk at one end, surrounded by fitted bookcases, and a couple of rather pedestrian couches and easy chairs at the other. The place looked comfortable and well used – almost homely, unlike the grandeur of the rest of the Palace. Philip, then in his nineties, bustled into the room, immaculately dressed in suit and tie, and asked me to take a seat. He got straight to the point. "Now, what is all this about you retiring? You're a young man." I did feel a bit of a twerp, but stuck to my guns and he accepted it in good grace, before going on to discuss the state of the world. A few years before the Duke had kindly invited Diana and me to the State Opening of Parliament, where we sat in the seats reserved for guests of the Royal Family, not in the anteroom bleachers, where most invitees sat, but right in the chamber of the House of Lords. It was the most spectacular event we have ever attended, carried out with the precision that only the British can achieve. The colours of the gowns and the sparkling jewellery on display were unforgettable; we were exceptionally privileged to witness this amazing piece of pageantry and proud to be British. I had written, thereafter, to the Palace to thank the Duke, but now, in this private meeting, I finally had the chance to thank him in person.

Not long after that meeting I was amazed to receive a letter from Buckingham Palace. This time it was from the Lord Chancellor, informing me that I was to receive the honour of Commander of the Victorian Order (CVO) and would be asked to attend the ceremony at Buckingham Palace. The next day another letter came from the Duke's office congratulating me, and on the following few days further letters from Anne, the Princess Royal, and Edward, The Earl of Wessex. Since all of the envelopes were clearly marked on the outside of the envelope 'Buckingham Palace', on the fourth day the postman actually rang the doorbell to hand me the post. "Blimey, mate. What's going on? You being knighted or something?"

At the formation of the charity Terry and I had taken the precaution of inviting the permanent secretaries of the Duke of Edinburgh and the Earl of Wessex to be trustees. As a result it was suggested that we hold our regular trustee meetings in Buckingham Palace, so I knew, therefore, the layout of the place pretty well. However, attending the award ceremony was something really special and I experienced the grandeur and importance of the Palace in a completely separate light. The invitation was for myself, Diana and two family members. Since we have four children, Diana immediately suggested that I should ask for two extra guest places. I resisted this on the basis that if everyone did so, there could be chaos. Diana knew this but she also knew that the decision as to which of the children I should invite would be difficult, since Sue and Simon (our eldest) were from her previous marriage and Sarah and Jonathan were from our marriage. I had no doubt that I should ask our offspring in order of age and that, should the eldest two accept, the bonds between us all were strong enough for the youngest two to understand. Although Sue would actually be in Italy on the day, and Simon in Dubai, both accepted to attend. I am sure that Sarah and Jonathan were disappointed but they never said so, only expressing their pride in their dad.

We arrived at the doors of the Palace at the same time as Rod Stewart and his wife, Penny. Upon entering, Rod and I were singled out and asked to follow a decoratively uniformed aide. Diane, Penny and offspring were sent to the ballroom where the investitures were to take place. It turned out, to my surprise, that Rod, I, with two others, were to be put through a rehearsal, which was somewhat different to the other medal recipients on the day. Rod was to be knighted and the other three of us were to be made Commanders, an honour marked with a hanging medal, as opposed to one that is pinned on. We were taken to a room where a rather brusque, but elegantly uniformed officer explained that he would demonstrate the procedure twice before letting us act it out. "Twice," he barked, "after which you may ask questions". With that he roleplayed the procedure once, then stepped back to his starting point. As he did so, Rod piped up with a question. "Not now, Roderick!" our instructor bellowed, deliberately rolling the r's," which put Sir Rod firmly in his place.

We were then escorted to a long room adjacent to the Ballroom to await our names being called. During the brief wait I seized the chance I had been waiting for. "How many of your children did you bring here today?" I asked Rod, knowing from the press that he had multiple offspring. "Two. I wanted to bring more, but I couldn't, could

I?" Well, I thought, if Sir Rod couldn't break the rules, what hope would I have had? The other thing that struck me was just how nervous Rod appeared to be, especially for one who performed in front of thousands of people. I completely understood this because I, too, despite having been in the Palace on so many occasions before, was also completely overawed. The building and the ancient ceremony seemed to connect me to history; I imagined all of the famous people who had also been through this pageant before – and I felt humbled. As anyone who has had the honour of participating in this ceremony will tell you, the sense of pride you get at being recognised by your country is overwhelming. Recognition is hugely satisfying. Ask anyone who has been fortunate enough to be honoured in this way, and they will tell you the same thing; that it was a real highlight in their lives. I am sure that this is very hard for most people to understand.

Several years later, we were dining with a group of friends in the Colombe d'Or, a beautiful and famous restaurant in Saint-Paul-de-Vence, in the south of France, when who should walk in but Rod Stewart, Penny and a couple of friends. They were seated with no fuss and politely ignored by the rest of the clientele. The Colombe d'Or is a place where celebrities can dine without the risk of being pestered. Notwithstanding this, towards the end of our meal, if only to show off to my party, I decided to go over to the Stewart's table and say hello. As I approached, I could see a look of annoyance flash over Rod's face, since he clearly did not recognise me – and why should he? Before he could say a word I put out my hand and said, mimicking the voice of the 'sergeant major' in Buckingham Palace, "Good evening, Sir Roderick," with much rolling of the r's. He looked at me a little quizzically. "Buckingham Palace!," I exclaimed. "Oh yes," he grinned, "Now I remember. What a day that was, wasn't it?" My friends, back at my table, were most impressed that Rod and I were mates.

Whilst running the charity took up a reasonable amount of time, I found that other retirement adventures would pop up. For example, I was sitting at my desk at home in London one day, with one eye and ear on Sky News, when I heard the sad announcement that Eric Morley had passed away. My association with Eric, initially through the Miss World pageant, which he and Julia owned, went back about ten years. During this time, I had gotten to know and like Eric very much. I knew that this particular year was to be the fiftieth anniversary of the Miss World pageant, which for its entire history had been run by Eric and Julia Morley. Although considered passé in the UK, the Miss World pageant still commanded huge audiences elsewhere in the world, particularly in the Far East, India, Africa and South America. For many years, Eric had been forced to find sponsorship for the pageant overseas, and now, for the fiftieth anniversary, he had planned to bring the show home to England, where, for this purpose, he had booked London's Dome.

As I listened to the announcement of Eric's passing that morning, I knew that the hundred or so competitors had recently arrived in London, because I had seen pictures of some of them in the newspaper, together with the normal controversy about beauty pageants. I knew that although Julia had been the other half of the Miss World management team, Eric had really run the business. As I watched the television that morning, I also knew, from my previous experience of having produced three Miss World pageants at Sun City, that 100 beautiful young ladies, many of whom would not be able to speak English, would be waiting for instructions as they rehearsed for the two-hour-long television show due to be beamed out to the world in less than a week's time. My God, I thought, how will Julia cope?

I picked up the phone and called the Morley's residence. Julia answered. It appeared that she had just walked in from the hospital, where Eric had died a few hours earlier. She was not aware that the media had broadcast the sad news, and was therefore taken aback by my call. Calmly, she told me how Eric had "gone to sleep" happily, having just watched his beloved Arsenal win a football match. She also told me that Eric, knowing that he was ill, was desperate for the show to go on, and that, one way or another, she was going to make sure that the pageant would take place the following week. I naturally offered my help, although I didn't want to intrude, knowing that at least one of her sons was involved in the business. She thanked me profusely and said that she would get back to me.

That evening, I had a call from Julia. The help she needed, it seemed, was not with the production of the show itself, but with her sponsors, an Indian television and communications company that apparently had been extremely difficult and uncooperative, and were now threatening to withhold large sums of money, thereby throwing the imminent production into jeopardy.

The next day, I went to see Julia, who was camped at the London Hilton, where the contestants were being housed, or, more exactly, 'imprisoned'. Julia prided herself that in all the years of Miss World production, no young lady had ever suffered any misfortune or embarrassment or gotten into any trouble whilst in her care. And Julia was right to be careful in this regard, because many of the contestants were eighteen and nineteen-year-olds who had never previously been out of Bangladesh or Sierra Leone or wherever.

Attending the Miss World finals as a contestant was, therefore, not all it was cracked up to be. Rehearsals for the television show were strenuous, and the two-week programme offered little social interaction for the contestants, except, of course, with each other or with their roommates at the Hilton. And just to make sure that nobody got up to mischief, a chaperone was attached to each group of four contestants, who were then closely monitored. This is not to say that the contestants did not have fun, because, for most of them, the focus was on the upcoming pageant and the hope that it held out for all of them. After all, preparing to be part of a worldwide television extravaganza is pretty heady stuff for most people. Julia was looking remarkably perky for a woman who had just lost her husband, but that was, of course, because she had to focus on the task at hand. Her grieving would have to go 'on hold'.

Between a multitude of interruptions, which were to be expected, Julia explained what she knew of the financial arrangements that Eric had entered into with the Indians. They were not easily understood. The immediate problem was their refusal to pay the fares or fees for the celebrity judges, as well as a large outstanding payment to the television production company. The television company was, naturally, refusing to carry on with the production unless it got paid. Everyone, it seemed, was blaming everyone else for this state of affairs, but only one man, Eric's accountant, Michael Macario, had really read and understood the contract, which, of course, was the governing factor. I gave what advice I could, and, thank God, the necessary payments were made so that the show could go on.

Unfortunately, in examining the paperwork that Eric had signed, Michael and I discovered a bigger problem, which for the time being we decided not to disclose to Julia. It seemed that Eric had entered into a three-year sponsorship deal with the Indians, which gave them the right to stage the Miss World pageant for this particular year and two to follow. Unfortunately, although the contract contained a detailed schedule for how payments of approximately one and a quarter million pounds should be paid in the first and current year, there was no schedule, nor indeed mention, of how payments were to be made for the ensuing years. Apparently, the Indians had missed all of the payment dates in the current year, evidenced by many demand letters in the files from Eric, and could, in my opinion, argue the case in the future that there was nothing more to pay for the second and third years. Worse still, the contract appeared to give them the right, but not the obligation, to put on the pageant in years two and three. It seemed to me that any dispute with Julia over money could lead to them simply saying that they would sit on the rights for the next two years and do nothing. If no pageants were to take place, I knew that Julia would be in breach of her contracts with all of the national pageant holders, which could lead to the end of the Miss World pageant as we knew it.

One of the nicest events connected to the Miss World pageant takes place a few days before the actual broadcast. It is called the Family Party, and only a few very privileged outsiders are allowed to attend. For several years past, Julia and Eric had been kind enough to invite Diana and me, and this year, of course, was no exception. The event is a private dinner party for all contestants, at which the most talented from the group entertain the others with an international cabaret. Although they are not, in the main, professional entertainers, many of the contestants have been models or dancers, and, in some cases, have trained as singers or musicians. The cabaret is always enchanting in its scope, enthusiasm and freshness. The contestants are very supportive of each other, and, by organising this event, Julia has managed to create an evening of unique charm.

On this particular occasion, Diana and I sat with Julia.

She was doing her utmost to stay in control, but it was obvious that the strain of coping without Eric was telling. I felt very strongly that, as soon as the pageant at the Dome was over, Julia should consider selling the Miss World Company, but I doubted very much whether she would listen to such advice.

The pageant itself went off without a hitch. Jerry Springer was the host, and he did a fine, professional job. Everyone involved, it seemed, had put in an extra-special effort, to help Julia, and the Indian sponsors were strangely muted. I was convinced that they were plotting. As it happened, Miss India won the competition. But for the fact that she sat next to Diana and myself at the after-pageant dinner and I can, therefore, vouch for her beauty, I, too, would have been suspicious of an Indian sponsor and an Indian winner. Poor Julia was to fly off to India within a day or two on a public relations exercise, and so I agreed to her request to meet her on her return, to help strategise for the future.

I had read and re-read the contract. I was convinced that the pages, which would have clarified the payments for years two and three, had been removed before Eric had signed. I felt sure that the earlier drafts, if they could be found, would have included additional payment schedules. I knew, from personal experience, that Eric would not have agreed to a payment of one and a quarter million pounds for three years, and even if he had, why would it all have been payable in the first year? No, there was not a question in my mind that the Indians had 'shuffled' the paperwork just before Eric, who was by then quite frail, had signed; and there was no doubt in my mind that they would soon be playing their hand against the recently widowed Julia. It was Michael who uncovered further evidence, in the form of a letter that Eric had written to the Indians one month after the signature date on the contract, advising them that there was an error in the contract, relating to the payment schedule. We could find no evidence in Eric's file of a reply. Julia was convinced that Eric's death had been hastened by the ongoing unpleasantness he had experienced with his sponsor, and I could not help but find myself agreeing with her.

We decided to have a confrontation with the local vice president of the Indian firm, the man, in fact, who had signed the contract. On the assumption that they would be desirous of staging the pageant for the second year, and on the assumption that the dates of the first year's payment schedule would be applicable in the second year, they would be required to immediately make a payment to World of half a million pounds. The sooner we were to find out whether they intended to pay, the better, because if they refused, we would have to get the contract overturned before we could look for an alternative sponsor.

The meeting was held in Eric's office at Golden Square in London. It seemed strange to be gathered around Eric's table, one at which I had often sat to negotiate past events with its owner. Julia asked me to sit at the head of the table and to 'chair' the meeting. Present, in addition to Julia, were Michael Macario, the head of the television production company, and the Indian, whose name now escapes me. I was also deeply conscious that Eric was 'present', and I silently promised him that I would not let him down.

I came straight to the point. I told the Indian that I had been advised by Julia and Michael that the sponsor's history of payment on time, during year one of the contract, had been abysmal, and had been the source of a great deal of stress to Eric. I asked him if they intended to exercise their option to sponsor the pageant again, and he confirmed that they did. I then told him that, since that was the case, they must now arrange to immediately pay World £500,000. The

Indian looked me straight in the eyes and said that there was no such payment called for in the contract. I had deliberately seated him immediately to my right, one removed from the head of the table—close enough, I thought, to be able to intimidate him.

With Eric spurring me on, I fixed him with the meanest look I could summon up, and said in a tone so firm that my intention could not be misunderstood, "I know that there is no payment scheduled in the contract, but I know that this was not the intention of the contract, and I know that you know this too. We both know that there is no way Eric would have agreed to a contract which offered no payments for years two and three. I don't know what you did at the time of the signing, but I do know that Eric has signed something that he did not negotiate with you, and to which he did not agree. That is something we both know, and so I suggest you acknowledge it now."

The man wriggled uncomfortably. "But the contract is the contract. What is written is what Eric signed. There is no more money to pay," he protested.

I cut him short. "In that case, why did Eric write to you five months ago, pointing out that there was a mistake in the contract?" I almost shouted, waving Eric's letter at him. "Why didn't you reply?"

"I know nothing of this letter," he meekly responded. "I know nothing of all of this. I must talk to my president.'

"I'll tell you what you can tell your president," I continued, my voice now as forceful as I could possibly be without actually shouting. "You can tell him that you are cheats and liars, that your behaviour has driven a man to his grave, and that under no circumstances, not even if you pay, can the Miss World organisation deal with you in the future. You may consider all arrangements you believe you have with World as cancelled. We will not deal with liars. Get out!"

He could not have been in any doubt that I meant what I said. He gathered up his papers, and without another whimper, left the room. For a while, there was an uneasy silence; the other attendees were stunned.

"Well, that's telling them," said Michael with a grin, breaking the tension, and Julia was clearly relieved.

Getting rid of the Indians was, however, not as easy as throwing one of them out of the room. On the face of it, the contract said what it said. We would have to prove that they had duped Eric. After discussions with Queen's Counsel, we brought an urgent application to have the contract overthrown, but our case was, initially, not strong. We also discovered that 'urgent High Court application' is an oxymoron. Bit by bit, we pieced together evidence that all indicated the Indians were lying. Somebody produced an internal budget that had been prepared by the sponsors which clearly showed budgeted payments of £1,250,000 in year one, escalating in year two and three by 5%. We also obtained an affidavit from an ex-employee at the company, who not only confirmed that she had heard in-office discussions about their conspiracy to trick Eric, but that she had left them because she could not countenance certain other activities in which they were engaged.

The president of the company, we had learned, was a high-profile individual of good standing in India. We did not think he would be thrilled to have our findings broadcast in the High Court in London, and we were right. At the eleventh hour, just before the case came to court, the Indians withdrew and renounced all rights to the pageant. Julia's first battle was over. She was free, but now she had nobody in the wings to pay for the pageant, because it had been impossible to talk to a replacement sponsor until the court case had been decided, and it was now getting too late in the year to attract a replacement. Most major firms put their annual marketing budgets to bed well before the start of each year. You cannot simply approach one halfway through a year and expect them to find a chunk of change large enough to sponsor such a major event at the end of the same year. Julia never gave up hope, but I could see that finding a replacement sponsor would be an impossible task.

Fortunately for Julia, although I had retired from any executive role with Sun International, I had remained as a director and non-executive chairman of Sun International Management, the company that operated all of the hotels in southern Africa, including Sun City. It had been some years since we had produced the Miss World pageant at Sun City, and recently we had experienced difficulty, due to the weakness of the rand, in promoting many international events there. Against my better judgment, and purely as one last favour to my old friend Eric, I persuaded the rest of my board to stage the pageant one more time at Sun City. This, I knew, would only grant Julia a temporary respite, so I set about trying to persuade her to sell the company. But, alas, together with a mutual friend, Tobin Prior, we had also mapped out a new plan for "modernising" the pageant in such a manner that Julia became incredibly excited about its future prospects. As a result, she steadfastly refused to entertain the idea of a sale, and so, little by little, I removed myself from any sphere of influence. I had, in my opinion, stepped up to the plate when I was needed; she must now do whatever she must do.

# Chapter Twenty-Four
## TORTUOUS INTERFERENCE

I also soon discovered that I was not done with Sun International. During the time that I had latterly been an officer of Sol's SIHL, the division of Sun that was listed on the New York Stock Exchange, I had also been a director of SIHL's largest investor, Royale Resorts, owned by Kersaf, which traded as Sun International in Southern Africa. All Sun International properties, whether belonging to SIHL in New York or Kersaf in South Africa, were marketed to the public as one brand, and part of my executive responsibility had been to manage the international marketing function on behalf of both companies. This frequently required me playing the role of arbitrator in regard to expenditures and emphasis of marketing effort. For example, if SIHL was opening a new hotel somewhere in the world, I would naturally focus the attention of the worldwide marketing force on that project, to the temporary disadvantage of others. Later, however, when the need for focus was on a property owned by Kersaf, I would ask the sales force to focus there. There could, as a result, be some bitching from the side of the company that was not getting the attention, but in the big picture, things balanced out and I felt that I was trusted in my judgments. Once I had resigned, it appeared that more distrust developed between both sides of the company, resulting in frequent arguments.

These arguments were exacerbated at a different level in the company. When SIHL had been formed, the initial shareholding had been one-third Kersaf, the South African company (through its overseas subsidiary, Royale Resorts); one-third Caledonian Investments; and one-third Sol Kerzner (through his family trust). Sol had been appointed chairman. As the company expanded, and was ultimately listed in the USA, the three founding members had agreed to vote together and to stay together, as a device to ensure continuing control. Kersaf also operated hotels and casinos under the Sun International brand in southern Africa, but had agreed, at the formation of SIHL, to use SIHL as the exclusive vehicle for the development of the Sun International brand everywhere in the world except southern Africa. In the beginning, this arrangement worked well. SIHL had soon listed on NASDAQ at a price equivalent to $12 per share and had subsequently transferred to the 'Big Board', i.e. the New York Stock Exchange. The Atlantis resort was opened successfully, and the Mohegan Sun contract was signed. The share value raced to $55. Being a "growth" company, no dividends were paid, but the Royale and Kersaf boards were happy to see their initial investment of around $30 million grow to nearly $200 million, particularly since at the same time, the South African rand was devaluing at roughly 10% per year.

After I left SIHL, things began to go wrong, although the first event has no bearing on the second. The Kerzners, against counsel from Kersaf's Buddy Hawton, made an investment in an obsolete casino property in Atlantic City, with the intention of rebuilding and relaunching it. The market, which had always valued SIHL as a hybrid between a resort and a casino company, immediately reacted badly, and started to rate the company in the casino sector, which was trading on much lower multiples, with the result that the share price started to tumble, eventually going as low as $18. Partly as a result of the falling share price, the company was now unable or unwilling to raise the capital to rebuild the Atlantic City property, and opted instead for a $55 million revamp. This had completely the wrong effect; it did not bring in new customers, but it did drive away many existing ones, who, it seemed, were quite happy to play in the rather shabby surroundings they were used to, rather than the new sanitised version. This had been one of the few occasions in Sol's career where he had failed to 'read' the market correctly, and the result was disastrous.

After a couple of years of mediocre results, the company decided to sell the Atlantic City property and took a write-off of over $200 million. By the time Kersaf's share of this loss was translated back into South African rand, the amount was huge, and Kersaf's shareholders began to question the wisdom of the arrangements its company had entered into with the Kerzners. To them, it seemed that Sol Kerzner was running SIHL as his private fiefdom, into which they were locked, with no effective right of veto, a falling share price, and no dividends. To add insult to injury, Sol reported, with all his normal rational explanations, cost overruns above budget in excess of $200 million in regard to the building of the Royal Towers at Atlantis; and Hawton found himself cast as a vociferous, but handcuffed, dissenter on the SIHL board. When Kerzner then attempted to persuade the board that SIHL should buy the Desert Inn in Las Vegas, Hawton did everything in his power to block the deal, egged on, of course, by his unhappy Kersaf board back in South Africa. The relationship between Kerzner and Hawton reached a real low, and any future cooperation between the pair seemed impossible. Hawton needed to free Kersaf from SIHL if he were to satisfy the Kersaf board, who no longer had faith in Kerzner, because Kersaf was inhibited, by agreement, from pursuing growth opportunities outside of southern Africa, since it could not use its own brand name, Sun International, and because all of its offshore funds were locked into SIHL.

Relationships went from bad to terrible. As a member of the Royale board, I was privileged to get an update on a regular basis at our quarterly meetings in Switzerland. With things at rock bottom, and with the SIHL share price close to its lowest, the Royale board decided that Kerzner might just think that this was a good time for him to buy out Royale, and, through intermediaries, a breakup of the control group of the company was proposed. As it happened, Kerzner also wanted to be free of the Kersaf dog yapping at his heels, and decided to bring matters to a head by initiating a damages claim against Kersaf/Royale, on the dubious basis that Royale had infringed the agreement not to operate under the name Sun International outside of southern Africa, by signing a management agreement with a wealthy Kuwaiti to operate a 900-room resort in Egypt at Marsa Alam. Despite Kerzner having repeatedly assured Hawton that he was not interested in SIHL managing this resort in Egypt, and thereby, under the terms of the agreement, freeing Royale to do so, Kerzner was now claiming that he had not been given an opportunity to properly review this matter, and that Kersaf had not formally advised SIHL of the potential opportunity in strict conformity with the agreement. As a result, SIHL was now suing Kersaf/Royale for $50 million for breach of contract, despite the fact that Royale was still the largest shareholder in SIHL.

The relationship between the principals was now so bad that this spat between old friends could no longer be settled face to face, so arrangements were put in hand for the two sides' lawyers to meet in London to discuss a settlement. Hawton's view was that there could be no settlement without divorce, and the Kerzners now seemed to welcome this. The discussions, naturally, had to involve the third partner in the control group, Caledonian, which was also interested in Kersaf/Royale gaining the right to sell its shares, because this could eventually set a precedent for Caledonian to do likewise. At the same time, Caledonian was extremely interested to see that Kersaf/Royale could not dump shares on the already thin market, and, as a result, drag down the value of Caledonian's own substantial shareholding.

It was, therefore, a large group of lawyers who met in London to work things out, with three groups of executives directing them from different headquarters not far removed. I was now drafted onto Kersaf/Royale's advisory team, partly because I was already in London, partly because I was a director of Royale, but mostly because I was deemed to have more knowledge of Sol 'in battle' than almost anyone else. To Kerzner, this must have seemed an act of betrayal and treachery, although, if I wished to remain as a director of Royale, I had little choice.

Our team closeted together in a basement war room at the St. James's Club, where my eldest son, Simon, was the manager, and where Kersaf directors had taken to residing when in London on other business. We knew that part of any settlement could involve the use of the brand name Sun International. Kersaf used the name broadly in southern Africa, where Sun International is a household name. We had to decide whether we wanted to own the name outright for worldwide use (which would, of course, be useful for our overseas expansion plans), or whether to let Sol keep it, with the possibility that we would have to get involved in an extensive and expensive rebranding exercise in southern Africa, or just risk confusion in the marketplace going forward. After some debate on this issue, Buddy Hawton handed his team (which, in addition to himself, consisted of Peter Bacon, David Coutts-Trotter, Frank Kilbourn and me) a blank piece of paper and asked us to write down how much we would each be willing to pay SIHL for the exclusive worldwide right to the name, if the decision was ours. Just like a party game, sitting in the lounge of the Saint James's Club, we all scribbled down our considered numbers, folded our papers in half, and handed them back to Buddy, who ceremoniously unfolded them and called out the results. The proposals varied from zero to $20 million. My suggestion had been $12 million, and, by chance, the average was also twelve.

The separation agreement being debated was complicated by the fact that its reach extended to South African law (Kersaf being a South African-listed company), Swiss law (Royale being a Swiss company), US law (SIHL being listed on the NYSE), Bahamian law (SIHL being a Bahamian company), English law (Caledonian), German law (Royale's minority partners were German) and Egyptian law (Marsa Alam). As a result of this, our legal team included lawyers from South Africa, England, Germany and the USA, with telephonic contact with others in Egypt and Switzerland.

One evening, we were working late in our underground bunker at the St. James's Club, and we decided to have dinner. Simon, on seeing the size of our group, and being fearful that we would completely disrupt his little restaurant, quietly asked me if I would mind taking them elsewhere. As a result, at about ten o'clock we all adjourned to an Indian restaurant a few blocks away, where Simon had managed to make a reservation. To everyone's surprise, and by amazing coincidence, SIHL's lawyers, who had obviously also been working late, were already there. There must be hundreds of restaurants in London. For the opposing teams of attorneys to pick the same one at the same time was remarkable. What was disturbing was that our team was substantially larger than theirs. "I bet Kerzner is glad he's not paying for your team," said their lead man as he passed our table on the way out.

"He might well be yet," piped up one of ours.

Complicated as it was, an agreement was finally reached. Kersaf/Royale finished up paying SIHL roughly $20 million for its freedom: freedom to sell its shares in SIHL (on a highly controlled basis); freedom from the Egyptian lawsuit; and, amazingly, for the right to use the name Sun International anywhere in the world. Under the agreement, SIHL would have one year to discontinue using Sun International, and Kersaf/Royale could not do business during that year in any place that SIHL was trading at the date of the agreement. To us, it seemed as if Kerzner had given up the name Sun International cheaply. We also assumed that, in so doing, he could not have been popular in territories where SIHL managed hotels for partners or third-party owners, because we knew that, year after year, he had stressed to them the importance of the brand and their need, therefore, to pay for its promotion.

Hawton and the Kersaf board were thrilled with the settlement. They were now free to pursue the growth of the Sun International brand outside of southern Africa, and by selling the shares in SIHL, they would have some substantial seed money to do so. Before the ink was dry, my retirement was placed 'on hold'. Would I (Hawton put to me) consider joining the board of Kersaf and taking up an executive position to spearhead the company's growth internationally, including taking charge of the resort in planning in Egypt? This is not what I wanted to do, but after some discussion with Diana, who, as always, encouraged me, I agreed to work for a period of eighteen months maximum, during which time I anticipated I could get some deals done and put an executive team in place, so that I could re-retire. And so, a whole new chapter in life was opened.

I quickly mapped out a plan, which was to establish Sun International Global Resorts, a chain of upmarket resort properties in Africa, the Middle East, and the Caribbean, to be managed and marketed under the known banner of Sun International. It was important to establish this network quickly, before Kerzner's quality SIHL hotels were rebranded, with the potential effect that the value of the name Sun International could be devalued. Touting the Sun International properties in southern Africa as the core and the base of a new chain, I began scouring the world for potential resort targets that might either be for sale, or in need of better management or marketing. I travelled so extensively in this endeavour that, at one point, I was met by two young ladies, in British Airways garb, at Gatwick Airport, who informed me that I had been, for the past few months, the most travelled passenger on the British Airways network.

"Do I get a prize?" I questioned jokingly.

"Yes," they replied, "two Concorde tickets to New York."

With my traveling salesman's hat on, I pitched the idea of Sun International Global Resorts to hotel owners in the chosen designated regions, hyping the synergy that would come from this tight association of the world's leading resorts. My message was well received, but the plan required a critical mass of properties to kickstart it, and it soon became apparent that these properties could not be restricted to southern Africa. I was not, therefore, unhappy when I was approached by some owners of hotels that were currently trading under the banner of Sun International, but managed by Kerzner's SIHL. It appeared that they had not been consulted by Sol or his executives about the sale of the brand to Kersaf, and, just as we had envisaged, they were extremely vexed that after years and years of financially supporting the brand, they were now being told that it was passé and would be replaced with another, yet to be agreed, within the next twelve months. Their view was simple. They had traded under the name Sun International for many years, and their main contact for much of that time had been me, and since Sun International still existed and I had been charged with developing it, they wanted to remain part of it.

I read and reread the restraints that we had agreed to in the separation agreement, and, on the urging of Buddy, took counsel's advice. Based on this, I informed the unhappy owners that we could not do business with them for the next eleven months, but that after that we would be happy to welcome them to the new Sun International Global Resorts group. I confirmed to them that until that time, they could legally continue trading under the name Sun International, and that if they were, during this period, able to free themselves from their contractual arrangements with SIHL, the eventual transfer of management and/or marketing could be a seamless affair.

Needless to say, Sol got to hear of my discussions, and within two months of the separation agreement having been finalised, he commenced legal action in New York against Kersaf and Royale, claiming that both Buddy and me had engaged in 'tortuous interference' with SIHL's business. "No sooner had the ink been dry," Sol's plea contended, than Hawton and Venison were indiscriminately breaching the agreement. The damages SIHL was seeking was $50 million: Sol's favourite number! The ensuing legal battle was costly, time-consuming, and at times vicious and vindictive. SIHL went to great lengths to monitor my movements, which could not have been easy, because I moved a lot. Sol's lawyers were even instructed to serve papers on me in New York at our son Jonathan's wedding (an instruction thankfully not acted on by his in-house lawyer). The Kersaf board (myself not included) became paranoid about anything else I might do that could "get us into trouble," and as a result seriously hampered my progress in establishing the global resort chain. The merits of SIHL's case, in my view, were very weak, but they hinged upon the meaning of the phrase 'doing business'. Was I, by speaking to (at their request) owners of hotels who had been badly treated (or worse, whose contracts had been breached by SIHL), 'doing business' with them? I thought that concept was ridiculous; our lawyers warned us that some judges might not agree with me.

As it turned out, the merits of the case were never put to the test, because our first line of defence was simply that the New York courts had no jurisdiction over this case, and that it should therefore not be heard before a New York jury. After all, the agreement that we were alleged to have breached had been negotiated in London; and the participants in the agreement were a Bahamian company, a Swiss company, a British company, a German company and a South African company. The alleged breaches had taken place in Greece, the Emirates, and Mauritius. The only connection with New York was that SIHL was listed on the New York Stock Exchange and that the company had a small sales office on Fifth Avenue.

The judge appointed to hear the case was described by our New York attorney as being "mentally and physically lethargic," which meant, we concluded, that he would take a long time to arrive at any decision. Time, when you deal with New York lawyers, means money! Irritatingly, the judge, whilst taking nine months to examine our claim that the case should not even be before him, ordered that the time-consuming process of discovery and affidavits should proceed. The longer this process continued, and the more the legal bills mounted, the more disturbed my board became. I remained confident that we would win. I knew, in my gut, that I had not done anything to be ashamed of. And win we did. Just as the Kersaf board was starting to think 'settlement', and, indeed, on the very day that we had dispatched David Coutts-Trotter to New York to negotiate a peace, the much-maligned judge ruled in our favour and threw the case out of his court.

We had won the battle, but there was no doubt in my mind that Sol had won the war. The deals that I had negotiated to bring Sun International Global Resorts to life had long gone cold. There could now be no hope of kickstarting the group with any of SIHL's properties, and the Kersaf board was no longer very supportive of the plan. In addition to this, and possibly at the instigation of the Kerzners, the institutional shareholders in Kersaf demanded several seats on the board. They, it seemed, were not interested in Kersaf's dreams to develop globally. They wanted Kersaf to bring back its offshore 'pile' to South Africa, to either pay down some local debt, or distribute back to the shareholders. I was neither willing to go along with this madness, nor to find myself working for a group of asset managers who had no passion for my business, so I resigned and re-retired.

Sol and Butch, on the other hand, marched on, and I was amused to see, within a few months, the emergence of my Sun International Global Resorts, this time called 'One and Only', as the resort arm of Kerzner Hotels International. I am sure that if I ever want to stay in one, I will be paying full-rack rate. Sadly, this period of success was not to last; indeed, it was to end in tragedy. Butch Kerzner, who's experience prior to joining his father had been entirely investment banking became more and more influential in the company. Having been brought up in an era of continuous upward trends in business, Butch was from the school of high leverage, i.e. the best way to expand a business is to utilise funds raised by borrowing heavily against your assets. This, you will recall, is not what his father had taught me on the day I joined him so many years ago, when he had warned me about the cyclical nature of the business. So, largely based upon the huge success of Atlantis, Butch and Sol were borrowing more and more to finance its expansion. They also borrowed heavily in an epic battle to take the company private in order to escape the regulatory environment of a US-listed enterprise. Unfortunately, the peak of this borrowing took place just before the financial downturn of 2000 and its ensuing recession. Room occupancy at Atlantis and the other hotels fell dramatically and the Kerzner's, now private, were unable to meet the debt payments. On top of this personal tragedy ensued. Whilst Butch was investigating a potential site in the Caribbean the helicopter he was in crashed, resulting in the deaths of all on board. Not only had Sol lost a business, he had lost something far more important—his eldest son.

# Chapter Twenty-Five
## CONSULTING

Shortly before the opening of the Royal Mirage in Dubai, just after the grand driveway had been finished and the Danie de Jaga camel sculptures had been embedded into the fountain at the porte-cochère , Dene Murphy, the project manager and driving force behind the project, and I were standing outside the main entrance doors when a red Ferrari thundered up the drive. This was odd, because the road had only just been finished and was not yet open to the public. Someone, obviously, had clout with the security men at the roadside gate.

Out of the car stepped a handsome 'dis-dashed' Arab, together with an attractive Arab lady, slickly dressed in Armani jeans, blouse, and exceptionally high heeled shoes. They looked important. They acted 'important'. The concierge came rushing out to greet them, having instantly recognised them as Sheikh Alabbar and his wife; Alabbar being, probably, the biggest property developer in Dubai. Dene and I introduced ourselves and offered to show the couple over the unfinished hotel and gardens. The little tour probably took about an hour, Dene with the Sheikh and me, following behind, with his wife. I could see Alabbar up ahead with Dene, asking many questions, but, at no point, did he seem impressed. Towards the end of the walkabout

I ventured to suggest this to Madam Alabbar. "No," she replied, "he will not like this building. It is too Arabic. It will remind him of his youth of poverty." Since the Royal Mirage was certainly one of the most opulent developments with which I have been involved, I found it quite hard to understand how it could be associated with poverty. She saw my dilemma and explained: "It is the style of building that he will not like; not the quality. His admiration is for steel and glass. He would like Dubai to look like New York. You know – modern." Well, he certainly got his way! Not, however, in regard to the Royal Mirage, which remains, over twenty years later, one of the most successful hotels in the city, despite its Arabian appearance. A low-rise development in Arabic style, now completely surrounded by steel and glass towers. An oasis in a desert of modernity, and one of which Dene and I were extremely proud.

A few years after this meeting with Sheikh Alabar, during the early years of my retirement, I was seated in the bar of the Mandarin Oriental hotel in New York when I was approached by a smartly suited Arab gentleman, whom I did not instantly recognise. It was none other than Sheikh Alabbar. I invited him to sit with me and share a cocktail. It turned out that this was not a chance meeting. He had found out that I was staying at the Mandarin and had deliberately approached me. He explained that he had recently signed an agreement with the fashion icon, Giorgio Armani, in which Alabbar would finance and build a chain of luxury hotels, to be marketed under the brand "Armani". Alabbar had, apparently, convinced Giorgio that he had the financial resources (which he did) to build a minimum of ten hotels, worldwide, in fairly short order, and that he had the management resources to plan, build, and operate these hotels (which he had not). Giorgio's task would be to design the interiors and have input into the architecture. Giorgio was to be paid a huge amount of money for his services and the use of his name. Alabbar's first commitment to Giorgio was to form a hotel management company and to produce, within six months, a complete operating manual for this embryonic hotel chain. Alabbar had decided, based upon recommendations from others in Dubai that I was the man to do this for him and had tracked me down to the bar in Manhattan.

Right there and then he offered me the job as President, Armani Hotels and Resorts, working for him, as chairman. It would be my responsibility to recruit the executive team, produce the operating manual, establish the brand, liaise with Giorgio in terms of design, and, ultimately, open and operate the hotels. The first two hotels were already in the pipeline; one to be a conversion of a block of apartments above the Armani showrooms in Milan and the other to be a section of the world's tallest building, then under construction in Dubai. I, and my team, would also be responsible for locating and acquiring other sites. Had I been twenty years younger this could have been a magnificent opportunity to stamp my mark on the international hotel business. I had the utmost respect for Armani, who had created and sustained, over several decades, an internationally recognised brand in the difficult and changing world of fashion. An international luxury hotel collection under the Armani name seemed like a very good idea indeed. However, I had no intention of starting another career and I made this clear to Alabbar. Nevertheless, I was intrigued by the idea and the thought of being involved, if only in the creation, was too attractive to turn down without consideration. Needless to say, Diana, was intrigued.

The upshot of the conversation was my agreement to work for Alabar as a consultant, with the task of setting up the new hotel company and recruiting a Chief Executive to carry on. It took a day or two to settle the terms of the consultancy, but within weeks I found myself with an office in Dubai and confronting a copy of a memorandum, sent to all of Alabbar's executives, announcing me as the new President of Armani Hotels and Resorts, with a copy, of course, to Giorgio himself. Naturally, I immediately objected in the strongest possible terms, but my objections fell upon Alabbar's deaf ears. "It is better that we let people 'think' that you are the boss," he reasoned. "I thought this would be helpful." "That's fine," I retorted, "with regard to your executives, but I want you to make it completely clear to Giorgio that I am not a permanent feature." "Of course," he lied, "I will tell him."

My first meeting with Giorgio was exceptionally interesting. Construction was proceeding apace in regard to the Dubai building, which was to be 165 storeys high. The hotel section would be from level six through to level twenty and, above that would be about 300 apartments to be marketed under the Armani brand. Giorgio had never before designed a hotel, nor an apartment building, although part of the deal was that the furniture for the apartments should be provided by Armani Casa, at that time a fledgling company. I had contacted Giorgio's office and explained to his assistant, Anthony, that I would need to meet with his boss every month over the next six of seven months for at least three days per month in order to complete the interior plans for the rooms and several restaurants, bars and lounges for both hotels. "Mr Armani will only be able to spare one half day per month," I was emphatically told by Anthony. "That will not work," I responded, but I decided, rather than negotiate with Anthony, that I should wait until I had met Giorgio, to whom I could explain the volume of work and detail required. So, the first meeting was set up – to be held in Giorgio's office in Milan.

The Armani headquarters is situated in an old Milanese building located almost opposite Giorgio's apartment. I was accompanied on this first meeting (and all subsequent ones) by Peter Van Wyk, a young and exceptionally competent project manager, already employed by Alabbar. We were met by the effusive Anthony and ushered into a large room with a long table surrounded by about a dozen chairs. Anthony, who spoke passably good English with a delightful Italian accent, asked Peter and myself to be seated, explaining that Giorgio would sit at the head of the table and that I should sit next to him on the side. Just as I was wondering what all of the other chairs were for a bevy of young Italian men arrived, were introduced by Anthony, and then took their seats around the table. Then Giorgio arrived, quite quietly, but with an enormous air of authority. The rest of the attendees stood up as a sign of respect, as did we, and remained standing until Anthony had introduced Peter and myself. There is little point in trying to physically describe Giorgio because I would be amazed if there are any readers of this book who have not, at some time in their lives, seen a picture of the silver haired, dark blue clad, fashion genius. He clearly commanded the utmost respect, boarding on reverence, from his employees.

I quickly found out that his English was (or, at least, appeared to be) very limited, so our conversations were carried out through Anthony's lyrical translations or with Giorgio and I in equally bad French. Luckily, we both understood the universal language of architectural drawings, plans, sketches and renderings. What Giorgio could not describe to me in language he certainly could with his pencil.

With regard to the building in Milan, he was, of course, completely familiar with it, since he had owned it for many years and the basement and first two floors were a showpiece for his brands. The building in Dubai, however, was a different challenge, because he had never been to Dubai and apparently had no intention of doing so. He also had little interest in getting to understand the complexities of the building, which were huge. To keep a building of 165 floors standing, especially one built on sand, means a massive amount of concrete is needed on the lower floors, which severely impacts their usefulness as lobbies and public areas, including restaurants. Since these lower floors had been allocated to the hotel section of the building, this left little scope for impressive lobbies or fantastic views from public areas. My disclosure of this seemed to come as a surprise and shock to Giorgio. Also, the building narrowed slightly as it rose, thereby changing the dimensions of the rooms on each floor, thereby making it hard to come up with cookie cutter design for the rooms. All of this increased the workload of interior design and it quickly became apparent to Giorgio that his contribution to the design would, indeed, take more than one half day's work per month.

"Vous est vrais," he exclaimed, after a few hours of travail, "I willa giva you onea whola day a montha." My first victory.

As the months went by, I became more and more impressed with Armani's ability, comprehension, attention to detail and his sense of humour. Indeed, I genuinely looked forward to our monthly planning sessions. Month after month we sat together hunched over his paper and pencil as I tried to point out all of the practical difficulties in his designs, which, on every occasion, after a little thought, he grasped, and picked up his pencil to redraw. Each time he did so with good spirit and would become totally immersed in seeking solutions. The men gathered around the table all addressed Giorgio as "Mr Armani" as did I, but after a day's work and growing respect for each other's ability, Armani suddenly turned to me and said, "Call me Giorgio," which I took as a huge compliment. Anthony was flabbergasted.

We did not, however, work uninterrupted. On one occasion a secretary came into the room and whispered into Giorgio's ear that a famous Italian actress had arrived for lunch with him. "Can't you see I'm busy with Peter," he said in Italian. "Tell her we can't have lunch today." The secretary explained that it had been a long-standing arrangement, but Giorgio brushed her off. As the actress received the bad news there was much screaming and cursing in the lobby. I detected a slight smile on Giorgio's lips.

On other occasions members of his staff would politely interrupt out meetings to show Giorgio products destined for his stores, of which he had 120 worldwide. Apparently, no item gets to see the light of day in a store unless Giorgio has personally inspected a sample and approved. Hence, there were many interruptions, when an, often nervous, underling would present him with an item of clothing, jewellery or whatever. Giorgio's approach was very tactile. He would almost stroke each item, even caress them. He would hold them to his skin, stretch them, scratch them and so on, almost as if each item were a personal pet. In some cases, he would reject them but, in the main, signed off with his approval. After a while, as certain items appeared for his review, he began asking my opinion. Naturally, I declined—with protestations that I was not competent in this area. My reluctance to comment continued for several months until, one day, foolishly, I offered an opinion on a certain item, stating that it was very nice. "Ugh, Calvin Klein!" retorted Giorgio, which I quickly understood meant the epitome of bad taste. Calvin Klein definitely meant inferior in Giorgio's eyes and my judgement obviously fell into that category. It has been hard since then for me to walk by a Calvin Klein store without a titter. But, as a result of this putdown, I did, later, ask Giorgio whom, in the fashion industry, he admired or respected. Without hesitation he shot back, "Ralph Lauren." I was somewhat surprised because the Lauren style seemed so far removed from that of Armani. But Giorgio explained that his admiration for Ralph Lauren was the man's ability to have developed such a full range of product with appeal to millionaires, high society, and the general public at all levels and all ages. The Lauren "reach" as he explained was tremendous.

Whilst things progressed well with Giorgio, back in Dubai they did not do so with Alabbar, who continued to insist that I should not look for my replacement, but should accept a longer-term role. He was also impatient to let the world know that there would soon be an Armani hotel chain and that he was to be the President. He kept asking me to advertise the chain, which I refused to do, since we had no hotels open, nobody to answer a phone and no way to make a reservation, thus making publicity, at this stage, not only pointless but distracting. He also wanted to me to open an office in Paris, which I considered to be a waste of time and money, and to produce some business cards proclaiming him as 'President'. I pointed out to him that all print and other design had to be approved by Giorgio, for brand protection. However, since for me this was such an insignificant matter, I did ask Giorgio to design a card for Alabbar, which he agreed to do. When the cards arrived, they were little square things, about the size of two postage stamps. The printing was almost too small to read that Alabbar was the President. Upon receipt of the cards, Alabbar tried to explain to me why it was important for him. "My name is not George or Henry or Peter. It is Mohamed. For a Mohamed to be President of an enterprise with the world recognition of Armani is a great honour and carries much prestige in my community." That, I thought, rather said it all.

My biggest problem with Alabbar had nothing to do with the planning of the two hotels in Dubai and Milan; it was in regard to the acquisition of new sites. During this period, I travelled extensively looking at possibilities in several major cities, including Paris, London and New York. This meant the involvement of other parties, be they sellers, brokers, auctioneers, etc. Often there was competition from other interested parties, so a prompt decision process was needed. Alabbar was particularly difficult in this regard and the whole process became exceptionally irritating and often too difficult for the third parties involved to tolerate. After losing several decent opportunities I was becoming increasingly frustrated. The straw that broke the camel's back came regarding a building in Paris, which was being auctioned. Through various contacts I had engineered the situation so that I thought we had the inside track at the auction. I had convinced my contacts that they would not be let down, but that I would need the final approval of Alabbar. As the crucial date approached, I could not get this and my contacts became more and more nervous. I gave Alabbar warning that if the approval did not come through before dawn on the auction day, we would lose the opportunity and severely annoy my contacts and damage my relationship with them for good. Having waited all night in a hotel room in Paris to activate things, should I receive the approval from Alabbar, I finally gave up and headed to Charles de Gaulle. I very reluctantly pulled our bid, much to the severe annoyance of my cultivated contacts. As I was boarding the plane to fly back to Dubai, with the intention of resigning, I got word from one of Alabbar's secretaries that I had his blessing for the deal. Too late!

When I terminated my consultancy Alabbar was most apologetic and tried to get me to change my mind, which I would not. Reluctantly, I agreed that I would endeavour to recruit my replacement. After a couple of months, I recommended a well-known figure in the hotel world, who was keen on the opportunity. In my discussions with him, I warned him that it would be difficult to deal with Alabbar, but he was insistent that he would be able to cope. A few months later he sued Alabbar for constructive dismissal and was paid off with several million dollars.

My only regret in giving up my responsibilities re Armani Hotels was the discontinuation of my monthly meetings with Giorgio. I had been constantly amazed at his capacity for hard work, his astounding attention to detail, his sharp sense of humour, his tenacious control of his business, and his uncluttered view of how to live his life. Rarely had I worked with such an impressive man. I did not want him to think that I was abandoning the enterprise so I decided to go to Milan to personally inform him of my decision to quit. He was very gracious and thanked me for my contribution to the project. He invited me to visit his Giorgio store to pick out an item, which I did. The tuxedo that I chose has been worn with pride on many occasions but is still as good as new.

As it turned out I was not through with the Middle East. Out of the blue one day came an offer of a consulting contract with MAF, the property- owning conglomerate of Majid Al Futtaim, which, although almost 100% owned by Majid, was operated as if it were a fully listed company, with all of the checks, balances and disciplines inherent in a public company. MAF owned the major shopping malls in Dubai, including the Mall of the Emirates (the one with the ski run with real snow), which included a 500 room hotel operated by Kempinski. Plans were afoot to add a further hotel to this mall with hotels in Bahrain, Beirut, Cairo, Doha, Oman and other Middle East countries. My consulting contract included a position on the board of directors, on which I happily served for over eight years. This entailed board meetings in Dubai at least four times a year and much Arabian travel. With a son and two granddaughters resident in Dubai this turned out to be more of a convenience than a hardship. The board did operate as if it were a listed company, but make no mistake, although Majid, the owner, did not actually sit on the board, it was clear that he had his fingers firmly on the pulse. It seemed to me that a common thread amongst all of the great entrepreneurs I had worked with was that they understood the product they were providing from the viewpoint of customers. Majid could be seen at night prowling around the malls noting which signs were not working or which floor tiles were cracked. He cared about the standards from a customer point of view. This change of emphasis in my life from hotels with shops to shops with hotels was a fascinating learning curve. If nothing else, I gained great insight into the business workings of the Middle East.

However, Greece was to rear its head once again in my life. The owners of the Loutraki casino were in trouble. This previously highly successful casino is situated about one hours drive on a motorway from Athens. Since the proposed Athens casino had not materialised (probably as a result of the connivance of some of the Loutraki owners), the Loutraki casino had consistently turned in a profit well north of €50 million a year. However, on the insistence of the European Union, which was bailing out a bankrupt Greece, that the Greek Government make serious efforts to collect taxes, certain new control procedures had been forced on businesses, such as the Loutraki casino. Apparently, the casino had been used by a large number of Greek businessmen, including small operators like taxi and shop owners, to launder their money. Suddenly Greek casinos were asked to report pay-outs and to ask all visitors to register with personal details, photos, etc. The effect on the business had been catastrophic and my help was sought to mitigate the problem and to come up with a new business plan.

Although the customers had all but disappeared the staff had not. The Greek laissez faire attitude to tax collection was one reason that Greece was bankrupt, but the other was that it was almost impossible to lay off unwanted workers. In a few days I had identified potential layoffs of at least 400 employees. I also came up with a plan to redirect the emphasis of the business into a broader resort, but the owners could not agree on how to finance the plan, so I decided that it was a lost cause. Despite all reasonable efforts to come to agreements with labour unions and the Government, I suspect that they will still be employed until the place is as bankrupt as the country.

It was not long, however, before Africa called again. They say that once you have drunk the waters of Africa, you will return. The opportunity that presented itself came as a result of the political transition of South Africa from black to white power. The new "Mandela" government was anxious to facilitate share ownership in public companies for previously disadvantaged citizens, which, naturally included black South Africans. Where possible, publicly listed companies were obliged to facilitate loans to blacks in order that they might purchase shares. Where licenses were required to operate businesses, Government had the clout to be able to insist in a large measure of black ownership. The casino business was one where Government had enormous leverage because the issue of new gaming licenses in South Africa proper was within their gift.

Peter J Venison CVO

Pre the 'revolution' in South Africa, casino gaming had been illegal. As a result, casinos had sprung up in the surrounding countries within easy driving reach of Johannesburg and other South African cities. Some of the 'countries', which had been spun off by South Africa, were not recognised by the rest of the world but, nevertheless, operated under a different legal jurisdiction, which did allow gambling. As a director of Sun International I had been totally involved in the development and operation of these 'homeland' casinos and was, therefore, extremely familiar with them. As part of the settlement between the African National Congress and the de Klerk government, the 'homelands' would be reincorporated into the new South Africa and the different laws would somehow have to be merged. It was not long, of course, before pressure was put on to the new Government to allow casino gambling in South Africa. Proper legislation was passed which would allow hotel companies in South Africa to compete for casino licenses in South African cities, provided that these new gaming companies were at least 51% owned by previously disadvantaged citizens (blacks).

Southern Sun, the company originally founded by Sol Kerzner, and which I had been Managing Director some years before, was now owned by South African Breweries, and had a portfolio of seventy hotels. Needless to say, SAB was in prime position to apply for casino licenses but would need to figure out how to 'sell' 51% of the company to blacks, whilst still exercising some control over the business. The basic plan was to lend the new black shareholders the money to buy 51% of the business but to restrict their control of the company until they had repaid the loans, which they would do through pledging their dividends. The problem was to identify the right blacks or black groups to qualify for share ownership.

Needless to say black groups of all sorts were lining up for the opportunity to finance their acquisition and control of the biggest hotel (and to be gaming) company in Africa. Somebody had to put together a group that would be acceptable to SAB, but also to the South African government. Without going into all of the details I found myself in the position of orchestrating this event by bringing together some of the competing black groups, which included a partnership between a society of small African traders and a black trade union from the garment industry. The African traders' association was run by one of the most charismatic men I have ever met—Sam Buthelezi, and the garment union by one of the cleverest men I had ever met—Johnny Copelyn, a white anti-aparthied activist lawyer. Buthelezi was basically in the driver's seat but was relying on me to advise him on the selection of either Copelyn or a group controlled by Cyril Ramaphosa, now president of South Africa. Much to the annoyance of Ramaphosa, I recommended to Sam that he join forces with Copelyn's garment workers union. Cyril did everything he could to prevent this, but Sam respected my judgement and, notwithstanding plenty of criticism, resisted some strong political pressure, and accepted my advice, which came down to my assessment of the ability of Copelyn, whom I could foresee would eventually run the company.

Sam Buthelezi, now sadly deceased, was a remarkable man. He was effectively the Mayor of Alexandra township, a huge sprawling black shanty town, which abutted some of the most expensive real estate in Africa in the northern suburbs of Johannesburg. I was somewhat familiar with Alexandra, since Diana had worked there as a volunteer in the clinic, prior to the Soweto Riots. He was also highly respected as the president of the African small traders' association, which operated mainly shops and shebeens in

African townships throughout the nation. Sam probably had the financial status to move out of 'Alex', but he chose to stay in his shanty house because this was his power base. Despite advice to the contrary, when I visited Sam, I would frequently drive there unaccompanied, through unpaved streets brimming over with wandering and ragged Africans, just like you see on the newsreels. Sometimes the mood seemed a little threatening, but as soon as I announced that I was going to see Sam, a sour look turned into a broad smile, and I was cheerily waved on my way. His house was, effectively, a shebeen or illegal pub. Anyone, rich or poor, was welcome. Whatever time of the day you visited him, the first thing he would do is to thrust a large glass of whisky into your hand. When the horse racing was on, his eyes were always glancing towards his one luxury, a giant television.

Despite his bonhomie, Sam was shrewd. He knew how to retain power and he knew how to use it. He had been through the 'struggle' and was well respected by and wired into all of the leading black politicians, including Madiba. Nevertheless, he was humble and warm-hearted. Notwithstanding all of the bad things that had happened to him during the white regime, there was not a racist bone in his huge body.

When the decision was taken to cut Ramaphosa out of the deal there is no doubt that Sam had to stand considerable political pressure, but stand it, he did. And when it came time for the deal to be done with SAB and for Sam to nominate Directors for the renamed Tsogo Sun Hotel and Gaming Group, he chose me. Ironically, despite all of the well-meaning efforts to restructure corporate South Africa, here I was, a white man, representing, one of the most influential black groups in the country. Hopefully, I represented them well.

Thereafter, Tsogo Sun had many successful years and

developed major casinos, hotel and entertainment facilities across South Africa. As a result, the loans to the black groups were swiftly paid off and the black shareholders were able to fully exercise their votes at board level. Johnny Copelyn, the white leader of the black union, became the Chairman and exercised shrewd leadership, After several years of flying up and down from Europe for quarterly board meetings I finally withdrew, but not without some small measure of satisfaction.

# Chapter Twenty-Six
## LOOKING BACK

What goes before is akin to watching the five-minute highlights show of a ninety-minute football match. I have attempted to pick out some of the best and worst moves in a forty-year career and subsequent retirement, but have, as a result, missed out much that went between. As in any highlights show, the tedious and boring passages are (hopefully) left out. To be successful in the hospitality industry, it is essential to concentrate on the details, and this can be extremely tedious. Highlight shows also fail to get over the sheer hard work and physical and mental effort that has gone into the real match, and, looking back at these pages, I realise that I have failed completely to impart just how much hard work it all was, not only by me, but by the many colleagues and friends that helped me along the way.

I also fear that I have tended to trivialise much of what has happened, without giving true weight to the achievements and failures. I have also not given due recognition to, nor in some cases even mentioned, the large number of friends and colleagues who have been the real source of satisfaction, support, and encouragement: the real reason why it has been such a pleasurable ride.

There is no doubt that the devil is in the details, and if you don't get the details right, the end result will go wrong, or, at best, be mediocre. It is also not possible to manage a hotel or entertainment business from your home or office; to be effective, you have to be where the services are being provided, and, by definition, this will take you away from home. This, of course, puts untold pressure on family life. Without the incredible support, love and advice from Diana, none of what goes before would have been possible.

As I look back on what has happened to me, as well as what I have made happen, I have tried to sort out what I have learned that might be useful for others just starting out. This is not supposed to be a book on 'how to manage' and who am I to preach? But, on reflection, there are a few things worth recording that have worked for me. They may not work for others, because one of the things I have learned is that there is no magic formula, and different people manage successfully in different ways, and different situations require different types of managers. For example, it is rare to find a manager who excels at developing and opening a new hotel, who is really good at running it thereafter. Opening a hotel is very task-oriented; the task is also obvious. A date has been set. There is a clear goal. Everything possible has to come together before opening day. Thereafter, the goal is less clear, less specific. In fact, part of the ongoing manager's job is to identify and communicate goals to the troops. Many managers don't do this well.

Effective communication is one of the keys to good management. There are things that all employees must know, things that they should know, and things that they could know. In rare cases, there are also things that they shouldn't know, or that, perhaps for regulatory reasons (such as insider-trading information), they must not know. In most cases, we don't even do a good job at telling our employees what they must know, let alone what they should know. We also tend to keep from them what they could know, and this is a big mistake, because by sharing this sort of information with our colleagues and employees we are, in fact, demonstrating our trust in them, and trust is something that goes two ways. Sharing facts, such as statistical or financial information as to how the business is doing, is a way of taking employees into your confidence, which helps to make them feel involved, understand the objectives, and feel part of the team. This seems rather obvious, but time and time again, I have run across managers who just don't do it. By giving information, you get information back, and, above all, you need information to run a business, whether it is information about why things aren't working or why they are. According to New York's then mayor, Rudy Giuliani, that city's remarkable decrease in crime at all levels, under his stewardship, was principally due to a system of information sharing that he called CompStat. Through CompStat, statistics on police performance were constantly shared, scrutinised, and compared. By studying the stats, the city government was able to pinpoint the problems and do something about them.

Sharing feelings is also pretty important. Letting people know exactly how you feel about things encourages them to do likewise, and whatever you can do to understand the feelings, hopes, fears, and aspirations of your employees will help you as a manager. Besides, having an opinion about something, whether it is agreeable or not, is normally positive. Being neutral or sitting on the fence is not, in my experience, regarded as a great leadership trait.

Not everyone is suited to work in hospitality. However, it is important for everyone to have some sense of passion about what they do. Professor Jim Collins, in his excellent bestseller *Built to Last* likens a great business to a "passion train." "If you don't share the passion for where the train is going, then get off," says Jim. And he is right. As a manager, I have learned that first and foremost, you must have the right people on your particular train. The right people, who share your passion, will not need motivating; they will be motivated. They will not wait for instruction; they will be making suggestions. It is a poor manager who is fearful of strong people around him, in case they are after his job. A good manager will welcome strong subordinates who challenge him. With people like that around him, success will follow, and he will soon have the next (better) job. Getting the right people on your passion train, however, is not easy. In recruiting them, their track record will tell you a lot, but not everything. It must be analysed very, very carefully. For me, first impressions are also very important, but again, they are not everything. You will undoubtedly, from time to time, find that you have hired the wrong person. If so, no matter how inconvenient and whatever the cost, take action, and part company. The longer you ride with an unwanted passenger, the more troublesome and costly it will eventually be. And besides, people who are traveling on the wrong train know it. They will be worried and uncomfortable. I have rarely fired people who were not actually relieved. I am still good friends with many of those that I have. Even the right people, however, need stroking. Nothing is more motivational than being told, either by a boss or a customer, that you have done a job well. Nothing is more demotivating than doing a job well and not having it recognised. We are, after all, only human.

Ultimately, in the hospitality business, as in almost every other business, we are only successful if our customers are satisfied. I have learned, over the years, that a satisfied customer is not the opposite of a dissatisfied one. In the hospitality business, a customer who is not dissatisfied is not necessarily satisfied—he is just not dissatisfied. For example, if you stay in a hotel, no matter what category it is, you expect to find a bed in your room with clean sheets; you expect to find hot water coming out of the hot tap and cold out of the cold tap; you expect to find a clean towel and a bar of soap, and so on. If these things do not exist, you will surely be dissatisfied. If they do exist, you will not be shouting for joy, unless, of course you have just come from a long trip in the Sahara. That is because these are things that you *expect*. They fall into your lowest category of needs.

The 'satisfiers' in our business tend to be the 'software' rather than the 'hardware'. A marvellous palace might blow the mind of your guest, but if the hot water runs cold, it will be for naught. Basic expectations must be met, but guests are only really happy with their stay if you exceed expectations, and, in my experience, most people who rave about a hotel are raving about the way they were treated. They rave about staff that went the extra mile, about staff that cared. These are the staff you need on your train, and if you want them to see how important it is, then you, the manager must be the role model. This means 'management by walking around', or, as I prefer to call it, management by 'being there'.

There are four major areas of focus for a manager in the hospitality business: guests (customers), human resources (employees), finances (prices, controls, accounts) and marketing. A hotelier who 'manages by walking around', particularly in areas where his guests are, will have the chance to monitor the first three very closely. By being where the customers are, you naturally get to see what is happening to them, and who is making it happen. You also get to see waste (or savings) well before they become apparent in the accounts. Accounts tell you what has happened after the fact; walking around lets you take corrective measures before the fact. You also get to talk to the guests, or, more importantly, to listen to them. Hoteliers and restaurateurs have fantastic opportunities to listen to their customers whilst, at the same time, making these customers feel welcomed and special. This is not space technology; it is common sense, but it does take an effort on behalf of the manager; it does take discipline.

George DeKornfeld, my boss at the Carlton Tower all those years ago, was a master of this discipline. Every morning, he took the daily guest arrival list and underlined ten names, at random. Come hell or high water, he would meet his 'ten' before the day was out. He would not go home until he had done so. Nothing was more important to him, for this was how he kept his pulse on the business. And it was catching. Pretty soon ten of George's subordinates, including me, were circulating the arrival list and underlining our own 'ten', so now 100 guests were being listened to every day—and, by chance, we had about 100 arrivals per day. It did not take long for problem areas to be spotted and corrected. It did not take long, either, for the 100 to talk to a 1000 about the hotel management "that cared."

Listening, of course, is only useful if, when necessary, action follows. Making lists of things to do is vital, but crossing the things off the list (once done) is more so. Not every problem, however, can be solved and crossed off the list so quickly. Some problems are not easily solved; some are endemic. They need special focus and planning to sort out, and management, therefore, is a constant process of goal-setting, action steps, and review. And all of us are better at some things than at others. Unfortunately, because it is more comfortable for us, we tend to spend more time doing the things we are good at than the things that we are not, with the obvious result that we don't get any practise at the things we do not do well, and, therefore, don't get any better. One of the interesting things about being a manager in the hospitality industry is that skills and knowledge are required across a very broad range. At one end of the range are detailed administrative tasks, such as stocktaking or bookkeeping, whilst at the other end, one might be expected to 'schmooze' with the guests. Luckily for me, my natural position on this scale was somewhere in the middle, which could mean that I was no good at the detailed administrative work and too reserved to schmooze. Only by pushing myself in both directions, and learning from others that were good at it, did I manage to expand my range of behaviour, knowledge, skill, and ability in both directions on the scale. Sometimes I found it difficult.

Learning to listen and *hear* is important, but so is learning to look and *see*. How many times have you run across a headwaiter who comes up to your table and enquires if "everything is all right, Sir or Ma'am?" and then is completely disinterested in the answer and blind to what is happening or not happening on the table? How many times have you seen a hotel assistant manager on his 'rounds' stick his head into the restaurant and fail to notice that the air conditioning has been set for the convenience of the waiters who are all racing around, rather than the shivering guests, or that the background music is repeating ad nauseam? If you are going to 'manage by walking around', then you must also look to see, feel, and sense what is going on around you.

And this brings us back to the details. Make no mistake: your customers notice the details. Your customers are not flitting in and out. They are sleeping in hotel rooms, using the shower or the telephone, sitting at restaurant tables, eating the food, etc. When half of your customers can't read the writing on the little bottles in the bathroom because the print is too small and they don't wear their glasses under the shower, they are irritated. When the instructions to the telephone don't coincide with the actual handset in place, it is annoying. When a lady has to get down on her hands and knees to open the safe in the room to find her jewellery just as she is dressed to go out, it is annoying. When the bell on the elevator goes bing or bong loudly in the corridor outside your room at night, or the ice machine in the hallway sounds like an intermittent thunderstorm, it is annoying. These are the details that matter. And these are the details that can, by and large, be thought through. These are the annoyances that can be eliminated, before they even happen, by careful planning and attention to detail.

Visualising how the architecture of a hotel will look when it is still on the drawing board is a 'gift'. Working through the details of how the hotel will actually function is a chore, but one which is well worth doing. This is something that I learned from Sol Kerzner. Sol is a genius at visualisation, but he is not beyond working out the details. He knows that a pretty building that doesn't function well is a waste of time.

You also cannot overprepare. Whether it is planning for a building, a function, or even a speech, one key to success is preparation. Preparation forces one to look ahead. It forces one to have empathy, to consider what is going to happen next, how people are going to react, what they will do, and what they will need. This process allows you to be ready for whatever curveballs are thrown.

Much of my work has taken place in Africa, and many of my successes, where I have had them, have been due to Africans. I would not therefore wish to leave the reader with the impression, which may have been created in the early chapters of this book, that Africans are slow, disorganised and therefore ineffective workers. I referred earlier to the saying in Africa that "the white man has the watch, but the black man has the time." On the face of it, the inference is that black men are slow. In my experience, what might seem to be a slur against the black African is, in fact, a compliment. It is not always wrong to take one's time, particularly as a manager or supervisor. Getting something done quickly does not always get something done right. This was impressed upon me recently during some training seminars that I was conducting in South Africa.

My training groups consisted of about a dozen people who were roughly representative of the Rainbow State: in each group there were a couple of whites, a couple of Asian Indians, someone of mixed race, and seven or eight black Africans. As part of the program, I required the participants to solve a problem, which involved them being assigned roles as bosses, supervisors and workers. I had utilised this exercise, with the identical problem, perhaps a hundred times elsewhere during my career in England, America, Italy, Australia, New Zealand, etc. No group had ever solved the problem in the time allotted, and the point of the exercise was to examine, through post mortem, what had gone wrong. To my utter amazement, a group to whom I had assigned a black African boss solved the problem, and I was even more amazed when, two weeks later, a different group, again with an African boss, did the same. When I told the group leaders and their 'workers' that they were the first people in the world, in my experience, to solve the problem, they were so proud of themselves that I thought they would burst. From then on, the confidence with which they tackled the issues before them, and their resultant success, was astounding.

This problem-solving exercise was part of a four-week training programme for junior supervisors. They were brought together in a central location, for one week at a time, at intervals, over a period of six months. On the first day of the first week, we, the trainers, asked the participants to give a prepared presentation to the rest of the group on a predetermined subject. Generally, they were so nervous and unsure of themselves that their presentations to their colleagues were extremely poor. On the last day of the fourth week of the program, we had warned the participants, they would be required to make a similar presentation to the board of directors of the company. I was also present on the final day. I could not believe that the people making the presentations, in the quite formidable surroundings of the company boardroom, were the same group that I had worked with six months before. The content and quality of the presentations were first-class; more noticeably, so was the self-confidence of the presenters. Africa must gain its self-confidence. When it does, it will be a different place.

Looking back, I feel privileged to have been part of the South African revolution, and somewhat ashamed that I did not have the confidence to realise that political change in the country could come about peacefully. Now, twenty-five years after the formation of the first democratic government, the progress has been considerable, although not nearly enough yet to satisfy everyone. Gradually, a new black middle class is being created and has been fuelling the market and creating jobs. To some extent Madiba's dream of a Rainbow Nation has come true but, under the surface, there are still underlying divisions between the colours in the rainbow. Much has been achieved in normalising society after the failed experiment of apartheid but the danger of this progress being derailed by crime and corruption is ever present. There still are massive hurdles to overcome. The most remarkable thing about the new South Africa is the pride in their country displayed by all South Africans, be they white, brown or black, and their determination to together make their country work. This, I believe, is the same 'can do' attitude that made America great. I hope I will be around long enough to see their success.

People often ask me who are the most impressive men or women that I have met. Without question I fire back; "Nelson Mandela and Muhammad Ali." Interestingly, they were both black. If you were to ask me who had most influence on my working life it would be a different answer entirely. The first was Professor Philip Nailon, the laconic teacher at my college of management theory. Philip was the man who made 'management' seem intriguing. Then, there was George DeKornfeld, the aristocratic hotel manager, and my forerunner and mentor at the Carlton Tower. It was George that gave me the freedom to experiment. Also, Alan Marsh, the jolly human resources director of Hotel Corporation of America, who put his considerable weight behind my early career and was the man who gave me, and then supported, my vision. But it was, of course, Sol Kerzner, the Sun King, who exercised by far and away the biggest influence. Sol taught me more about running a business than any other person and for that I am extremely grateful. He also gave me some of the toughest years of my life, when I acted as a sort of human buffer between him and so many others, who could not cope with him. This book, *Out of the Shadow of the Sun* is a revision of a previous one, *In the Shadow of the Sun*. The change from *In* to *Out of* may not seem much, but it is very meaningful. I now realise that I, like many other people, was condemned to spend my après-Kerzner years in his shadow. Luckily, as time went by, I learned that I could perform quality work without reliance on him. In fact, much of what I am most proud has been achieved without his influence, guidance or interference. I like to believe that I am now out of his shadow and have grown and prospered as such. Nevertheless, my appreciation of what I learned in the shadow is immense and I shall always be grateful for that.

When I half-heartedly started into the hotel and

hospitality industry at the age of seventeen, part of my rationale was that there would always be a job available. At the very worst, I reasoned, people would need to be fed and, in some cases, housed. In my wildest dreams, I could not have envisaged the massive growth over these sixty-five years in travel, both domestic and overseas, and the huge related growth, therefore, in the industry of transporting, housing, feeding and entertaining these travellers. On my second date with Diana, I took her to the movies. The film we saw was *Breakfast at Tiffany's*. The theme song from the movie was 'Moon River', which included the words, "I'm off to see the world; there's such a lot of world to see." As we left the cinema, I promised Diana I would show her the world. I had no idea how right I would be. By sticking with this industry, I have visited over a 120 countries, and done business in many of them. I have kept my word and taken Diana to most of them too, at least the ones she wanted to see. We have met kings and queens, presidents and prime ministers, film stars and celebrities, and hundreds and hundreds of other nice folk. We have witnessed breath-taking scenery. We have seen unbelievable hardship and poverty. We have been encouraged and discouraged. We have laughed and we have cried. We have, in short, seen and done things that we would not have thought possible. Luckily, in the main, we have been able to do it together, and there is no doubt at all in my mind that I could not have done it alone.

# Chapter Twenty-Seven
## EPILOGUE

As this book was going to press, we learned of the sad passing of Sol Kerzner, who is featured prominently in these pages. The death of Sol is a great loss for South Africa and the world. He was an extraordinary person whose creativity, ability and determination changed the face of the hotel and entertainment industry in South Africa and, to a large extent, much of the rest of the world. I should know, because I worked with him for twenty years, travelled thousands of miles with him alone in the company jet, and even lived, for a while, in his house. Sol was one of those rare men who could turn vision into reality through single minded leadership, as evidenced in the Lost City at Sun City, Atlantis (in the Bahamas and Dubai), the Mohegan Sun, USA, and many more. His interests were twofold; business and family. No matter how busy we were or on whatever time zone, Sol would always take time out to talk to his family – and understood if you needed to do the same. He was a demanding and highly focused boss. As I have said in this book, he could enter a room where his executives had been struggling over a problem for hours and immediately point to the solution. His ability to hone in on the crux of the matter was uncanny. In all aspects of the business, save for actually cooking the meals, he was equal to the experts. He could visualise one-dimensional plans into three-dimensional images, a gift that astounded many architects and designers. He did not excel at small talk, unless it was about sport, but was not without a great sense of humour, including jokes about himself. He was good to his friends, especially those that were less well off. Beyond that, he was quite closed and rarely shared his feelings, either personally or in regard to philosophy, religion, or politics. He did not tolerate foolish behaviour or laziness in his business. He could be very tough on his employees and associates. His speech was famously colourful. He was the only man I have ever met who could use the 'F' word as a noun, verb and adjective all in one sentence. Even executives and employees that left him on bad terms, which many did, still recognised him as a great entrepreneur and maintained their admiration for his ability and iconic leadership. Many of us have learned much from him and, from time to time, I do believe that he learned something from us. It is a shame, therefore, that these qualities which drove him forward, were somewhat diminished by his habit of wearing out his executives.

Sol was definitely one of the great players in the hospitality industry, right up there with the Hiltons, Marriotts, and Wynns of the world. His go it alone approach may have been his greatest strength, but perhaps it also may have held him back from being the greatest hotelier ever. That said, very few men have come so far from such humble beginnings. We will miss him greatly, but the mark he has left on the world with his buildings will be with us for a long time to come. And for those that knew him well, the mark of his personality will remain with us until we, too, move on. May he rest in peace.

www.ingramcontent.com/pod-product-compliance
Lightning Source LLC
Chambersburg PA
CBHW032145080426
42735CB00008B/592